CLOTHING FOR MODERNS

_____

MODERN

Fifth Edition

Mabel D. Erwin
Late Professor Emeritus of Clothing and Textiles
Texas Tech University

Lila A. Kinchen
Associate Professor Emeritus of Clothing and Textiles
Texas Tech University

Macmillan Publishing Co., Inc.
New York

Collier Macmillan Publishers
London

Earlier editions copyright 1949, © 1957,
and
copyright © 1964 and 1969
by Macmillan Publishing Co., Inc.

Macmillan Publishing Co., Inc.
866 Third Avenue, New York, New York 10022

Collier-Macmillan Canada, Ltd.

Printing: 1 2 3 4 5 6 7 8   Year: 4 5 6 7 8 9 80

Library of Congress Cataloging in Publication Data

Erwin, Mabel Deane.
  Clothing for moderns.

  Includes bibliographical references.
  1. Dressmaking. 2. Clothing and dress.
I. Kinchen, Lila A., joint author. II. Title.
TT518.E7   1974   646.4'3'04   72-12458
ISBN 0-02-334210-2

Preface

This book is designed for anyone who is interested in developing or improving abilities and skills in dress selection and construction. It assumes some previous experiences in the field of clothing and textiles, but the form is sufficiently basic to meet the needs of the less experienced person while providing challenges for the more advanced.

The primary purpose of the book is to broaden the base of understanding of clothing construction, with special emphasis for the college or university student who anticipates not only her own personal clothing needs, but also work in a related professional field where she may be assisting others with such problems. The presentation in breadth and depth can be significant to those in the educational field—in secondary schools, extension services, business, and other areas. A basic knowledge of clothing can contribute to the capacities of social workers active in youth organizations, in Head Start, in centers for the handicapped, and in the developing countries.

v

In Part One, the first chapter presents a brief review of the factors recognized as determining or affecting clothing choices and contributing to the explanations of clothing behavior. The following four chapters deal with dress in relation to art, wardrobe planning, consumer education, and the tremendous increase in fashion sewing by individuals. Little technical information relative to some of these subjects or to textiles is involved. For such information, study of a comprehensive text on the subject is recommended. However, many suggestions for making choices are to be found here. Some additional references are mentioned or listed. Readers are encouraged to keep informed of new products and techniques, and to evaluate them in terms of their potentialities.

Part Two deals with clothing construction, including the selection of patterns and fabrics, pattern alterations, fitting, organization of work, and details of construction, with emphasis on concepts and reasons for choices and techniques. Construction processes are presented, as nearly as possible, in the order of use. Many new sketches and photographs have been included.

The approach used in various parts of the book leads the student in thinking through a process or in evaluating an appropriate procedure. Educators and students are equally concerned with clear concepts, with finding relationships among concepts, and with stating conclusions in the form of generalizations or principles that may be applied to the solving of other problems. The terms *concept* and *generalization* are not always used, but the approach can be recognized. Where questions or problems are presented, it is to the student's advantage to stop reading and think through the problem, as directed. Suggested solutions are provided for help in evaluating decisions.

Previous experiences in the clothing field have provided the student with many concepts that will be clarified and expanded in college. In high school, the emphasis begins with basic concepts; in college, the student is ready for higher levels of learning, of comprehending relationships, and of verbalizing generalizations. The latter, naturally, are not to be presented at the beginning of the study of a problem, but used to check one's understanding at its close. Generalizations are listed at the ends of many chapters—offered as a nucleus upon which the thinking student can build.

It is human nature to revel in discovery and find joy in learning; the "discovery" technique is exciting. Still, it would be expensive in time, money, and human capabilities to present every problem in this manner. The discoveries of others are made available through the printed word, family life experiences, association with enthusiastic, experienced teachers, and through the mass media. This book presents recognized standards and tested methods for achieving them.

Emphasis is placed on an organization of work that provides for a preliminary overview of all the tasks to be accomplished. The plan is based on two or three fittings, and presents a grouping of construction problems around fittings, for fast, expedient, and efficient handling. Visualizing the total relationship between construction and fitting—or between any of the various procedures—offers many advantages. Research findings show that the ability to visualize is one of the key factors in achievement.

Appreciation is expressed to those persons and organizations, recognized by the proper courtesy lines, who so generously contributed photographs and other materials. Special recognition is extended to family members and friends for their assistance and encouragement, to Billie Wolfe and Peggy Benton Young for their respective contributions in photography and sketching, and to Jackie Williams for her assistance in many areas.

L. A. K.

Contents

ix

PART TWO

Clothing Construction

PART

ONE

Clothing Selection

1

The Significance of Dress

A growing awareness of the significance of clothing is evident. Study of the factors that influence both the individual and society reveals involvements in momentous, far-reaching, and complex facets of human activity.

The value of clothing in meeting certain human needs—physical protection, modesty, and decoration—has long been recognized. Today, its role in satisfying other needs is being more clearly perceived. Research is confirming the importance placed upon clothing by the individual, although the reasons for this importance are vaguely sensed or unknown. There is, perhaps, the complex blending of instinct, emotion, racial inheritance, sense of values, religious conviction, and social relations with other members of the human race.

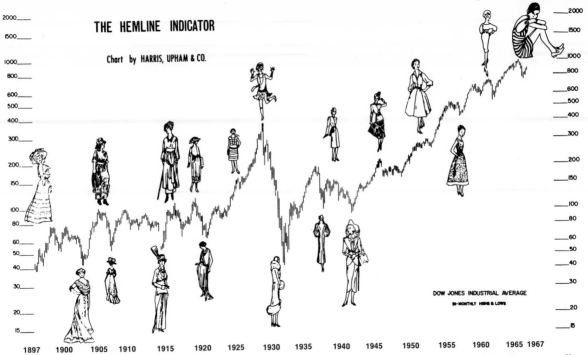

THE HEMLINE INDICATOR

Chart by HARRIS, UPHAM & CO.

DOW JONES INDUSTRIAL AVERAGE
BI-MONTHLY HIGHS & LOWS

1897 1900 1905 1910 1915 1920 1925 1930 1935 1940 1945 1950 1955 1960 1965 1967

Figure 1-1. What relation do you find between the stock market and hemlines, as well as other style features? (Courtesy of Harris, Upham & Co.)

There is abundant evidence that one's clothing behavior is influenced by the same forces—social, psychological, and economic—that affect other areas of endeavor. Fashion tends to parallel events in history (Fig. 1-1).

Horn observes that because clothing behavior can be interpreted from many points of view, an interdisciplinary approach is required for its study. Relevant disciplines include anthropology, history, sociology, psychology, economics, art, philosophy, and the physical aspects of clothing.[1]

The scope of this book does not permit study of these factors in detail but it seems appropriate to recognize them. To become more aware of the influences clothing has upon us, to analyze reasons for our choices, and to survey situations that are affecting the design, production, and supply of clothing can, possibly, broaden our comprehension.

Excellent references are available for continued, recommended study; current research is constantly adding to the present store of knowledge on this subject.

Anthropological and Historical Influences

Culture and Clothing

Culture encompasses all that man learns as a member of society—his concepts, habits, arts, beliefs, knowledge, skills, morals, and so on. The clothing worn will depend partly on social inheritance. It may show a mixture of cultural influences

[1]Marilyn J. Horn, *The Second Skin* (Boston: Houghton Mifflin Company, 1968), p. 18.

6

1460 1530 1560 1620 1630

1760 1796 1800 1825 1860

1885 1895 1902 1925 1960's

Figure 1-2. Five hundred years of costume display varied silhouettes and countless details. Careful scrutiny indicates that many are still favored for different occasions.

Figure 1-3. Greek sculpture, fifth century B.C. One piece of cloth draped simply and in beautiful proportions. It formed the basis of our concept of classic beauty. (Courtesy of The Metropolitan Museum of Art.)

and be modified by changes that constantly occur in a society. Silhouettes of the complete costume have been characteristically different in the various periods of history, periods that may have extended over centuries (Fig. 1-2). Rapid changes in transportation and business have shortened their duration.

Clothing is influenced by physical environment, resources, and the ability to use these resources. An example can be seen in a fashion change that occurred at the end of World War I. The cotton and woolen mills of France had been badly damaged, making fine cottons and woolens very scarce. It had been the custom for ladies' underwear to be made of fine batiste, nainsook, and handkerchief linen. To meet this situation, France turned to its silk mills at Lyon, where production had not been interrupted. As a result, silk underwear came into the market, and the new couture design for 1927 was the ensemble: several silk dresses could be worn under the same straight, simple coat of wool. This custom introduced the era of crepe de chine, flat crepe, and satin dresses, with wool suits almost completely out of fashion. Few people knew the reasons for this radical change in style.[2]

Various societies have developed unique ways of making their textiles and designing their clothing, Horn recognizes an interesting fact: From the technical standpoint, "there are only three basic patterns of dress: the tailored garment, the

[2]Ermina Stimson, Rhea Bower, and Alice Lessing (Compilers), *Sixty Years of Fashion, 1900–1960*, (New York: Fairchild Publications, 1963), p. 7.

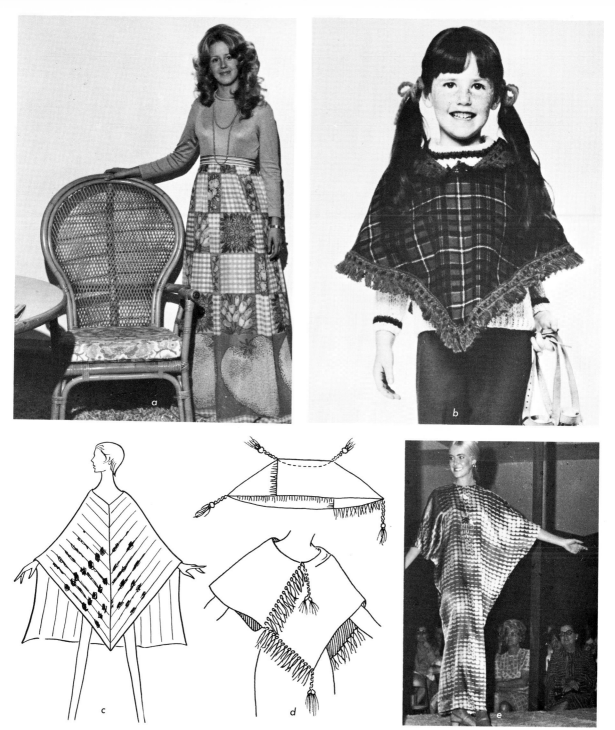

Figure 1-4. Geometric shapes that involve little sewing: *a*, dirndl; *b* and *c*, ponchos; *d*, quexquemtl (keks-kamtl), small version of the poncho worn by women of Mexico, made of two scarves with the end of one sewed to the side of the other; *e*, caftan. (Courtesy of Janet Heineman, *a*; The Wool Bureau, Inc., *b*; Vivian J. Adams, *d*; Margaret's, *e*.

Figure 1-5. Knitted fabrics for men's suits present challenges in yarn and fabric construction. (Courtesy of Blue Bell, Inc., Greensboro, N.C.)

draped garment [Fig. 1-3], and a composite type which combines some of the characteristics of the other two. In the thousands of years of man's existence, no fundamentally new or different pattern has evolved."[3]

Rudolfsky advocates a return to the use of plane geometric shapes, as squares and rectangles, with little or no sewing.[4] Beautiful examples of such shapes include the cummerbund, dirndl, huipil, kilt, manilla, penung, poncho, rebozo, sari, sarong, sash, serape, caftan, and toga. Some of these shapes are shown in Figure 1-4.

Not until this century, and the advent of man-made fibers, were there any significant changes in the fibers used for clothing; for centuries man had depended on natural fibers. Also, not until this decade had the construction of fabric for general use in women's outer garments and in men's wear varied greatly from the

[3]Horn, op. cit., p. 23.
[4]Bernard Rudolfsky, *Are Clothes Modern?* (Chicago: Paul Theobald, 1947), p. 200.

woven construction developed centuries ago. The knitting process, long known and used in the production of such special articles of clothing as sweaters, has taken on added importance in the great volume and variety of knitted fabrics now available (Fig. 1-5). This development illustrates the point that raw materials and tools influence the design of clothing. With modern technology, new designs are constantly evolving through innovations in materials, tools, and processes.

FOLKWAYS AND CUSTOMS

Folkways and customs are social habits that become rooted in tradition—with customs the most deeply rooted—through long periods of usage. Both are passed from one generation to another. An outstanding example in women's dress is the Indian sari (Fig. 1-6).

MORES AND LAWS   Social habits that involve morals or ethics can be defined as mores. These are folkways that are considered conducive to the welfare of society and that, through general observance, develop the force of law. They may be controlled through strong social sanctions, or, if the force is sufficiently strong, the rule may become a law.

Figure 1-6. For centuries, women in India have worn the sari, a six-yard length of beautiful fabric draped on the body. (Courtesy of Arati Prabhakar.)

Figure 1-7. The granny dress in this decade is not related to one's morals in the same manner as it might have been decades ago. (Courtesy of Celanese.)

In the world's societies, the sexual taboos and restrictions have influenced clothing, making it a reflector of the moral standards of the culture. Horn notes that "In general, the relationship between clothes and sex centers on the degree of exposure, concealment, or emphasis given particular parts of the body. The exposure of almost every part of the human anatomy has been considered 'indecent' or 'immoral' in some period of fashion history."[5]

The '70s version of the "granny" print, with boots, provides a completely covered effect, but for reasons different from those that might have been held by one's great-grandmother (Fig. 1-7). She wore high-topped shoes with her long dress and was careful to keep her skirt hem in the "proper" location. To expose the leg above the shoe top was looked upon as questionable decency.

It is interesting to follow fashion history through the centuries and to study dress—or lack of dress—among various groups of peoples. Such a study can provide a basis for an objective view of the standards of decency and morality in one's own culture (Fig. 1-8).

Sumptuary laws were an attempt in Europe in the Middle Ages to control

[5]Horn, op cit., pp. 60–61.

Figure 1-8. For centuries, short skirts have been rare—almost always worn for sport—probably owing to a variety of social and psychological factors. *a,* Prehistoric cave dwellers wore the same style of garment and hair-do. *b,* Loin cloth and long hose were highly decorated with net sash and beaded fringe in Crete, 1450–1375 B.C. *c,* Diana, goddess of the chase (note Psyche knot). *d,* Teutonic, prehistoric style; note strap device for one shoulder. *e,* Black, hand-woven wool garment common among early American Indians about A.D. 1650. (Note similarity of *d* and *e.*) *f,* South Pacific Islands grass skirt. *g,* Mrs. Amelia Bloomer, who tried to get nineteenth-century women to adopt short skirts; however, the bloomers were what made a hit. *h,* The middy blouse and pleated skirt below the knee, 1920s. *i,* In 1967, girls were undecided whether to wear shorter mini-skirts. In 1968, pants, tights, leotards, and long hose were considered necessary accompaniments.

dress in order to distinguish one class from another. The bourgeoisie had become more wealthy than the ruling classes, and to maintain their preeminence, the latter made laws regulating yardages, costs, colors, points on shoes, lengths of sleeves and sashes, and amounts of gold, jewels, laces, and furs that could be used for decoration; separate norms for different classes were established. Laws of a similar nature were pronounced in the early American Colonies.

Relics of such attempts can be seen today in the protocol of coronations and of university academic processions. During World War II, rulings were passed to regulate the kind and amount of consumer goods a citizen could purchase. Clothing manufacturers were limited in the materials to be used—required to keep skirt lengths at the point where fashion had them located at the time, and hems no wider than two inches.

VALUES

Another characteristic of the individual, learned from his culture, is his possession of a body of ideas and beliefs as to what is valuable and important. It is generally accepted that one's values are acquired in the family, especially during his early years; in schools and peer groups; and through mass media.

The ideas that a person holds to be of value are indicated indirectly through clothing choices. Some recognized values are an interest in beauty; the desire to feel good in clothes, considering both the physical and psychological aspects; and the desire for obtaining social approval, leadership, prestige, and influence.

Value patterns change with new experiences and circumstances. In the United States, many long-held values are disappearing and new ones are emerging. Changing patterns include attitudes toward the length of service to be given by clothing. Many persons in an affluent society provided with long-wearing fibers in clothing no longer expect to wear a garment until it reaches a threadbare condition. Another significant change is the trend toward more casual, informal, and comfortable dress.

Value patterns are influenced by age. For example, teen-agers attach greater importance to clothing as a means of gaining acceptance and approval than do mature persons. Even though both groups—the young and the mature—hold more or less identical values, the order of importance is different.[6]

SOCIOPSYCHOLOGICAL FACTORS

CLOTHES AND SELF   Clothes are an outward expression of how people feel about themselves and the world around them. Clothing is recognized as an intimate part of an individual—an expansion or extension of the bodily self. Recent research is clarifying the importance of clothing as related to one's concept of self, defined by Ryan as, "the individual's perception of his own characteristics, his abilities or his failings, his appearance, and the total organization of characteristics which he perceives as distinguishing him as an individual."[7]

In changing the body size and shape, clothing may give an increased sense

[6]Ibid., pp. 81–84.
[7]Mary Shaw Ryan, *Clothing: A Study in Human Behavior* (New York: Holt, Rinehart & Winston, Inc., 1966), p. 82.

Figure 1-9. Clothing conveys moods and feelings. (Courtesy of J. P. Stevens & Co., Inc.)

of value and importance. This feeling may be experienced in an especially elegant, full-length dress, in pleated or circular skirts (Fig. 1-9, *a*), in capes, padded bras, and wigs. Clothing can convey moods and feelings—it can give a joyous sense of motion, vivacity, and freedom. Reich describes the feeling experienced in wearing bell bottoms (Fig. 1-9, *b*): "They express the body as jeans do, but they say much more. They give the ankles a special freedom as if to invite dancing right on the street. . . . A touch football game, if the players are wearing bell bottoms, is like a folk dance or a ballet." [8]

A person's feelings about his self-worth are largely the result of his social situation. Clothing assists in the process of "finding one's self" and in identifying that self to others. Clothes are an important force in the enhancement of the self, leading to greater self-confidence and self-esteem (Fig. 1-10). Humphrey, Klaasen, and Creekmore found that "clothing can reflect either feelings of self-worth or feelings of insecurity." [9]

[8]Charles A. Reich, *The Greening of America* (New York: Random House, Inc., 1970), p. 255.

[9]Carolyn Humphrey, Mary Klaasen, and Anna M. Creekmore, "Clothing and Self-Concept of Adolescents," *Journal of Home Economics*, **63**:4 (April 1971), p. 250.

Figure 1-10. Clothing can reflect feelings of self-worth or feelings of insecurity. (Courtesy of The Wool Bureau, Inc.)

Figure 1-11. Clothes can communicate much about a person. (Courtesy of Blue Bell, Inc.)

CLOTHING SYMBOLS

One's appearance affects not only his feelings and behavior, but also serves as a nonverbal symbol, projecting a revealing impression to those with whom he comes in contact. A visual first impression often can convey in a few seconds much information about a person: his role or place in society, his sex, age, situation, nationality, profession, social stratification, economic status, and possibly something about his personality traits. Someone has said, "Clothes communicate. Being without what they tell would be like losing the language" (Fig. 1-11). Time may reveal errors in judgment, but the appraisal often may prove quite accurate, depending upon the judge's level of perception. Persons who are well acquainted with an individual tend not to use these clothing cues.

ROLES AND STATUS

Role refers to one's place in social relationships; status refers to one's place on a scale of prestige.[10]

[10]Horn, op. cit., p. 131.

16

In a society, certain guides are provided for its members regarding what is considered desirable behavior in various circumstances. An individual is expected to perform his role within these limitations—to gain approval and admiration, rather than contempt and ridicule. Age, sex, and occupation are among the factors considered by society in determining standards for social behavior. Ryan concludes that, "In a complex society such as ours there are a wide variety of cultural roles. Each individual plays more than one of these roles and is aware of what others expect of him in each of them—expect in dress as well as behavior. The individual tries to live up to these expectations."[11]

Roles change as a person advances through various stages of life and as his environment changes. Changing social patterns modify beliefs as to what constitutes appropriate dress. It is generally accepted that dress is influential in enabling one to move from one role to another.

CLASS DISTINCTIONS

One strong reason for dressing as we do is attributed to the status factor. In our democracy today no sharp lines of distinction exist; there is a similarity at all class levels, but there are also differences.

At the beginning of the '50s, Barber and Lobel found that the American social class system could be differentiated into three classifications and that the clothing for each class followed a set pattern. In the group at the top were the families with long lineage and high occupational position—the "old money" families. Women in this group had little need to compete; they tended to stress the aesthetic function of clothes, were not quite so conscious of fashion, and wore their quality clothes for a long period. They were thought of as aristocratic and well-bred.

The next level of social class included the "high fashion," couture-conscious style leaders. Wealth and high living were symbolized, rather than family ties. They tried to avoid obvious ostentation. Prestige labels for this group were "sophisticated" and "chic."

For the middle and lower-middle classes, respectability was the symbol. Clothes worn by its members were conservative and "smart."[12]

An interesting comparison can be made between this situation and that which existed in the United States in 1867, when *Harper's Bazar* (as it was then spelled) published its first issue. For reasons different from today's there was great uniformity of dress—"so many elegantly dressed women." Everyone was wearing crinolines—not just the ladies of fashion, but their maids, city dwellers, sod-house dwellers, and those who worked in the fields—all wore clothes of the same material and cut. *Harper's* editor proclaimed, " 'The uniformity that results is not favorable to the picturesque'—and announced with pride that it had established connections with the leading European fashion journals."[13]

[11]Ryan, op. cit., pp. 77–78.

[12]Bernard Barber and Lyle Lobel, "Fashions in Women's Clothes and the American Social System," *Social Forces,* **31**(1952), 124–131.

[13]Russell Lynes, *The Tastemakers* (New York: The Universal Library, Grosset & Dunlap, Inc., 1954), pp. 76–77.

Vertical social mobility—that is, the movement up and down the ladder of income and prestige—is quite marked in American society. Clothing facilitates this movement.

Clothes hold an important place as status symbols. Conspicuous consumption—"keeping up with the Joneses"—a theory expounded by Veblen, is still clearly discernible. This economic phenomenon is criticized because it results in waste, both for the individual and for society. Basically, it represents a conflict between classes. The status factor is indicated in any clothes that give the wearer a feeling of approval, recognition, and belonging—either in his own class or in the class above.

Persons with ambitions toward social mobility aspire to move upward—not to a lower class. It is within the middle class that the greatest emphasis is placed upon clothes and appearance. The bulk of fashion followers are here, many continually reaching for a higher status, with the visible evidence of the stage reached presented in their clothes, furnishings, fashionable addresses, and other consumer commodities. The middle group is more status conscious than either of the other groups. Fashions are largely set by those in the upper middle class, who have money and occasions to wear various types of garments. This may be partly owing to the diminishing size of the upper group and the phenomenal growth of the middle group as affluence increases in our society. Also, as was pointed out earlier, persons in the upper group whose social status has been established for generations are less likely to care about presenting this evidence of status.

Persons in the lowest class tend to attach little importance to the social significance of clothing unless they are interested in social mobility toward the middle class.

It is against this background involving status that many persons, especially the young, have reacted negatively within recent years. The question remains: is an individual free of status when he adopts the tattered jeans that others in his group are wearing?

As clothing becomes increasingly available to all persons, it becomes a less reliable indicator of social class and has the effect of speeding changes in fashion. Horn observes that "the accelerated change which takes place in fashion today is the direct result of the democratization of fashion. . . . In our society, fashions are copied quickly into low-priced lines, . . . Fashion leaders are thus forced to change their styles more frequently in order to maintain a distinction from the masses."[14]

Conformity and Individuality

Seemingly contradictory to the need for conformity is the need for expressing individuality. How these two are interrelated is illustrated in the popularity of jeans today, with the individuality and creativeness of the wearer demonstrated in the selection of other garments, fabric, and/or accessories to give a personal touch. Adolescents often express the need for conforming or belonging to their

[14] Horn, op. cit., p. 16.

peer groups by choosing clothing that is being worn by most of the others in the group; adults might express this need by selecting current fashion trends valued by their social group. As one becomes more mature, less need is felt to conform and greater emphasis may be placed on individuality.

Conformity in clothing leads to the development of the self-confidence that one acquires through being accepted by and identified with peers. The "right" clothes can free a person from disapproval and ridicule and give a feeling of adequacy and poise. Getting a new hair style, or slimming the figure if one is overweight, can produce the same effect.

Hambleton, Roach, and Ehle found that with fashion-emphasizing mass media there is a tendency among teen-age girls to wear the latest fashions, rather than conform to the mode of the peer group. This tendency is in contrast to the behavior of teen-age boys, who are likely to be less conscious of new fashions and satisfied to simply look like the rest of the crowd.[15]

Conformity of masses of people is a necessity before a design can become "fashion." It must first be approved by persons of high social status, as pointed out earlier—possibly a leader within a peer group who sets up a counternorm—and then be accepted by the masses.

SOCIAL CHANGE AND FASHION

Numerous factors can be credited with influencing fast-moving and momentous changes that are related to clothing and fashion in our free society. Fashion changes are occurring more rapidly in our democracy because of the behavior of the consumer in rejecting the dictates of fashion designers; the youth market; the freedom of industry to produce acceptable consumer goods; the affluent conditions resulting from increased incomes of much of the population; more leisure time, with corresponding needs in clothing; greater culture contacts in a world with easy and extensive communications, which result in ethnic adaptations such as the Chinese influence stimulated by events related to the entrance of China into the United Nations; education, because it opens doors to new experiences and encourages the acquisition of more fashionable clothing; the greater freedom of women; a general appreciation and desire for change and progress; and the high degree of development of our technology.

Economic Aspects of Clothing

CLOTHING EXPENDITURES—THE FAMILY

Per capita income rose during the 1960s. Even though prices of goods and services advanced also, the real income was increased, and it is still rising in the '70s.

Distribution of the family dollar has continued to show a slight decrease in percentage of clothing expenditures, although with higher incomes the amount is

[15]Kay Brogger Hambleton, Mary Ellen Roach, and Kathryn Ehle, "Teen-Age Appearance," *Journal of Home Economics,* **64**:2 (February 1972), 33.

greater in actual dollars. Some factors involved in this percentage decline include the following.

1. The trend toward casual dress, which is less expensive than more formal clothing.
2. The development of man-made fibers that are long-wearing and easily cared for, reducing cleaning costs.
3. The phenomenal rise of home sewing, cutting costs somewhat (subject to the number of garments made).
4. Increase in the number of family members under 18 and over 65, since these groups spend less than those in between.
5. The failure of cost of clothing to increase commensurately with increases in income.

SOCIOECONOMIC CHANGES

Consumer expenditures for clothing are being influenced by various factors.

1. The growing number of working women.
2. The increase in family income.
3. The affluence of young people.
4. Sales of used clothing.
5. Increased leisure.
6. Population changes—new families resulting from the earlier baby boom—which are expected to diminish during the '70s.
7. Decreasing family size.
8. Greater discrimination on the part of quality-conscious shoppers.
9. A consumer reluctance to purchase high-fashion, expensive clothes.

GROWING CONSUMER INFLUENCE

Affluent consumers are in a more advantageous position than ever before to influence the type and quality of clothing available in the market. If they fail to buy a retailer's merchandise, they can put him out of business.

Women are growing more independent—they feel free about choosing or rejecting what the market has to offer. Consider the midi, offered as a new fashion at the beginning of the '70s, and expected by many in the industry to usher in a return of the cycle brought into fashion by Dior in the '40s. Women were not ready for this style so they turned to pant suits in phenomenal numbers. When short pants—shorts—were due to be replaced in fashion, young people preferred "hot pants," sometimes compromising by covering them with long slit skirts (Fig. 1-12, *a*). From hot pants they went on to "short suits" (Fig. 1-12 *b*)—in fashion terminology.

What about the midi? "Give it more time," said some people experienced in the fashion world. It will be interesting to watch this influence through the '70s.

Fashion tastes have become more sophisticated because of exposure to mass media. The retailer who is indifferent to the consumer's needs and desires can

Figure 1-12. In the early 1970s, young women preferred "hot pants" to the midi. (Courtesy of Celanese)

expect her to patronize his competitor, who may be more aware. Competition for the fashion clothing dollars increased tremendously during the '60s, leading customers into such new places as variety stores, discount houses, and supermarkets. The freedom to reject ready-to-wear may be reflected partly in the tremendous increase in home sewing, and the growing realization in the industry that over-the-counter fabrics require up-grading to the standards of those in ready-to-wear. Because clothes last longer, the consumer who is unable to find what she wants may postpone purchasing clothing and spend more on nonfashion merchandise—home furnishing, travel, and art objects.

The Clothing Industry—United States

The textile and clothing industries combined rank among the largest in the United States. Approximately one half of the amount spent by Americans annually for clothing is spent on women's fashion merchandise.

The industry has been characterized by outstanding leadership in the development and production of man-made fibers since World War II, leading to innovations in fibers, fabrics, and finishes. These have greatly influenced construction, care, and use of clothing. More adequate information about textile products has been made available and the Federal Trade Commission (FTC) has set up rulings to protect the consumer from deceptive practices.

A real problem in the apparel industry is the high cost of labor in a non-automated industry. Apparel industry leaders expect a high degree of intensive automation within fifteen years. But the cost of installing automatic machinery will be exceptionally high.

The Gerber Scientific Instrument Company has introduced computerized pattern grading, cloth cutting, and sewing. The computerized cutter can cut 100 to 200 ply of cloth at a time. The sewing machines involve the use of a punched tape that can be designed to guide the equipment through a limitless variety of operations, without an operator, functioning on the principal of the old player piano. The operating speed is ten times that of home sewing machines. First put into use by the Arrow Company, these machines can sew collars on shirts in about one half the time required by traditional methods. The president of this company, in pointing to many high-technology firms that are high in sales abroad and in the doldrums at home, observes that costs can be lowered if 100 operators can be replaced with computerized sewing machines. This statement deserves some thought. Why will the cost go down? Because the labor cost has been eliminated? What will happen to the laborers who lose their jobs to the machine? Will they be able to get new jobs?

Within recent years, many smaller mills and apparel manufacturing plants have consolidated or gone out of business for reasons in addition to outdated machinery: the increase in imports, creating an oversupply of products and lowered prices that makes it impossible to raise wages and compete in the labor market; and changed consumer buying patterns, requiring the rapid delivery of merchandise to the retailer who orders a relatively small number of garments at one time because he is unwilling to risk a large and possibly unmovable inventory. This places the textile manufacturer at a disadvantage. He has to predict the amounts and types of fabrics needed in his inventories—dependent upon consumer acceptance. Only the best-organized large industries, well supplied with the newest and most efficient machinery, and capable of meeting the challenges presented in a fashion consumer's market, are able to survive. Anything the manufacturer can do to reduce the time between the order and the delivery will cut costs. With fashion unpredictable, short-interval scheduling is an absolute necessity for the producer. Some of the leading retailers are reported to be near a complete inventory-control system, with an automated management system utilizing electronic data processing to take much of the guesswork out of retailing operations and reduce mounting costs. The system is designed for quicker sales transactions, giving customers faster service and a greater merchandise selection and retailers reduced operating costs.[16]

The 1960s witnessed increased competition, more affluent consumers who demanded new and sophisticated techniques in merchandising, and a phenomenal growth in the construction of garments in the home—fashion sewing.

[16]John Osbon, "Sears Near Decision on EDP System," *Women's Wear Daily* (April 12, 1971), p. 29.

The 1970s are viewed as a challenge to the industry's experts to recognize the potent force that "consumerism" has become and develop the high-quality products and easy-care handling that our leisure-oriented society requires.

The implications of projected changes in such factors as population, income, age groups, and college-educated persons for the '70s suggest these developments: "More sophisticated, richer, better-educated consumers will demonstrate a more pronounced tendency toward individualism and, possibly, less interest in possessions. There will be greater stress on all forms of recreational expenditures. . . . National brands will be stronger than ever. Price lines will appeal to the middle and upper income groups."[17]

Designer Geoffrey Beene sees a trend in the '70s for regrettably smaller and more frequent collections. In his opinion, "people buy more impulsively than they ever have before. . . . It's a visual way of buying now where it used to be more practical. . . . Customers buy too quickly, too impulsively, and too often."[18]

Donald Brooks looks into the '70s: "The boutique growth will be driven by 'the unit price being less expensive, hopefully because of its dash and because it is designed for a young market, . . .' The couture . . . will be bought by women 'who don't want to look like other people and want durability . . . Women won't buy labels blindly . . .' stores should have a 'more open mind as to what customers want to wear, as opposed to what the buyer wants to buy. . . . At the point of retail, whole design concepts should be presented to the public instead of a picked-over selection of a buyer'."[19]

Here are some points from Bill Blass: "In this country, there's a tremendous number of women who want designer clothes. Not for the labels—we all agree that's dead—but she wants the authority of expensive clothes that are well-made, and good-fitting. . . . It's wrong to think there is a radical change needed in fashion. One of the things contributing to women's lack of confidence is the feeling something she buys will be outdated in six months. . . . A woman interested in clothes doesn't want to see the whole collection in August. . . . We're seeing more European rtw [ready-to-wear], but it's not really important. . . . We make clothes for most of America."[20]

Oscar de la Renta comments that "Great quality is not of so much importance anymore. Not for the great majority. The people who buy couture clothes are a very small segment in our society. They do care for a certain degree of quality. Young people love quality too, but in a different way. They will love a bag embroidered in Pakistan . . . quality, too, but a different value."[21]

Chester Weinberg expresses this idea: "The concept of clothes at any price just doesn't relate to today. Women will think of buying a painting, some furniture

---

[17] Samuel Feinberg, "The Changing Retail Profile—Look to 1980," *Women's Wear Daily* (March 5, 1971), p. 15.

[18] "Surviving the Seventies," *Women's Wear Daily* (March 5, 1971), p. 13.

[19] Ibid., p. 13.

[20] Ibid., p. 4.

[21] Ibid., p. 5.

or several other things before spending $1,000 or $1,500 for a dress or costume."[22]

THE INTERNATIONAL MARKET

Reasons for international trade are complex and far-reaching. These three are basic.

1. The consumer is provided with a wider range of choice, and possibly with commodities, that could not be produced in his own country for one reason or another.
2. Differences in raw materials, labor, talents, climate, tools, and machinery available may build up surpluses or result in scarcities of certain commodities; therefore, an exchange of commodities can balance and ease the situation to the advantage of both nations involved.
3. Liberal trade policies improve foreign relations and raise economic levels and clothing consumption for all.

The buying of imported goods versus products made in the United States is a controversial subject with some Americans. Recently, a drop in unemployment in the U.S.A. was attributed to imports. Whether that attribution is correct or not, depends on many factors that will require careful study before conclusions can be reached. No doubt, the very poor business conditions in the textile mills are partly due to the excessive importing of textile products, especially low-quality materials from Japan. On the other side of the question, an analysis by Lawrence Krause concluded that very little of unemployment in the U.S. (first quarter of 1970 through first quarter of 1971) was related to foreign trade. The reason for this is that many exports from the United States had a higher labor content than the product displaced by U.S. imports. For example, capital goods, which account for about 35 per cent of U.S. exports, generally use a far higher ratio to capital than do autos and many other types of consumer goods that the U.S. imports.[23]

The International Couture

Paris has been considered the world center of fashion for the last half century. Within recent years, its position has appeared to weaken. The couture admits that the market has decreased in size and that women cannot be depended on to follow its lead completely.

For economic reasons many designers have added couture ready-to-wear and opened boutiques. Dior was among the first to spread his name over an empire of fashion-related businesses. One realistic designer has expressed the opinion that many houses would close, "should Americans stop buying their perfumes." Growing inroads are being made on the high-fashion couture by these boutiques.

Some houses are closing the couture and going exclusively to ready-to-wear, whereas others are attempting to maintain both. The reputation for creation and

[22]Chester Weinberg, "Fashion for Less," *Women's Wear Daily* (May 5, 1971), p. 1.
[23]Sanford Rose, "Our Strange Hard Line on Trade," *Fortune* (November 1971), p. 139.

inspiration in the field of fashion is considered an advantage for the ready-to-wear phase of the business, and the couture label is valuable for the boutique.

One of the fundamental problems existing for the couture is the difficulty and rising cost in getting the hand labor needed. Another, and perhaps more significant, problem is the behavior of today's consumers, who show a tendency to shy away from the purchase of expensive clothes.

SOME DESIGNER'S OPINIONS

In defense of the trend toward couture ready-to-wear, André Oliver, co-designer for Cardin says, "The couture can never regain its authority over the way people dress. The days are over when a couturier . . . could cause women deliberately to make themselves ugly to be in fashion. Women are free to choose now. The designer can reach women who like his style through his ready-to-wear."[24]

Marc Bohan of Dior still sees haute couture in terms of the private client, existing along with ready-to-wear: "Haute couture creates a climate. It gives fashion an authenticity."[25]

Givenchy believes that there will always be enough women with money to spend in the couture.

Helene of St. Laurent states that "Couture just cannot die, for the basic and simple reason that it is and will always be a laboratory of research."[26]

Since the above statement was made, Yves St. Laurent has closed his couture. After fourteen years at the top as one of the great names in high fashion, he chose to concentrate on his ready-to-wear market.

Art and Dress

Art involves not only the ability to paint a beautifully dressed body, or to chisel a sculpture of her; it focuses also on developing the talent to choose, construct, or assemble garments and accessories displaying imagination, creativity, and an appreciation for beauty.

Lynes observes that "The marriage of the practical and the aesthetic was an idea that Americans liked in the nineteenth century just as well as they claim they do now—that there needed to be nothing top-lofty about art and that it was a commodity that people could use and enjoy without pretentions or large bank accounts."[27]

The art principle of the ancient Greeks was that of enduring beauty through simplicity and harmony. The classic draping, which was comprised of a rectangle of cloth held by beautiful pins and girdles, has been preserved in sculpture (Fig. 1-3), furnishing the basic concepts in simplicity and grace to which fashion design-

[24]G. Y. Dryanksy, "Couture Happy for Season But Wary on Future," *Women's Wear Daily* (Aug. 6, 1971), p. 1.

[25]"Ready-to-wear vs. Couture," *Women's Wear Daily* (Feb. 8, 1971), p. 1.

[26]Claude de Leusse, "Fitting the Bill," *Women's Wear Daily* (June 21, 1971), p. 13.

[27]Lynes, op. cit., p. 79.

ers return most frequently. Originality came in rearranging, just as it does today. A new fashion almost always is an evolution. The "new" lies more in fresh combinations than in a change of silhouette itself—by cutting into sections, by reviving a type of decoration, or by using the newer types of fabrics.

The Romans adopted ideas from the Greeks, and the French adapted the costumes of all Mediterranean civilizations to their own way of life. The rest of the world has been affected by French dressmaking. But American designers and mass production are exerting a powerful world influence. Together, the styles of European and American costume are known as *Western dress*.

The modern dress designer has a philosophy of art, fashion, and history plus imagination. A wide knowledge is helpful in making satisfying and beautiful choices.

The various art principles involving line, shape, size, texture, and color influence the image projected by the individual. This image can be enhanced or altered through illusory procedures. Techniques will be presented in greater detail in Chapter 2.

The Physical Aspects of Clothing

The physical aspects of clothing involve (1) factors affecting physical comfort and well-being, and (2) clothing in relation to physical appearance.

Well-chosen clothing functions as a control of the environment: to insulate and protect the body from extremes in temperature; to provide comfort through absorption or evaporation of moisture; to avoid restrictions of body movement caused by tightness in the garment; and to prevent irritation from fibers or construction processes.

Glossary

Avant-garde [Fr.] (àvahn *gard*), ahead of fashion, a trend.

Boutique [Fr.] (*boo*-tēek), a small retail store in which miscellaneous items are sold, including accessories.

Couture [Fr.] (*koo*-tür), sewing or needle work; the product of a dressmaker.

Couturier [Fr.] (kōō tü *ryā*)—male dressmaker; designer; head of a dressmaking house.

Couturière [Fr.] (koo tü *ryār*), woman dressmaker; designer.

Fashion, the prevailing mode or style.

Haute couture [Fr.] (*oat*-koo-tur), high fashion; creative fashion design; couturier houses as a group.

High fashion, the newest or latest fashion.

Style, a characteristic form, outline, design, or dress; for example, a princess style, A-line skirt, set-in sleeve, turtleneck.

ANSPACK, KARLYNE. *The Why of Fashion.* Ames, Iowa: Iowa State University Press, 1967.

KEFGEN, MARY, AND PHYLLIS TOUCHIE-SPECHT. *Individuality in Clothing Selection and Personal Appearance.* New York: Macmillan Publishing Co., Inc., 1971.

MCLUHAN, MARSHALL. *Understanding Media: The Extensions of Man.* New York: McGraw-Hill Book Company, 1964.

ROACH, MARY ELLEN, AND JOANNE B. EICHER. *Dress, Adornment, and the Social Order.* New York: John Wiley & Sons, Inc., 1965.

2

Color, Line and Shape, Pattern, and Texture

One may become a designer who plans and makes beautiful clothes, or a "selecting and arranging" designer who buys and wears clothes in harmony with her wishes, personality, and figure, appropriate for the occasions in her life-style.

Dorothy Shaver, president of Lord and Taylor for many years, is given credit for coining the phrase, "The American Look," that look associated with perfect grooming, simplicity of dress, and attention to detail to give a *casual* effect.

29

This chapter will review briefly ways in which clothes influence appearance. For a more detailed study of the factors involved, suggested readings are listed in footnotes and at the end of the chapter.

Color

The generally accepted theory in making a color choice is to give first consideration to what you like in color—the effect the color has on you and your personality. Second, consider your personal coloring. Then take into account the occasion, function, climate, and weather.

In the past, great importance was attached to the *symbolism* of color—and that varied with different cultures. Today we accept the fact that color does have a *psychological* effect on both the wearer and her observers. Dingy, dull, and sedate colors may make the wearer feel weary or uninspired and give others an impression of dullness, inadequacy, or primness when the very opposite may be true of the person's personality.

THEORIES OF COLOR

Psychologists and physicists use charts to explain color in terms of vision and of colored lights (of special interest in the theater and in store displays). The Munsell color theory uses five colors: yellow, green, blue, purple, and red. The Prang system (Plate I) uses six colors: three *primaries*—yellow, red, and blue—which in pairs make the three *secondaries*—orange, green, and purple. Opposites are *complements* because each completes the other; however, in pigments they make gray—in colored yarns woven closely the resulting fabric is almost gray—but used side by side in larger amounts, in fabrics and costumes, one enhances or emphasizes the other.

Hue (H) refers to the name of the color on the color wheel (not the fashion term necessarily).
Value (V) refers to the lightness or darkness of a color.
Intensity (I) refers to the brightness or dullness.

It is more important to discern not only differences in hue but also in value and intensity. Half close your eyes to see value differences. All hues in fabric can be varied in dyeing by the use of water (white in paint) to make them lighter, by black to darken them, or by the use of their complements to gray or soften them. Making value and intensity scales will give you a further understanding of the many subtle qualities of color to be considered.

Black is the darkest, white is the lightest, with the middle value halfway between. A *value scale* is a gradation from (black) low dark, dark, high dark, middle, low light, light, to high light (white).

Between neutral (gray) and the full intensity of a color may be an indefinite number of intensities, but four steps make a practical way to express the amount, as $\frac{1}{4}N$ (neutral), $\frac{1}{2}N$, $\frac{3}{4}N$, N, $\frac{3}{4}I$, $\frac{1}{2}I$, $\frac{1}{4}I$.

Because we do not all see colors alike, artists usually describe them in terms of hue (location on the color wheel), value (light, medium, or dark), and intensity (bright or dull). Fabric or yarn dyers follow names on the Standard Color Card. Fashion designers and advertisers use glamorous names: peach-blossom on the Standard Color Card was called "Stifled Sigh Pink" by one designer; in art class you would probably call it a grayed, light yellow-red.

A *monochromatic* color scheme implies the use of one color in various degrees of light and dark—in values of the color.

An *analogous* color harmony uses those colors next to each other on the color wheel; they are related because they contain a color in common. The more closely related the set of colors, the easier they are to combine. These harmonies are generally more interesting than monochromatic color harmonies.

Complementary colors are opposite each other on the color wheel, as red and green. Used next to each other, they appear brighter. Green placed next to florid skin, makes it appear even more red.

Split-complementary colors involve the use of a color with the colors on each side of its complement.

The *triad* harmony is a combination of three colors placed equidistant on the color wheel; the *tetrad* uses four colors equidistant on the color wheel.

Warm and Cool Colors

Observe Plate I (following p. 38). The primary colors yellow and red are regarded as *warm* colors because of their effects upon us, probably through our association with the warm or hot rays of the sun and the color and heat of fire. Orange is warm, being composed of yellow and red.

Blue, or the other side of the color wheel, is cool. Although green and purple are mixtures of cool and warm colors, they are generally classified as more cool than warm. When blue predominates they are, naturally, more cool than the colors that result when the mixture approaches pure red or yellow.

Selecting Colors for Your Type

Here is a basic guide for selecting becoming colors: if your personal coloring is warm, use warm colors; if your coloring is cool, select cool colors. *Key your color choices to your natural coloring.*

Your natural coloring is determined by skin, hair, and eyes, with the skin probably of first importance because of its larger area. If the undertone of your skin is yellow, the skin will be cream in color, making you a warm type; if you are without yellow in the skin, the undertone is blue, and the coloring is cool; you will find pure white harmonious with your coloring, rather than creamy white. Hair and eye colors are keyed by nature to skin tones.

Check the side of the color wheel from which you will choose most of your colors; from the opposite side select colors for accents or accessories.

The best way to learn which colors in your group look best on you is to try them. Drape them around your body in a good light, both natural and artificial, since they may appear quite different in these two situations. Select the colors you like, in the values or intensities that look best on you. (Plate II following p. 38.)

THE COLOR KEY SYSTEM

The Color Key System, developed by Robert Dorr, involves a simplified plan for choosing and combines the colors most becoming to an individual. Basically, it operates on the same principles incorporated in the presentation of warm and cool colors, designating the colors keyed to blue undertones as Key 1, and those keyed to yellow as Key 2. The individual chooses the key that harmonizes with his natural coloring.

Research supporting the Color Key System has indicated that "each person during his early teens forms a pattern of color choice that remains constant during his entire lifetime. . . . It has been proven that when an individual, male or female, selects the key he prefers, the colors in that key are his most becoming and comfortable."[1] The colors in each key are scientifically related to each other by the basic pigments in their composition, and the individual's natural color is made from these same colors.

USING COLORS

1. If you are warm in coloring and you like blue, select a blue that has been modified by a warm color—such as yellow—to give a warm greenish-blue that will key to your warm color.
2. Eyes can be emphasized by wearing a bit of the same, but not brighter, color near the face, as the latter choice tends to drain color from the eyes.
3. Light hair is emphasized by dark colors; it may appear faded with colors that are extremely bright.
4. Color and sheen in hair are enhanced by contrasting colors or by the same color.
5. Blonds who are delicate in coloring may wish to avoid pale, dull colors, which give a monotonous effect. Clear colors are best.
6. Wear colors darker than the skin, unless you wish to emphasize its darkness or suntan. Pastels and white accent dark skin coloring.
7. Dark skins with dark hair look good in dark, rich colors.
8. Where there is an excess of yellow in the skin, resulting in sallowness, avoid yellows, yellow-greens, and purple; natural coloring is emphasized by wearing a repetition of the color or its complement.
9. Where coloring approaches neutral, it may be safer to use a combination of warm and cool, using colors that look best with your skin and eyes—with some dark values to contrast with the hair. Avoid neutral colors such as tan, dull gold, or gray. Try clear blue-greens and corals. Select brown or cocoa if you are the warm type, in preference to tan and beige, in order to provide value contrast.
10. The figure appears larger in white, bright, and warm colors—these seem

[1]Mary Kefgen and Phyllis Touchie-Specht, *Individuality in Clothing Selection and Personal Appearance* (New York: Macmillan Publishing Co., Inc., 1971), p. 282.

to advance. Dark, dull, and cool colors tend to minimize, as they give the impression of receding.

11. When several colors are used in one composition, arrange them in pleasing proportions. Equal amounts are monotonous.

12. The Law of Areas suggests the use of the stronger color (in hue, value, or intensity) in smaller amounts, to attract attention to some desirable center of interest.

13. Repetition of a color should create a smooth, rhythmic eye movement. It is more pleasing not to repeat a contrasting bright color more than once or twice in a costume, even then possibly changing the tone.

14. A girl with a quiet personality may be eclipsed by large areas of bright color, or her personality may be enhanced—the most important point to be considered is how she feels in this color.

Line and Shape

DESIGN

A design is a deliberate, well-considered plan for creating something beautiful. Although each person is a potential designer, to be excellent one learns to create beauty through order and harmony. All designers work with the elements of line, space, texture, and color. The elements are not used alone but are combined in useful, appropriate ways to produce interesting and graceful effects (Fig. 2-1).

Figure 2-1. This fifteenth-century tapestry, *Courtiers with Roses,* is considered one of the finest examples of the weaving art. The medieval headdress (hennin) balanced by the sweeping robe of a slender figure has been the inspiration of many traditional wedding gowns. Not only the figures, but the shapes and space divisions (stripes of red, white, and green) exemplify harmony and pleasing proportions. (Courtesy of The Metropolitan Museum of Art.)

Figure 2-2. Structural design composed of integral parts—pants with wide bottoms and cuffs, lines of a blazer jacket with patch pockets, and knitted turtle-neck sweater—with stitching in contrasting color, adding *a*, structural decoration; *b*, saddlestitching in contrasting color emphasizes bodice edges and pleats; *c*, decorative design in embroidery showing Chinese influence. (Courtesy of Celanese, *a*; Donovan-Galvani, *b*; National Cotton Council, *c*.)

The design of a garment involves two elements—*structural* and *decorative* design. These are often inseparable. Structural design includes the over-all design of a garment—its outline shape or silhouette—plus all those lines and details involved in assembling the sections of the garment, such as seams, darts, tucks, and pleats. These may also add a decorative quality—structural decoration—especially where they are emphasized by a line of top stitching, as on a welt seam or an edge. This may be given further emphasis by introducing thread of a contrasting color (Fig. 2-2, *a* and *b*).

Decorative design refers to decoration applied to a garment. It is not an integral part of the structure (Fig. 2-2, *c*). Applied decoration may include various types of trims, as braids, embroidery, buttons that do not fasten, and tacked-on bows. Unless these are properly related to the structural design, the effect may be displeasing.

THE SILHOUETTE

The silhouette can reveal one's natural body contour or distort it, as fashion has sometimes decreed. Hooped skirts, bustles, extreme blousiness, and pinched waistlines are examples of such distortion. Consider the wedding dresses in Figure 2-3; compare the sleeve of *a* with the back skirt fullness of *b*; the bustle effect in this case is properly subordinated to give a pleasing effect. The silhouette is definitely related to points of movement—natural, body division lines. The fashionable shifts of the '60s, tending to be shapeless and somewhat out of harmony with the body shape were made more imaginative by the designer's use of belts (although placed lower than the waistline and loosely adjusted), long bishop sleeves, small soft collars, and applied decorations (Fig. 2-4). Structural seamlines may suggest the natural location of such body features as waistline, neckline, and the hinges joining the arms to the shoulders. The long torso style of the 1920s frequently divided the design into equal oblongs; the chemise styles of 1963 improved the idea by suggesting a rounded bust and the normal waistline; and although the shift of the late 1960s and the miniskirt often revealed unsightly knees, the right hose, shoes, or boots minimized this effect.

Vertical lines tend to slenderize when the eye is led up and down—referred to as vertical movement. Use *horizontal* lines and shapes where width is desired (Fig. 2-5). With skill, horizontal lines and spaces can be arranged to suggest vertical movement. Gradation of sizes is helpful in achieving this result; they serve as a ladder to greater height. Also, bold stripes, even used vertically, may widen the figure. The effect produced by lines and spaces, therefore, will depend upon the direction of eye movement in perceiving the total design. Wide belts do not slenderize but may call attention to a small waistline. Broad collars accent shoulders (good to balance wide hips); avoid an appearance of top-heaviness. *Curves,* giving the effect of roundness and a softer, feminine feeling, may broaden (Fig. 2-6). *Diagonal* lines, to be transitional, connect some point in the design to another point; they are good harmonizers, especially if slightly elliptical instead of yardstick straight.

Repetition of a line or shape and extreme contrast both emphasize. Appropriate hair styles and necklines vary with the shape of a face (Fig. 2-7). What effect

Figure 2-3. Wedding dresses of today involve simpler silhouettes, decorative details, and dressmaking than formerly; large sleeve, *a*; bustle effect, *b*.

Figure 2-4. The shifts of the 1960s, rather shapeless, were made more imaginative by the use of low-placed loose belts and applied decoration. (Courtesy of Cotton Producers Institute, *a*; Howard Wolf, *b*.)

Figure 2-5. Vertical lines add height. Figure *b*, with the V turned upward, appears taller than *a*. The horizontal lines across *a* and *e* emphasize the width of the figure at these points. Two lines, *c*, increase the vertical movement; the spreading of lines, *d*, emphasizes the shoulder width and narrows the waistline by contrast.

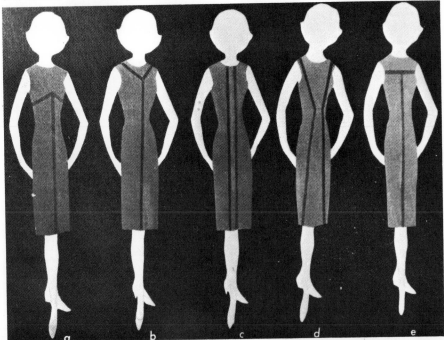

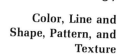

Figure 2-6. Curves and ruffle tend to increase apparent size. (Courtesy of Cotton Producers Institute.)

Figure 2-7. Repetition and contrast both accent shape; therefore, it is wise to select transitional lines or shapes that are related and harmonious. Shown are, left to right, square, round, oval, long, and heart-shaped faces with appropriate hair styles. Square and round faces can also be narrowed by long straight hair, partly covering the sides of the face.

Figure 2-8. Hue or value contrast tends to cut height. The short person appears taller in *b*; with its greater length of skirt, *a* is better for her than *c*, which can be worn by the tall, slender person.

would result if the chin lines were repeated in these necklines? A square jaw and broad shoulders are accented by a square neckline, high yokes, bangs, heavy-rimmed glasses, and square shoulder lines.

RHYTHM

Repetition of a design in rows of trim, buttons, and seamlines permits a smooth, rhythmic eye movement. The eye automatically connects points in space; if there are many spots not in a direct, flowing line, the eye movement jumps. A white dress with black earrings, black necklace, black buttons, black belt, black gloves, and black shoes would appear "spotty." Efficient planning also involves the careful consideration of color and value contrasts in such cases to give a pleasing, rhythmic arrangement of details and smooth movement.

PROPORTION OR SCALE

The relationship in size between a part and the whole is referred to as scale or proportion (Fig. 2-8).

With striking intensity or value contrasts, spaces may be less pleasing when widths or lengths are equal. However, interesting effects can be achieved with evenly spaced stripes in dull or dark colors, with a series of related colors, or with chevron cuts.

The *tiers* in fiesta-style skirts seem more imaginative and interesting in unequal, graduated widths: they may be graduated with equal decoration, or equal tiers

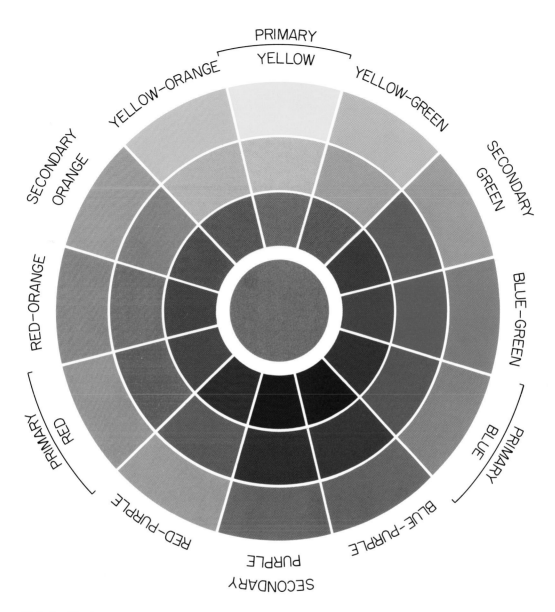

Plate I. The Prang color wheel consists of three groups of colors, primary, secondary, and intermediate. The primary colors—yellow, red, and blue—when paired, make the three secondaries—orange, green, and purple. The primary colors, paired with secondaries, yield six intermediate colors. (Reprinted by permission from Dorothy Stepat-Devan, *Introduction to Home Furnishings,* Macmillan Publishing Co., Inc., New York, 1971.)

Plate II. One of the most satisfying ways to learn what a color can do for you is to try it on. (Courtesy of, *top row, left to right,* Jane Euresti, Sherilyn Jackson, Barbara Price, Jackie Williams, and Jan Jennings; *middle row,* Debbie Brown, Bonnie Baldridge, Anita Owens, and Jan Stephens; *bottom row,* Joyce Stockton, Patricia Boyce, and Sharice Adams. Color background courtesy of Poly-SiBonne! by Armo, 206 West 40th Street, New York City, New York.)

may have graduated decoration, or graduated decoration may be applied to graduated tiers.

Optical illusions are created by changing spaces to enhance the attractive, or to camouflage a proportion that you wish were different. The hipline in *c* will make the hips appear wider as the eye follows this line across the body. A full sleeve ending at this point would further increase the feeling of width at the hips, because the sleeve widths would provide an extension of the line. This condition applies to any part of the silhouette: sleeves puffed at the shoulder would increase shoulder width; elbow-length sleeves, full at their lower edges, could be expected to increase the apparent width of the body at the bust line.

EMPHASIS

Emphasis involves the most eye-catching part of a garment or outfit. Many good designers place the main point of emphasis near the face or in a position to lead the eye to the face; through lack of emphasis, undesirable features are minimized. (Consider Figs. 2-2, b and 2-5.) Unbroken lines from shoulder to hem, as in princess lines, keep eyes away from the waistline; darts in a bodice matching gore lines in a skirt do the same. If hips are too prominent, call more attention to the face with unusual necklines, collars, and necklaces; radiating lines at the neckline attract attention to the face. A blond's appearance is enhanced by a dark value worn next to her hair.

Triangles are employed to lead the eye to areas needing emphasis and away from undesirable features. The eye finds the wide end of the triangle a stable base on which to rest, causing the whole design to appear wider there. A skirt too narrow at the bottom makes wide hips look wider; a flared skirt with the base of the triangle near the hem seems more balanced and keeps the hips from looking so wide. Placing the base of the triangle at the shoulders emphasizes them and minimizes the hips.

An object gains emphasis if given enough plain space for a background; a lace collar is lost on a printed dress; most jewelry or flowers are not effective on prints. What kind of pin or necklace might be worn on a printed dress?

Emphasize one center of interest and subordinate the rest of the costume to that. For example, make a cuff narrower or less decorated than the collar (Fig. 2-9).

Eleanor King, author of *Glorify Yourself,*[2] is responsible for the "Rule of 14," which suggests a maximum of fourteen eye-arresting elements in a street costume—only one should dominate. Too many centers of interest give an overdecorated and spotty effect.

SPECIAL FIGURE PROBLEMS

What does your full-length mirror reveal about you? Does it make you wish for a more perfect figure?

There is no such thing as a perfect figure, according to conclusions derived from a survey based on the opinions of 40,000 women. The composite perfect figure

[2] Englewood Cliffs, N.J.: Prentice-Hall, Inc., 1948.

Figure 2-9. Emphasis created by applied decoration. (See also Figure 2-7.)

that existed in the minds of these women does not exist in reality. This is evident from the study of measurements of the so-called perfect figures of royalty, the fashionable set, actresses, and fashion models—all considered to be among the most beautiful women. The public image of a woman of fashion is extreme slenderness to the point of emaciation. But the chunky, chubby girl can be as popular, loved, respected, and happy as the others by attention to grooming, careful choices, fit, and an interesting personality.

Beauty cannot be measured solely in inches. There are many conflicting ideas of what constitutes this quality. The Greeks' idea of feminine beauty is immortally portrayed in the Venus de Milo, which has influenced our concepts of beauty through the ages. Each culture—Japanese, African, or any other—has its own conceptions of what makes a woman beautiful. In each one we find small variations. Figures can vary somewhat and still be beautiful.

Accept the facts of your basic shape. You may want to improve your own special lines through posture, properly fitted undergarments, or optical illusions in dress. The body silhouette of "Norma" approximates the natural youthful figure (Fig. 2-10).

For the *petite* (short, tiny) girl with flat chest and thin arms, the semifitted princess or shift style is better than the fitted waistline, because it gives the illusion of height. Other lines that are excellent choices are narrow yokes and collars and short, fairly loose jackets and short skirts scaled to her size; moderately full peasant-type sleeves to hide thin arms—not balloonish, as this amount of fullness

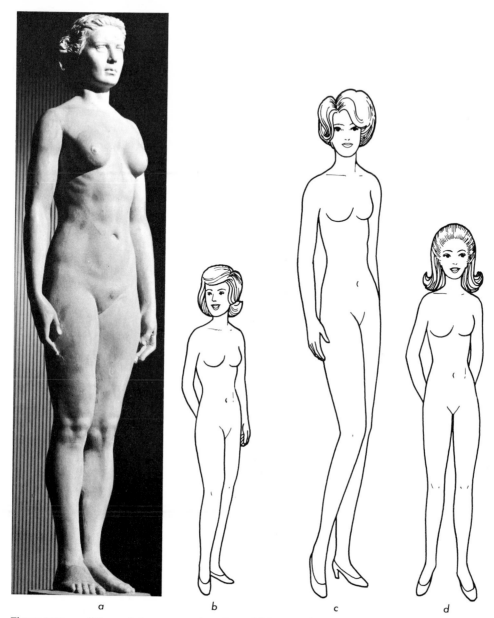

Figure 2-10. *a*, "Norma," the average American girl (16 years), modeled by Abram Belskie under the direction of Dr. Robert Latou Dickinson. The average American girl measures bust, 33.9 inches; waist, 26.4 inches; hip, 37.4 inches; height, 5 feet, 3.6 inches; weight, 123 pounds. She is four inches shorter than most fashion models, larger in bust, girth of hip, thigh, calf, ankle. (Courtesy of American Museum of Natural History.) *b*, Fashion model. *c*, Sketching model for advertising. *d*, Average American college girl.

41

would be out of proportion for her; soft, kimono-type sleeves, not too voluminous; textures should be neither too flat nor too shaggy. If clinging, the flat texture would accent her thinness and hollows, unless underlined; shagginess to a point would add pleasing curves to her figure, provided the bulk were not too extreme. Small accessories are generally appropriate, but for her, too many of them might over-emphasize the effect.

The person with a *short, heavy* figure can improve her appearance by holding her head erect, keeping her neck free of clutter to gain height and her hair neater to achieve elegance. A wise investment would be a cincher girdle to make the waist-line smaller and neater.

The *short, chunky* type of girl will try to aim at the inconspicuous costume, with accents on her most attractive features and details inside the silhouette. Well-placed lengthwise and diagonal lines are flattering because they lead the eye in a vertical direction. She must avoid both too snug and too full, bunchy, bulky areas; they extend the silhouette, and increase the appearance of size. She requires narrow panels or gores and soft, neat fullness, such as groups of pleats or flare in the skirt, rather than a gathered skirt. A slight flare at the lower skirt balances width of bust, hips, or waist, and gives a youthful swing. She shuns yokes, flounces, peplums, off-the-shoulder effect, wide flowing sleeves, and flaring or contrasting cuffs to avoid apparent increase in width.

She looks good in coat styles, shifts, button-down-the-front styles, and narrow self-belts, better worn slightly lower than normal, but not at hipline, to avoid accenting width—a higher line can give the illusion of a smaller hipline. Half-size or custom-size patterns and garments may fit, but they are usually too matronly in style. She looks best with normal armholes, fitted as high under the arm as possible, to give the illusion of height and slenderness, and skirts not too short.

In coats, a straight-line, *single-breasted* Chesterfield type is more flattering than a fitted princess cut. If a princess style is chosen, it must be only semifitted, to avoid emphasis on her curves. If she has a short neck, she will find that garments that button up high or with stand-up collars may seem to shorten her neck. Cardigan styles are very good for her. A closely fitted jacket or snug skirt empha-sizes heavy hips or thighs. She looks better in a short semifitted jacket or bolero so that the length of the skirt showing will make her appear taller; a three-quarter topper conceals the hips, but it should not flare much or be in contrasting value or hue. An overblouse is better than tuck-in styles. A mannish shirt usually adds apparent bulk.

She needs heavy fabrics that fall into straighter lines. Clinging, lightweight fabrics, bold prints, bright colors, and stiff, shiny fabrics tend to increase her size. A contrasting blouse and skirt will make her look broader and shorter. Heavy jewelry and a large flat bag make her seem smaller by contrast.

The *stocky figure,* which is taller yet broad, will want to avoid close or too-loose cuts (a dirndl skirt, a peg-top skirt, or long full sleeves would increase her apparent size). She would benefit from skirts cut in several gores or sections; modified flares, pleats below the hipline, princess shifts, button-down-the-front styles; narrow collars, long V-necks, a slight ease rather than a snug fit in the lower bodice; three-quarter or long straight sleeves; diagonal lines, heavy fabrics, and narrow belts. To reduce the buxom look, she needs simple collarless styles, softly draped bodices, softly flared skirts, dark boxy jackets, and simple, semifitted garments. Fussy trims, puffed sleeves, ordinary or bold prints, checks, plaids, fleece coats, and bright colors are not for her. Sophisticated large-scale or textured prints make good choices. Better choices, even in gay colors, result if the background is neutral, dark, or closely related to the colors in the print.

The *tall, thin girl* has fashion on her side. She has the opportunity to play up her small, slender waist and use more horizontal lines than other types. If graceful she can wear striking designs and colors. She can have large accessories—big bags. If very tall, she looks good in shorter skirts, lower heels, and hats with brims.

She can easily wear shifts, cages, separates, long-torso designs, full skirts, flounces, frilly collars and bows, capes, swagger coats, contrasting colors used horizontally, wide belts; horizontal off-the-shoulder lines, yokes, and insets; double-breasted coats, broad shoulder lines, deep armholes, and loosely cut elbow or three-quarter sleeves—anything to add width. If her neck is thin or long, she will prefer high, soft, full, or deep collars.

As a rule, princess styles need to be broken by horizontal or diagonal lines to improve her proportions and add femininity. Tight bodices, tight-fitted or very short sleeves, and narrow skirts—lengthwise lines—would emphasize her height.

A person with a *flat bust* or *hollow chest* can use full shifts and blouses, boleros, capes, and such decoration as pocket flaps and gathered, pleated, or frilled fronts.

One with a *large bust* looks better in garments with just enough fullness below the bust to conceal the size without adding extra bulk. A very neat fit is required, but extreme tightness is revealing. Fairly broad shoulders and a flaring hemline attract attention away from the bust. In general, breast pockets and deep yokes tend to accent the bust. Princess and shift styles are satisfactory for her. Short jackets and cardigan style sweaters form transitional lines and give a feeling of movement from shoulder to hipline (the eye does not pause at the bust). Pearls to fit a high natural neckline are better than a three-strand, bust-length necklace. Try a silver or gold chain ending with a pendant *below* the bust. Try a high-cut, under-armhole line, rather than a kimono sleeve for a slenderizing effect; however, well-cut gussets can give the same result.

If you have *round shoulders,* work on your posture. Wear dresses with backs slightly bloused, gathers at the waistline, semifitted jackets, and small collars. The shoulder seam may lie half an inch back of the highest shoulder point. Learn proper pattern alteration.

With a *sway back,* select princess or shift styles, overblouses, bloused bodices, capes, and bolero jackets ending below the waistline. Fill in the hollow with belts buckled at the back, and soft girdles with ties at the back. In both the back bodice and skirt, make the darts shorter and narrower and ease in or gather the extra width to conceal the hollow. Avoid tight-fitting bodices or sweaters.

If *broad shoulders* are your problem, avoid narrow skirts, and severe high necklines. Balance the shoulders with flared hemlines. A bateau neckline will emphasize width of shoulders; use oval or V-necklines.

With *large hips,* avoid straight tubes and bulky fullness; use several gores with some flare at the hemline to balance the hips. It is a mistake to wear a tightly fitted skirt. Let the darts enter the waistline to match the darts of the bodice. As for a sway back, it is better to have a slight amount of ease at the waistline than to remove it all in darts. Lengthwise pleats and panels attract the eye away from the silhouette, unless they are located too near the hipline, where they may emphasize width.

Shallow skirt yokes, about 3 inches below the waistline, attract the eye away from the larger circumference of the normal hipline. A garment with the torso line placed between the waistline and hipline modifies the small waist and large hip by establishing a compromising circumference line. To break the larger area gives a more pleasing proportion. Since this is a conflict between the big hipline and the small waistline, it can be treated in the same way as the sway back: fill in the waistline with a crushed belt and soft blousing. You accent the width of your hips by resting your hands on your hips or by wearing wide sleeves and wide or contrasting cuffs. Before a mirror, decide on the best kind of handbag for you and the best position for carrying it. Helpful suggestions include a narrow, matching belt, if any, and a short loose jacket, with the waistline not closely fitted. A firm foundation garment and well-fitted slip will enable one to appear smart in rather snug skirts if made of firm materials. Emphasis at the shoulders tends to minimize hips by attracting attention away from them.

Pattern in Fabric

Patterns in fabric influence selection, construction, and use of garments.

With counters in stores full of patterned fabrics ranging from the bizarre, sprawling, dramatic types through the host of florals to the precise little all-overs and dainty pin-dots, how can one be sure of a choice that will bring distinction or charm to a dress?

WHAT IS A DISTINCTIVE PRINT?

When sprawling florals have been fashionable, the change to an abstract, simple geometric design may attract us, or vice versa. But to be new or different is not enough to make a print distinctive (Figs. 2-11 and 2-12). Some characteristics of prints with distinction follow.

1. Good designs are planned or *organized* units arranged in an interesting, not monotonous, order.
2. The units are discernible, not crowded, blurred, or smeared; they are not too sketchy or scratchy in drawing, nor carelessly scattered.
3. The individual units of a design may be quite simple—such as dots, squares, triangles, or abstract shapes—but to be distinctive they are arranged in some unusual, imaginative, orderly form or consist of some unusual color combination. Even seminaturalistic floral patterns may be distinctive if arranged in an orderly way to form a pattern; naturalistic pink roses sprinkled hit-or-miss would be poor in design, but the same shapely roses arranged in well-proportioned stripes might be distinctive. They might be highly

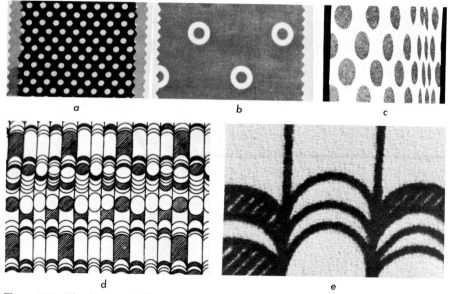

Figure 2-11. The dot can yield a variety of designs: *a*, ordinary as to proportion and interest; *b*, rings are better spaced and have more interest; *c*, more imaginative and rhythmical; *d* and *e*, much imagination indicated, interesting variations in shapes, value, and texture, in velvety flocks on heavy wool crepe.

Figure 2-12. Florals are often naturalistic, rather than stylized or conventionalized: *a*, these are also out of harmony with the geometric background; *b*, naturalistic, crowded and unorderly; *c*, Liberty print—stylized, neat and uncrowded.

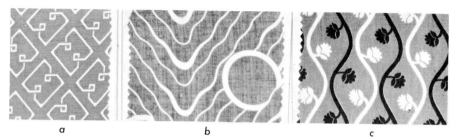

Figure 2-13. Careful designing from abstract to conventionalized floral.

stylized if changed in hue and arranged in a diagonal or definitely rhythmical formation (Fig. 2-13).

4. Small elementary designs, such as a five-petaled daisy and a heart-shaped leaf that a child could draw, are to be avoided. Rather, find the flower and leaf drawn or arranged precisely by an artist with imagination yet with simplicity. Also, avoid pictorial ideas treated in a photographic manner—naturalistic scenes, flowers, or animals. Rather, choose such ideas treated in a highly abstract, conventionalized, or stylized manner. Avoid designs shaded to give perspective; the general effect should be one of flatness to harmonize with the flatness of the cloth.

5. The lights and darks are so spaced that the darks lead the eye into light and light into dark without sudden changes or jerky eye movements.

6. One clear but unusual color, with a neutral such as white, beige, gray, or black, is generally most satisfactory; it is clean-looking, orderly, and easily combined with other fabrics (Fig. 2-14). A mixture of colors tends to be confusing. If more than two colors are used, one color should predominate, but all should be harmonious. Dainty baby colors are not in harmony with intense colors.

7. In selecting a solid color to combine with a print, it is better to select the predominating color for a more harmonious effect. If you select a minor color, it is ordinarily better to use it in lines such as binding, piping, or a belt than in spots or areas such as pockets and collars.

Selecting Patterned Fabrics

To judge a design and see its true effect, especially its rhythm, examine it from some distance and in a large piece rather than from a small sample. A useful trick is to squint as you study a design; if many masses stand out here and there or vie for importance, rhythm is lacking. Colors often neutralize each other or blend together, producing an entirely different hue or value. A red- and blue-checked material at even a short distance had a purplish cast that did not harmonize with the pure red belt chosen for it when the owner tried to match the small red checks.

Remember that backgrounds of advancing colors, as warm tones of ivory and beige tend to unify the patterns placed on them; cool, receding tones, as blue, white, and cool grays, tend to make the patterns stand out.

Study the personality of the wearer. The athletic type, the sophisticated type, and the extrovert do not look right in dainty geometric or floral prints but require stronger, more abstract, dramatic designs. The quiet type may look best in a medium-sized design in related colors. The average active girl would choose a medium-sized print, but could use more contrast in color and value, as in jade green and white stripes widely spaced. The nervous, overactive type of person may wish to avoid active prints such as stripes, checks, and fluttery, choppy designs. Too bold stripes would accent a long masculine stride. Polka dots, checks, and plaids make a confused design with freckles, bulging eyes, or ringlets in the hair.

In Figure 2-15, the size, and in this case the ages, of the wearers are in harmony with the scale of the plaids. The man could wear either, but the boy would be overpowered by the fabric in the man's jacket. The limited amount and arrange-

Figure 2-14. Japanese wood block printing—perfect examples of rhythm; never dated. (Courtesy of Art and Architecture Division; The New York Library.)

ment of value contrast in the boy's plaid minimizes the size of the squares. If the lighter yarns had been placed in the wide crosswise stripes, the scale would have been greatly increased, making it out of proportion for the smaller figure.

Small designs are suitable for both the small and the large person, but with this difference: the small person can wear a small floral, which would be a poor choice for the larger person. She is likely to appear commonplace or old in pin-dots or in any other extremely small pattern. A good choice for her would be a medium geometric or abstract design to give a texture effect of body or weight. She may wear larger designs with rhythmical lines if there is no great contrast of light and dark.

Consider the pattern in relation to the age of the wearer. Geometric and abstract prints are excellent for the active general wear of college and business girls. However, they are a little too active and businesslike for older women, who probably will look better in graceful floral (but conventionalized) designs and the more sophisticated types of prints.

If the motifs in themselves are distinctive, "spaced" prints are best reserved for the dramatic type and the average or tall figure. They are more effective on a dark or neutral background. In cutting the dress, be careful to place the motifs to their best advantage, avoiding too-prominent features and attracting the eye to more desirable locations (Fig. 2-16).

Texture of Fabric

Texture refers to the surface appearance of the fabric, plus its characteristic body or "hand"—the feel of it. Often we know how it will feel even if we do not touch it. Sight and previous experiences in handling have provided information: it is rough or smooth, soft or harsh, stiff or limp, thick or thin, spongy, sturdy, crisp, hairy, fuzzy, shiny, dull, ribbed, felted, or cobwebby.

Figure 2-15. The sizes of plaids are in harmony with the sizes of the wearers, although the adult could wear either size. (Courtesy of The Wool Bureau, Inc., *a* and *b*.)

Figure 2-16. Large designs are reserved for the dramatic type and the average or tall figure. (Courtesy of Cotton Producers Institute.)

These characteristics are created by different fibers such as cotton, wool, or synthetics; by yarns that are varied in size, ply, twist, uniformity, or lack of uniformity; by various constructions—knitted, woven, felted, bonded; and by their surface finish—napped, starched, embossed, or glazed.

Occasion and Texture

Texture is probably the most important single guide for choosing what is appropriate for the occasion. The different textures project a feeling of fitness: luxury—swish and rustle; cleanliness—crispness and smoothness; efficiency—firmness and pliability. Whatever the impression created by a fabric, its characteristics must be considered in relation to the intended use, one's personality and figure, and the silhouette indicated by the dress pattern. These points will be considered further in Chapter 7. Some textures have an appropriate relationship to the weather, climate, and season.

Materials used for clothing may be classified as to texture in three categories:

1. Heavy, rough, harsh, sturdy, dull.
2. Medium weight and roughness, soft, pliable, dull.
3. Fine, smooth, sheer, shiny, velvety, sparkling.

Fabrics in the second group are usable with those in the first and third groups; those in the first and third may be too unlike to be harmonious—care would be required in teaming fabrics from these two groups. For example, a heavy wool skirt might be worn with a nylon jersey or fine cotton broadcloth blouse from the third group, but it would not be harmonious with a silk chiffon or satin blouse from that group.

The gradations of texture indicate to a certain extent their suitability for various occasions, ages, and personalities. Hard usage and active sports require heavy, firm, coarse, and rough textures; for casual wear, smoother and more interesting textures and less sturdy fabrics may be chosen; for special occasions "after five," one may prefer the finest textures, as lace, brocade, velvet, chiffon, and satin.

Using Fabrics

1. In combining textures, avoid inharmonious extremes, or those so much alike that the combination lacks variety and interest.
2. Texture affects color: rough textures and sheerness tend to subdue the effect of a color; shiny textures brighten it.
3. Fabrics that are shiny, stiff, or bulky and those with large patterns tend to increase the apparent size of a person and may overpower the small or petite figure.
4. Because fabrics that are soft and clingy reveal the body contours, they are most appropriate for persons with pleasing proportions. The effects of these fabrics can be counterbalanced somewhat with the use of underlinings.
5. Medium and fine fabrics seem more harmonious for feminine types and for dressier occasions.

Fabric Design Terms

TRADITIONAL FABRIC DESIGNS

Bayadere, (bä ya dēr) a fabric with horizontal stripes.

Hound's tooth, small irregular design of broken "district" checks.

Liberty prints, small all-over patterns, quaint calico types; all-over, small Victorian florals; earlier examples, naturalistic but imaginative; currently conventionalized, modernized, bolder.

Paisley, pine and pomegranate (Persian) motifs made popular in Paisley (Scotland) shawls. Current ones more stylized, not crowded (Fig. 2-17).

Roman stripe, wide stripes in rich colors; usually in silk scarves.

Shepherd's check, small, even, black and white checked fabric; one of the so-called district checks.

Tartan plaid, distinctive for each Scots Highland clan. Extensively used today for kilts as well as for other sport clothes.

Tattersall, checks about one-half inch apart, two sets of dark lines on light ground.

Windowpane plaid, simple large bars larger than Tattersall.

DESIGN TERMS

Abstract-art patterns, no literal reproduction of nature or actuality, but shape, line, color to act on the consciousness; often a variation of geometric shapes (see Fig. 2-13).

Art Nouveau, (àr nōō-vō), Turn-of-the-century design that stressed conventionalized design in contrast to the Victorian naturalistic; characterized by long curving lines of leaves, flowers, and flickering whirls of color. Revival 1965–69 stressed bolder colors, unexpected stripes, swirling arabesques, lines long and slenderizing; colors clear but not always bold, often of the same value and intensity.

Baroque, (bà rōk), Italian art style of the late seventeenth to early eighteenth century; extravagantly ornate; irregular, rough, imperfect pearls.

Conventionalized design, forms stylized into imaginative shapes, somewhat related to nature forms but imaginative, with more attention to arrangement.

Cubism, early twentieth-century art style emphasizing formal structure, reducing natural forms to geometric equivalents—organization of engineered planes independent of camera representation.

Engineered designs, designs fitted to cut of garment, placing most important lines to stress body shape or cut of pattern—idea adaptable to cage and shift styles.

Florals, may be naturalistic (Victorian, girls' finishing school art), or stylized into flat motifs, conventionalized.

"Granny" prints, small all-over patterns, quaint calico type; most are too naturalistic; used during popularity of the muu-muu (see Fig. 1-7).

Impressionism, a nineteenth century art style characterized by a fluctuating appearance of shapes, usually small, many bright touches of color that partially fuse when viewed at a distance, a rhythmic vibration that scintillates, yet merges tone.

Naturalism, designs with forms almost photographic in shape and color of flowers, leaves, and so on; shaded to show perspective.

Op art, a style of abstract art in which forms and space are organized to produce illusions of an ambiguous nature as advancing and receding forms on a flat surface; dramatic design based on optical idea of geometric figures. Developed from Bauhaus and Cubism trends of 1920s; some ideas borrowed from baroque and rococo (Fig. 2-18.)

Psychedelic designs (sī-kē-*del*-ik), designs denoting calm and state of aesthetic entrancement and creative impetus (pleasurable perception of the senses).

Rococo, (rō *kō* kō), art style that evolved from baroque, but more refined; delicate over-all shellwork, foliage and so on.

Trompe l'oeil (trômp-*lā*), visual deception. Example: a printed shift with collar, pocket, and seamlines printed rather than sewn.

African Influence

Adinkra, printed cotton cloth made in Ghana by the Ashanti. Carved gourds are dipped in native brown dyes as in block printing.

Caftan, Turkish and Arabic long coatlike robe usually tied at waist for women by a long sash; worn on street without sash by men. The neck is usually rounded with a low slit down the front through which the buttons and stripes of the vest may be seen. Much copied for evening and lounging wear of an elegant nature.

Kente cloth, Ashanti *weavings;* formerly handwoven in four-inch narrow strips, then sewn together, often in staggered arrangement; imitations now for tourists (Fig. 2-19).

Safari, wild game hunting in Africa. In textiles, brown prints, swirls; khaki, brimmed hats, knickers.

Modern Fabric Designers

Larsen, adapts current art influences to both fabrics and garments; engineers, as Mondrian influence on a poncho.

Lesur, Parisian designer famous for wool and silk fabrics; especially known for poodle cloth.

Luksus, a woolen and silk fabric designer, using bold shapes and color especially for straighter-cut blouses, pajamas, dresses; similar to Art Nouveau, but more modern.

Marimekko, company making designs for fabrics and clothes. Finnish in origin. For hand-printed shifts—bold, colorful, but often muted to blend with grayish landscape; strong geometrics, unfussy florals but sophisticated simplicity; stresses freedom from fashion. Many dots and stripes inspired from folk costumes; bubbles, ends of a woodpile, not unlike Japanese tie-dye use of pebble and mushroom shapes.

Pucci (pōō'-chee), Florentine designer famous for pull-over jersey dresses, accessories, bold, colorful prints, geometrics. Perfectly cut, close-fitting, yet with freedom of movement; one design developed in countless color combinations. **Rodier** (Rŭd-yā'), famous Parisian designer of fabrics.

REFERENCES

PATRICK, JULIA MOCKETT. *Distinctive Dress.* New York: Charles Scribner's Sons, 1969.
KEFGEN, MARY, AND PHYLLIS TOUCHIE-SPECHT. *Individuality in Clothing Selection and Personal Appearance.* New York: Macmillan Publishing Co., Inc., 1971.
HORN, MARILYN J. *The Second Skin.* Boston: Houghton Mifflin Company, 1968.

a   b   c   d

Figure 2-17. Traditional Asian designs: *a*, the pine-and-pomegranate pattern (source of Paisley shawl designs), originally from Persia (Iran); *b*, all-over cotton print from Bangkok for a sarong or skirt; *c*, typical hand-blocked sari (6 yards long) from India; *d*, stylized Paisley motifs simplified in a modern manner.

Figure 2-18. Op art. Great ingenuity is required to adapt such patterns to garments. They need few or no accessories.

Figure 2-19. African influence: Kente cloth from Ghana is woven in 4-inch strips, then sewn together often in staggered arrangement. At right is Adinkira, printed by hand from carved gourds, usually brown on white or natural cotton about calico weight. A line system of production is used. (Courtesy of Ghana Information Service.)

Coordinating Your Wardrobe

The concept of a coordinated wardrobe implies a collection of clothes that fit your life-style, from which you can assemble a complete outfit for each of your occasions. This is accomplished by drawing from your stock of interchangeable garments and accessories; it offers assurance of making the desired "first impression" on your various audiences.

Knowing that your wardrobe is adequate for any situation increases self-confidence and the enjoyment of each day's activities. Clothes can be both becoming and appropriate for the occasion, whether you have much or little money to spend.

The kind of college you have chosen, its location, and your activities will influence your planning for wardrobe additions; feeling right in your clothes is dependent, somewhat, upon their similarity to what others are wearing. In case you are in a new or unfamiliar situation, a check on current patterns of dress is a first step. This provides a background for balancing the factors of conformity and individuality in your planning, to determine the degree of each that is right for you.

BASIS FOR A COORDINATED EFFECT

Plan your wardrobe around several basic outer garments to insure coordinated outfits. Your interests and needs will determine how many of the following groups you might wish to include.

1. Coat—year-round topcoat.
2. Suit—versatile in style (possibly with both skirt and pants).
3. Separates—skirts, pants, shorts, blouses, sweaters, jackets.
4. Casual dress.
5. Afternoon dress—informal, semidressy dress.
6. After-five—
   a. Informal entertaining at home.
   b. Short party dress.
   c. Long formal.

Eliminate any of these groups that do not fit your life-style, then plan to have at least one complete outfit in each group that your style of life suggests.

Owning a basic wardrobe does not mean that you are to limit yourself to one in each group. Its object is to assemble a limited number of garments that look right together. For example, the basic coat could possibly be chosen for wear with all other items on the list—normally with items 2, 3, 4, 5, and 6.

With a basic wardrobe provided, supplementary items can be added that appeal to you as a special means of expressing yourself—your moods, your feelings, the many facets of your personality. This is accomplished also with your basic suit or dress, through your selection of blouses, scarfs, and jewelry.

Basic Wardrobe Color

A wardrobe that will insure one's being well-dressed requires long-range planning based on a color scheme that carries through from season to season and year to year.

The basic color may or may not be your most becoming color; if it is not, it can be chosen to combine well with the many colors you have found to be becoming.

Black is not flattering to all skins but can be relieved by accents of becoming colors next to the face. It combines well with gray, beige, white, and clear tones of green, yellow, violet, light blue, aquamarine, red, and pink. Black is a perfect background for jewelry and really fine accessories.

Brown is worn best with brown, beige, tan, green, rust, yellow, white, turquoise, or light-to-medium blue; not wine-red but coral, copper, and salmon-red;

gold, cream, and orange. Brown, tan, or natural accessories are necessary. This family of colors belongs to one of warm coloring.

One with cool coloring may choose navy blue and accents of lighter blue, jade, green, white, gray, burgundy, American Beauty, cerise, coral, flesh-pink, violet, or lime; tan leathers and brown furs; rust, orange, beige, and cream; black or navy blue accessories; and a cherry-red coat. Navy blue is more youthful than black. In spring it is at its best with accents of washable white.

Gray is not as practical as beige and the other darker neutrals for a basic color choice. Beige combines with brown, cocoa, coral-red, black, green, blue, violet, red, and yellow—to be more specific, coral, jade, aquamarine, canary, raspberry, and rust. Softly textured tweedy types in this color are more flattering and practical than flat weaves.

A satisfactory plan is to choose a coat, suit, dress, and at least one set of accessories (shoes, bag, gloves, and hat—if a hat is needed) in the basic color. This plan need not produce monotony because there can be variety in value, intensity, and texture among all the parts. With each new season, consider these factors to determine how you can best add new garments to give variety, distinction, and this season's "new look" to your basic wardrobe.

You may want to use the same color for accessories—such as black or brown—through the four years of college. It is expensive to change. Many college girls have chosen brown as a basic for campus and black as a basic for dressier occasions. Others might choose navy for spring, white for summer, and black for winter. Navy blue shoes are not pleasing with black and their use is limited with many other colors, but black shoes and bag—especially in patent—could be used with navy. Brown with black is best when the style and quality of materials are above par. Browns in various tones usually blend together better than the various blues and may be more readily available in the markets.

The Basic Coat

A basic coat is the year-round, full-length type of coat. In severe climates an insulated or extra lining can be zipped in. It will satisfy longer if it is classic in style, full-hanging like a greatcoat, or straight-line like a Chesterfield. If you are to have only one coat, the most satisfactory choice will be one that is not too dressy or too sporty. If you have both a dress coat and a sport coat, it is better to have them related in color, so that some of your accessories and dresses can be worn with either. For example, a green dress coat and a tan or brown sport coat would be wiser selections than a navy dress coat and a brown sport coat. A white coat has many uses.

A good type of basic coat is made of wool of above-average grade and is well-tailored and simply cut (Fig. 3-1). Raglan, kimono, or dolman sleeves are roomy for wear over a suit. Check the armholes of set-in sleeves for roominess. The coat buttons, preferably, should not show a value or color contrast with the coat, because less-dominant buttons offer less interference with its versatility. In difficult situations, one might consider replacing the buttons to improve the design.

Figure 3-1. Unbelted, single-breasted coats, *a* and *b*, lend themselves to the informality of being worn open; *c*, polo coat may be a suitable design as a basic if sport clothes are usually worn; *d* and *e*, with set-in sleeves, would require careful checking on roominess for wear over other garments. (Courtesy of Pendleton, *a* and *d*; Montgomery Ward, *b*; The Wool Bureau, Inc., *c*; Hemphill-Wells Company, *e*.)

Decorative features that are subtle, such as seams, do not conflict with accessories. Shawl collars and cardigan styles are softer and more versatile than pointed lapels. Flares and shapes in sleeves will date the coat. Large patch pockets are more sporty; welt pockets less so.

The basic coat serves more purposes if made in the basic wardrobe color or in a color related enough to harmonize with most other parts of the wardrobe. A fairly soft texture—monotone tweed, Shetland, or fleece—is better than a deeply flocked tweed, plaid, or a flat-surfaced gabardine. A red or natural chinchilla may be basic enough, but black, blue, gray, beige, or a grayed lemon yellow are better. In contrast to camel's hair, a closely sheared soft-nap fabric such as Melton or Shetland is more satisfactory if many dressy occasions are involved.

Plaid, fur, or white coats may be desirable extras but are not basic. A plaid fits well into wardrobes that have many items in solid, harmonious colors that can be worn with it (Fig. 3-2, *a*). An all-weather coat belongs in this group, *b*.

The Basic Suit

A well-chosen basic suit—or dress and jacket with a suit-look—is an excellent choice of garment to serve for several different occasions by a change of accessories to suit the situation and your mood (Fig. 3-3). To form such a background, a suit, or suit-look garment, should meet the following standards:

1. It is in your basic color, or one harmonious with your coat.
2. It is made in a fabric of weight and texture suitable for summer or winter in most climates and is not patterned; it is a lighter weight than a coat fabric.
3. It is classic or conservative in cut—not dressy, yet not severely tailored.

Figure 3-2. Desirable extras in coats may include a wide range: *a*, brushed wool plaid; *b*, all-weather coat in quilted blue denim with fake lamb's fur; *c*, swinging wool topper balmaccan. (Courtesy of The Wool Bureau, Inc., *a* and *c*; Cotton Incorporated, *b*.)

a

b

c

Figure 3-3. *a*, A suit, or suit-look ensemble, in an unpatterned fabric, presents many possibilities for creative expression in various combinations of blouses, scarves, and other accessories. *b*, Suitable in cut for a basic, *b* is used here as an extra in an interesting patterned fabric. (Courtesy of National Cotton Council, *a* and *b*.)

4. It may be collarless; it should not have extreme mannish collar and lapels.
5. It is without contrasting decorative features that would prevent the use of colors in accessories. Buttons, preferably, match the jacket in color; they may be self-covered, plastic or bone—not rhinestones or in fancy designs.

Suits in the spring markets usually make better basic suits than those in the fall, because they are not so warm and bulky. Extra time and money may be required to purchase or make a basic suit, but it is a good investment because the garment may be worn for several years.

Both designs, *a* and *b*, would have similar uses and identical appearances, whether they are jacket and skirt or jacket and dress combinations. In design *a*, the jacket is combined with a short-sleeved dress, in design *b* with a sleeveless dress.

SEPARATES

The versatility of short coats and jackets can greatly extend the wardrobe in combinations with separates (Fig. 3-4). Suits, in addition to being basic, hold a significant place among separates: their parts, teamed with skirts, pants, blouses, sweaters, jumpers, and various accessories can multiply the number of outfits available to the person who has planned well (Fig. 3-5).

A challenging and creative project is involved in assembling items in the present wardrobe and planning additions that will lead to further coordination. One blouse chosen in an appropriate color—solid or patterned to fill a gap—may provide many more combinations (Fig. 3-6).

Figure 3-4. *a*, Pea jacket in fuchia wool chinchilla, pants in yellow chinchilla, worn with yellow polka dot blouse; *b*, brushed wool plaid shirt; *c*, short jacket with deep-cut raglan sleeves; *d*, wrap-around jacket. (Courtesy of The Wool Bureau Inc., *a*, *b*, and *c*; J. P. Stevens & Co., Inc., *d*.)

| a | b | c |

Figure 3-5. *a*, Suit with a sport coat look, in wool fleece; *b*, knitted wool in denim blue with white saddle stitching on lumberjacket and front-pleated skirt, combined with a red sweater; *c*, vested blazer suit in wool flannel provides three parts for mix-and-match. (Courtesy of The Wool Bureau Inc., *a* and *b*; J. P. Stevens Co., Inc., *c*.)

The Basic Dress

The basic dress is one that can be changed to serve various occasions; it is a good background for jewelry and, possibly, a great variety of other garments that may be combined with it (Fig. 3-7). It is chosen in the basic wardrobe color with a silhouette that you like; it is distinguished by simplicity; it is casual (but not as tailored as the shirt style or as informal as the skirt and sweater), yet not dressy; and it is evidently in the current mode without being extreme. The design should be one that can be worn at any time of day in any season and without a special set of accessories. Skirt and sleeve lengths depend on the occasions for which the dress will be worn and the current fashion. Prime requisites are a moderate silhouette, a collarless neckline, and, of course, no sewed-on trimmings. It should not be too plain, but, rather, enhanced by a somewhat clever use of seams and darts, with becoming fullness, self-fabric belt, and fastenings. The basic dress with jacket or full length coat to match is often a popular choice, *c* and *d*.

The fabric should be a solid, never a print. Seasonable fabrics include crepe, crash, flannel, shantung, or knits, available in natural fibers, synthetics, and blends. It is an easy garment to make.

CASUAL DRESS

Dresses and pant suits in this classification are tailored, simple in design, informal, and are characterized by comfort, durability, and easy care.

If classic in design, the casual dress has great versatility. In a well-chosen fabric, it may go anywhere in most localities—to church, luncheon, and afternoon social affairs (Fig. 3-8). Custom often decrees some restraint for the general solemnity of the church service, making dressy, after-five clothes and very casual attire inappropriate.

SEMIDRESSY—THE AFTERNOON DRESS

This type of dress is optional in wardrobes based on informal styles of living. As is apparent from the preceding discussion, a well-chosen garment in the casual group may be used for the more special social occasions also. If there are quite a few of these occasions in your life, however, you may want to include clothes that are slightly more dressy than the clothes you might wear shopping, but not as dressy as those you might wear after five (Fig. 3-9).

AFTER-FIVE CLOTHES

Clothes for after-five occasions may be dressier than those worn for an afternoon social occasion. The glitter of rhinestones is reserved for this period of the day. If these types are needed in your wardrobe, they can be chosen for their adaptability to various situations, whether you are going out or entertaining at home (Fig. 3-10).

The informality on many campuses has eliminated the need for the décolleté formal dress (Fig. 3-11). If one has a need for this type of garment, its usefulness may be greatly extended by covering its low-cut neckline with a jacket.

AT-HOME CLOTHES

Informal entertaining at home in a dress or pants in a gay design and colors can contribute to the fun of expressing moods and feelings in a setting possibly not experienced during other occasions in the day (Fig. 3-12).

ACTIVE SPORTS

Discover the most appropriate clothes for the sports you participate in; the types will vary somewhat for different sections of the country (Fig. 3-13).

Weddings

Wedding dresses should be modest, with the neck and arms only partially uncovered. The standard bridal attire requires a head covering of some kind, preferably a veil or flowers, long sleeves or long gloves, and a moderately high neck. On the traditional white wedding dress, the long sleeves should fit snugly at the wrist to achieve a graceful effect. If you want to use the wedding dress as

a

b

c

d

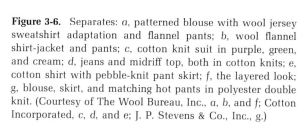

Figure 3-6. Separates: *a*, patterned blouse with wool jersey sweatshirt adaptation and flannel pants; *b*, wool flannel shirt-jacket and pants; *c*, cotton knit suit in purple, green, and cream; *d*, jeans and midriff top, both in cotton knits; *e*, cotton shirt with pebble-knit pant skirt; *f*, the layered look; *g*, blouse, skirt, and matching hot pants in polyester double knit. (Courtesy of The Wool Bureau, Inc., *a*, *b*, and *f*; Cotton Incorporated, *c*, *d*, and *e*; J. P. Stevens & Co., Inc., *g*.)

Figure 3-7. *a*, A simple basic dress serves as a background for a variety of belts, scarves, and jewelry; *b*, design satisfactory for a basic dress, except for the patterned fabric; *c* and *d*, basic dress and coat ensembles. (Courtesy of J. P. Stevens & Co., Inc., *a*; Donovan-Galvani, *b*, *c*, and *d*.)

an evening dress later, there are many possible adaptations. You might replace long sleeves with short sleeves; a sheer yoke could be removed; or the dress could be altered later to street length (Fig. 3-14). If you are to be married in a suit or afternoon type of dress, the best choice is a basic style; wear gloves and a small hat with a modest veil. The design of the costume should be classic in simplicity, and the style of hairdress and hat beautifully harmonious with the shape of your face. Photographs taken of you should be beautiful enough for your grandchildren to display proudly, with no remarks about the grotesque styles of yesterday.

Planning a wedding involves your sense of values as well as those of other members of your family. Will it be simple or elaborate? A modest home wedding may keep more sacredness in the occasion for you and leave more money to be spent on your apartment. For example, in modern Japan, young people prefer spending money for a honeymoon and an apartment over the time-honored reception for all the relatives. Simple home, garden, and chapel weddings suggest cottons—in suits and simple styles.

Bridesmaids' dresses, selected with care, can also serve for future occasions.

Travel

The concept of the basic wardrobe is identical to that of the travel wardrobe, although the types chosen for travel often will be limited to fewer than those included in the wardrobe plan.

The most suitable clothing for travel has been found to be suits, pant suits, mix-and-match separates, simple tailored dresses, and a topcoat. Specific styles and fabrics depend on activities and locality.

Easy-care and wrinkle-resistant fabrics make knits the favorites; comfortable shoes are a must!

Periodicals concerned with travel and suggestions from travel companies recommend condensing wardrobes to a minimum of five to eight outfits.

Wardrobe Planning

A sensible way to get started on planning for a new season's additions to the wardrobe is to answer these questions about yourself:

1. What image do I want to reflect?
2. What are my assets—physical characteristics, personality, present wardrobe, money?
3. What new clothes do I need? How many?
4. How can I shop wisely, to insure satisfaction with my selections? (This point will be considered further in Chapter 4.)

Your Resources

MONEY

Young people are more numerous, better educated, and richer than ever before. Based on findings of the Census Bureau, the 14 to 24 age group comprises one fifth of the total population of the United States. More time is being spent in getting

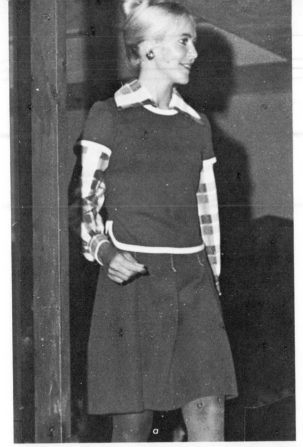

a

b

c

d

Figure 3-8. *a,* Two-piece dress accented by blouse; *b,* shirt-waist dress in nylon tricot; *c,* polyester knits in skirt, blouse, and sleeveless cardigan; *d,* wool knit T-shirt dress with long sleeve and cardigan vest; *e,* jumpsuit with jacket; *f,* color-coordinated knits; *g,* pantsuit. (Courtesy of Margaret's, *a* and *e;* J. P. Stevens & Co., Inc., *b;* Donovan-Galvani, *c;* The Wool Bureau, Inc., *d;* Hemphill-Wells Co., *f;* Montgomery Ward, *g.*)

Figure 3-9. *a*, A wool georgette dress, appropriate for wear to weddings, dinners, and parties; *b*, basic dress and jacket. (Courtesy of The Wool Bureau, Inc., *a*; Krieg, *b*.)

an education; the trend now is toward later marriages; 35 per cent have part-time jobs—as compared with 20 per cent in 1960; and the median family income for households headed by a full-time worker under 25 is almost three fourths that of the average American family.[1]

College Costs

More young Americans are working their way through college than previously. With the rising costs of higher education, the squeeze on the family's income is increasing. Government figures show the median income before taxes to be, roughly, $10,600. At this level, taxes take out about one fourth of the total. A student attending even a state-supported college and living on campus will probably need another one fourth, necessitating earning part of the college expenses, in many cases.

Spending Patterns for Apparel

The Family

Before 1950, the average percentage distribution for American family expenditures for clothing was 10 to 12 per cent. Since 1950, the average has remained approximately the same for younger persons. The trend has been slightly downward from 10 per cent, for older persons.

[1]"The 'Now' Generation in U.S.," *U.S. News and World Report*, March 22, 1971, p. 64.

Figure 3-10. After-five clothes: *a*, wool jersey pajama-skirt with striped taffeta smoking jacket; *b*, bouclé knit dress with kimono-sleeved evening sweater; *c*, low-cut halter dress in wool flannel with cropped shirt jacket; *d*, velveteen hot pants with embroidery, available also with a long skirt; *e*, tricot knit dress and jacket. (Courtesy of The Wool Bureau, Inc., *a*, *b*, *c*; Cotton Incorporated, *d*; Montgomery Ward, *e*.)

This does not mean that less money is being spent for clothing; in actual dollars, more is being spent because incomes have increased. In general, as income rises, the amount spent for clothing rises up to a certain level, above which families use more on recreation, savings, investments, or contributions to charitable, civic, or professional organizations. Perhaps the durability and use value of garments has improved, affecting this figure.

THE COLLEGE WOMAN

Available studies show an increase in the wardrobes of college women during recent years, reflecting the relative affluence of families and, no doubt, the increase in home sewing.

PRESENT WARDROBE The amount to be spent for new clothing will depend, somewhat, on the status of the present wardrobe, so the next step implies evaluation. Consider your assets and liabilities.

ASSETS—WHAT DO YOU HAVE? Analyze your present wardrobe to provide a realistic picture of your situation. Now is the time to weed out mistakes. Check the articles that you want to continue using.

WARDROBE LIABILITIES

Concentrate on each item you consider a mistake and ask yourself some questions: Why is it a mistake? Is it the color, the fabric, the trim, or the style? Is it unbecoming and unsuitable (or just, "it doesn't do anything for me")? Could it be improved with different accessories? Could it be teamed with some other

Figure 3-11. Miss Wool of 1972—Barbara Ward—wearing a formal with halter neckline. (Courtesy of The Wool Bureau, Inc.)

Figure 3-12. *a*, Cotton Paisley design, with quilted skirt and velveteen vest; *b*, an Asian-inspired design in cotton, with crop-top and wrap-pants; *c*, colorful suit in cotton blend; *d*, floor-length T-shirt; *e*, puffed-sleeve empire style. (Courtesy of Cotton, Inc., *a*; Vanity Fair, *b*; Hemphill-Wells Company, *c*; J. P. Stevens & Co., Inc., *d*; Sears Roebuck & Co., *e*.)

a

b

c

d

Figure 3-13. *a*, Jeans in ribless corduroy, with crocheted tank top over sweater; *b*, fast-drying polyester stretch-knit terry; *c*, cotton knit tunic or swim suit topper; *d*, cotton knit; *e*, canvas jacket suit with a knit shirt; *f*, a variety of garments for the skier; *g*, tricot knit dress. (Courtesy of J. P. Stevens & Co., Inc., *a*; Vanity Fair, *b*; Cotton, Inc., *c* and *d*; Kodel, *e*; Neiman-Marcus, *f*; Sears Roebuck & Co., *g*.)

Figure 3-14. *a*, Bridal gown with illusion veil complementing the Watteau paneled train that falls from the Empire bodice decorated with lace and beads; *b*, the Juliet look—pure silk gros de Londres, capelet embellished with pearls; molded body, cathedral train; *c*, for bridesmaid or wedding guest in summery cotton lace with bright red or blue belt; *d*, cotton piqué with organdy and wide satin belt—for bride or bridesmaid. (Courtesy of Miss Betsy, *a*; Priscilla of Boston, *b*; Cotton Producers Institute, *c* and *d*.)

item in the wardrobe or a new purchase to give a new, fashionable look? Could it be restyled or refitted? Did you shop in too much of a hurry? Did someone else exert pressure on you? Was it a gift? Do you have too many of certain kinds of clothes and too few in another category?

Now that mistakes have been recognized along with reasons *why* they are mistakes, you are in a better position to plan for additions.

Lay out, or try on, a whole outfit to decide whether it needs supplementing. Decide on how much more wear you can anticipate from the more important articles. A coat, suit, skirt, sweater, or jacket can be expected to last from two to five years if the style is simple; if it has a good fit and is becoming; if it has quality in fabric and workmanship; and if it still has fashion quality.

PLAN AHEAD   How far ahead and in how much detail does one make a wardrobe plan? A good method is to plan over a three-year period for major expenditures such as a coat or suit. Make detailed plans for only one season at a time.

CONSIDER EXPENSIVE GARMENTS FIRST   Plan the most expensive things first; then plan the rest of the wardrobe around them. Plan your coat before your dresses; your dresses and suits before hat and shoes; and a hat before shoes (unless you seldom need a hat). After your plan is made, you can wait for the sales on coats and still be reasonably safe in getting some of your dresses earlier. It is a good plan to buy your purse and shoes the same season, as the next season usually finds a new shade in vogue, making the older article look shabby or even inharmonious.

It is always a good idea to rotate the major expenses, not selecting all of the most expensive items the same year.

PLAN FOR VERSATILITY   The greater number of basic or classic garments you choose in harmonizing designs, textures, and colors, the greater your wardrobe's expansion. Indicate the garments you will want to be classic in style. After choosing these, you are ready to select whatever else your money and desires dictate—the seasonal, the gay, the less-durable items to provide variety; supplements to vary your classic suit or dress; or whatever is in the current market to give you the feeling or the "look" that you want to project.

CONSIDER FASHION TRENDS   Your concepts of good design and style related to your clothing will be fundamental in guiding your choices, but fashion trends are also of some importance. Learn to recognize the status of a fashion. It is an advantage in selecting becoming styles in basics to know which of these will probably be in good fashion for at least three years. If you buy a style at full price when it is coming in, it will bring you more satisfaction and value than if you pay half price for it when it is going out. Adapt the fashion in a practical way to yourself and your needs.

Table 3-1
SUGGESTED WARDROBE PLAN

COAT	SUITS	DRESSES	SKIRTS	BLOUSES	SWEATERS
Fall coat					
Spring coat					
Jacket or sport coat					

Table 3-1 (Cont.)

HAT	GLOVES	BAG	SHOES	SCARF, NECK-PIECE, ETC.	JEWELRY	COLOR	FABRIC SAMPLE

STEPS IN WARDROBE PLANNING

Step 1. Base your plan on your life-style—think of your morning-to-night activities, your likes and dislikes, and your hobbies.

Step 2. List the inventory items that you will continue to use on a form such as that shown in Table 3-1, or on one of your own adaptation.

Step 3. Decide on the items to be added; list them in the table used in Step 2.

Step 4. Key accessories to the basics. With one set of *major accessories*—hat (?), shoes, bag, and gloves—in the basic wardrobe color, one can branch out in an indefinite number of combinations, usually wearing three of the four, but at least two of them. True, if coat, dress, and major accessories are all brown, the outfit is monotonous. At least one contrast is desirable, maybe two, but not three. The contrast can be in value, such as beige gloves; in hue, such as a turquoise scarf; or in intensity, such as a tangerine scarf. Keying accessories to the basic wardrobe refers to the use of harmonious elements in relation to the whole. Accessories other than the major four merit discrimination in selection and assembling. You certainly need a set for casual wear and a set for dress-up.

Step 5. Plan for design and color. Make your wardrobe plan.

COORDINATING ACCESSORIES

Although a girl has a pleasing figure and well-chosen clothes, she must wear them in just the right manner to achieve a look of smartness. Adding the best accessories requires up-to-date information and careful planning.

The total look should create a simple effect with some accent of interest. In striving for simplicity, it is not necessary to look plain or uninteresting. Find an individual or original touch to avoid monotony. To achieve the effect of simplicity, avoid wearing too many accessories and having too many centers of interest.

For a basic set of accessories, the most satisfactory plan is to select shoes, bag, and gloves in the same color, with possible variations in value—shoes and bag might be selected in black, with gloves in black or white; or shoes and bag in brown, with beige gloves. Because these are basic accessories, they are simple in line and design, with decoration kept to a minimum. The gloves and hat may contrast in color with the rest of the outfit. If gloves are chosen in the same color or value as the bag, spottiness is avoided. This is sometimes a consideration when the garment is of contrasting value or color. Bags may be chosen according to your needs in various sizes and shapes.

At formal luncheons, teas, weddings, and receptions, guests wear gloves.

With winter suits and coats, the glove should be long enough to reach the sleeve.

Be discriminating in your choice of jewelry. Definitely save glitter for after-five.

Accessories, carried in bag or purse, afford quick changes for after-work hours.

Summary

The object in planning a coordinated wardrobe is to provide a supply of apparel that is harmonious in all its parts. It should be becoming to the individual and be adequate for each type of occasion in his life. This does not necessarily imply a different costume for each occasion; it means that the wardrobe is so well planned that clothes can be reassembled and used for different occasions.

The extensiveness of a wardrobe is influenced by the number of basic or classic garments included and on the degree of their coordination.

When these basic needs have been met, additional garments in types appropriate to the interests of the individual may be added to provide variety and fulfillment of the human need for expression.

References

Chambers, Helen, and Verna Moulton. *Clothing Selection*. Philadelphia: J. B. Lippincott Co., 1969.

Kefgen, Mary, and Phyllis Touchie-Specht. *Individuality in Clothing Selection and Personal Appearance*. New York: Macmillan Publishing Co., Inc., 1971.

4

The Consumer's Point of View

Clothes are being purchased today not only as a necessity but as a popular form of luxury, making the United States the world's largest manufacturer of apparel. The clothing industry's increasing growth is attributable, in part, to the growing spending power of the younger age group.

Although home sewing has been increasing and there has been an emphasis on this outlet for creativity in the individual, the need remains even more to know how to buy ready-to-wear intelligently. Making clothing may provide a greater opportunity for creative expression, but the development that can come through the selection of ready-mades to achieve a harmonious and satisfying wardrobe is also creative expression. Even though one is able to sew, a decision is often demanded as to what to make and what to buy ready-made.

The Consumer

Growing consumer dissatisfactions have been evident during recent years. A *Good Housekeeping* poll of 1,000 members of the magazine's Consumer Panel found the chief ground for discontent to be quality, followed by price, performance, and size of clothing. Information, or lack of information, given in product advertisements elicited further reasons for discontent.[1]

Fifty-four per cent of the respondents in this survey reported difficulties when shopping. Workmanship and size presented the leading causes for complaint in women's clothing. Other complaints were fraying seams; poor finishing; inadequate hem allowances; stitching that comes out in the laundry; poor thread; uneven hems; unsatisfactory buttons and buttonholes; crooked stitching; improperly sewn zippers; cheap linings; unmatched plaids and stripes; extremely limited stocks in half sizes, large sizes, and extra-small sizes; imported clothing frequently not running true to size; panty hose tending not to wear or fit well; and lack of permanence in labels.

RECOGNITION OF CONSUMER INTERESTS

The early '70s were characterized by an unparalleled recognition of consumers' interests. Through legislation, various rulings, and organizations that function to protect the consumer, much progress has been made and efforts continue in this direction.

PERMANENT CARE LABELS

The regulation of greatest significance to the clothing consumer is the FTC ruling requiring that apparel must bear permanent care labels, clearly disclosing washing and cleaning instructions for the products. This rule became effective July 3, 1972, and covers articles leaving manufacturers' plants after that date. It applies to both domestic and imported goods. The rule also requires that textiles that will be used by home sewers to make apparel must be accompanied by care labels that consumers can affix permanently to the finished product. Items excluded from the ruling include shoes, gloves, and headwear. The instructions must be provided in such a manner that they will remain legible for the reasonable life of the article, and be readily accessible to the user. Some companies have voluntarily furnished such labels on their merchandise for many years (Fig. 4-1). Manufacturers have expressed the opinion that permanent labels will be advantageous for the manufacturer as well as the consumer, since better labeling can gain better-satisfied customers.

This labeling is of great value because of the large number of products on the market, each with different care-performance characteristics, making it almost

---

[1]Good Housekeeping Consumer Panel, *Good Housekeeping*, October 1970, pp. 179–180.

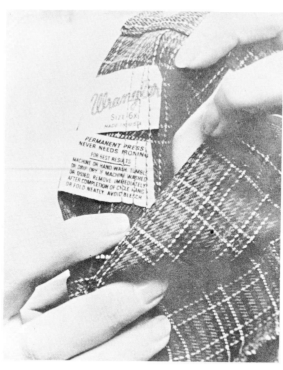

Figure 4-1. Permanent care labels were stitched into ready-to-wear voluntarily by some manufacturers before this practice was made mandatory. (Courtesy of Blue Bell, Inc.)

impossible for consumers to be properly informed. In this age of new products, the traditional source of care information—personal experience based on trial and error and possibly handed down from earlier generations—no longer meets the needs of today's consumer.

OTHER REGULATIONS

The "truth-in-lending" provision of the Consumer Credit Protection Act, effective in July 1969, requires that cost of credit be revealed in uniform, easy-to-understand terms. The law requires that all important credit costs be clearly disclosed to the consumer before he signs a credit agreement. The creditor must disclose both the *finance charge*—which tells in dollars and cents how much the credit costs—and the annual *percentage rate.*

Another advantage for today's consumer is "cooling off" legislation; it allows the revoking of a purchase contract during a three-day period after signing—an important means of defense against the wiles of the door-to-door salesman.

Laws have been passed that prohibit the use of highly flammable fabrics in children's sleepwear; these laws cover product safety, truth-in-advertising, and tighter warranty regulations. Class-action law, for the first time, allows a group of consumers to pool their resources and sue the creditor.

The outlook for this decade is promising, with indications pointing toward emphasis on better quality, reliable service, and honest advertising—a significant turn for both shoppers and business.

Consumers' Rights and Responsibilities

The four basic rights listed here were expressed first by President Kennedy in 1962. Rights carry responsibilities.

Right to Be Informed—Responsibilities

To be aware of available product information.

To study advertisements in detail.

To understand performance claims.

To read care instructions before purchasing.

To have questions answered before purchasing.

To keep informed about new developments.

Right to Choose—Responsibilities

To understand the reasons for your choices.

To make selections carefully.

To check sources of merchandise for reliability.

To do comparative shopping.

Right to Safety—Responsibilities

To evaluate merchandise for safety features before buying.

To follow use and care instructions.

To observe warnings.

To report poor performance to retailer.

Right to Be Heard—Responsibilities

To know when you have a legitimate complaint.

To know what you can do about it.

To understand why you should act.

To be familiar with sources for help.

How to Make a Complaint

What we, the consumers, do about our valid complaints can play an important part in improving merchandise and marketing practices—industry has to please us in order to stay in business. This places a responsibility on each consumer to make his opinions known. Each time we buy an article we are casting a vote for it—whether it is good or bad. Business appreciates and often solicits the opportunity to learn of both our likes and dislikes.

Steps in Making a Complaint

1. **Try to solve the problem locally.** Begin inquiries with the merchant from whom the product was purchased. (Avoid store rush hours.)

2. **Go to the manufacturer.** When the complaint concerns a product, complain to the manufacturer. Write a businesslike, courteous letter directly to the company—to the appropriate department if possible, or to the president of the company. For the address, check the tag or booklet that accompanied the product, or go to the public library. Send a second letter if you fail to hear from the company within a month.

3. **Go to a protection agency.** Choose the most appropriate source.
   a. With a valid complaint concerning major appliances, contact Major Appliance Consumer Action Panel (MACAP).

   > Chairman of MACAP
   > 20 North Wacker Drive
   > Chicago, Illinois 60606

   b. Direct your inquiry about unfair or deceptive merchandising practices such as misleading advertising, labeling, or guarantees, to your state office, if possible, or to the national office of the U.S. Department of Health, Education and Welfare, Consumer Protection and Environmental Health Service.

   c. Direct your inquiries when in doubt about what to do or where to get assistance to your

   > Congressman, U.S. House of Representatives
   > Washington, D.C. 20515
   > or
   > Senator, U.S. Senate
   > Washington, D.C. 20510

   d. In case you have been unable to resolve your complaint by any other means, address

   > The Presidents' Committee on Consumer Interests
   > The White House
   > Washington, D.C. 20500

4. Consumer complaints frequently concern specific problems that are handled by a local, state, or federal agency. You would go directly to one that you are aware of in your state as an agency connected with consumer affairs; in some states the Attorney General's Office has a consumer protection division.

SUGGESTED SHOPPING GUIDES

1. Have a wardrobe plan, but permit yourself freedom to change it, providing that you have well-considered reasons for revision.
2. Carry a shopping list of sizes, amounts needed, and samples for matching.
3. Try not to shop at busy hours.
4. Consider giving reasons for not buying in a courteous, informative manner. The store buyer may relay your reasons to the manufacturer or select other products more in harmony with your wishes the next time he goes to market.

WHERE WILL YOU SHOP?

There are approximately a dozen different kinds of stores today that handle varying amounts and types of clothing and textiles. These include department stores, chain ready-to-wear stores, mail-order houses, yard goods stores, drug stores, neighborhood stores, sample or manufacturers' outlet stores, "wholesale" stores, supermarkets, discount and closed-door discount stores, and boutique and specialty shops.

Considering volume of business, the large mail-order stores and the discount houses are enjoying tremendous growth. The discount stores have the advantage of low markup, self-service, lower-cost plant and display, fast turnover of merchandise, locations on or near major traffic thoroughfares, and shopping for many kinds of goods under one roof. By the mid-'70s, discount shopping malls are expected—shopping centers made up exclusively of discount tenants.

Boutique customers may be given a little more individual attention, and merchandise may be more unusual or unique than that offered in the department store. The latter often has a boutique area, however. The difference between buying in a department store or a boutique is that department stores tend to buy many pieces of one item; boutiques buy a "few of this and a few of that," giving customers the feeling that they are not so likely to meet the dress on another person.

Department stores, generally, have been slow in responding to the youth market. This is not true of the big chains, whose strength seems to grow daily among the young. The key clothing market in the '70s includes persons in the 12 to 34 age group.

DIRECT MARKETING A rather new concept in merchandising, direct marketing, is expected to attain phenomenal growth during the '70s. Increased convenience and lower sales costs are making it appealing to both buyers and sellers.

Direct marketing involves the use of mails, newspapers, magazines, radio, or TV for the purpose of soliciting a response by telephone, mail, or personal visit from a customer.

The growth of customer credit cards and the computer have paved the way, it is believed, for the era of direct marketing—merchandising that bypasses the wholesaler and the retail store and brings goods and services directly to the attention of customers, thereby cutting costs.

CREDIT RATING Most people have a credit rating on file under their name. Passage of the Fair Credit Reporting Act, which became effective on April 25, 1971, makes one's credit rating available to anyone who has been denied credit.

BRANDS An awareness of brand names can present an avenue of information relative to the quality of merchandise. The reputation of a brand may not be synonomous with the quality advertised, but it can be an indication. With personal experience in using merchandise, brands are an advantage in making the decision to choose or reject the item in the future, as familiarity with brands furnishes a basis for evaluation. Sometimes the best brand of one manufacturer is inferior to the products of another. Not all brands or brand names represent a stationary quality. Read the ads, watch TV promotions, or listen to radio advertising. Either way, the information gained will be more accurate than ever before, because of the recent regulations mentioned earlier. But, the consumer is still responsible for studying the fine print, in the ad or on the label.

LABELS   The wide variety of fabrics available today have different characteristics that affect their appearance as well as their suitability for varied purposes. In order to use these successfully, we need to know what fibers they are made of and how they will perform. Two types of labels that can be of assistance are *brand* and *informative* labels. The first is used to identify the merchandise of a particular seller. Informative labels identify fiber content and provide varying amounts of information concerning fabric structure, special finishes, and directions and precautions on proper use and care.

It is to the advantage of the consumer to make use of the information provided on the label. Much effort on the part of the conscientious manufacturer has gone into study and research in order to provide a more satisfactory product (Fig. 4-2).

The Textile Fiber Products Identification Act of 1960 and the permanent care rulings effective in 1972 are of tremendous importance to the consumer. Although many companies have furnished much voluntary information, usually on hang-tags but sometimes in permanent forms on the clothing, having this information available on every garment and on yard goods will make comparative shopping more effective and strengthen one's prospects for greater satisfaction in using the garment.

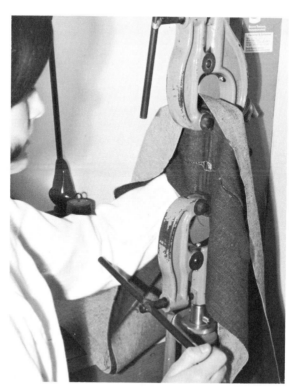

Figure 4-2. The Scott Tester is being used to determine the breaking strength of machine stitching in a seam. (Courtesy of Blue Bell, Inc.)

Figure 4-3. An information file on wear and care records can be useful not only during the life of a garment but also when purchasing a replacement. (Courtesy of Celanese.)

Be alert to new developments, new terms on labels, and new definitions; the information gained can be valuable when planning and caring for the garments in the wardrobe (Fig. 4-3).

BARGAINS

A shopping hazard to watch for in hunting bargains at sales is the practice of fraudulent preticketing. This is the trick of artificially marking up the so-called list prices in order to show a large reduction on sales prices. Not all merchants are dishonest, but this practice has become widespread in the retailing world. Check all prices advertised as sales prices, if possible, by comparing them with prices of the week before. Sometimes sales prices are markups rather than markdowns.

When you buy tempting bargains that soon prove to be shoddy merchandise, you are not only cheating yourself, but you are helping to undermine conditions for all producers: the farmer who grows the cotton or wool-bearing sheep; the people who spin and weave the thread and cloth; and those who sell it. If consumers never bought poor merchandise, there would be no market for it and manufacturers would cease to make it. Consumer resistance to prices too high for the quality will help considerably in price control.

SHOPPING FOR READY-MADES

Today's shopper may become confused in trying to recognize those items that will bring her the greatest satisfaction from the sea of consumer goods offered. She needs the ability to recognize quality to meet her requirements. There is frequently little or no correlation between quality and price; there are fewer salespersons to help with her selection, and if the selection is unsatisfactory, it may be time-consuming or even difficult to return the merchandise.

FABRICS Information concerning the inherent properties of fibers, the fabrics in which they are used, and suggestions for general handling and care will be treated in some detail in Chapter 7.

Coats and Suits

Before buying a coat, decide how much you can afford to spend, approximately how long you will want to wear it, and what color and design will be most suitable. Is it to be a basic coat or an extra? (Fig. 4-4.) If the coat or suit is striking in cut, color combination, or texture, it cannot be used so interchangeably with other wardrobe items.

Coats of tweed, Shetland-type woolens, melton cloth, and close-napped fabrics are excellent for general-wear coats. They wrinkle less. However, if these fabrics are poor in quality, they tend to lose shape. Gabardine and hard worsteds are better for suits, especially for very tailored ones. They wear well but often show shine and spots. The fleece woolens, popular in the polo type of sport coats, have been satisfactory in good qualities. The poor grades fade, sag, and pill. If you can hold it to the light, you may see thick and thin places in a lower grade. Camel's hair and other specialty fibers are soft, lightweight, and warm, but are more expensive

Figure 4-4. Selecting a coat requires careful consideration of one's present wardrobe and life-style. (Courtesy of Patricia Hargrave.)

than wool. They are best in natural colors. Softer napped fabrics, such as suede, bouclé, and broadcloth, are for dressy wear and are not so serviceable. Tropical worsteds, blends of wool with silk, mohair, and polyester, give excellent service for suits.

If the cloth stretches much, it will soon get out of shape. A well-balanced weave without long floats, loops, or heavy knots will not sag or wear out quickly. Look for a label that guarantees against fading, shrinking, sagging, or pilling. One hundred per cent virgin wool is an excellent choice.

If you do not purchase at the first of the season but wait for the sales, you may get a better buy for your money in a classic or conservative style; however, there will be fewer garments available from which to choose.

There are, of course, gradual changes from year to year, but classic designs and patterns continue in good fashion. Few fashion experts can date, to the year, a basic greatcoat. Selecting a current style will insure a coat good for two or more years ahead. Consult fashion periodicals with dependable forecasts.

Acetate makes a durable lining. Check to see whether it is perspiration-resistant and slip-proof. The lining should not show from the right side of the coat. Zipped-in linings or interlinings of wool or wool-blend are practical in cold but changeable climates. Woven interlinings are less bulky than quilted ones.

Be critical of the tailoring and fit. Alterations are expensive. It pays to select the correct size. If the garment has a set-in sleeve, the most important point to observe is the fit in the shoulder-armhole area. It should be smooth, neither too narrow nor too wide. The sleeve should be free of wrinkles, eased smoothly into the armhole, set straight, and balanced. If full-length, the sleeve should cover the wrist bone when the arm is bent. Check the fit of the neckline. The lapels should not have crease lines pressed in. The outer edge of a turn-back collar should cover the neckline seam. A standard collarless neckline should not bulge away from the body, unless it is designed that way, as in a cowl effect. The front facing in a good jacket or coat does not show on the right side of the coat along the edges. The collar and lapels do not curl, and their underside is not visible along the edges. The lower edges of a jacket and sleeves in the better grades have a bias muslin interfacing. These lower edges should show no evidences of sewing.

See if the designs match from right to left, if the garment is cut on the grain, and if it sets in balance from front to back, as well as from right to left.

Checking to determine whether the threads in the fabric—the grain—are the same on the two sides will furnish valuable information as to how you can expect it to perform. Understandably, in the process of manufacturing, many layers of fabric must be spread one on top of the other (Fig. 4-5). If this, and the cutting process that follows (Fig. 4-6) are not done carefully, the fabric grain is not true in some parts of the garments, causing it to hang or set differently.

Cheaper coats show such defects as (1) sleeves set in armholes so that the side seam of coat and sleeve are joined in one operation; (2) the collar joined in one seam between coat and facing, creating the bulk of six layers; (3) the seam edges not graded; (4) threads not matching the fabric; the lining rarely being tacked to the coat along seams; (5) the seams underpressed or not pressed open; (6) the lining

Figure 4-5. Spreading the cloth for cutting many garments at once. (Courtesy of Blue Bell, Inc.)

Figure 4-6. Cutting garments for the ready-to-wear market. (Courtesy of Blue Bell, Inc.)

attached at lower edge in a long coat; (7) fraying buttonholes; and (8) cheap fasteners.

The lining in a better coat has a full-length pleat at the center back; it is tacked along each seam; it is hemmed separately from the coat and tacked loosely at the seams to the coat; and it is neatly attached to the front facing, neck edge, and armhole. Jackets have the lining slip-hemmed at the lower edge far enough back to guarantee looseness without sagging.

Become acquainted with brands of coats and suits in your favorite stores. In what price range does each come? Read all tags and labels. Save them for future protection. Reliable firms and manufacturers make good their claims.

If you have the time and talent, you could save money by *making a coat.*

Dresses

Look at clothes in windows, on mannequins, and on racks. Confine most of your looking to your price range. Do not try on a dress if it is definitely poor in design, has a poor color combination, is too high-priced, is distinctly below your standards of workmanship or fabric quality, or is not what you need. Remember, some of the best-fitting clothes—owing to their simplicity—do not look their best dangling limply on a hanger. They need to be tried on to be appreciated.

Examine the material, the workmanship, and the labels. Judge the fabric quality by the same standards you apply in purchasing yard goods (Chapter 7). If labels are missing, ask for them. You want to know which fibers you are getting and what percentages of fibers are present; whether the fabric is wrinkle-resistant; colorfast; permanent press; whether it will shrink or stretch out of shape; and how to care for it.

Good construction in a garment implies that it was not cut skimpily in size and that it was cut correctly as to grain. If off-grain, the garment does not feel comfortable, hold its shape, wear well, or hang correctly. If one sleeve sets well and the other does not, the dress is probably off-grain and fitting seldom can help it. Do stripes and plaids match?

Are seams, pleats, and hems wide enough to set correctly and permit needed changes? Avoid seams that pucker or bulge. There should be little evidence of piecing. Are the stitchings, fasteners, and plackets neat and strong and suitable for the material or kind of dress? Are facings and hems too conspicuous? Do they draw?

Try the garment on for correctness of size, how becoming it is, fit, and ability to combine with the rest of your wardrobe. For fit, look first at the shoulder-armhole area, then at the length of the waist and of the skirt. The latter two are easier to alter, but see if there is material with which to do it. Does the neckline bulge away from the body? Avoid sleeves set too high on the shoulder or those falling off the shoulder. Sit, walk, and reach to see if the dress is full enough to be attractive and comfortable. You either have the wrong size or a poorly cut garment if it is too tight at the hip- and bustlines; the waistline is too high; the back and armholes draw; or the sleeves twist and are short and tight. Try the next size larger. Decide whether you or the store can make a professional-looking alteration. What are the charges?

The very tiny girl (under 5′2″) should look for a junior size, which is smaller in the waist and hips and shorter and more youthful in style. The short, full figure can be fitted best in half sizes or custom sizes; they have more fullness in the waist, hips, and sleeve cap, a shorter waist, and narrower shoulders.

Sizing of ready-mades has been improved, but some lack of standardization remains. Mail-order concerns are following a classification based on measures from the Women's Army Corps: four classes (misses', women's, juniors', half sizes); three heights (tall, regular, short); and three hips (average, slender −, full +). Of course we would not expect every dress design to be carried in all thirty-six possibilities. Formerly, we expected a size 14 in the bargain basement to be comparable to size 12 in the more expensive lines. It will be a great advantage when size 14 is not tagged a size 10 in coats, 34 in blouses, 36 in sweaters, and 5 in panties. You can help to bring this about, with courteous complaints and suggestions.

If style and attractiveness are more important than durability—as in an evening dress—you can overlook somewhat the quality of the fabric, stitching, and finishing details; but if you do, you should pay less. For casual wear do not permit fashion, a novelty fabric, or a style that will be dated the next year to cloud your judgment. But do get some element in it up-to-date!

Consider the cost in time, money, and energy to keep the dress fresh and good-looking. Read the label to find out how it is to be cleaned.

What changes in fitting, construction, or decoration can you make yourself and which ones are to be expected at the price paid? Learning to fit garments is one of your most valuable assets.

Frills and cheap decorations can blind you to other faults. Well-executed dressmaking details found in better dresses include a neat placket; taped waistline; lingerie straps; high-grade, smooth buttons; reinforced pockets; buttonholes rather than snap fasteners; and an inconspicuous hem. Some of these may mean more to you than others. They each add to the cost.

Specific evidences of cheaper grades in dresses include (1) a seam allowance less than one half inch; (2) seams chain-stitched and cord-stitched; (3) topstitching unevenly spaced, long stitches fewer than 14 per inch, poor tension, thread not matching in color, low-grade thread, loose thread ends; (4) holes punched at ends of darts, waistline seam made before underarm seams, hem at bottom of sleeve made before lengthwise seam; (5) puckers in neck binding or facing; (6) skimpy pleats, uneven width in pleats; (7) plackets less than 9 inches long, buttonholes wrong size, cut off-grain, corners not finished neatly; (8) poorly designed buttons that are not sewed on well or "thoroughly" reinforced; and (9) hems that are conspicuous, narrow, uneven, or finished with cheap tape.

The mass-produced clothes of today have a degree of chic and sophistication, simplicity in design, even some touch of originality and flair. Although they are not dramatic, accessories can be added to make them so.

Skirts

Apply the same principles in buying skirts that you use in purchasing dresses. Select a skirt by hip measure. Sit and walk in a skirt to test it. If it rides up, a serious alteration problem may be indicated, making the purchase questionable. A well-fitted skirt should balance on the figure from right to left and front to back. There should be no crosswise or diagonal wrinkles caused by too snug a fit through the hips or waist. The zipper will be well hidden. Some recent designs in knitted fabrics have elastic in the band without a placket.

All-wool skirts, if of a good grade, wrinkle less, are superior in color, and stay in press longer than skirts of low-grade wool. Good-quality wool feels soft and spongy, and is fairly firm in weave. A wool skirt should be dry-cleaned unless the label indicates it has received one of the shrink-resisting finishes. Less expensive materials include man-made fabrics. Many are washable, require little ironing, and may be more comfortable than wool for some persons. Blends are available in beautiful colors: solids, plaids, stripes, and printed designs. They look like wool but cost less. Double-knits, corduroy, denim, and many other fabrics give excellent service.

Blouses

For suit blouses, avoid materials that crush or wrinkle easily and designs with bulky sleeves. Details in the better blouses include matching thread and 14 to 16 stitches per inch. Tops of pockets are neatly reinforced. Piped buttonholes are narrow, neat, and flat. Machine-made buttonholes have close stitching with firm, durable ends. Buttons, if pearl, are not scaly, but uniform in thickness and sewed on with a shank with stitches in the same direction as the cut of the buttonhole. There should be sufficient overlap to prevent the underslip from showing through the buttonholes.

Sleeves are not skimpy in width and are neatly eased into the armhole. Long sleeves have the wrist placket and cuff neatly attached. The neckline or collar finish is well tailored. Collarless blouses are easier to launder and set off jewelry well. Look for wide facings. Will it launder or must it be dry-cleaned?

It is not possible to find many of these details on an inexpensive blouse.

Pants

Because of their greater comfort, stretch fabrics have been most popular for pants. The most widely used are polyester double knits, which are machine washable. Polyester and cotton blends are also machine washable. Various blends of acetate, rayon, and nylon in double and jersey knits, usually require more careful handling; hand washing or dry cleaning is often recommended. A blend of cotton and acetate in a seersucker weave provides cool comfort during warm days. Elasticized waists provide an easy fit.

Construction details that apply to dresses and skirts apply, also, to pants.

Sweaters

Sweaters in many styles are practical additions to the wardrobe. Acrylics or blends are probably more popular than wool, because of ease in washing.

Cashmere sweaters cost more than wool; but they are finer and softer.

Cotton and linen yarns make beautiful, practical sweaters. In buying, try the sweater on to secure long enough shoulder seams, the right sleeve length, ample fullness in the bust, yet snugness at the waistline (or looseness, if it is a hiplength style). Look for firm ribbing; avoid uneven or overly bulky seams. Fine-gauged sweaters are more resilient than coarse-gauged ones, which may shrink and lose their shape. Stretch the garment to see that it is elastic and springs back to its original size and shape. Pockets and openings, if any, should be flat and firm, buttonholes reinforced, and buttons aligned and evenly spaced. Styling is best built in by full-fashioning, rather than by seams.

Hand-knit sweaters are to be treasured. However, they often lack the style of a factory-made sweater. Yokes and puffed sleeves seem out of place on sweaters and complicate the cleaning.

Washing is easy if you are careful; dry cleaning is better if you do not know how to wash. Keep sweaters laid flat in a box or drawer, rather than on hangers. Underarm perspiration causes wool to fade and mat.

Knits continue to gain in popularity and are to be found in full-length coats, suits, dresses, and separates. Double-knits are considered excellent for holding their shape and are reasonably priced. Ribbon knits are packable, but they are bulky and expensive. Italian-type knits are often highly regarded for fashion quality.

Stretch Garments

Stretch fabrics are being made in a great variety of weights and constructions—in both knit and woven fabrics. A stretch fabric stretches under tension, when a body movement pulls it out of line. It goes back into shape when the tension is released. It may stretch vertically, horizontally, or in both directions. To check on the amount of stretch, pull the fabric, being sure you are pulling in the direction of the stretch. Keep the hands about a foot or more apart, as stretch is not easily perceptible in a short distance on the fabric. Be sure it has more stretch than you require. Fabrics stretched to their limit may become distorted in wear. Stretch fabrics eventually "grow" to some extent and fail to return to their original size after being stretched. Hence, garments should be purchased in your regular size.

Stretch fabrics are wrinkle resistant and resist bagginess if large enough. Neck, wrist, and waistbands in stretch sweaters keep their shape well.

Select stretch-wear garments with as few seams as possible, because seams reduce the amount a garment will stretch. The most durable seams are chain stitched or single stitched with 12 to 16 stitches per inch. Seams made with longer stitches or with lock stitches are not elastic enough to stretch adequately when the fabric stretches. Seams should be finished to prevent fraying.

The best type of lining is tricot or any other fabric that will stretch.

Rainwear

A wide variety of fabrics are available for rainwear, depending on the fashion. For occasional showers, the inexpensive plastic raincoat is satisfactory. Although a plastic raincoat is waterproof, it generally stiffens and becomes uncomfortable in cold weather because it is nonporous. A better investment is a water-repellent, windproof coat that will cover your suit or dress completely. It may be reversible and need not be drab in color. A lightweight, closely woven fabric is best. Examine the seams, pockets, ventilators, and the amount of overlap; a double layer across the shoulders affords twice the protection. Consider its use as well as its appearance. You could have an ordinary coat made water repellent at the dry cleaner's.

Accessories

SHOES

The most important purchase you make is that of a pair of shoes, for they affect your ensemble, your posture, and your comfort.

Have your feet measured for size—while standing—each time you buy. Test to see if the length is right; the ends of your toes should never touch the end of the shoe. There should be no pressure on top of the toes from a cap that is built too shallow. See if the ball of the foot lies over the widest part of the sole. The sole should not be more than one fourth inch narrower than the foot. Step down and raise the heel; the bend in the sole should come directly under the big toe joint. Test to see if the heel fits. It should be snug but should not slip when you raise your heel. A combination last may help; for example, you might want a narrower heel in proportion to the rest of the shoe. Test to see if the top of the pump binds or bulges away from the foot.

Shoes that need alterations to make them comfortable, such as stretching, heel lifts, gores, or inner soles may be disappointing. Try the shoes on both feet and walk around in them when your feet are tired or swollen.

Wedge heels are often in fashion for casual wear, which is fortunate, because the wedge is also a corrective for fallen arches. Toeing straight ahead as you walk is also helpful.

Well-tailored, soft, and pliable shoes are generally made on the better lasts, which means better, more natural shapes and comfortable fit. Cheap shoes are usually stiff, overdecorated, and may not fit well.

Shoes are kept in shape by walking with toes straight ahead, having heels straightened when necessary, and keeping the leather soft and clean.

HANDBAGS

In buying a utility handbag for general use, it is wiser to match it with your shoes in color and, if possible, in leather. Calf, cowhide, and goatskin are good buys. Pig, seal, and alligator are more expensive. Suede is not as durable and fades, except in the guaranteed, high-priced bags. A combination of suede and smooth leather in a classic shape may result in a more versatile type. Patent leather generally gives good service. A leather lining is most durable but costs more; avoid light colors and poor stitching. A zipper compartment adds to the convenience and safety of the bag. Look for firm seams and reinforcements, ample gussets, a strong frame, a safe closing, and the absence of a cheaper trim. Hand tooling limits a bag to sport wear. Adjustable shoulder-strap handles add versatility and are good for travel. A bag with a handle should be carried high to prevent its dangling below your skirt hem.

Hats

With the trend to informality, fewer hats have been worn, although headgear in great variety—such as scarfs, turbans, floppy straws or felts, gypsy, cowboy, and sombrero style hats—has been available.

Should you go shopping for a hat, wear the dress and coat with which it will be most frequently worn. Stand before a full-length mirror to observe the total effect. The appearance of the hat on you is what gives it style, but the quality of the materials is also to be considered.

A fur felt is better than a wool felt. The latter will feel grainy, rough, and stiff, whereas a fur felt is soft and silky. The stiffness in a wool felt is due to shellac, and after a while it tends to lose its shape and color.

Gloves

For casual wear, knit gloves are popular and are available in wool and acrylic fibers. With leather palms or finger grips, they are comfortable for driving. As a result of the popularity of bicycle riding, gloves can now be purchased with padded palms, for gripping the handle bars.

Gloves have become a relatively scarce item in some wardrobes during recent years, except for the varieties worn for warmth.

Fabric gloves are practical, and they can be fitted as neatly as kid gloves. Outseam stitchings are good on sport gloves and shorties, but they make the hand appear larger. Look for durability and flexibility in fasteners or buttonholes. A knitted fabric will fit better than a woven one. In either case, a close, fine construction looks and wears better than one noticeably loose or sleazy. String gloves are serviceable for general wear but are not harmonious with fine fabrics or prints.

For sports and winter wear, capeskin and pigskin are good buys. For dress, suede synthetic substitutes are available and glacé kid are excellent, but expensive.

Good leather feels soft and supple, not stiff or papery. Look for a guarantee against crocking (color rubbing off) or fading, especially in black suede. Some leathers are washable, others are not; so read labels. Chamois and doeskin are usually washable; avoid those with thick and thin places. Investigate special glove shampoos—they are good even for kid gloves.

Glove length is measured in buttons—one to twenty—with each button representing one inch from the base of the thumb.

Hosiery

Stretch nylon hose give great satisfaction because of their elasticity, great strength, sheerness, and ease of laundering. To fit well, hose require a size corresponding to your foot measure and to leg length and girth (Fig. 4-7). Full-fashioned

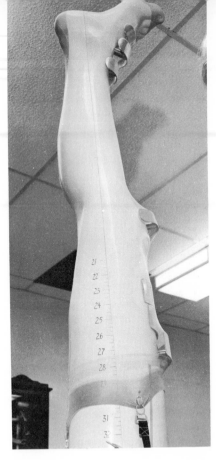

Figure 4-7. Special equipment is used for determining whether hosiery meets the manufacturer's standards. (Courtesy of Burlington Hosiery Company)

shaping with a seam up the back provides a good fit and a slenderizing effect; seamless hose, however, are currently more popular. If knitted too narrow, hose will wrinkle around the ankles. They should be a little longer than the foot for comfort, unless they are stretch types.

Sheerness depends on gauge (knitted loops per one and one-half inches around the hose) and denier (fineness, diameter, size, or weight of the yarns used). The higher the denier, the heavier the yarn; fine (12 to 15 denier) is used in sheer hose. For a service weight, 51 gauge, 30 denier is most commonly used; and 60 gauge, 15 denier is most often used for a dress sheer.

Determine the kind of hose now available on the market suited to your uses and your budget. Buying three pairs of the same color and size is economical. Select the grayer tones if black or blue are your basic colors, beige for warm basics. The tones should blend in a transition between skirt and shoes. Mesh hose are runproof, but snags in them enlarge to holes. Seconds and irregulars are usually very poor bargains. Seamless hose attain a bare-leg look and are made to fit by the size of the knit stitch rather than by full-fashioning. Cantrece (nylon) hugs the ankle well and retains its fit.

Fibers used in socks range from mercerized and combed cotton through various blends, with synthetics to stretch nylon; the latter is generally used. Reinforcement in the heel and toe adds durability.

PANTYHOSE

Many complaints have been made relative to the poor fit and short life of pantyhose. Efforts toward standardized sizing have greatly improved this situation. Ill-fitting hose tend to develop runs. Although the demand for sheer hosiery is great, this type of hose is more prone to run—up and down. Run-resistant stockings will run in one direction only. A hole may appear in nonrun hose, but they will not run. You might be able to continue wearing the latter, if the hole develops where it isn't noticeable.

Many manufacturers label pantyhose as to height, weight, and hip measurement, so it is wise to check the package for this additional information (Fig. 4-8). Because brands vary in size, it is a good idea when you find a size that fits comfortably to stay with it. Opaque types, made of heavier yarns, are less likely to run.

Unsized pantyhose (referred to as one-size-fits-all), which are made to stretch more, are growing in popularity, but they usually do not fit the petite or the large figure very well. Because of their great degree of stretch, they snag more easily than other types. Proportioned pantyhose, when you have determined the brand and size best for you, offer the best combination of good fit and wear.

Innovations of pantyhose with heavier panty or support tops provide greater comfort and figure control, preserving the sheer look on the leg, while smoothing the tummy and hip area somewhat. Some combinations have a cotton panty section.

First, locate your height in the column at the left. Then, move across to the square under your weight. And there you are:

P—Petite
PM—Petite Medium
M—Medium
MT—Medium Tall
T—Tall

(If you are 6 feet tall, or 5'11" and over 155 lbs., you should wear Extra Tall, which is available in Hanes® style 950.)

HEIGHT	WEIGHT															
	90	95	100	105	110	115	120	125	130	135	140	145	150	155	160	165
4 11"	P	P	P	P	P	P	PM									
5'0"	P	P	P	P	P	P	PM	PM								
5'1"	P	P	P	P	P	PM	PM	PM	PM							
5'2"	P	P	P	P	PM	PM	PM	PM	PM	M						
5'3"		P	P	PM	PM	PM	PM	M	M	M	M					
5'4"			PM	PM	PM	PM	M	M	M	M	M	MT				
5'5"				PM	PM	M	M	M	M	M	MT	MT	MT	MT		
5'6"					M	M	M	M	MT	MT	MT	MT	MT	T		
5'7"						M	M	MT	MT	MT	MT	T	T	T	T	
5'8"							MT	MT	MT	MT	T	T	T	T	T	T
5'9"								MT	MT	T	T	T	T	T	T	T
5'10"									T	T	T	T	T	T	T	T
5'11"										T	T	T	T	T		

Figure 4-8. Size chart for women's hosiery products, pantyhose. (Size chart adopted by Hanes Corporation, Winston-Salem, N.C.)

Heel and toe reinforcements extend the wear period, but barefoot designs are desirable with sandal shoes. For longer wear in any type, follow the directions suggested by the manufacturer for putting on the pantyhose.

JEWELRY

The opportunity to express yourself is most apparent in costume jewelry. If you choose soft, feminine clothes, you will find more delicate jewelry in harmony. For rougher fabrics in sportswear and pantsuits, more massive pieces in such materials as heavy silver, copper, leather, wood, and lucite may give a desirable touch. For the peasant look that has been popular, tassels, bangles, and beads fit the situation. Ethnic fashions usually are accompanied in the market by appropriate symbols in accessories.

Rather than invest in large quantities of costume jewelry, you may want to consider a few real semiprecious stones, which cost no more than a lot of imitation jewels. Jewelry of this type can give basic garments—well-tailored solids and simple tweeds—an elegant look. Good jewelry is lost on big plaids and prints. Basic dresses create a demand for pendants; blazers and dresses call for pins; the "little black dress" revives or maintains interest in pearls and semiprecious stones.

A leading jewelry designer says, "Jewelry for young people should be simple and small." He believes that jewelry need not change as rapidly as fashion, because jewelry "goes with the person, not with the clothes."

FURS AND MAN-MADE FURS

A fur coat or fur trimming on a coat is a luxury. Because furs are more costly than cloth and there are so many bargains, it is good to learn as many helpful facts as possible before making such an investment. It is better to buy from a local reputable dealer who is likely to observe the rules and regulations established to protect the consumer.

It is a good plan to *buy the best grade in a price range that you can afford,* including man-made furs, not a low grade of a more expensive type. For example, buy a good grade of rabbit, pony, goat, or calf, rather than a low grade of lamb or squirrel. A good seal-dyed muskrat (Hudson seal) is better than a low-grade, poorly finished, real seal; a good grade of seal-dyed coney (rabbit), called Sealine, is better than a low-grade Hudson seal. It is certainly true that a good cloth coat is a better buy than a coat of cheap, mangy-looking fur. Red fox, monkey fur, bright colors in furs, or strong contrasts of color in the same piece are likely to be conspicuous or to be imitations.

In buying a fur coat, be sure that (1) the size is ample, (2) the lining carries a guarantee, (3) the style is conservative enough to last several years, (4) the leather part does not feel brittle or stiff, (5) the leather and nap both feel uniformly thick throughout, (6) there is not too much irregular piecing, and (7) the edges are folded over on the wrong side like hems (the lower grades have seams right on the edge). Tipping, blending, pointing, dropping, and leathering are legitimate processes that cut the price to you and, therefore, should be mentioned on the label.

A good fur should not shed much; it should not look mangy, dull, matted, or lifeless, but appear lustrous and bright.

The greatest enemies of fur are moths, heat, sun, and friction. Air your fur frequently, but not in the sun. Avoid friction caused by jewelry or a purse. A soft scarf will double the wear of the collar. Cold storage is the best moth preventive, but a big box in a cool place is safe if a generous amount of dichloricide is used. Have the coat cleaned by a reputable cleaner.

Long-haired furs like raccoon or fox do not look attractive on short, stocky figures. Also, fur stoles are too matronly for college women. Abbreviated capes and jackets are more youthful. Dyed mouton-processed lamb is an inexpensive and attractive type for college girls. Fake furs make excellent coats at budget prices.

Lounging and Sleepwear

The selection of robes and sleeping garments involves many of the same considerations as those involved in the selection of casual dresses and underwear. In general, the garments should be light in weight and easy to care for. Knitted and perma-pressed fabrics are popular in robes, needing little, if any, ironing.

Although many items of sleepwear are in knits, woven fabrics are also comfortable and practical. The increase in the use of woven fabrics can be attributed to durable-press finishes for cotton and other fabrics and the advent of man-made fibers and blends with their shape-holding qualities.

Blended polyester and cotton fabric has become a leader in the sleepwear field within recent years, making great inroads on brushed nylons, flannels, and tricot knits. Knits that are brushed or napped to form a long, soft, bulky outer layer often become matted and unsightly after a few launderings, contributing little to warmth.

Undergarments

SLIPS

In lingerie, the difference in price between similar garments is usually the difference in workmanship. Check carefully for details showing good construction.

Nylon has been almost as popular in lingerie as in hosiery, because of its light weight and ease of washing. The most popular fabrics for slips are satin, crepe, and textured tricots. Some are opaque and some have a lustrous look, derived from special nylons, such as Antron. Nylon "taffeta" tricots behave well under knits because they cling less than regular nylon tricots.

Polyester tricots, satins, and taffetas are now on the market; all of these have a nonstatic, noncling finish. Acetate and rayon slips, although cooler than nylon, do not dry as quickly, and rayon requires ironing.

Cotton slips are preferred by some for summer wear, because of their coolness and absorptive quality. Blends of cotton and polyester are popular because of their strength and absorptive quality.

When buying a slip in a new design, it is best to try it on. Buy by bust measure and length and see that it is well fitted at the underarm and bust.

Bias-cut slips are suitable for slight figures. If the bias garment is too tight, the seams ripple, and the slip cups and rides up easily.

More recent designs in lingerie include the bra slip, the pant liner, and the body suit. Bra slips are sized like regular bras. Body suits give a smooth, all-in-one look.

Adjustable shoulder straps should be attached to the fabric, not to the lace trim only. Other good features include tight lock stitches, flat facing, and nylon lace for long wear. Poor quality is indicated by thick binding, hemmed tops, narrow seams, ragged embroidery, and coarse lace with ribbon straps.

Half slips may be preferred with long bras, or body suits. Without these, a full-length slip gives more protection to the dress and a greater softness between bra and dress. Fewer slips are worn today, also, because of underlined garments.

PANTIES

Panties come in many designs to fit a variety of pants, as well as skirts. Price is no indication of quality in panties. Many of the more costly have novelty trims that bear no relation to the value or service you will get. Gift sets are especially poor buys at holiday times or at special sales. The sizes are now marked by actual hip measurements. Use a tape measure or hold the garment up to your waist. The waistband should stretch out to your hip measure. See that the elastic is fastened well at the ends so that it will not tear out. The back of the garment should measure wider and longer than the front to allow sitting room. The leg finish should not show through the dress, and the crotch should be reinforced. Discover brands proportioned as you are. Some girls need longer seats, others need longer legs. For quality and fabrics, see the preceding section about slips. Nylon is more durable than cotton or rayon and washes easily. Cottons or rayons may be preferred in warmer climates because they have greater absorbency. Some styles in stretch nylon, such as the bikini, are made in one size that fits all. The most generally used fabrics in panties are tricot knits in nylon, rayon, and acetate.

BODY SUITS (TANKSUITS)

The versatile body suit in a knit makes a satisfactory undercover aid to wear with the very low-cut or bare back design, in addition to serving as a top for a variety of garments, as skirts, pants, and jumpers.

Foundation Garments

BRAS

Look for fitted darts and good construction in bras as in slips. It is best to try on bras for a good fit. Measurements are included here for determining size. For a bra, take a snug measurement just under the bosom and add 5 inches to it (for figures over 38, add 3 inches). For a cup size, measure the chest above the breasts and subtract from bra size: if the difference is one inch, wear an A cup; 2 inches, B; 3 inches, C; 4 inches, D.

Wearing the proper cup size helps to eliminate pressure on the shoulder from the bra strap. Bras shaped with underwires may contribute to proper fit for the person wearing the larger cup sizes. Also, long-line designs with stretch elastic sides and built-up back straps are recommended for a comfortable, youthful profile for the slightly larger figure. Stretch straps add comfort in wearing.

Knit fashions and sheath styles require adequate foundation garments for a smooth appearance. The trend has been away from the uplifted, pointed bosom toward softer, rounded shapes, but not as flat as in the 1920s. Popular fabrics have been tricot and double knits. The latter can be made in a single, soft layer with very narrow seams.

A cincher contributes to neat, tiny waistlines, rib-cagey wide belts, and well-shaped skirts.

GIRDLES

Only the very firm, slim figure looks right in a revealing dress without some type of foundation garment. Girdles are made in many styles, and in thin, light-weight fabrics. Shop for this type and try for a comfortable fit to give a smooth unbroken line. Let the saleswoman fit you correctly.

Garterless girdles hold stockings satisfactorily, if the leg length of the stocking is correct. They should end at mid-thigh, and fit snugly but not bind. For the slightly heavier figure, an "action back"—a mesh insert below the back waistband—allows the waistband to remain in place as the body moves.

SUMMARY

A breakthrough in the early 1970s resulted in an unprecedented legal recognition of the plight of the consumer: poor quality products, deception in advertising, exorbitant credit costs, inefficient and costly service, and misleading guarantees.

As a result, government and industry are both working toward improvement; laws have been passed and new regulations set up for the consumer's protection. A knowledge of one's rights and responsibilities as a consumer adds to the individual's ability to handle consumer problems.

Tentative determination of one's needs, familiarity with market offerings in relation to those needs, an understanding of quality in merchandise, and a knowledge of available sources of information are desirable prerequisites for shopping.

REFERENCES

BLANDFORD, JOSEPHINE M., AND LOIS M. GUREL. *Fibers and Fabrics.* Washington, D.C.: U.S. Department of Commerce, 1970

HOLLEN, NORMA, AND JANE SADLER. *Textiles* (2nd ed.). New York: Macmillan Publishing Co., Inc., 1968

JOSEPH, MARJORY L. *Introductory Textile Science.* New York: Holt, Rinehart & Winston, Inc., 1966

Textile Handbook (4th ed.). Washington, D.C.: American Home Economics Association, 1970

Fashion Sewing

The phenomenal growth of home sewing—fashion sewing—during the latter half of the 1960s and continuing on into the '70s has made a tremendous impact on the sale of patterns, fabrics, notions, sewing machines, and other related products. By the early '70s, fashion sewing was the second fastest growing industry in the country.

The Simplicity Pattern Company estimated that the nation's 45 million home sewers contributed 350 million women's garments to the 1,250 million made in the United States in 1970. This number represents about half of all females 12 years of age and older. The chances are that every fourth woman seen on the street is wearing a made-at-home garment (Fig. 5-1).

The volume of business of the Simplicity Company doubled during the last

Figure 5-1. These fashion sewers received national recognition for their garments, submitted in the 1972 Make It Yourself with Wool contest: *a*, first place, senior division, Eileen Hawes; *b*, junior, Susan White; alternates, *c*, Ruth Hunt and, *d*, Carla Bass. (Courtesy of The Wool Bureau, Inc.)

five years of the '60s. Pattern companies reported record sales of $150 million in 1969.[1]

This trend began in the early '60s, apparently as a result of teen-age interest in sewing, which is seen as one of the remarkable aspects of the home sewing boom.

SHE SEWS AT HOME

1. Her median age is about 23—it was 40 in 1960.
2. She is highly individual and fashion oriented.
3. Her clothes don't look "homemade."
4. She and her like are spending more than $3 billion annually on home sewing supplies and equipment.
5. Six out of seven teen-age girls now sew with reasonable proficiency.
6. Sewing is their number-one hobby.

WHY SEW?

No attempt has been made to arrange the following list in order of importance, because this would vary with the individual's interests and situation.

[1]Peter Tonge, "On Sewing for Herself," *The Christian Science Monitor* (Jan. 23, 1971), p. 1.

1. **To save money.** Women are dollar-conscious today. According to the clothing industry, the final cost of a ready-to-wear garment may be divided roughly into three equal parts: for labor, fabric, and design. With labor "free" and a pattern costing no more than $5, the home sewer can save almost two thirds of the cost of a ready-to-wear garment.[2]

2. **To resist spiralling costs.** The cost of good ready-to-wear apparel and its upkeep increased 16 per cent between 1967 and 1971, according to the U.S. Bureau of Labor statistics.

3. **For individuality.** The fashion sewer is not likely to meet herself in a dozen places, as may be the case with a ready-made manufactured and sold in volume. She has more freedom of choice as to design, fabric, and color.

4. **For greater self-expression.** This theory is supported by the fact that all home-craft industries are enjoying a boom. Many women sew as an outlet for their creative ability. Creativity involves the use of imagination to find the best solutions to problems, leading often to original ideas and applications.

5. **Because styles are simple.** Clothing is simple in style today and comparatively easy to make. One of the fortunate influences for fashion sewing was the advent of the shift dress, which cleared the way for simple, fashionable patterns. Young people want simplicity.

6. **Because fabrics are easier to handle.** Bonding and special construction and finishing processes have simplified sewing techniques, although couture designs are no deterrent for many fashion sewers.

7. **To meet the demand for variety.** The demand today is for a greater variety of clothing. The budget will stretch to provide more clothes if the fashion sewer makes them.

8. **Because good equipment is available.** The push-button sewing machine and other available sewing equipment facilitate sewing.

9. **For immediate use.** More and more fashion sewers have a tendency to sew for "right now"—sew it today and wear it tomorrow.

10. **Because home-sewing is "accepted."** There is no longer a stigma about wearing made-at-home clothes. "Homemade," for many, used to mean a dress to wear around the house. Now, a home seamstress is more likely to vacuum the house in a discount-store garment and step out dressed for important occasions wearing her own artistic creation.

11. **To relieve tensions.** Psychiatrists recognize the importance of doing work with the hands to relieve tensions.

12. **To strengthen family ties.** Sewing can be a bond for knitting family ties closer together. Social values are expressed in sewing for loved ones or in participation in a community sewing project.

THE POSITION OF THE INDUSTRY

Fashion sewing is being looked upon in industry as a movement, not as a fad.

[2]Josephine Ripley, "Why Such Enthusiasm for Sewing?" *Christian Science Monitor*, Aug. 9, 1971, p. 2.

With the rise in the cost of living expected to continue, the basic need for home sewing will remain. No matter what the economic cycle may be, according to this theory, fashion sewing will continue to be important. If money is available, consumers will want to sew more clothes to be more fashionable; if the supply of money should be reduced, there will be a more crucial need than ever for the fashion sewer to make her own clothes.

Combine the affluent teen-ager's predilection for "do your own thing" with the important youth market, and teen-age sewing promotions become inevitable. These promotions, tied in with magazines, pattern companies, and often a fabric company, have met with great success. Much of the market is directed to the young creative consumer.

Most fashion magazines have sections on fashion sewing. *Seventeen* launched a new magazine called *Make It,* which emphasizes sewing and related crafts.

The large pattern companies and other companies related to the sewing industry are giving away enormous quantities of free sewing guides and educational materials.

"How to" books on dressmaking are mushrooming. *The Vogue Sewing Book* sold 125,000 copies during its first nine months. Even so, the Vogue-Buttrick company published another book for the nonsewer and novice. *Ready, Set, Sew* is geared to the younger reader.

Pattern companies are doing an excellent job of interpreting fashion. Until recent years, home sewing was always a year behind ready-to-wear. Now, the pattern companies have corrected that lag.

There is a great increase in the number of fabric shops. The Singer Company has added a line of fabrics. Spadea is now a major source for imported fabrics as well as designer patterns. Diversification into the home sewing market has given Bobbie Brooks, Inc., extensive experience with fabric quality, purchasing, and design preferences, the company has reported.

Earlier, most of the exciting and more desirable fabrics were in wholesale lines only. Now, many companies have open lines and will sell to anybody. The state of the economy at the beginning of this decade influenced this tendency, but it was also influenced by the awareness, in industry, that persons who sew are interested in fashion. Although better-quality fabrics are available to the home sewer, colors have not kept pace, and the color range for piece goods is more limited than that offered to wholesalers. Sometimes colors for the two markets are not even the same. Ironically, fashion sewers are usually more sophisticated in their color choices than the person who does not sew.

Fashion sewing classes abound. Many have waiting lists. Dressmaking is the most popular course of all among women and girls at evening classes, according to the pattern industry. Some classes are free, but for the most part there is a charge. Classes are being conducted by the Singer Company, the pattern companies, and others.

Doubtless, the large number of girls learning to sew in home economics classes in the public schools and in the 4-H Extension Service clubs has had a part in bringing about this upsurge in sewing.

A new organization has come into being, illustrating the growing emphasis on fashion sewing: The American Fashion Home Sewing Council was organized in 1971 for the purpose of promoting the fashion sewing industry from every level. The Council is serving as a clearing house for the questions of retailers regarding such things as which thread to use for a certain fabric and other valuable information to be passed on to the consumer.

A new and unique development occurred in 1971 when the McCall Pattern Company began offering a free sewing course for male executives in the home sewing field—for the "men making their living from this field without knowing a thing about it." The course consisted of six two-hour classes; all the basics of sewing were taught, including operating a sewing machine, fabric in relation to pattern, pattern placement, cutting, and sewing. The course was not designed to make dressmakers of salesmen and editors but to give them a better understanding of their field. Response to the classes was overwhelming. None of these "new pupils" had ever done any sewing. The vice-president of one large company is quoted as saying, "Big grown men look clumsy sitting behind a sewing machine, but now I can understand some of the problems of the company."[3]

SPECIAL CONSUMER ADVANTAGES

More services are being made available in the larger cities and by mail, because of increased interest in sewing. Fabrics can now be custom pleated, and mail service for bound buttonholes is anticipated.

Promising developments may be hoped for as a result of the sewing classes for the men executives already referred to. Their actual participation in construction has revealed a greater awareness of some of the problems that have annoyed home sewers for years. The gentlemen were unable to understand the guide sheets, so improved ones were prepared for their patterns within a few months; the difficulties in handling off-grain fabrics were points of enlightenment and surprise; improvements can be hoped for in that area.

The increase in the number of fabric shops offers great opportunities for young people in sales and even in a fashion direction. With so many young people sewing, companies like to have young salespersons on their staffs, along with mature persons. Many sewers feel that an older person is more knowledgeable about fabrics, but the young people often like to talk to a young salesperson when making decisions on what to buy, especially as to design.

[3]"Execs Enter 'Eye of Needle,'" *Women's Wear Daily*, March 16, 1971.

PART TWO

Clothing Construction

Pattern
Selection

Successful dressmaking begins with a pattern as nearly correct in size as possible. Both the size and type of pattern selected will influence the possible difficulties to be encountered in making a well-fitted garment and on the time to be spent in accomplishing this goal.

It is relatively easy to alter a pattern and cut a garment to fit; it can be very difficult, or impossible, to get the extra length or width needed after the garment has been cut, especially where there is only a $\frac{5}{8}$-inch seam to work with. Although the method or the principle back of the method is the same in paper as in cloth, it is safer to correct the pattern. Careful alteration can result in a better product, save time, and provide greater satisfaction in sewing with fitting problems eliminated or, at least, minimized.

There are a number of decisions to be made before the pattern is selected:

the purpose or need for the proposed garment; the style of pattern that fits this purpose; consideration of the pattern, and availability of the pattern in the type and size that most nearly conforms to the body measurements.

PRELIMINARY PLANNING

Observe ready-to-wear garments during a "window-shopping" trip and study fashion magazines and newspapers for the season's style trends and fashion details. This is not to suggest a slavish following of fashion, but you will want to be informed in this direction before making a selection.

Consider several possible designs. Which will be most becoming to you? Which will be best suited to the fabric being considered? Which will be suitable for one with your experience? Which will be the most challenging—offering learning opportunities in proportion to your capabilities?

BRANDS OF PATTERNS

The great variety in the more commonly offered brands of patterns—the types, proportions, and sizes—provides a wide field from which to choose. You are aware that some patterns are designed especially to be easy-to-make, suitable for the inexperienced person but also for the experienced seamstress who wants to make a dress in a short time. Many patterns include three or four variations of the design and possibly more than one design, as a dress and coat. Designer patterns are becoming more available—patterns by the leading designers of many countries. The winning designs from contests that are open to young designers are also often available.

Computer patterns may eliminate the need for pattern alterations, as they become more available in stores. Many persons require only simple alterations in commercial patterns, but for severe figure difficulties, the computer pattern may be a great advantage.

A difficulty in supplying this type of pattern is the necessity for very accurate measurements to be fed into the computer. The customer cannot take these measurements for herself and few people are sufficiently skilled in the science of anthropometry to avoid mistakes in measuring. In some cases, measurements are taken by a trained person in the store.

The volume of available designs is limited, but the person who has a knowledge of flat pattern design could develop her own designs or use her basic computer pattern in adapting commercial patterns to her own needs.

Available computer patterns cost several times as much as conventional commercial patterns, but are likely to be subject to a great deal of reuse, which tends to offset the initial cost.

The Spadea Pattern Company has added a series of European-style printed patterns. These are printed on both sides of the paper—two are available for the price of one. Overlapping lines in a maze must be traced and transferred to another sheet of paper in order to segregate the pattern sections.

Patterns with a different approach have been introduced into the United States within recent years. These feature European methods based on measure-

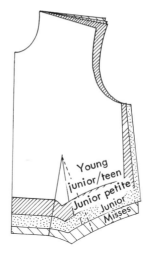

Figure 6-1. Patterns are available in a variety of types. Find the one that best fits your figure.

ments—a pattern drafting technique. This concept involves the use of a miniature pattern. Dots placed at certain points on the edges of this miniature mark the appropriate points for charting the body measurements of an individual and provide the guide for completion of the pattern. Theoretically, this technique can easily and speedily eliminate, or reduce the need for pattern alterations. Designs may be somewhat limited in relation to other brands, but the method could open new avenues for the person interested in this technique. It might be a distinct advantage to someone with unusually difficult fitting problems and involve the purchase of fewer patterns. One example of this type of pattern is the American Way, Tru-Fit Pattern.

Figure Types and Pattern Sizes

Four patterns are shown in Figure 6-1, one superimposed upon the other. They represent four of the seven teen and adult figure types of patterns produced by most pattern companies. Selecting a pattern in the proper size is a most important step toward sewing with satisfaction; using a pattern in the correct size eliminates much pattern alteration and garment fitting.

WHICH FIGURE TYPE ARE YOU?

Study the information presented in Figure 6-2, and analyze your own body proportions and shape. The figure types do not refer to age, although Young Junior-Teen and Junior Petite are designed for the younger, smaller figure. Height and back waist measurements are the keys to your figure type. Read the descriptions of the body types, and tentatively decide which of these best fits you.

In Table 6-1 figure types are classified on four measurements: three basic circumference measurements—bust, waist, and hip—and the back waist length. Patterns are designed on a standard scale of measurements, approved by the

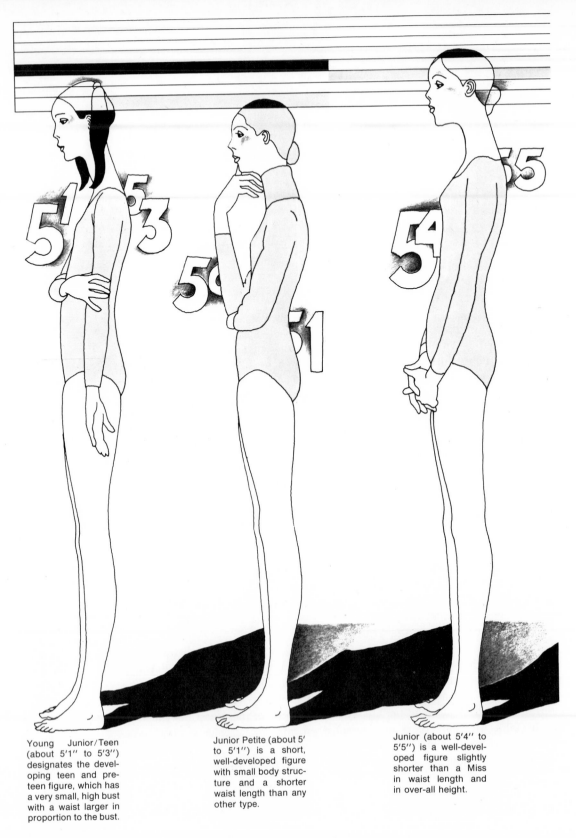

Young Junior/Teen (about 5'1" to 5'3") designates the developing teen and preteen figure, which has a very small, high bust with a waist larger in proportion to the bust.

Junior Petite (about 5' to 5'1") is a short, well-developed figure with small body structure and a shorter waist length than any other type.

Junior (about 5'4" to 5'5") is a well-developed figure slightly shorter than a Miss in waist length and in over-all height.

Figure 6-2. Body types. (Courtesy of the Simplicity Sewing Book, Simplicity Pattern Company.)

Miss Petite (about 5'2'' to 5'4'') is a shorter figure than the comparable Miss size, but longer than the corresponding Junior Petite.

Miss (about 5'5'' to 5'6'') is well proportioned, well developed in all body areas, and is the tallest of all figure types. This type can be called the "average" figure.

Half-Size (about 5'2'' to 5'3'') is a fully developed shorter figure with narrower shoulders than the Miss. The waist is larger in proportion to the bust than in the other mature figure types.

Woman (about 5'5'' to 5'6'') is a larger, more mature figure of about the same height as a Miss. The back waist length is longer because the back is fuller, and all measurements are larger proportionately.

Table 6-1

BODY MEASUREMENT CHART

Approved by the Measurement Standard Committee of the Pattern Fashion Industry

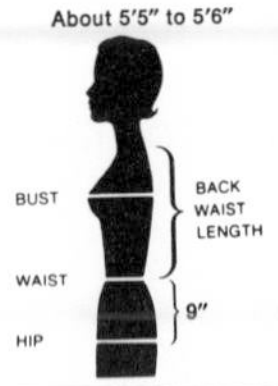

MISSES'

Misses' patterns are designed for a well proportioned, and developed figure; about 5'5" to 5'6" without shoes.

Size	6	8	10	12	14	16	18	20
Bust	30½	31½	32½	34	36	38	40	42
Waist	23	24	25	26½	28	30	32	34
Hip	32½	33½	34½	36	38	40	42	44
Back Waist Length	15½	15¾	16	16¼	16½	16¾	17	17¼

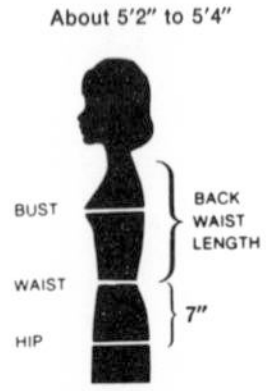

MISS PETITE

This size range is designed for the shorter Miss figure; about 5'2" to 5'4" without shoes.

Size	6mp	8mp	10mp	12mp	14mp	16mp
Bust	30½	31½	32½	34	36	38
Waist	23½	24½	25½	27	28½	30½
Hip	32½	33½	34½	36	38	40
Back Waist Length	14½	14¾	15	15¼	15½	15¾

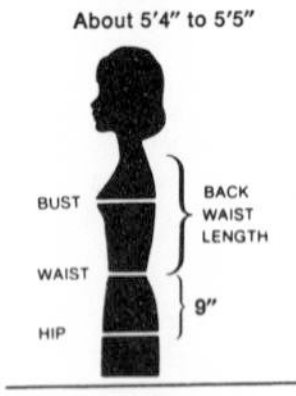

JUNIOR

Junior patterns are designed for a well proportioned, shorter waisted figure; about 5'4" to 5'5" without shoes.

Size	5	7	9	11	13	15
Bust	30	31	32	33½	35	37
Waist	22½	23½	24½	25½	27	29
Hip	32	33	34	35½	37	39
Back Waist Length	15	15¼	15½	15¾	16	16¼

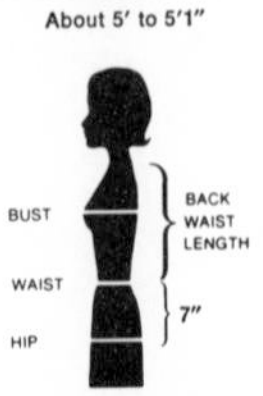

JUNIOR PETITE

Junior Petite patterns are designed for a well proportioned, petite figure; about 5' to 5'1" without shoes.

Size	3jp	5jp	7jp	9jp	11jp	13jp
Bust	30½	31	32	33	34	35
Waist	22½	23	24	25	26	27
Hip	31½	32	33	34	35	36
Back Waist Length	14	14¼	14½	14¾	15	15¼

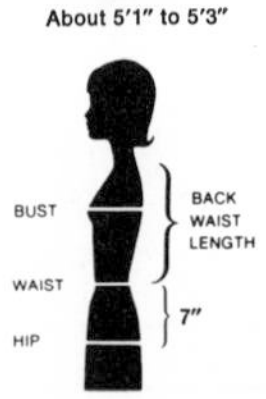

YOUNG JUNIOR/TEEN

This size range is designed for the developing pre-teen and teen figures; about 5'1" to 5'3" without shoes.

Size	5/6	7/8	9/10	11/12	13/14	15/16
Bust	28	29	30½	32	33½	35
Waist	22	23	24	25	26	27
Hip	31	32	33½	35	36½	38
Back Waist Length	13½	14	14½	15	15⅜	15¾

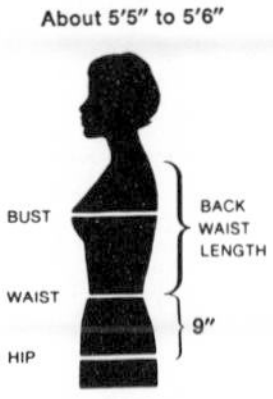

WOMEN'S

Women's patterns are designed for the larger, more fully mature figure; about 5'5" to 5'6" without shoes.

Size	38	40	42	44	46	48	50
Bust	42	44	46	48	50	52	54
Waist	35	37	39	41½	44	46½	49
Hip	44	46	48	50	52	54	56
Back Waist Length	17¼	17⅜	17½	17⅝	17¾	17⅞	18

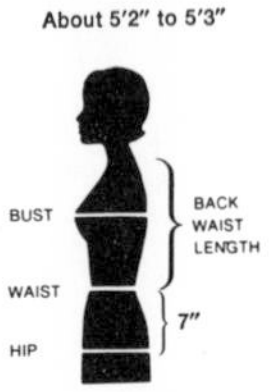

HALF-SIZE

Half-size patterns are for a fully developed figure with a short backwaist length. Waist and hip are larger in proportion to bust than other figure types; about 5'2" to 5'3" without shoes.

Size	10½	12½	14½	16½	18½	20½	22½	24½
Bust	33	35	37	39	41	43	45	47
Waist	27	29	31	33	35	37½	40	42½
Hip	35	37	39	41	43	45½	48	50½
Back Waist Length	15	15¼	15½	15¾	15⅞	16	16⅛	16¼

HOW TO TAKE BODY MEASUREMENTS FOR PANTS AND SHORTS:

Stand evenly on both feet. Measure snugly over undergarments you usually wear with pants. Side length is from waist to desired finished length.

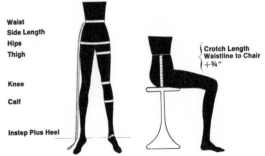

SKIRTS, SLACKS & SHORTS:

Select by waist measurement. For hip-hugger patterns OR if hips are much larger in proportion to waist, select size by hip measurement.

Misses'
Waist 23 24 25 26½ 28 30 32 34
Hip 32½ 33½ 34½ 36 38 40 42 44

Miss Petite
Waist 23½ 24½ 25½ 27 28½ 30½
Hip 32½ 33½ 34½ 36 38 40

Junior
Waist 22½ 23½ 24½ 25½ 27 29
Hip 32 33 34 35½ 37 39

Junior Petite
Waist 22½ 23 24 25 26 27
Hip 31½ 32 33 34 35 36

Women's
Waist 35 37 39 41½ 44 46½ 49
Hip 44 46 48 50 52 54 56

Young Junior/Teen
Waist 22 23 24 25 26 27
Hip 31 32 33½ 35 36½ 38

SOURCE: Courtesy of the *Simplicity Sewing Book*, Simplicity Pattern Company.

Measurement Standard Committee of the Pattern Fashion Industry, and are used by practically all pattern companies.

Pattern sizes are based on actual body measurements. To determine your size, take your measurements and compare them with those listed on the chart. If yours are the same as those listed—the standard measurements used by the pattern company—you are fairly safe in assuming that the garment will have a fashion-right appearance on your figure. Each pattern has an allowance in excess of basic body measurements—minimum ease to provide for comfort and action, and styling

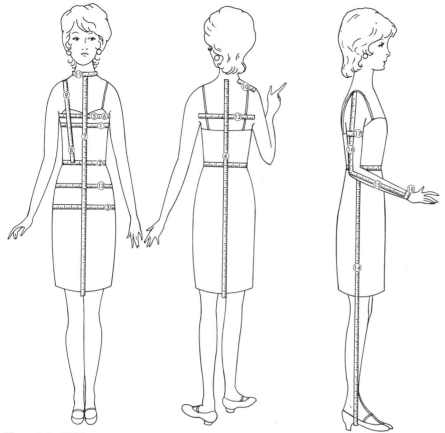

Figure 6-3. Taking measurements.

ease for design interest and current fashion. Therefore, the actual measurements of the pattern will be somewhat in excess of those given on the pattern envelope.

How Many Measurements Do You Need?

The four measurements already referred to—bust, waist, hip, and back waist length—may be sufficient for you in determining your pattern size. If you are aware of any problems you have experienced with garments that fit improperly, you may need to take additional measurements to assist you in making this decision.

Taking Measurements

It is preferable to take measurements over smooth, well-fitted undergarments, the types that will be worn with the garment; shoes may be worn. You will need assistance in taking the measurements. Keep the tape measure snug.

Some positions on the body at which measurements are taken are shown in Figure 6-3. The locations are numbered to correspond with the directions that follow. Start with the four measurements that are generally used in determining

Table 6-2

Measurements for Pattern Selection

	MY MEASUREMENTS	STANDARD MEASUREMENTS	DIFFERENCE + OR −
Bust			
Waist			
Hip			

Back waist length _____

Type of pattern indicated
  (as Misses or Junior Petite) _____

Sizes indicated
  for: blouse, dress, or coat _____

  for: skirt, or pants _____

pattern type and size, and record them in Table 6-2. In column 2, record the corresponding standard measurements from Table 6-1.

How to Measure

1. **Bust.** Measure over the fullest part of the bust and straight across the back.
2. **Waist.** Measure at the natural waistline (the smallest part of the trunk) keeping tape parallel with the floor; lap tape and pin it flat, allowing one end to hang at side seam; leave it in position while other measurements are taken. Or, tie a string around your waist.
3. **Hip.** Take this measure seven or nine inches below the waistline as directed for your probable figure type—nine inches for Misses and Junior types and seven inches for Miss Petite, Junior Petite, Half-Size, and Young Junior/Teen figures—or, if in doubt, take both. Keep the tape parallel with the floor, after locating its proper level on the tape hanging from the waistline.
4. **Back waist length.** Measure at center back, from the prominent neck bone to the middle of the waistline tape.

If you found that your body measurements—bust, waist, hip, and back waist length—conformed to those of one of the sizes given on the measurement chart, you are ready to make a decision regarding your pattern type and size, especially if your weight or figure has not changed since your previous experience in using patterns.

In case there is evidence that additional measurements are needed before you can make a decision, record them in Table 6-3, matching the location numbers on the figure to the item numbers on the table.

Metric conversion charts are provided in Table 6-4.

Table 6-3
PERSONAL MEASUREMENT CHART

	1 STANDARD MEASUREMENTS	2 MY BODY MEASUREMENTS	3 DIFFERENCES BETWEEN 1 AND 2 + OR −	4 EASE RECOMMENDED	5 SIZE OF COLUMNS 2 AND 4	6 PATTERN MEASUREMENTS	7 DIFFERENCES BETWEEN 5 AND 6 + OR −
1. Bust				3–5 in.			
2. Waist				1 in.			
3. Hip				2 in.			
4. Back waist length				½–1 in.			
5. High bust							
6. Chest							
7. Front waist length— center front				½–1 in.			
8. Front waist length— over bust				½–1 in.			
9. Bust depth							
10. Shoulder length				Back shoulder at least ½ in. longer than front			
11. Neck circumference				¼–½ in.			
12. Back shoulder width				½–1 in.			
13. High hip—2–4″ below waist				1 in.			
14. Skirts, shorts, or pants length				Hems as desired			
15. Arm length—shoulder to wrist							
16. Arm length—shoulder to elbow							
17. Upper-arm circumference				2–3 in.			
18. Wrist circumference				½–1 in.			
19. Crotch depth—waist to seat level				¾ in.			
20. Ankle							

Table 6-4

METRIC EQUIVALENCY CHART
CONVERTING INCHES TO CENTIMETERS
AND YARDS TO METERS

This chart gives the standard equivalents as approved by the Pattern Fashion Industry

INCHES INTO MILLIMETERS AND CENTIMETERS
(SLIGHTLY ROUNDED FOR YOUR CONVENIENCE)

mm—millimeters   cm—centimeters   m—meters

INCHES	MM		CM	INCHES	CM	INCHES	CM
$\frac{1}{8}$	3mm			7	18	29	73,5
$\frac{1}{4}$	6mm			8	20,5	30	76
$\frac{3}{8}$	10mm	or	1 cm	9	23	31	79
$\frac{1}{2}$	13mm	or	1,3cm	10	25,5	32	81,5
$\frac{5}{8}$	15mm	or	1,5cm	11	28	33	84
				12	30,5	34	86,5
$\frac{3}{4}$	20mm	or	2cm	13	33	35	89
$\frac{7}{8}$	22mm	or	2,2cm	14	35,5	36	91,5
1	25mm	or	2,5cm	15	38	37	94
$1\frac{1}{4}$	32mm	or	3,2cm	16	40,5	38	96,5
$1\frac{1}{2}$	38mm	or	3,8cm	17	43	39	99
$1\frac{3}{4}$	45mm	or	4,5cm	18	46	40	101,5
2	50mm	or	5cm	19	48,5	41	104
$2\frac{1}{2}$	65mm	or	6,5cm	20	51	42	106,5
3	75mm	or	7,5cm	21	53,5	43	109
$3\frac{1}{2}$	90mm	or	9cm	22	56	44	112
				23	58,5	45	114,5
4	100mm	or	10cm	24	61	46	117
$4\frac{1}{2}$	115mm	or	11,5cm	25	63,5	47	119,5
5	125mm	or	12,5cm	26	66	48	122
$5\frac{1}{2}$	140mm	or	14cm	27	68,5	49	124,5
6	150mm	or	15cm	28	71	50	127

YARDS TO METERS
(SLIGHTLY ROUNDED FOR YOUR CONVENIENCE)

YARDS	METERS	YARDS	METERS	YARDS	METERS	YARDS	METERS	YARDS	METERS
$\frac{1}{8}$	0,15	$2\frac{1}{8}$	1,95	$4\frac{1}{8}$	3,80	$6\frac{1}{8}$	5,60	$8\frac{1}{8}$	7,45
$\frac{1}{4}$	0,25	$2\frac{1}{4}$	2,10	$4\frac{1}{4}$	3,90	$6\frac{1}{4}$	5,75	$8\frac{1}{4}$	7,55
$\frac{3}{8}$	0,35	$2\frac{3}{8}$	2,20	$4\frac{3}{8}$	4,00	$6\frac{3}{8}$	5,85	$8\frac{3}{8}$	7,70
$\frac{1}{2}$	0,50	$2\frac{1}{2}$	2,30	$4\frac{1}{2}$	4,15	$6\frac{1}{2}$	5,95	$8\frac{1}{2}$	7,80
$\frac{5}{8}$	0,60	$2\frac{5}{8}$	2,40	$4\frac{5}{8}$	4,25	$6\frac{5}{8}$	6,10	$8\frac{5}{8}$	7,90
$\frac{3}{4}$	0,70	$2\frac{3}{4}$	2,55	$4\frac{3}{4}$	4,35	$6\frac{3}{4}$	6,20	$8\frac{3}{4}$	8,00
$\frac{7}{8}$	0,80	$2\frac{7}{8}$	2,65	$4\frac{7}{8}$	4,50	$6\frac{7}{8}$	6,30	$8\frac{7}{8}$	8,15
1	0,95	3	2,75	5	4,60	7	6,40	9	8,25
$1\frac{1}{8}$	1,05	$3\frac{1}{8}$	2,90	$5\frac{1}{8}$	4,70	$7\frac{1}{8}$	6,55	$9\frac{1}{8}$	8,35
$1\frac{1}{4}$	1,15	$3\frac{1}{4}$	3,00	$5\frac{1}{4}$	4,80	$7\frac{1}{4}$	6,65	$9\frac{1}{4}$	8,50
$1\frac{3}{8}$	1,30	$3\frac{3}{8}$	3,10	$5\frac{3}{8}$	4,95	$7\frac{3}{8}$	6,75	$9\frac{3}{8}$	8,60
$1\frac{1}{2}$	1,40	$3\frac{1}{2}$	3,20	$5\frac{1}{2}$	5,05	$7\frac{1}{2}$	6,90	$9\frac{1}{2}$	8,70
$1\frac{5}{8}$	1,50	$3\frac{5}{8}$	3,35	$5\frac{5}{8}$	5,15	$7\frac{5}{8}$	7,00	$9\frac{5}{8}$	8,80
$1\frac{3}{4}$	1,60	$3\frac{3}{4}$	3,45	$5\frac{3}{4}$	5,30	$7\frac{3}{4}$	7,10	$9\frac{3}{4}$	8,95
$1\frac{7}{8}$	1,75	$3\frac{7}{8}$	3,55	$5\frac{7}{8}$	5,40	$7\frac{7}{8}$	7,20	$9\frac{7}{8}$	9.05
2	1,85	4	3,70	6	5,50	8	7,35	10	9,15

Table 6-4 (Cont.)

AVAILABLE FABRIC WIDTHS				AVAILABLE ZIPPER LENGTHS					
25″	65cm	50″	127cm	4″	10cm	10″	25cm	22″	55cm
27″	70cm	54″/56″	140cm	5″	12cm	12″	30cm	24″	60cm
35″/36″	90cm	58″/60″	150cm	6″	15cm	14″	35cm	26″	65cm
39″	100cm	68″/70″	175cm	7″	18cm	16″	40cm	28″	70cm
44″/45″	115cm	72″	180cm	8″	20cm	18″	45cm	30″	75cm
48″	122cm			9″	22cm	20″	50cm		

SOURCE: Courtesy of Butterick Fashion Marketing Company—Vogue Patterns and Butterick Patterns.

ADDITIONAL MEASUREMENTS

5. **High bust.** Measure around the body high under the arms, keeping tape parallel to the floor.

6. **Chest.** While the *high bust* tape is in position, take a reading across the front, from arm crease to arm crease.

7. **Front waist length.** Measure at center front, from the base of the neck to the middle of the waistline tape.

8. **Front length over bust.** Measure from the middle of the shoulder seam over the point of the bust to the middle of the waistline tape. Take two readings: the full length from shoulder to waistline, and the shoulder to the point of bust. Record the latter figure under number 9.

9. **Bust depth.** This measurement is taken from the shoulder to the point of bust (described in number 8).

10. **Shoulder length.** Measure from base of neck to the shoulder bone socket. (It probably will be more accurate to take this measurement from a well-fitting dress with set-in sleeves.)

11. **Neck circumference.** Measure around fullest part of neck. For an accurate measurement, allow tape to stand on one edge as it circles the neck.

12. **Back shoulder width.** Measure the distance across the back from arm crease to arm crease, four inches below the prominent neck bone, with arms hanging at ease. (Take this measurement from a well-fitting dress with set-in sleeves, if possible.)

13. **High hip.** Measure two to four inches below the waistline over the hip bones, with tape parallel to the floor.

14. **Skirt, shorts, or slacks length.** Measure from the waistline tape to the desired length for center back, center front, and right- and left-side seams.

15. **Arm length, shoulder to wrist.** Measure from the arm socket over the bent elbow to the wrist bone.

16. **Arm length, shoulder to elbow.** Measure from the arm socket to the point of the elbow.

17. **Upper-arm circumference.** Measure around the fullest part of the bent arm above the elbow.

18. **Wrist circumference.** Measure around the wrist at the bone.

19. **Crotch depth.** Sit in a straight, hard chair; with a ruler resting on the edge

of the chair beside the figure, take a reading at the middle of the waistline tape from waist to seat level. Add ¾ inch.

20. **Ankle.** Measure over the instep and around the lower back heel.

PROPORTIONED PATTERNS

If your circumference measurements (bust, waist, and hip) conformed to those on the chart, but your back waist length varied, you may find a basic proportioned pattern an advantage for you. Proportioned patterns provide adjustments for short, average, or tall figures.

PATTERNS FOR KNITS

There are many patterns that can be used for knits. These fall into the following three classes.

THE REGULAR, CONVENTIONAL PATTERN The heavier double knits, which tend to have less stretch than the others, can be used satisfactorily with the conventional pattern. They may require tighter fitting, however, because some of the ease allowed for woven fabrics may not be needed. If this type of pattern is to be used for a very stretchy fabric such as a sweater knit, it might be advisable to buy a smaller size. The design should be uncomplicated in detail, without gathers and draped lines, and with emphasis placed on decorative top stitching.

A RECOMMENDED-FOR-KNITS PATTERN This is a regular pattern, designed in a simple style that adapts well to knits. As pointed out earlier, the garment may require larger seams or the purchase of a smaller pattern, depending upon the fabric chosen.

THE FOR-KNITS-ONLY PATTERNS Patterns that are designed especially for knitted fabrics will not have the excess ease that is present in the regular patterns. These patterns are to be selected by body measurements.

Another type of pattern is available for the person who wishes to be creative in designing her own pattern. This is a master pattern—a special knit pattern—that may have several different sizes in one envelope. Measure the bust or chest of the pattern to determine which is the best size for you.

WHEN CIRCUMFERENCE MEASUREMENTS VARY

If some of your measurements are different from those on the pattern, which of them should be used in making your selection?

Many persons have measurements that vary from those listed on the measurements charts. Note the lines in the basic pattern (Fig. 6-4). Ask yourself these questions:

1. For larger or smaller hips, would it be easier to adjust a gored skirt pattern if the hip measure is correct, or if the waist measure is correct? It would be relatively easy to make the waistline smaller or larger by changing the darts and seams located there; therefore, buying by hip measure would simplify the alterations.

Figure 6-4. Basic dress pattern.

2. Would the answer to the first question be the same if the skirt were designed with considerable fullness, as with gathers, unpressed pleats, or wide circularity? The best measurement to use in that case would be the waist measure, as there would be no problem with the hip size.

3. For a larger bust, can the same principle be used in buying a blouse, dress, or jacket pattern as that used in deciding on a skirt pattern size? It is clear that the principle would be the same. With darts and seams at the waistline, adjustments could be made easily; therefore, it would be an advantage to select this pattern by bust measure.

4. In selecting a dress pattern with the waistline seam for a person with both larger bust and larger hips, which measurement would probably be better? Perhaps it is clear to you now or it will be after you have learned more about pattern alterations, that changing a pattern for a larger hip may be less involved than changing it for a larger bust; therefore, it is generally recommended that the bust measure be used rather than the hip measure for selecting a dress pattern. But you cannot be sure that the bust measure will be your only consideration. The following problem illustrates this point.

5. The girl shown in Figure 6-5, *a*, bought her pattern for this overblouse by bust measure. Was this size a good selection for her?

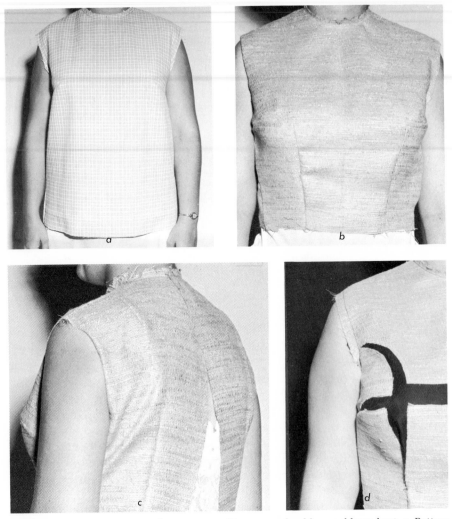

Figure 6-5. Selecting a pattern for a person with narrow shoulders and large bust. *a*, Pattern selected by bust measure; *b* and *c*, for shoulder-chest width; *d*, alteration to correct for bust.

There is sufficient ease at the bustline because the pattern was selected to conform to her bust measurement, size 14. Note the chest area: the pattern is too wide here; the shoulder seams are too long, throwing the armholes out of position. It is obvious that this pattern would require alteration for narrow shoulders and possibly a smaller neck, if the collar is to fit closely; alteration of these lines may interfere with the fit of the collar and sleeve patterns.

In this case one can see that consideration of the bust measurement alone was not a satisfactory plan. Through the shoulder and chest area, this student measured size 12, shown in the bodice in *b* and *c*—correct in size through the shoulders and chest, but so small at the bust that it does not reach around the figure. An alteration for a larger bust resulted in a bodice that fit, *d*; this alteration in the pattern would eliminate the need for changes on any pattern section except the front.

This student will find it to her advantage to select a pattern size that is more nearly correct in the chest and shoulder width, rather than in the bust measure.

YOUR FINAL DECISION

You are now ready to decide on the type and size of pattern you believe will most nearly fit you. To further confirm this belief, you may want to consider checking on a few other points.

1. Is the type and size of the pattern you have decided on justified by any previous experiences in using patterns (assuming that your figure and weight have not changed). In case there is a discrepancy, it is wise to recheck your measurements for possible error. No means of determining your correct size can be better than positive information based on experience (not just a hazy idea of what your mother or your dressmaker may have been using and possibly altering). Also to be considered in this connection is the question of whether you have developed a discriminating judgment about a correctly fitted garment. How sure are you of this?

2. In case you have had no previous experience in using patterns, perhaps you are wondering whether it is safe to select a pattern in the same size that fits you in ready-to-wear. This is quite possible but yet not conclusive. It was not until after the adoption of New Sizing by the pattern companies during the latter part of the 1960s that the sizes of ready-to-wear and patterns became more nearly comparable—when the Misses size 32 (approximate) bust measure was designated as size 10, rather than size 12. The standardization of sizes by the pattern companies has contributed toward reaching this goal.

3. With limited information regarding your possible best selection of a pattern size, a quick method for an accurate determination is to try on a shell (a basic garment), if these test garments are available in your clothing laboratory. If they are not available, and your figure varies considerably from the standard measurements used by the pattern company, it might be time-saving and safer for you to cut a basic test garment in muslin or another inexpensive fabric in order to learn more about your figure, especially if you have plans for a large investment in your fabric. Another alternative is to select the size that appears to be the best selection; then, as you prepare to cut the garment, compare your measurements with the pattern measurements and alter if necessary.

THE PATTERN—SIMPLE OR COMPLICATED?

The difficulty of a design at this point in your experience depends on your ability and somewhat on your preferences. If you have had little or no experience in sewing, it will be to your advantage to select an easy-to-make pattern. This way you will be able to get good results and keep up with your classmates. Even if you have sewed some but have not been completely satisfied with your standards in construction techniques or the speed you have attained, keep the design simple. It would seem wise to improve your sewing techniques on simple designs and then use more complicated patterns as you try to develop speed in various areas.

If you have had considerable experience and have been successful, you may be in a position to select a more difficult and challenging design.

The purpose of the following exercises is to assist you in learning by reviewing what you have already learned about pattern designs in relation to complications in construction. Such evaluations of choices, in line with your present skills, plus the challenges you wish to accept can greatly influence satisfactions to be gained.

Judging Difficulty in Construction

Study the designs sketched in relation to construction in Figure 6-6. Which design, *a* or *b*, would be simpler to construct? Why?

It is evident that skirt *a* would be easier to construct, as it has fewer parts to be joined together and, therefore, fewer seams. Both skirts (we assume) have side seams. More time would be required to make the additional seams in *b* than to make the darts in *a*, especially if the fabric used required finishing the seam edges. Side plackets in the two skirts would be equal in difficulty. The waistline of skirt *a*, stitched to the belting, would be simpler to construct than *b*, with an interfaced band attached. Both skirts would be relatively easy to fit, with *a* probably easier.

Compare the waistline of *b* with *c*. In *c* the wider, low-slung, fitted band or yoke, with top stitching crossing it at the placket, would involve a few more complicated techniques than those required in *b*; there would be different problems in interfacing and in handling the somewhat bias edges of both the pants and yoke sections in the seam that joins them together. The placket in *c* would be a great deal more complicated to construct than in *b*. Fitting, also, might be more involved in *c*.

Consider *d*, to be made in a plaid fabric, with bias trim (wide piping) on the pockets, bias cuffs, and buttoned band. This design would be time-consuming and complicated for an inexperienced person, although it is not extremely difficult to construct.

Could one find a simpler problem than *e*, which has no placket and is hemmed at the waistline to encase the elastic?

Pleats and top stitching complicate Figure 6-7, *a*; simple, easy-to-make features include the neck and armhole facings and machine buttonholes. What is unique about design *b*, which shows a Chinese influence? With the right and left fronts unlike, and fabric buttonholes to be made on varying fabric grains, this design is more involved, both in pattern placement and in construction, than the front bodice of *a*. The mandarin collar would be simple to make, and the degree of difficulty to be encountered in setting these sleeves would depend on the choice of fabric (see Chapter 7). If difficulty is anticipated in making the buttonholes on the bias grain at the curve, they could be relocated on the grain.

Contrast the complication of designs *a* and *b* in Figure 6-8. Making the top-stitched collar and setting the sleeves in *a* would provide challenging problems,

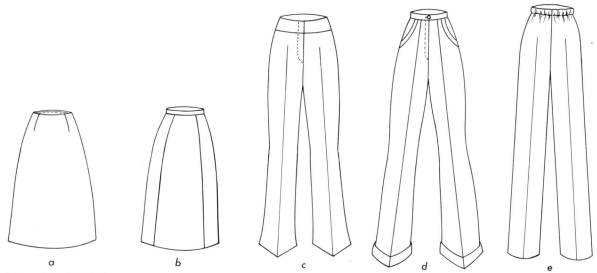

Figure 6-6. Which designs are simpler to construct?

Figure 6-7. Evaluate construction problems.

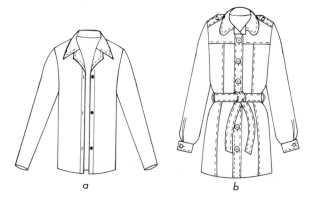

Figure 6-8. Which is more complicated to construct?

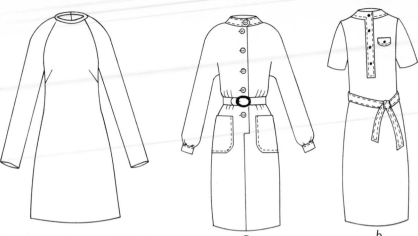

Figure 6-9. An easy design to construct.

Figure 6-10. Compare sleeves and necklines.

a

b

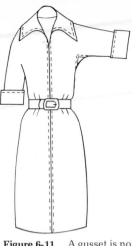

Figure 6-11. A gusset is not difficult—it requires the ability to match seam lines with perfection.

but the quantity of work to be accomplished in the construction of *b* would make it a much lengthier process. Considering the sleeves in the two garments, a simple hem or facing at the wrist of *a* can be made in a fraction of the time that would be necessary for the cuff treatments in *b*. However, sleeve *b* will be easier to set in than sleeve *a*—assuming that *a* has the normal set-in sleeve—because *b* is a shirt-type sleeve with a short cap and less fullness to be eased into the upper half.

Would you expect to spend much time making the dress in Figure 6-9? How would the time involvement in constructing and joining these sleeves to the body of the garment compare with the normal set-in sleeve? You could expect these raglan sleeves to be easier to attach because of the absence of fullness to be eased in.

The kimono sleeve in Figure 6-10, *a,* is a part of the dress, resulting in a very simple problem for this loose, roomy sleeve. The wrist bands would require some time, although they are simple to make. Compare the neck treatments and front closings of *a* and *b*. Although the front closing of *a* is longer, the closing in *b* would be a more complicated line to construct because of the skill and precision necessary to secure flat, smooth, corners, both at the end of the opening and at the neckline. Neat, straight top stitching would involve careful handling in stitching through varying thicknesses of fabric.

Are you able to distinguish a feature in Figure 6-11 that would require a high degree of precision handling and an accurate matching of seam lines for a quality product? The gussets at the underarms can add much comfort and convenience in wearing this type of kimono sleeve, cut as high as it is under the arm. It is not difficult to construct, with precision-marked and matched seam lines.

Study Figure 6-12, designs *a, b,* and *c*. What do they have in common that the designs we have already considered did not have? Each of these has seams on the bias, varying degrees on the bias, that make them more complicated and difficult to handle in construction. Which of the three would require the most skill in handling? No doubt you chose *c*, with its darker inset seamed to other parts

132

of the garment with many areas on the bias. The fact that it is made of crepe might add further challenges in handling.

PATTERN CHARACTERISTICS

A number of design features that influence the relative difficulties in garment construction have been pointed out. Summarized lists follow.

SIMPLE DESIGNS

Relatively few pattern pieces.
A limited number of simple, fairly straight seams and other construction processes, such as patch pockets.
Parts for the right and left sides of the body are cut alike.
No topstitching.
Machine-made buttonholes.
Darts.
Sleeveless and collarless designs.
Kimono, dolman, raglan, or shirt-type (short cap) sleeves.

MORE COMPLICATED DESIGNS

Precision topstitching.
Intricate seams—bias, curved, and angular.
Profuse gathers, tucks, and pleats—especially pressed pleats.
Fabric buttonholes.

Figure 6-12. Bias seams complicate a design. Which would be most difficult to construct, *a, b,* or *c?*

Set-in sleeves.
Collars and cuffs.
Gussets.

This attempt to recognize relative characteristics is incomplete. There are other factors to be considered, including the choice of fabric, which will be considered in Chapter 7.

Plan for Self-evaluation

Growth in any undertaking is achieved through the frequent appraisal of day-by-day progress. Table 6-5 is a suggested plan for self-evaluation of the various procedures involved in selecting and making a garment.

This is not intended as a score card for use at the end of the construction process, but as a guide for checking your progress as you go along, or to assist you in developing your own plan for such an evaluation.

An important consideration in checking your progress will be your ability to manage your activities and keep up with your classmates. If you find that you are a slow worker, try to improve your organization of work, or do not insist upon the highest degree of perfection for yourself at this stage in your experience. It is more important to gain a mental concept of standards and good management; perfection in manipulative skills is acquired with practice.

Table 6-5
EVALUATE YOUR PROGRESS*

	CHOICE OF PROBLEM			Score
	1	2	3	
1. Design	Commonplace or too extreme for wearer; poorly adapted to fabric and occasion.		Up-to-date but not extreme; suitable for individual; well adapted to fabric and occasion.	1._____
2. Fabric	Unattractive, uninteresting, poor texture; color unsuitable for wearer and occasion.		Attractive, satisfactory in color and design, interesting texture.	2._____
3. Trimming	Uninteresting, does not harmonize with the garment; unsatisfactory texture and color.		Interesting, harmonizes with garment; pleasing texture and color.	3._____
CONSTRUCTION OF GARMENT				
4. Thread	Does not match color of fabric; incorrect size.		Matches color of fabric; correct size and type.	4._____

Table 6-5 (Cont.)

	1	2	3	Score
5. Machine stitching	Not straight and even, not alike on both sides; improper length for fabric.		Alike on both sides, proper stitch length for fabric; even, accurate; tension adjusted to fabric.	5._____
6. Stay stitching	Not well placed in relation to seam line; not stitched in direction of grain.		Correctly placed in relation to seam; stitched in direction of grain; used where needed.	6._____
7. Interfacing	Poor choice; inadequate use.		Correct weight for fabric; used where needed.	7._____
8. Darts	Uneven or abruptly tapered; not well placed; threads not tied or points retraced.		Evenly and gradually tapered; well placed; threads tied.	8._____
9. Gathers	Unevenly distributed; coarse.		Evenly distributed, fine.	9._____
10. Seams	Unsuitable, uneven, bulky, puckered; improperly finished.		Correctly placed, even, smooth, flat; edges properly finished.	10._____
11. Fabric buttonholes	Lips uneven, corners not square; hand hemming stitches on back too long; not hemmed to cover stitching line.		Lips even, corners square; hand hemmed along stitching line; hand hemming stitches $\frac{1}{16}$–$\frac{1}{8}$-inch, and inconspicuous.	11._____
12. Collar	Interfacing is wrinkled; not understitched; facing shows; enclosed seam too wide; bulky corner; collar points tend to roll upward.		Interfacing properly attached; evenly understitched; seam hidden under edge of collar; enclosed seam trimmed and notched if necessary; bulk removed from corner; sharp, well-turned corner; collar points and edges lie fairly flat.	12._____

Table 6-5 (Cont.)

**Clothing
Construction**

		1	2	3	Score
	13. Armhole facings	Unsatisfactory width; poorly finished; improper joinings; stretched; show along edge.		Understitched properly, slashed; edge finished properly; seams joining facing section pressed open and trimmed to $\frac{1}{4}$-inch, satisfactory width, hidden.	13._____
	14. Sleeves	Puckers along seam line; only one line of stitching; seam unfinished.		Ease distributed so there are no puckers; double-stitched in lower half; bias strip attached to upper half if needed; armhole seam correctly finished.	14._____
	15. Waistline seam	No stay; pressed toward bulky side; uneven.		Straight strip of fabric or seam tape stay; pressed in direction of least bulk; smooth set.	15._____
	16. Placket	Does not lie flat; stitching uneven; threads not fastened; zipper not concealed; opening too short.		Lies smoothly; front lap completely conceals slide fastener in side placket; opening about $\frac{1}{2}$-inch longer than metal; threads tied at ends of stitching on front of garment; stitching even distance from seamline.	16._____
	17. Hem	Conspicuous; uneven in width, improper width; bulky; poor distribution of fullness at top of hem.		Inconspicuous; even and proper width; smooth; fullness well distributed or removed.	17._____
	18. Fasteners	Inappropriate; not placed where needed; unevenly spaced; insecurely attached; incorrectly attached.		Satisfactory for garment; placed in space correctly; securely and properly attached.	18._____
	19. Grain	Off-grain at center front and back.		Grain straight down center front and back.	19._____

Table 6-5 (Cont.)

137

Pattern Selection

	1	2	3	Score
20. Snugness of fit	Too tight or too loose.	Fitted snugly but not too tight.		20._____
21. Shoulder seam	Does not follow shoulder line.	Sets correctly at shoulder.		21._____
22. Underarm seam	Crooked or slants to front or back.	Straight and perpendicular to floor.		22._____
23. Bust darts	Do not point to fullest part of bust; too long; crossing full part of bust.	Point to fullest point of bust and end one to two inches from full part.		23._____
24. Bodice	Wrinkles point to shoulder or bust; too tight or loose.	Smooth set; correct amounts of ease; all lines in correct locations.		24._____
25. Sleeve	Wrinkles point to top of cap; grain line uneven; unbalanced; too tight or loose.	No wrinkles; balanced; ease evenly distributed; straight grain.		25._____
26. Hemline	Uneven.	Even.		26._____
27. Time schedule	Was unable to keep up with the class.	Time and work schedule was efficiently organized.		27._____

GENERAL APPEARANCE

	1	2	3	Score
28. Individuality	Ordinary; does little for wearer.	Has fashion quality and interest.		28._____
29. Attractiveness	Color and line are poor for wearer.	Well-fitted and satisfactory in color and line.		29._____
30. Professional effect	Poor handling of fabrics and processes.	High-quality workmanship, pressing, and neatness.		30._____
31. Ensemble	Accessories poorly chosen.	Accessories add up to a pleasing total look.		31._____

* In evaluating the quality of your work, choose number 2 if your work is better than the standards in the left-hand column, 1, but does not measure up to the standards listed in the right-hand column, 3. Record 1, 2, or 3 in the blank at the right. Check the chart items as you work on the various steps.

7

Fabric Selection

The romantic story of textiles has extended through some 12,000 years of history. During that period the number of natural fibers used for clothing gradually increased to reach a total of four major ones—flax, wool, silk, and cotton. Not until this century did man begin to add his own production to nature's store. The development has been phenomenal. The number of man-made fibers on the market today is many times that of the natural fibers.

You may already have a thorough knowledge of the inherent properties of fibers and fabrics and their suitability for various uses, plus an appreciation of their serviceability and beauty. This book is naturally limited to a brief review. For more extensive treatments of the subject, references are listed at the end of the chapter.

Textile Fibers

The following classification includes the major fibers used in apparel textiles, limiting man-made fibers to those produced in the United States. A partial list of trade names follows the generic terms listed here.[1]

NATURAL

Cellulose: cotton, flax (linen).
Protein: silk, wool, specialty hair fibers.

MAN-MADE

Acetate: Acele, Avisco, Chromspun, Celanese, Estron.
Triacetate: Arnel.
Acrylic: Acrilan, Creslan, Orlon, Zefran.
Anidex: Anim/8.
Metallic: Chromeflex, Durastran, Lamé, Lurex, Nylmet.
Modacrylic: Dynel, Verel.
Nylon: Antron, Cantrece, Caprolan, Cumuloft, Enkalon, Nyloft, Qiana.
Olefin: DLP, Herculon, Vectra.
Polyester: Avlin, Dacron, Fortrel, Kodel, Trevira, Uycron.
Rayon: Bemberg, Coloray, Cupioni, Fibro, Fortisan, Jetspun, Avril, Nupron, Zantrel.
Rubber: Lactron, Lastex.
Saran: Lus-Trus, Velon.
Spandex: Glospan, Lycra, Spandelle, Vnel.
Vinyon: Avisco Vinyon HH.

Fiber Blends and Combinations

The conclusion can be drawn from a study of fiber properties that no single fiber can meet all needs. By blending or combining two or more, new fabrics can be produced that maximize the most desirable characteristics of the fibers and minimize those less desirable.

1. *Cotton* and *rayon* are combined with other fibers to increase absorbency and comfort, decrease static buildup, improve dyeability, and reduce construction costs.

2. *Acrylics* improve softness and warmth without adding weight.

3. *Nylon* adds strength.

4. *Acetate* improves drapability and texture.

5. *Polyester* contributes wash-and-wear qualities, abrasion resistance, wrinkle resistance, and dimensional stability.

Proportions of fibers vary with fiber properties and intended end uses, but a general rule for satisfactory performance is that a fabric should contain at least

[1]Generic names and definitions in this section were established by the FTC under Rule 7, Rules and Regulations Under the Textile Fiber Products Identification Act, 1959.

50 per cent of that fiber having the major characteristic desired. No hard-and-fast rules for care of blends and combinations are possible. It is wise to follow the manufacturer's instructions conscientiously. Should care instructions not be available, handle the product according to procedures recommended for the most sensitive fiber present.

TEXTILE FIBER OUTLOOK

Projections for the '70s predicted a limited emphasis toward bringing additional new man-made fibers into the market. Interest is expected to be centered more on the further development and improvement of the qualities of fibers already in use. Continued research with yarn, blends, and finishes may yield solutions to such problems as static buildup and snagging in double-knits. New versions of blends of synthetic fibers, of synthetic with natural fibers, novel textured yarns, and various forms of construction in unusual surface textures will be offered.

QUALITY IN FABRICS

Quality in a fabric is dependent upon many factors: inherent characteristics of the fibers, fabric construction, finishes, and uses in harmony with these qualifications. In Table 7-1, some of the properties of the various textile fibers and fabrics are presented. Colorfastness, shrinkage control, wrinkle resistance, and wash-and-wear properties are among the most desired characteristics in clothing.

COLORFASTNESS   It is important in judging colorfastness to have some kind of guarantee. "Colorfast" on a label is better than no statement at all, but more specific statements are preferable: "fast to sun and washing," "fast to perspiration," and "will not crock." The term *vat dyed* indicates satisfactory colors. No colors are absolutely fast—merely relatively so. A swatch may be washed or tested—attached to a piece of white fabric—in an attempt to discover its tendency to fade, bleed, run, or crock, but information secured from a label, based on tests in a Launder-Ometer, Fade-Ometer, or Crockmeter with a guarantee, is more reliable and saves time. Extensive laboratory test procedures based on expected-use conditions are better able to predict the fabrics's performance. Generally, more severe tests are established for fabrics that will be laundered commercially. "Washable" does not insure that the fabric will not fade or shrink in washing. Generally, yarn-dyed fabrics, such as gingham, hold their color better than piece-dyed fabrics, such as printed cottons.

Colorfastness to *fumes* is of increasing importance in a polluted atmosphere, especially with acetates, requiring continued research to overcome these problems.

DIMENSIONAL STABILITY   You will want to know that the fabric will hold its approximate shape and size during wear and cleaning—that it will not shrink, stretch, or slip at the seams. Shrinkage can be controlled in the factory by special processes. *Sanforized* labels guarantee "maximum residual shrinkage of less than 1 per cent" when the fabric is air dried. Such terms as *preshrunk* and *supershrunk* on labels were indefinite and misleading and, therefore, are no longer permitted by the FTC.

Table 7-1
CLASSIFICATION OF COMMONLY USED FIBERS FOR APPAREL

FIBERS	CHARACTERISTICS—FIBERS AND FABRICS	GENERAL HANDLING AND CARE
Cellulosic Cotton Linen	Comfortable to wear because of absorbency; stronger when wet; low resiliency and elasticity with tendency to wrinkle unless treated; resin finishes may improve shrinkage, crease retention, and wrinkle resistance; ignites readily and is not self-extinguishing; can be made flame-resistant.	Can be washed in hot water, machine-washed and tumble-dried; bleached, although bleaching tends to weaken linen fibers; some cotton finishes cause the fabric to yellow when exposed to chlorine bleach. Can be ironed at high temperatures— 400°F. Easy-care finishes may not require ironing. Linen ironed damp for best results.
Rayon	The first man-made fiber; the least expensive, and most widely used fiber. Very versatile, used extensively in blends. Comfortable because of absorbency, lustrous, good drapability; weaker when wet. Newer types of viscose rayon are stronger and more dimensionally stable, with greater similarity to cotton in over-all properties (as Avril, Nupron, and Zantrel). Colorfast to dry cleaning and washing. Fair to poor in resiliency, wash-and-wear qualities, and resistance to abrasion, mildew, and wrinkling. Ignites readily.	Can be washed as cotton or linen, but should be ironed with a moderate ironing temperature—fibers will not melt but might scorch at high temperatures. Rayon blends may require more gentle treatment when heat-sensitive fibers are included.
Protein Silk Wool Specialty hair fibers	Fabrics hold their shape well, resist wrinkling; are comfortable to wear in cool, damp weather because of absorbency; weaker when wet, harmed by dry heat, oxidizing agents, and alkalies; attacked by moths; silk yellowed by sunlight, strong soaps, and age; do not burn readily.	Dry cleaning more successful than washing, but can be washed with care; use moist heat in pressing and moderate ironing temperatures; avoid chlorine bleaches; use neutral soap.
Acetate	Luxurious, soft feel; silky appearance; excellent draping qualities; and good dimensional stability. Fair to poor in absorbency, colorfastness, pressed-in crease retention, resistance to abrasion and wrinkling, and wash-and-wear qualities. Ignites readily and is not self-extinguishing.	Can be hand-laundered, using warm water and gentle agitation— do not soak, wring out, or twist. Can be dry-cleaned and pressed with a cool iron. Protect from nail polish and paint remover, because these substances may dissolve the fibers.

Table 7-1 (Cont.)

CLASSIFICATION OF COMMONLY USED FIBERS FOR APPAREL

FIBERS	CHARACTERISTICS— FIBERS AND FABRICS	GENERAL HANDLING AND CARE
Triacetate	Similar to the most desirable qualities listed for acetate. In addition, triacetate has good resistance to heat and wrinkling, and good wash-and-wear qualities. Ignites readily and is not self-extinguishing.	Can be machine-washed and tumble-dried and ironed, if necessary, with a hot iron—450°F.
Acrylic	Good to excellent in colorfastness, dimensional stability, wool-like qualities, pressed-in crease retention, resiliency, warmth, wash-and-wear qualities, and wrinkle resistance. Fair to poor in abrasion and pilling resistance and in strength; ignites and burns readily and has low absorbency; pleats and creases can be heat set; is subject to static buildup; burns readily.	Can be machine-washed and tumble-dried at low temperatures, and dry-cleaned; safe ironing temperature 300–325°F; can be bleached.
Anidex	Synthetic elastic fiber; excellent in flexlife and resistance to aging, body oils, chlorine bleaches, dry-cleaning solvents, heat, and light. Good holding power and strength; contributes properties of stretch and recovery to blends, reducing or eliminating sagging or bagging in hosiery, knit and woven outerwear, lingerie, and stretch fabrics.	Can be machine-washed and tumble-dried at normal settings; bleached with chlorine bleaches; safely pressed at 320°F.
Metallic	Metallic yarns and fabrics are nonabsorbent, nontarnishing, and extremely sensitive to heat.	Fabrics can be washed when the amount of metallic yarns is small; dry-cleaned, and pressed with a cool iron, unless otherwise specified by the manufacturer.
Modacrylic	Good to excellent in colorfastness, resiliency, softness, warmth, wash-and-wear qualities, and resistance to sunlight and wrinkling; fair to poor in dimensional stability and strength and in resistance to abrasion and pilling; fabric is flame-resistant and generally self-extinguishing; blended with other fibers to reduce flammability; can be made to resemble fur.	Can be machine-washed and tumble-dried at low temperatures, ironed if necessary at low temperature, 200–250°F; and dry cleaned; the fur cleaning process is recommended for deep-pile fabrics.

Table 7-1 (Cont.)

CLASSIFICATION OF COMMONLY USED FIBERS FOR APPAREL

FIBERS	CHARACTERISTICS— FIBERS AND FABRICS	GENERAL HANDLING AND CARE
Nylon	Outstanding in versatility; good to excellent in colorfastness, dimensional stability, elasticity, resiliency, strength, and resistance to abrasion, mildew, moths, and perspiration. Fair to poor in absorbency, and resistance to pilling, sunlight, and wrinkling. Can be heat set. Chief contributions to blends are strength and abrasion resistance.	Can be machine-washed and tumble-dried at low temperature; bleached with chlorine bleach; and ironed at 300–375°F (depending on type).
Olefin	Good-to-excellent resistance to abrasion, pilling, stains, sunlight, wrinkling, and aging. Fair to poor absorbency and dyeability. Very light in weight and provides better thermal insulation than wool.	Can be machine-washed in luke-warm water; tumble-dried at low temperatures *except* when the fiber is used as a filler in quilted pads and has not been treated with a wash-resistant antioxidant by the manufacturer. In this form, heat may build up in the filler, resulting in fire. Can be bleached at low water temperatures (below 150°F), and dry cleaned. Articles made of 100 per cent olefin cannot be ironed, but blends can be ironed at low temperatures.
Polyester	This fiber brought in wash-and-wear qualities; does not shrink or stretch appreciably; heat-set pleats and creases stand up extremely well; good to excellent in colorfastness, resiliency, strength, and resistance to abrasion, sunlight, and wrinkling. Owing to outstanding wrinkle resistance and dimensional stability, it is used extensively in blends, especially with cotton (durable-press textiles), rayon, and wool. Fair to poor in absorbency, pilling, and snagging; high affinity for oily soil and oil-borne stains, making soil-release finishes desirable.	Can be machine-washed and tumble-dried. Articles containing fiberfill (polyester filler or padding) can also be machine-washed and dried, depending on the cover fabric; may be bleached with chlorine bleaches (follow directions on hang tags), dry-cleaned, and ironed at 300–350°F. Remove oily stains before washing (look for cleaners on your supermarket shelf).
Rubber	Rubber-core yarns are used where stretch or elasticity is required (Anidex, Spandex, or natural rubber); high elongation; good elasticity and holding power; low resistance to body oils, cosmetics, light and perspiration; and low strength.	Launder in accordance with manufacturer's recommendations, if available. Wash with water at low temperature; avoid high concentrations of bleaches, heat, and exposure to sunlight. Do not dry-clean or dry in automatic dryers.

FIBERS	CHARACTERISTICS— FIBERS AND FABRICS	GENERAL HANDLING AND CARE
Saran	Low absorbency and high resiliency; because of low resistance to heat and poor stability, its use in apparel fabrics is very limited—mainly used for handbags and shoes.	Can be washed with soap or detergent and bleached with chlorine bleach, but water must be kept at 100°F. or lower.
Spandex	Synthetic elastic fiber; excellent elasticity and resistance to cosmetic lotions and body oils, flexing, and sunlight; Spandex core-spun yarns retain holding power better than those of covered natural rubber yarns; foundation garments are soft and provide great freedom of movement; desirable for sewing foundation garments and swim suits at home—little danger of damage from needle cutting. Yellows with age and with temperatures above 300°F.	Can be machine-washed and tumble-dried at low temperatures; bleached, except with chlorine bleaches; dry-cleaned; and ironed, if necessary, at temperatures below 300°F.
Vinyon	Because of low strength and extreme sensitivity to heat, principal use is as a binder agent that softens, shrinks, and bonds to other fibers in the presence of heat and solvents. Excellent for use in bonded and nonwoven fabrics.	Can be washed in warm water with a mild detergent and drip-dried. Do not tumble-dry or iron.

WASH-AND-WEAR FINISHES—DURABLE- OR PERMANENT-PRESS

Efforts to develop wrinkle-resistant finishes can be credited with the present volume of durable- or permanent-press products in our markets and the continuing work toward further improvements in this direction.

As a result of the poor resilience of cellulose fibers, wrinkle-resistant finishes (generally synthetic resins), have been developed for cotton, linen, and rayon fabrics. Blends of these fibers and combinations with various other fibers are also treated with these finishes, which improve not only wrinkle resistance, but shape retention, durable crispness, control of relaxation shrinkage, and the possibility of durable creases and pleats in finished garments. Two methods of finishing are involved in the latter. The process, applied and cured before the fabrics are shipped to the manufacturer, is termed *precure*. In *postcure* finishing, the finish is applied and dried or partially cured before the fabric leaves the mill. After the garment has been finished by the manufacturer, the final curing of the finish is completed by means of oven baking or pressing with high temperatures and pressures.

SOME PROBLEMS Difficulty in altering the garment is a limitation imposed by the postcure process, whereas difficulty in obtaining a well-pressed appearance is a limitation with the precured process, whether the garment was factory-made or custom-made. Other problems encountered are chlorine retention by some finishes, causing white fabrics to turn yellow; an off-grain condition that cannot be straightened; reduced strength and abrasion resistance; and greater retention of oil-borne stains. Labels on wrinkle-resistant fabrics should be checked to see whether or not a chlorine bleach is safe.

EVALUATE FINISHES Wash-and-wear finishes provide easy care, comfort, and aesthetic and economic qualities for a fabric. However, a number of considerations may be involved in such an evaluation: whether the finish will function as claimed; require special handling; is permanent for the life of the garment; and can withstand washing, dry cleaning, or both. Careful reading of the label will be helpful in this assessment.

EXAMPLES OF FINISHES A finish or process may have a trademark name as Sanforized-Plus (Sanforized Company, Division of Cluett, Peabody & Company), or may be indicated by a fabric name such as Belfast (Deering Milliken, Inc.); Perma-Pressed (Avondale Mills); Tebelized (T.B. Lee Company, Inc.); or Wrinkl-Shed (Dan River Mills, Inc.).

Sanforized-Plus is a finish for the control of shrinkage plus crease recovery. Sanforized-Plus-2 embodies shrinkage control on durable-press fabric.

Some durable-press trademark names are Coneprest (Cone Mills); Dan Press (Dan River Mills); Penn Prest (J. C. Penney Co.); and Perma-Prest (Sears, Roebuck and Co.).

Examples of other finishes include stain-and-spot-resistant finish—Scotchgard and Zepel; soil release—Wash Ease, Soil-Out, and Danclean; perspiration-resistant finish—Sanitized; reflective finish—Milium; water-repellent finish—Cravenette; and waterproof finish—Reevair. Slip-resistant finishes and stretch-and-sag-resistant finishes are widely used on fabrics of man-made fibers.

OTHER INDICATIONS OF QUALITY

Plain and twill weaves are the most durable. Satin weave can be durable if the floating yarns are short and the yarn count is high. Long floats passed over too many yarns are easily snagged and torn. Heavy cords, as in some dimities, rub against finer yarns, resulting in slits in wear. Novelty weaves and fancy yarns cannot be expected to give great durability. They often are chosen for variety and for their beauty in texture where exceptional durability is not demanded (Fig. 7-1).

Smoother and longer-wearing woven fabrics are made of combed yarns. Ply yarns also add to the strength of fabrics. A balanced, or near-balanced, yarn count indicates durability—that is, a fabric is stronger if an equal, or almost equal, number of warp and filling yarns are used per square inch. When comparing yarn

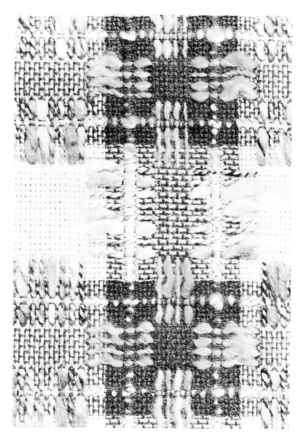

Figure 7-1. The long floats in this fabric add interest in texture, color, and pattern; their tendency to snag suggests limited uses, as in short sleeved or sleeveless blouses or jackets.

counts in an effort to determine quality, fabrics must be comparable; compare one grade of gingham with another gingham, not with denim.

Knowledge about fiber content and *blends* is of great importance to the consumer, owing to the extensive use of the latter with the introduction of synthetic fibers. Since the Textile Fiber Products Identification Act became effective, consumers know the percentage, by weight, of each fiber present in a fabric. To use this information intelligently, it is helpful to know not only the general characteristics of each fiber but also something of the carry-over of the fiber properties into the blend and the effectiveness of this carry-over. For instance, cotton and rayon are valued for their absorptive power, rayon for its low cost, and acetate for its draping qualities. Other man-made fibers besides rayon and acetate are valued for their strength, quick drying, and wrinkle resistance, with polyesters particularly desirable for their resistance to wrinkling when damp and acrylics for their bulky softness. However, because it is impossible for consumers to estimate the worth of percentages, they must rely on the label not only to tell what is in the cloth but how it will perform. The harsh curing conditions of durable-press cotton, with the resulting damage, necessitate the use of about 25 to 65 per cent of nylon or polyester fiber blended with the cotton. Millions are being spent on research in this area, so that each year more is learned about the best proportions. For a number of years now, a satisfactory proportion of polyester to cotton in many blends has been 65 to 35 per cent, or near this ratio.

INTERPRETING LABELS

Improved labeling of textile products has been of great assistance to the consumer who knows what to look for and the meanings of the terms used.

An extensive discussion of the consumer and related concerns has been presented in Chapter 4. A review of relevant subject matter in this chapter is recommended.

Information on labels may identify the manufacturer of the fiber, or the fabric (or both), and the seller, possibly involving brand names or symbols and trademarks. In some cases the label may indicate that the product has been tested in a laboratory and given a *seal of approval* label, or that the product has been manufactured to meet certain standards. This type of label is designated as a *certification* label. The amount and type of information presented will determine its adequacy for the consumer who wants sufficient information for guidance in making wise purchases and knowledge of how to care for the merchandise.

Consumer information falls into two classes: *mandatory*—required by law— and *voluntary*—provided of his own volition by the manufacturer.

Mandatory information includes (1) fiber content and percentages, (2) name or identification number for the manufacturer, and (3) a permanent-care label attached to the garment, sufficiently durable to last the reasonable life expectancy of the garment.

Voluntary information may include any additional information as fabric structure, special finishes, appearance, and sewing instructions.

A survey of the labels shown in Figure 7-2 indicates that one cannot necessarily expect to find all of the information provided on one hangtag.

Examine *a*. This label contains little more than the mandatory information: (1) the brand name of the product, which meets the criteria for manufacturer identification, (2) the fiber content, and (3) directions for care, which in ready-to-wear must also be permanently attached to the garment. The only significant item of voluntary information on this label refers to the construction of the fabric—it is a knit.

Many labels provide voluntary information that can be of assistance in the interpretation of labels. For example, label *b* carries the name of the retailer—a large mail-order firm—on its opposite side. Two fibers blended in recognized percentages for demonstrated comfort and durability give some credence to the claims of super qualities. "Sanforized for minimum shrinkage" has significant meaning for many consumers, but more specific information might be helpful to many others—that the Sanforized garment with no more than 1 per cent shrinkage will not shrink out of fit. (A garment can usually be worn with shrinkage up to 2 per cent. Five per cent shrinkage amounts approximately to a change from one size to another.) However, the widely spread knowledge that "Sanforized" generally insures a satisfactory degree of dimensional stability minimizes this uncertainty.

Figure 7-2. How much information does the label contain?

Figure 7-3. Permanent care label with lettering woven into the fabric to be stitched into the garment. (Courtesy of Celanese.)

Labels *c* and *d* provide other examples of voluntary information supplied by the manufacturer.

Permanent Care Labels

Permanent care labels had been attached to clothing by many manufacturers before this requirement became mandatory. The advent of man-made fibers added emphasis to the need to give assistance to the consumer regarding their use and care, which often respond to varied conditions, unlike the natural fibers whose properties had become familiar through many generations of use. An example of a permanent-care label to be stitched into the garment is found in Figure 7-3. This label is very tightly woven with the wording woven in. All mandatory information has been provided, plus the names of the fiber used and the fabric construction.

Another type of permanent-care label covers twenty-seven different situations (Fig. 7-4). The fabric used in the labels shown is approximately the weight of muslin

Figure 7-4. Very firm fabric with printed information. (Courtesy of Celanese.)

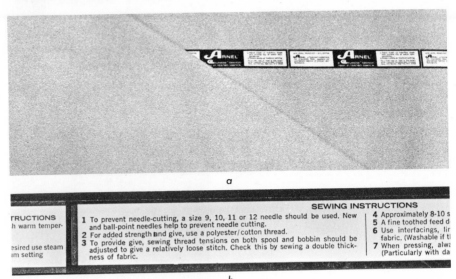

Figure 7-5. *a,* A strip with label information is rolled into a bolt of fabric; *b,* close-up, providing both care and sewing instructions. (Courtesy of Celanese.)

sheeting, very firmly woven with an apparent crease-resistant finish. The information is printed on the labels.

What labels, in what forms, does the shopper find on yard goods? Information can be found on the bolt board or roller, on an accompanying label or hangtag, or identification may be woven into or printed on the selvage. As a result of the advent of permanent-care labeling, information may be found on a strip rolled into the bolt of fabric (Fig. 7-5, *a*). A close-up of this label is seen in *b*. You will note that sewing instructions are also included.

Consumer-Care Guide for Apparel[2]

A care guide to help the consumer interpret the care instructions on permanent-care labels is presented in Table 7-2. It should be remembered that performance claims for a garment are valid only if the recommended care instructions are followed.

[2]Consumer Affairs Committee, American Manufacturers Association, 1969.

Table 7-2

CONSUMER CARE GUIDE FOR APPAREL

This Guide is made available to help you understand and follow the brief care instructions found on permanent labels on garments. Be sure to follow all care instructions.

	WHEN LABEL READS:	IT MEANS:
MACHINE WASHABLE	Washable Machine washable Machine wash	Wash, bleach, dry and press by any customary method including commericial laundering
	Home launder only	Same as above but do not use commercial laundering
	No bleach	Do not use bleach
	No starch	Do not use starch
	Cold wash Cold setting Cold rinse	Use cold water from tap or cold washing machine setting
	Warm wash Warm setting Warm rinse	Use warm water 90° to 110° Fahrenheit
	Hot wash Hot setting	Use hot water (hot washing machine setting) 130° Fahrenheit or hotter
	No spin	Remove wash load before final machine spin cycle
	Delicate cycle Gentle cycle	Use appropriate machine setting; otherwise wash by hand

	Durable
	  press cycle
	Permanent
	  press cycle
		Use appropriate machine setting; otherwise use medium wash, cold rinse and short spin cycle

	Wash separately	Wash alone or with like colors

	WHEN LABEL READS:	IT MEANS:
NON-MACHINE WASHING	Hand washable Hand wash	Launder only by hand in luke warm (hand comfortable) water. May be bleached. May be drycleaned
	Hand wash only	Same as above, but **do not** dryclean
	Hand wash separately	Hand wash alone or with like colors
	No bleach	Do not use bleach
HOME DRYING	Tumble dry Machine dry	Dry in tumble dryer at specified setting high, medium low or no heat
	Tumble dry Remove promptly	Same as above, but in absence of cool-down cycle remove at once when tumbling stops
	Drip dry Hang dry Line dry	Hang wet and allow to dry with hand shaping only
	No squeeze No wring No twist	Hang dry, drip dry or dry flat only
	Dry flat	Lay garment on flat surface
	Block to dry	Maintain original size and shape while drying
IRONING OR PRESSING	Cool iron	Set iron at lowest setting
	Warm iron	Set iron at medium setting
	Hot iron	Set iron at hot setting
	No iron No press	Do not iron or press with heat
	Steam iron Steam press	Iron or press with steam
	Iron damp	Dampen garment before ironing
MISCELLANEOUS	Dryclean Dryclean only	Garment should be drycleaned only, including self-service

	Professionally
	  clean only
	Commercially
	  clean only
		Do not use self-service drycleaning

	No dryclean	Use recommended care instructions. cleaning materials to be used.

A  ® ELANESE REPRINT   This Care Guide was produced by the Consumer Affairs Committee, American Apparel Manufacturers Association and is based on the Voluntary Guide of the Textile Industry Advisory Committee for Consumer Interests. *Copyright 1971, The American Apparel Manufacturers Association, Inc.*

SOURCE: Courtesy of Celanese and of The American Apparel Manufacturers Association, Inc.

"Over-the-Counter" Tests

After studying the label, you are ready to make "over-the-counter" tests. These involve sight and touch. Examine the fabric. Perhaps you will conclude from this examination that the fabric in question is of firm, even weave and free of flaws; shows no indication of slippage; and does not wrinkle when crushed. This information, added to what was learned in studying the labels, will furnish a satisfactory basis for your decision making.

TO DETERMINE:

1. Slippage.

2. Stretching.

MAKE THIS TEST:

1. Stretch the cloth between your two thumbs and two forefingers—both crosswise and lengthwise (Fig. 7-6). If the threads shift apart readily, slippage troubles can be expected.

2. Notice whether there is stretching when fabric is pulled as in test for slippage. What special care will be needed in stitching?

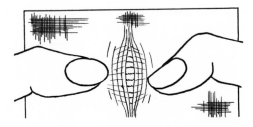

Figure 7-6. The slippage test.

3. Wrinkle resistance; resiliency.

4. Evenness of yarn, weave, and color.

5. Relative lengths of fibers present.

6. Strength of foundation in napped cloth.

7. Pilling.

8. Workability.

3. Crush in the palm of hand to determine degree of wrinkling. For wool:
   a. Good wool feels alive, springy, soapy, and soft; does not crease.
   b. Poor wool feels lifeless, boardy, harsh, and matted; does not recover quickly from wrinkles.

4. Scrutinize surface of fabric for flaws; hold up to light to detect uniformity or irregularities in yarn, weave, and color.

5. Fold the fabric and hold the fold up to a good light. A great deal of fuzz on a firm type of cotton or linen indicates use of short or low-grade fibers. Examine torn end.

6. Hold to light and stretch to determine whether napping has been excessive and overdone. Examine the wrong side. Does it appear sleazy or cloudy?

7. Rub fabric briskly. If nap rolls up into pills or rubs off, you cannot expect the most satisfactory wear.

8. Drape or fold fabric as it will be used in the design. Will it pleat, press, or stitch well or with ease?

9. Check end of fabric to determine whether it follows the crosswise thread. (Ask salesperson to cut or tear, if possible.) Fold fabric smoothly, with selvages parallel. Do crosswise threads in the two layers of folded fabric lie parallel to each other? If not, what are your chances for straightening it? For using the off-grain fabric successfully? Purchase would be a questionable procedure, even with a plain fabric, and most unwise where the pattern is off-grain.

Fabric Types

WASH-AND-WEAR AND PERMANENT-PRESS FABRICS

The characteristics that give wash-and-wear and durable press fabrics their desirable characteristics can create difficulties in sewing. The resin finishes give a smoother, harder surface, making the fabric less pliable and more resistant to easing-in, to scissors, pins, and needles; they do not press well—to give flat seams and sharp, clean edges; and seams have a tendency to pucker. Therefore, these fabrics are more satisfactory for simple patterns. Avoid intricate seaming and design details with topstitching. Seams made on the bias, even on a slight bias, tend to produce a smoother look.

If sharp, flat edges or pressed pleats are desired, they must be edge-stitched for the best results. It is better to choose patterns with darts to remove fullness, than try to ease in fullness. For the same reason, avoiding set-in sleeves eliminates problems.

Permanent press can also be achieved without the use of resin, if a large proportion of the easy-care fiber is used, as 80 per cent polyester and 20 per cent cotton. Both polyester-cotton and polyester-rayon blends have been proved very successful in durable-press fabrics.

Permanent-press fabrics that are off-grain probably cannot be straightened and, therefore, are poor choices, especially when the printed or woven pattern makes this defect conspicuous. In a plain fabric with no perceptible weave, this condition could be accepted. Where the fabric lacks flexibility because of resin finishes, making its grainlines inflexible the poor hang or set of the garment might not be as pronounced as it would be in an untreated fabric. There might always be some question, however, as to satisfactory results.

Knitted Fabrics

Knits have become popular because they are comfortable to wear, easy to care for, wrinkle-resistant without special finishes, and available in a variety of textures and patterns (Fig. 7-7).

Figure 7-7. A great variety in textures and patterns characterizes knitted fabrics, with firm, durable constructions for men's wear (swatched on bottom row).

The quality and serviceability of these fabrics, constructed with an arrangement of interlocking loops of yarns, are influenced by the type of knitting used, the fiber, the fineness or closeness of the knitting, the dimensional stability of the fabric, and special finishes.

Circular or Flat Knits

This type of knit has loops running across the fabric and is often purchased in tubular form. It is lighter in weight than the double-knit and does not keep its shape as well; it is unsuitable for pants and straight skirts without a supporting fabric. It can be made into casual, sporty, or dressy garments depending on the fabric. It adapts well to the skinny look in sport tops, as in T-shirts. It is satisfactory for designs with soft fullness, as in gathered skirts and dresses. Such details as collars and cuffs need interfacing for body.

Warp Knits—Tricot and Raschel

Warp-knitted fabrics are usually flatter, less elastic, more run-resistant, and knitted more closely than circular knits. Because of their firmness, they are less apt to snag than double-knits. The variety of fibers and yarns used permits a wide range of garments, from men's wear, dresses, tops, pants, and skirts to lingerie, sleepwear, and lounging wear.

Raschel is a type of warp knit by which intricate, lacy, and openwork designs are produced.

DOUBLE-KNITS

These fabrics are firm, heavyweight knits that are really two single layers knitted together. The two sides appear the same except in textured designs. They have more body and durability than single knits and are less likely to sag or lose shape.

Because of the weight of double-knits, patterns with simple lines are best—decorative seams, darts, pocket details, topstitching, and eased fullness. They are generally too bulky for gathers or a large number of pleats. It is best to avoid bias-cut skirts in knits, unless the fabric has been made shrink-resistant or you are prepared to make frequent adjustments for stretching.

Double-knit is suitable for any type of garment that requires a firm, heavy fabric, such as dresses, suits, pants, skirts, shirts, jackets, and coats.

KNIT-PAPER FABRICS

A high-strength paper yarn can be knitted into a variety of constructions for use in apparel. These are pliable and can be sewed on the home sewing machine. They are washable and wrinkle-resistant; they maintain their shape and do not lose strength when wet; and they can be dry-cleaned.

Nonwoven Fabrics

NONWOVEN DISPOSABLE PAPER PRODUCTS

Fibers in nonwoven paper are held together either chemically or mechanically by fast, economical production methods. Disposables sometimes are convenient selections, because they require no laundering or care. However, they would be more expensive than other textiles over a long period of use.

INTERIOR SECTIONS OF APPAREL   In clothing construction, nonwoven paper fabrics are limited largely to shaping, reinforcing, and padding. One can select fabrics varying in weight, bulk, controlled tear strength, flexibility, and stiffness or softness, depending upon the purpose for which it is to be used.

BONDED FABRICS

Bonded fabrics are light but firm and require no underlining because of the tricot (knit) that usually is fused to the back of them. They can be lined if stretching is a problem. Bonded fabrics do not ravel. An especially important point to check before buying bonded fabric is whether the lengthwise and crosswise yarns are at right angles to each other. *Fabrics bonded off-grain cannot be straightened.* If the fabric is correct as to grain, it does not matter whether the tricot is correct, because the knit construction is flexible and can stretch in all directions. Therefore, the appearance or wear of the garment will not be affected.

Napped Fabrics

The nap characteristics of a fabric affect the yardage needed.

Nap refers to pile fabrics, such as velvet; to fabrics with fuzzy surfaces, such as fleece; and to textured fabrics, such as brocade, satin, and knits. They appear different in the up-and-down directions, depending on the reflection of light. Nap also refers to fabrics whose designs are in definite up-and-down directions.

UP-AND-DOWN

Designs are often one-way or directional, with the up-and-down direction obvious, as in design a in Figure 7-8. Every section of the pattern would require placement with the motifs pointing in the same direction, either down or up. This characteristic is also evident in b. More careful examination is needed to determine the directional condition in c. Start with any prominent line across the fabric and explore the space above and below it. If the stripes are unlike in width, color, or texture on either side of the starting point, the fabric has an up-and-down design. The correct pattern yardage needed for such fabrics as a, b, and c will be labeled for fabrics with nap.

RIGHT-AND-LEFT

Determining the type of design across the horizontal direction involves checking on each side of a vertical line. Start with the center of the line of motifs or the line of space between the motifs in Figure 7-8, a. The pattern is identical in left and right directions at any given point. However, the design repeat with its variations in value and hue would require careful matching in the seam in order to place the darker or lighter motifs next to their counterparts. Extra yardage would be required for matching this relatively large repeat, even though the pattern has few seams.

With a right-and-left uneven plaid, as c, the design progresses around the body, except in cases where there is no difference between the right and wrong sides of the fabric. In this case, the designs on right and left sections could be made identical only if a seam were placed at the center and one side cut wrong side out.

EVEN OR BALANCED PLAIDS

In an even plaid, the design matches when the corner is folded back across the center of any repeat (Fig. 7-9). The stripes are the same width and color in both lengthwise and crosswise directions. Balanced plaids are easier to match than those that are unbalanced, and are suitable for pattern placements labeled "without nap"—provided the pattern is simple, with few cutting lines.

Because the multiplicity of lines in plaids produces a confused design when the pattern has many seams, some patterns are labeled not suitable for plaids.

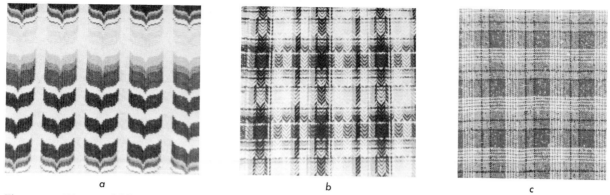

Figure 7-8. Directional fabrics: all have up-and-down direction; *b* and *c* also have horizontal direction. All would require pattern placements labeled "with nap."

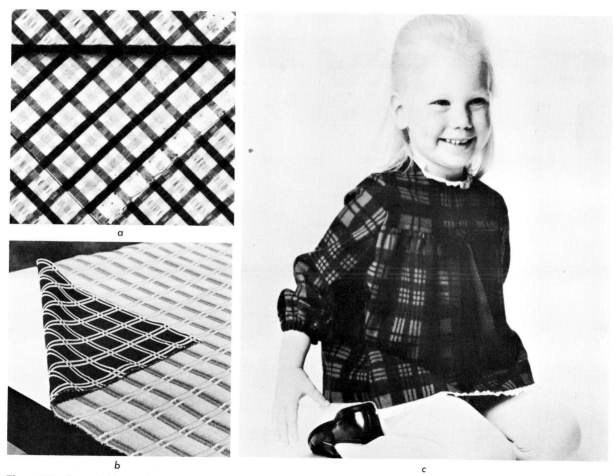

Figure 7-9. Even plaids match when a corner is turned back: *a*, woven fabric; *b*, knit fabric. *c*, Plaids, whether even or uneven, may require more fabric for matching. (Courtesy of The Wool Bureau, Inc., *c*.)

157

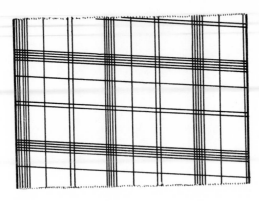

Figure 7-10. Design printed off the grain.

STRIPES

The balance in a striped design is determined in the same manner as in the plaid. Both situations present an arrangement of stripes, with both vertical and horizontal stripes to be considered in the plaid.

DESIGNS PRINTED OFF-GRAIN

Avoid a fabric in which the printed-on design is not in line with the threads in the fabric (Fig. 7-10). The lines in this plaid do not coincide with the crosswise threads along the torn end of the fabric. The person who makes such a selection is starting the project with a handicap, as she is immediately confronted with liabilities, regardless of the procedure chosen for the steps ahead.

TWILLS

Twills are unsuitable for a kimono, or any type of sleeve cut in one piece with the blouse. Note the effect obtained along the shoulder seam on this kimono sleeve (Fig. 7-11).

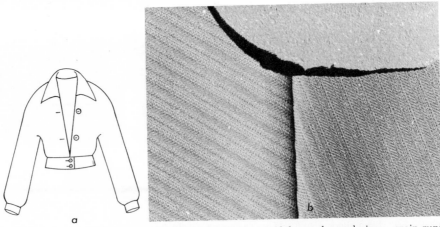

Figure 7-11. Twill fabrics are unsuitable for kimono or dolman sleeve designs—grain runs in different directions at the shoulder seam and down the sleeve, *b*.

YARDAGE INCREASES FOR NAPPED FABRICS

The nap characteristics of a fabric affect the yardage needed. The extra amount required for matching napped fabrics will be determined by the size of the repeat, the number of lengths of garment to be matched, and the size of the pattern. An additional $\frac{1}{4}$ to 1 yard may be required.

For a very large repeat, it is advisable to tentatively locate the motif at one end of the garment, in order to estimate the total number of repeats and yards to be purchased. The dominant part of a design is usually located at the hem or near the hemline.

FABRIC WIDTHS

Occasionally, yardage widths indicated for a pattern may not correspond to the width of the fabric that has been selected. The Fabric Conversion Chart (Table 7-3) can be helpful in such situations.

Supporting Fabrics

Supporting fabrics include *underlining, interfacing,* and *lining.* These fabrics, hidden underneath the outer fabric, are used for a variety of purposes and in a diversity of garments with different design, fiber content, construction, texture, and weight—all of which influence their selection and use. Some designs may require two or three different types of supporting fabrics to create the effects desired and others will require none.

Table 7-3
FABRIC CONVERSION CHART

Fabric Width	35″–36″	39″	41″	44″–45″	50″	52″–54″	58″–60″	66″
Yardage	1 3/4	1 1/2	1 1/2	1 3/8	1 1/4	1 1/8	1	7/8
	2	1 3/4	1 3/4	1 5/8	1 1/2	1 3/8	1 1/4	1 1/8
	2 1/4	2	2	1 3/4	1 5/8	1 1/2	1 3/8	1 1/4
	2 1/2	2 1/4	2 1/4	2 1/8	1 3/4	1 3/4	1 5/8	1 1/2
	2 7/8	2 1/2	2 1/2	2 1/4	2	1 7/8	1 3/4	1 5/8
	3 1/8	2 3/4	2 3/4	2 1/2	2 1/4	2	1 7/8	1 3/4
	3 3/8	3	2 7/8	2 3/4	2 3/8	2 1/4	2	1 7/8
	3 3/4	3 1/4	3 1/8	2 7/8	2 5/8	2 3/8	2 1/4	2 1/8
	4 1/4	3 1/2	3 3/8	3 1/8	2 3/4	2 5/8	2 3/8	2 1/4
	4 1/2	3 3/4	3 5/8	3 3/8	3	2 3/4	2 5/8	2 1/2
	4 3/4	4	3 7/8	3 5/8	3 1/4	2 7/8	2 3/4	2 5/8
	5	4 1/4	4 1/8	3 7/8	3 3/8	3 1/8	2 7/8	2 3/4

Add Additional $\frac{1}{4}$ Yard:

- For wide span conversion in fabric ● For nap or one-directional printed fabrics
- For styles with sleeves cut in one piece with body of garment

SOURCE: Courtesy of Cooperative Extension Service, Rutgers University—the State University of New Jersey.

All inner fabrics are chosen in harmony with the outer fabric as to probable length of life and handling and care required: washability, dry-cleanability, similarity in responses to pressing and steam pressing, equality in shrinkage possibilities, and in wash-and-wear qualities.

1. In order to follow the lead of the outer fabric in its expression of inherent qualities, lining and interlining fabrics should be as pliable, soft, and light in weight—or slightly more so—as the outer fabric. (This would not apply in situations where a great deal of shaping is required.)

2. Where support of shape is desired, a firm-bodied, resilient fabric is essential, as in a mandarin collar.

3. To eliminate undesirable stretch in the outer fabric, underline it with a firmly woven fabric.

4. Where body only is needed to preserve the shape and grain of a loosely woven or limp fabric, a soft underlining will best retain the soft hand and draping qualities of the outer fabric.

5. Consider the use of self-fabric in certain situations, in order to best preserve the hand, drape, or color effect desired.

6. To evaluate a supporting fabric, place it under the outer fabric and handle it to determine whether it provides the qualities desired for the design to be used. Consider the effect in draped or shaped sections, any possible change in color or design in the outer fabric, the relative merits in using one of the many fabrics marketed for this purpose or self-fabric, and the possibility of eliminating supporting fabrics altogether.

UNDERLININGS An underlining is cut exactly like the garment; its purpose is to add body and support, to give and retain shape, and to reduce wrinkling in the outer fabric. The two are stitched in the seams as one fabric. The underlining protects the outer fabric and lengthens the life of the garment. It can help to build a silhouette in a design that is to stand away from the body, as a great coat or bell sleeve, or simply preserve the shape and grain of a loosely woven or limp fabric, depending on the type of interlining chosen. Facings, interfacings, and hems can be hand-sewn to the underlining, so that no stitches show on the right side of the garment.

Because an underlining fabric for one garment might be suitable as an interfacing in a garment of different design and fabric, these two types of supporting fabrics are listed together in Table 7-4.

INTERFACINGS An interfacing is a layer of fabric used to give body, support, shape retention, firmness, strength, stability, and smoothness to such parts of a garment as collars, cuffs, lapels, front edges, pockets, necklines, armholes, shoulder areas, yokes, belts, buttonholes, and hems. It prevents stretching and gives body or crispness without bulk. It can cushion bulky seam allowances or edges to prevent imprints on the right side of the garment. (Table 7-4).

Table 7-4
UNDERLININGS AND/OR INTERFACINGS

FABRIC NAME	FIBER CONTENT	TYPE	WEIGHT	WIDTH	COLOR	USES	CHARACTERISTICS
About Face		Woven	Medium soft, crisp		All colors	Underlining for soft hand.	Machine-washable, dry-cleanable.
About Face Basic Liner		Woven	Light		Natural, black, and white	Shaping for light- and medium-weight fabric.	Machine-washable, dry-cleanable, crease- and wrinkle-resistant.
Acro	Polyester/ rayon/mohair	Woven	Medium	25 in.	Ecru	For medium- and heavyweight cotton, medium-weight wools, and heavyweight knits.	Machine-washable, dry-cleanable.
Armoflex	Nylon/poly-ester/rayon	Woven	Light but firm	1¼ in., 1½ in., and 2 in.	White	For waistbands.	Machine-washable and dry-cleanable; twists, bends, and flexes with body movement; does not curl.
Armo Press	Polyester/ rayon	Woven	Light	22 in. 45 in.	White	For light- and medium-weight polyesters.	Permanent-press interfacing for all easy-care fabrics, machine-washable, shrinkage-controlled.
Bisque	100 per cent polyester	Woven, crisp	Light	44 in.	All colors	With permanent press, crisp for shaping.	Machine-washable, 1 per cent maximum shrinkage, perspiration proof, anti-static finish.
Detail Pelomite	95 per cent rayon	Nonwoven	Light	17 in.	White and black	To reinforce and sta-bilize small detail areas during con-struction: fabric but-tonholes, gussets, and slashed areas.	A regular nonwoven with a polyethylene adhesive on one side. Stiff when pressed on, so it should not be used as an interfacing.

Table 7-4 (Cont.)
UNDERLININGS AND/OR INTERFACINGS

FABRIC NAME	FIBER CONTENT	TYPE	WEIGHT	WIDTH	COLOR	USES	CHARACTERISTICS
Earlaire of Reemay	100 per cent polyester	Spun bonded	Light structural	44 in.	Several colors	Lightweight for underlining and interfacing; structural weight for shaping in jackets and coats.	Great seam strength, washable, 1 per cent maximum shrinkage, dry-cleanable, fast-drying, retains shape, white stays white.
Fino Hair Canvas	88 per cent wool 12 per cent mohair	Woven	Medium	25 in.	Natural, black, and white	Interfacing and underlining for silks and medium-to-heavy wools.	Dry-cleanable, highest quality hair canvas.
Finolight Hair Canvas	43 per cent wool 40 per cent cotton 17 per cent mohair	Woven	Lightweight	25 in.	Beige	Silks, wools, and other lightweight fabrics that are not to be washed.	Dry-cleanable.
Formite Sheer Canvas		Woven	Light	25 in.	Natural, black, and white	Interfacings in lightweight wools and permanent press.	Machine-washable.
Instant Armo Press-on	Cotton/rayon	Woven	Light	19 in. 38 in.	White and black	Shaping small detailed areas in lightweight wool, cotton, synthetics, and blends.	Machine-washable, dry-cleanable
Interlon L R H	Rayon/nylon	Nonwoven	Light Regular Heavy	25, 37 in. 25, 37 in. 25 in.	Black and white	Interfacing or interlining for various weight fabrics.	Resilient, easy-care, and compatible with all types of fabrics, including synthetics and blends.
Bias	100 per cent polyester		Bias feather-weight	25 in., 37 in.	White only	For any garment cut on the bias, knits, polyesters, and all lightweight fabrics requiring stretch or "give."	Has no grainline, so pattern can be laid out and cut in any direction. No raveling or fraying. All types are washable, dry-cleanable, shrinkage-controlled, and noncrushable.
Durable Press	Rayon/ polyester			25 in.	Black and white	Light- and medium-weight durable-press, polyester and easy-care outer fabrics.	Durable press tumble dries without wrinkling; 1 per cent maximum shrinkage.

162

Name	Fiber content	Construction	Weight	Width	Colors	Uses	Characteristics
Keynote Plus	65 per cent polyester 35 per cent combed cotton	Woven	Light	44 in.	All colors	Underlining for permanent-press fabrics.	Machine washable, 1 per cent maximum shrinkage, dry cleanable, wrinkle-resistant.
Marvelaire	100 per cent polyester	Woven, soft	Light	44 in.	All colors	Wash-and-wear, permanent-press; soft hand for draping.	Machine washable, 1 per cent maximum shrinkage, perspiration proof, anti-static finish.
Pellon Regular	Rayon/nylon	Nonwoven	Light, medium, heavy	25, 37 in.	White and black	For interfacing scoop and V-necklines to prevent stretching; waistbands, tabs, welts, and flaps. Medium-and heavy-weights generally used in accessories, crafts.	Have no "give"; firm support, washable and dry-cleanable.
All bias	100 per cent polyester	Nonwoven	Feather-weight	25 in.	White and gray	For all light- to medium-weight fabrics for soft, subtle shaping. For medium- to heavy-weight fabrics where firm shape is desired. Underlining for light-weight knits (back lining when heavier outer fabric is used), coats, ski wear, lounge-wear. Interfacing for lingerie, bra dresses, and swimwear; for quilting, trapunto; rolled hems, sleeve caps.	Bias types give in all directions, resulting in flexible, supple shaping and molding; are crease- and crush-resistant; light and porous, washable and dry-cleanable, can be stitched or fused.
			Lightweight	25, 37 in.	White and gray		
			Fleece	45 in.	White		
Permanent Press lining	65 per cent polyester, 35 per cent cotton	Woven	Light	44 in.	All colors	For underlining permanent-press fabrics; also suitable for linings.	Machine-washable, tumble-dry, 1 per cent maximum shrinkage; combed cotton batiste.
Poly-SiBonne	Rayon	Woven	Soft, crisp	45 in.	All colors	Lining and underlining lightweight fabrics; cotton, linen, lightweight wool.	Machine-washable, tumble-dry, 1 per cent maximum shrinkage, dry-cleanable; antistatic.

Table 7-4 (Cont.)

UNDERLININGS AND/OR INTERFACINGS

FABRIC NAME	FIBER CONTENT	TYPE	WEIGHT	WIDTH	COLOR	USES	CHARACTERISTICS
Siri	Rayon	Woven	Four weights	45 in.	All colors	Underlining for wool, linen, cotton, and synthetics.	Machine-washable, tumble-dry, shrinkage controlled, dry-cleanable; antistatic.
Suit-shape	Cotton/rayon	Woven, fusible	Medium	22 in.	Natural and white	Interfacing to give body to men's and women's tailored garments.	Compatible with polyesters, wools, blends, linen, cotton, corduroy, and velveteen. Lends a natural hand to knits and woven fabrics.
Tri-Dimensional (3D)	100 per cent polyester	Nonwoven			White, gray, and tan	With all knits.	Does not change the hand of even soft knits; adds body and shape, but with a grainline. Curved lines as contour belts and funnel collars can be shaped after finishing.
		Granular, fusible	Light and medium				
		Web, fusible	Light and medium				
Undercurrent	100 per cent Avril rayon	Woven	Medium, soft and crisp	45 in.	All colors	An underlining to support, shape, and prevent stretching in knits and loosely woven knits.	Compatible with all outer fabrics, machine-washable and dry-cleanable; no preshrinking needed.
Veriform Durable Press	Polyester/rayon	Woven	Light, soft, crisp	45 in.	Black and white	To be used as interfacing or underlining in all permanent-press and polyester fashions.	Washable, 1 per cent maximum shrinkage, dry-cleanable.

Table 7-5
LINING FABRICS

FABRIC NAME	TYPE	WIDTH	USES	CHARACTERISTICS
Butterfly	100 per cent polyester	44 in.	Very lightweight garments.	Guaranteed for life of garment, lightweight, crease-resistant, anti-static; machine washable, maximum shrinkage 1 per cent, drip-or tumble-dry, dry-cleanable.
China silk	Lightweight silk		Soft silk, rayons, lightweight wools for soft silhouette.	Dry-cleanable.
Ciao	100 per cent polyester crepeon	45 in.	Loungewear and blouses; lining for polyester knits and easy-care fabrics.	Will not slip or slide, antistatic; machine-washable, tumble-dry, maximum shrinkage 1 per cent.
Earl Glo				
Acetate faille, taffeta	Acetate	44 in.	Medium-to heavyweights.	All acetates hand-washable; perspiration- and gas-fading proof, Sanitized, dry-cleanable.
Acetate satin, plain and Milium	Acetate	44 in.	For suits and coats.	
Crepe black satin, plain and Milium	Acetate/ Rayon	44 in.	Medium-weight linings.	
Rayon twill	Rayon	44 in.	For coats and suits.	
Quilted satin	Acetate	45 in.	Coats, permanent-press robes, loungewear, and skirts.	
Crepe de chine	100 per cent polyester	44 in.	Coats, suits, skirts, robes, and loungewear.	Machine-washable, minimum shrinkage; perspiration-proof; wrinkle-resistant.
Permanent Press lining	65 per cent polyester, 35 per cent cotton	44 in.	Lightweight fabric for permanent press.	Cotton content is combed; machine-washable, tumble-dry, 1 per cent maximum shrinkage.
Tritessa			For lightweight garments.	Silky and luxurious; machine-washable, dry-cleanable.

LININGS   A lining is an inner garment that is assembled separately and sewed into the garment. It hides and protects seams; helps to preserve shape; prevents stretching; reduces wrinkling; extends the life of the outer fabric; provides an attractive, smoothly finished interior; and adds warmth to the garment (Table 7-5).

INTERLININGS   An interlining is used specifically to add additional warmth. It may consist of a layer of fabric placed between the garment and the lining, as in jackets, coats, and suits. Several types of interlining are available. A flat wool fabric and cotton outing flannel are types that have been used. Lining and interlining materials are often combined: a satin fabric may have a fleece back, a metallic back (Milium), or a flannel back. Dacron fiberfill may be quilted to the outer fabric or to the lining fabric to provide the desirable warmth in a ski jacket, coat, or

Figure 7-12. *a,* Dacron fiberfill is often quilted to lining or outer fabric; in *b,* man-made fleece and outer fabric were constructed together; in *c,* two fabrics used together.

a winter lounging robe, adding bulk and warmth with minimum weight (Fig. 7-12, *a*). In *b,* this fabric, with its own man-made fleece, is ideal for such garments as *c,* and also for unlined coats and jackets.

WHERE SUPPORTING FABRICS ARE UNDESIRABLE

Numerous instances can be found where supporting fabrics are unnecessary and undesirable. Examples include many knitted garments, as a T-shirt, tank top, or other knitted garment where an underlining might interfere with the fabric's desirable stretch qualities.

Desirable effects in sheer fabrics may depend on the merits of the fabric alone, as in billowy sleeves, or where plain, sheer fabric floats over an underdress of patterned fabric that is visible underneath.

One of the advantages in wearing sheers—to provide a cool summer garment—

is lost or minimized when the garment is given the added warmth of an underlining.

An underlining fabric that is nonabsorbent would feel clammy and uncomfortable.

Coordinating Fabrics and Patterns

The pattern you are considering or have decided upon will influence your choice of fabric. A very important source of information is the list of fabric suggestions for your design in the pattern catalogue or on the pattern envelope. For what reasons are some fabrics suitable for a design and others not?

The following discussions of fabric choice in relation to pattern will be confined largely to texture, weight, and hand or drapability of the fabric, with some consideration of design. Suggestions are also given for the selection of appropriate supporting fabrics. Refer to the Glossary (pp. 175–76) for assistance in identifying any fabrics mentioned in the following exercises.

Consider the sketches in Figure 7-13 in relation to fabrics. What types of fabrics are suitable for *a*? One could list many fabrics whose inherent properties would work well in this simple, tailored chemise—fabrics with natural body and weight such as linen, double-knits, wool flannel, seersucker, garbardine, cotton piqué, and waleless corduroy. In heavier weights, these fabrics might give satisfactory results without an underlining.

Consider such lighter-weight fabrics as wool jersey, shantung, and synthetic mixtures in comparable weights. These lack the body necessary to give a smooth, sculptured appearance, but with the added body of an underlining very good results could be expected. For strength and stability along the front closing with its buttons and buttonholes, an additional medium-weight interfacing might be needed; the latter would also be satisfactory for the neckline and armholes (possibly optional for the armholes—the underlining plus the armhole facings might provide

Figure 7-13. Construction lines in these dresses present varied needs for supporting fabrics.

a　　　　　　*b*

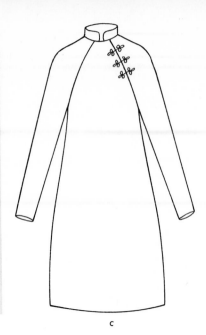

a   b   c

Figure 7-14. These collars would require very different interfacing fabrics.

sufficient body for these edges). The line of topstitching along the upper edge of pocket would tend to stiffen this line, so that interfacing might not be needed, but this would depend on the fabrics used.

Fabrics considered for *a* would be suitable for *b,* with those requiring no underlining possibly the best selections, because of the crosswise topstitched seam. The added bulk of underlining layers might result in a bulky, less attractive seam, as well as make it more troublesome to construct. However, this would depend somewhat upon the fabrics used. The open V-neckline would require a crisper and slightly heavier interfacing than *a* to give and hold this V-shape well. In a permanent-press fabric, the pressed pleats would not be sharp without stitching along their edges. Without an underlining, armholes would require interfacing.

Design *a* in Figure 7-14 obviously is made in a soft, drapable fabric with a fluid line that gently follows the curves of the body; this design will require the same type, but slightly lighter weight, of underlining to provide the needed support. Try to visualize this dress with a heavier, less flexible underlining. The stiffened combination might stand away from the body to produce angular folds underneath and interfere with the smooth fluidity.

The soft, folded turtleneck collar in *b* would require a very lightweight, soft, flexible interfacing, cut on the bias. A collar of this type, with a low stand, might maintain its shape with an underlining fabric only. To make a decision, fold the fabrics together and handle them in different dimensions and thicknesses to determine which plan is best.

The same, or similar, fabrics would be desirable for *c,* except for the collar, which would require an interfacing fabric providing more shape. This Mandarin collar would require a heavy, slightly flexible interfacing fabric.

How does the fabric influence the construction processes in sleeves? Consider the raglan sleeve in *c*. One can expect relatively little difficulty with this design, as the seams attaching sleeves to dress will be handled in the same manner as ordinary seams.

The set-in sleeve in Figure 7-15 is a somewhat more complicated problem. Why? The armhole seam, making a circle around this moving joint, must have length in the sleeve cap in excess of that in the armhole in order to provide comfort and fit smoothly over the curved end of the shoulder. This extra length in the sleeve cap seam, from notch to notch in the upper half, must be eased onto the shorter seamline of the armhole. Easing this fullness in to give a smooth, unpuckered sleeve can be a difficult task if yarns of the fabric are closely packed together, or are so stabilized by fabric finishes that they cannot be crowded together any more closely. Knitted fabrics can be eased without difficulty.

Would a heavy double-knit be satisfactory for *a*? This design requires a lighter-weight fabric because of the gathers in the skirt. A soft fabric such as crepe, a lightweight knit, or a soft voile would hang and drape well. Also, the crushed tie would be bulky and disappointing in a heavy fabric.

Which supporting fabrics are indicated for *a*? A very lightweight, soft underlining, used, possibly, in the bodice only to stabilize the area and add support for the weight of the skirt, might be sufficient. The rolled collar would need treatment similar to that in Figure 7-14, *b,* but the tie and skirt might be more satisfactory without an underlining, which would be optional in the sleeves. The best possible underlining might be the self-fabric, with an interfacing in the collar.

The set-in sleeve in design *a* probably would not be difficult to attach to the dress in the fabrics suitable for this design. However, some lightweight woven fabrics with a high yarn count, such as a fine broadcloth or tightly woven cotton

Figure 7-15. Sleeve problems.

muslin, would be difficult to handle in easing the extra fullness in the upper sleeve cap to obtain a smooth unpuckered appearance.

How does the sleeve problem in *b* compare with that in *a*? With the seam dropped below the end of the shoulder and the general looseness here, there is no problem of easing the sleeve—it will be approximately the same length as the overblouse where they are joined together. Choose any fabric without concern about this sleeve design. This is an excellent choice for fabrics whose yarns cannot be shifted, as in closely woven gabardine and those fabrics with finishes that fix the yarns in an inflexible condition.

The short-cap sleeve in *c* is cut with enough flare to provide adequate cover for the knob of the shoulder, without the necessity for easing-in the sleeve cap; this construction can be handled satisfactorily in any fabric. A successful plan in a lightweight fabric is to cut the sleeves double, to avoid finishes at the lower edges. This neckline, with a set-in yoke and buttoned opening, would require careful handling in construction, because of the bias seam—with one side the convex edge of the yoke and the other the concave edge of the bodice—plus the corners along the opening. A fairly firm fabric would be desirable.

The sleeve in the chemise smock in *d* would be easy to set into the armhole because the darts in the sleeve cap have removed the extra length in the sleeve to approximate the length of the armhole seam, eliminating the necessity for easing the sleeve into the armhole. Suitable fabrics would include a wide variety as flannel, gabardine, canvas, and double knits.

Note the sleeves in *e*. Here the gathers have reduced the length of the sleeve-cap seam as the darts reduced it in *d*, simplifying the setting of the sleeves. It is obvious that a soft, drapable fabric would be in harmony with this design. The fitted midriff inset, and possibly the entire bodice, would require underlining for stability, but this might be optional for the remainder of the dress, provided the fabric chosen has a great deal of body. In case underlining is not used, a neck interfacing or facing might be desirable to add stability and strength to this bias-bound neckline. The opaqueness of the fabric should be checked carefully for a possible change of color or faint visibility of seams, if some parts are underlined and other parts are not.

Design *a* in Figure 7-16 would require either a stiff fabric such as faille, or a stiff interlining fabric for support. To give this silhouette in the skirt, widened by godets, further support might be needed in an undergarment such as a stiffened taffeta slip. Easing the sleeve cap into a smooth line would present a challenge in this heavy-bodied fabric with closely packed yarns. For greater success in this area, it would be an advantage to keep the circumference measurement in the sleeve at a minimum for comfort—less is needed in this dressy type of garment—so that the resulting sleeve cap would have less fullness to be eased in.

Filmy georgette or chiffon is indicated for design *b*. The desirable floating airiness in the skirt and sleeves would probably eliminate underlining for these areas. These sharp, flat pleats at the waistline and hip areas would not be possible with the bulkiness that would result from underlining. Consider self-fabric as a possible underlining for the bodice.

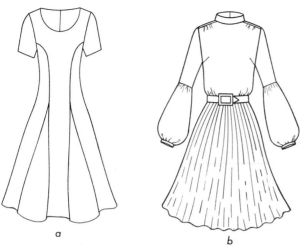

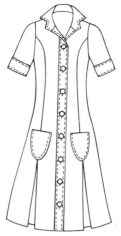

Figure 7-16. Designs indicating need for firm and soft fabrics.

Figure 7-17. Unsuitable for a bulky fabric, with top stitching through numerous layers of fabric.

Evaluate wide-wale corduroy as to its suitability for the design in Figure 7-17. This would be a poor choice of fabric for a design with so many construction lines and so much topstitching through numerous thicknesses of fabrics across bulky seams.

In Figure 7-18, the design, *a*, would require a soft fabric such as voile, batiste, gingham, or a lightweight knit. A simple way to handle the ruffle is to make it double, without underlining or interfacing. In a patterned fabric, fold and check to determine whether the resulting effect is pleasing, in case the fabric is so thin that the pattern shows through.

Which would be more effective for design *b*, a solid color or an all-over patterned fabric? The interesting structural line in the yoke would be lost in a patterned fabric and not worth the effort and time necessary to make this detailed yoke line, complicated because of the plain seam used. A solid-color, firm, non-raveling fabric—or an underlining in a firmly woven, or possibly nonwoven, featherweight fabric—would be desirable for this intricate shape. A medium-weight double-knit would be an excellent choice because of the knit's nonraveling quality.

Is *c* a satisfactory design for a plaid? Matching plaids in so many seams would be a tremendous chore. Would you expect the general effect to be any more pleasing than that of the plaid fabric joined in a minimum of seams? It appears doubtful in this case. There is more justification in designs where some sections might be cut on the bias.

NOTIONS

While shopping for pattern and fabrics, it will be an advantage to select any other sewing materials needed, such as thread, seam binding, and zipper.

Figure 7-18. *a*, In lightweight fabrics, ruffles can be cut double; *b*, choose a solid-color fabric; *c*, an unsuitable design for plaid.

THREAD

1. Thread is selected to harmonize with natural or man-made fibers, in a size suited to the weight of the fabric and to the purpose of the garment.

2. The color chosen should be slightly darker than that of the fabric, because thread appears lighter in a line of stitching than when on the spool.

3. For multicolored fabrics, such as prints, thread is selected in a color to harmonize with the predominant hue.

4. Try using both colors of a check or plaid—one color on the top and the other on the bobbin.

COTTON THREAD   Cotton threads most used for apparel are mercerized, heavy-duty mercerized, and Bel-waxed sewing cotton. These threads are strong, smooth, and shrinkage-resistant. Heavy-duty cotton is suitable for use on very heavy fabrics such as canvas, work denim, and corduroy. Waxed or glazed threads are excellent for hand sewing because tangling is reduced.

SILK THREAD   Silk A thread is desirable for stitching silk or wool fabrics. It is strong, durable, lint-free, and elastic. The last property, plus its smoothness, will probably require a slightly tighter tension adjustment on the machine, for woven fabrics. Silk D—buttonhole twist—is used for topstitching, tailor's buttonholes, and other fastenings.

SYNTHETIC OR COMBINATION THREADS   Synthetic thread, or combinations of synthetic fibers with cotton, have the elasticity and strength needed for sewing on synthetic, knit, bonded, stretch, and permanent-press fabrics. They can be used on any fabric but are especially good on those containing man-made fibers.

Polyester/cotton thread is made with a polyester core wrapped in cotton—the core yarn provides strength and elasticity while the cotton wrap shields it from heat and increases the range of colors possible. Examples of this type of thread are Dual Duty and Polyspun.

One hundred per cent polyester threads are noted for high strength and

Table 7-6
NEEDLES AND THREAD

FABRIC TYPE AND WEIGHT	THREAD	NEEDLES
Very light: chiffon, georgette, net, organza, brushed nylon, polyester crepe, underwear and sleepwear tricots	Cotton: sizes 60, 70, or 100, or mercerized sewing thread Silk A Synthetics or combination	Machine: sizes 9 or 11 Hand sewing: sizes 9 to 12
Light: voile, batiste, dimity, sheer crepe, synthetic jersey, matte jersey, lacy knits (such as stretch lace), raschels	Cotton: sizes 60, or 70, or mercerized sewing thread Silk A Synthetics or combination	Machine: size 11 Hand sewing: sizes 8 or 9
Medium light: gingham, challis, taffeta, satin, surah, sheer wool crepe, lightweight double knits, bonded lace	Cotton: sizes 60 or 70, or mercerized sewing thread Silk A	Machine: sizes 11 or 14 Hand sewing: sizes 7 or 8
Medium: piqué, linen, shantung, flannel, velvet, lightweight corduroy, poplin, faille, wool jersey, heavy double knits, bonded fabrics	Cotton: sizes 50 or 60, or mercerized sewing thread Silk A Synthetics or combination	Machine: size 14 Hand sewing: sizes 6 or 7
Medium-heavy: denim, tweed, gabardine, terry, quilted fabric, burlap, vinyl-coated cloth, fleece, brocade, fake fur, imitation leather, girdle fabrics that contain rubber or Spandex	Cotton; size 40, or mercerized sewing thread Silk A Synthetics or combination	Machine: sizes 14 or 16 Hand sewing: size 6
Heavy: sailcloth, ticking, heavy-backed vinyl, corduroy, heavy wools	Cotton: sizes 24, 30, or 40, or mercerized Heavy Duty Silk A Synthetics or combination	Machine: size 16 Hand sewing: sizes 4 or 5
Very heavy: canvas, duck, work denim, wide-wale corduroy, leather, suede	Cotton: sizes 8, 16, or 20, or button and carpet thread Nylon: Nymo	Machine: sizes 16 or 18 Hand sewing: sizes 1 to 5

elasticity, plus stability to high temperatures and durability through repeated washings and dry cleanings. These threads will not shrink when laundered, to cause a puckered seam. Available brands include Spun Polyester and Poly-Bond.

Nymo is a nylon thread.

SEAM BINDING

Seam binding is available in wash-and-wear rayon, iron-on, and bias types, in one-half- and one-inch widths. The latter may be desirable on bulky or loosely woven fabrics. Care must be taken in using the iron-on type, which is unsatisfactory on lightweight fabrics such as silks, knits, lightweight wools, and other soft fabrics. They may stiffen the fabric and show an imprint on the right side. A selvage from your fabric can serve as a waistline stay.

For cotton fabrics, cotton bias binding may be the most satisfactory selection, especially on curved hems. Look for Sanforized or fully shrunk binding, or make plans to shrink it.

Nylon lace may be substituted for seam binding to give a lighter, less conspicuous, and decorative effect. It is stretchable and can easily be shaped to fit curves. It responds well on stretch fabrics. Bias binding also gives sufficiently for use on stretch fabrics.

ZIPPERS

Three types of zippers are available.

1. The regular zipper has teeth visible on both right and wrong sides, and comes in two weights, that commonly used on apparel, and one for heavy-duty purposes.

2. The zipper with covered teeth, which eliminates the tendency for the fabric to catch in it.

3. The invisible zipper is designed to be inconspicuous in the seam; the teeth are hidden on the inside of the garment.

In addition to metal, teeth or coils are made of nylon and polyester, which can be dyed to match the zipper tape. It is a good idea to place a cloth between the zipper and the iron in pressing the latter type, unless there is assurance that the synthetic teeth will not be damaged by heat. Follow directions for the type being used.

For buttons and other types of closings see Chapters 24 and 27.

NEEDLES

Do you have the correct size and type of needles for the fabrics you will be using?

For stitching knit and stretch fabrics, ball-point needles are recommended. With a rounded point, this needle tends to push the yarns aside, rather than split or cut them when the needle goes through the fabric.

Suggestions for Selecting Yard Goods

1. When several grades are available in a fabric, the middle grades are often the best buys from the standpoint of durability. It is an advantage to learn the characteristics of high, medium, and low grades, as the best grade in one store may be average in another.

2. It is wiser to purchase the best quality in a price grouping within the budget than a lower grade in a more expensive class of merchandise.

3. Remnants at half price are not economical if you buy too much or too little or produce a garment of ordinary design.

4. An economical procedure in garment construction is to consider fabric in

relation to pattern. Purchase the pattern first; make alterations, and then buy exactly the amount of fabric needed. A saving of only one sixth of a yard may enable one to have better buttons or other accessories. Double-breasted coats, great coats, and very circular bias, draped, or pleated skirts require more cloth than straight cuts and therefore cost more. Also, cleaners charge more for skirts with many pleats.

5. Napped fabrics, large repeats in florals or plaids, up-and-down designs, and stripes require more time in planning the layout and usually require more yardage.

6. Pieces cut on the bias require about one third more yardage.

7. Collars, pockets, belts, and ties can sometimes be lined with another fabric to make these parts less bulky, or to cut costs.

8. Ready-made decorations are timesavers but are expensive if distinctive. Try three handsome buttons rather than five or six ordinary ones. Self-trims, such as loops, belts, buckles, covered buttons, arrowheads, set-in pockets, frogs, and tassels—if well made—add distinction. Such work reduces the costs of decoration but increases labor costs.

9. When estimating the final cost, divide the total by the number of wearings. Consider the cost of cleaning in making the original investment.

THE FINANCIAL INVESTMENT

After deciding on the type of fabric you wish to use, consider the cost from several viewpoints. You are aware that the garment you make in class is a learning experience. Therefore, better fabric might be purchased than you normally would buy, if it will give you an advantage in breadth of learning. Regard the extra cost as an educational item in your budget rather than as a wardrobe addition.

GLOSSARY OF TEXTILE TERMS AND FABRICS

alaskine, wiry, somewhat lustrous texture; silk and worsted yarns.

Armo, trade name for well-known interfacing fabrics.

Ban-lon, trademark name for heat-set, textured nylon or Dacron yarn.

Belfast, a nonresin type of finish for wash-and-wear cottons. White cottons with this finish will not turn yellow from use of chlorine bleach.

Bemberg, trademark for rayon yarns and fabrics made by the cuprammonium process. Valued for coolness.

blend, yarns composed of two or more fibers mixed before the yarn is spun.

bonding, the use of synthetic resin for binding two or more fabrics together; the backing is usually tricot knit.

broadcloth, a closely woven fabric with very fine ribs.

brocade, an embossed appearance, with rich designs in raised figures.

calico, a plain woven cotton fabric heavier than muslin. All cotton goods were called calicos until the end of the seventeenth century.

carded, process of separating and partly straightening short fibers in preparation for spinning.

cashmere, a very fine quality of goat hair.

Celanese, trademark for cellulose acetate yarns and fabrics.

challis, soft, supple, lightweight, plain weave fabrics.

chambray, cotton fabric in plain weave combining colored warp and white filling yarns.

chiffon, (shee-fŏn′), Sheer plain weave of silk or synthetics.

China silk, a soft, lightweight, plain-weave fabric used for linings and scarves.

chinchilla cloth, a heavy, twill-weave coating fabric, with a napped surface rolled into little balls.

chino, a twilled cotton fabric, used mainly for sportswear.

Chromespun, trademark for solution-dyed acetate fiber. Colorfast to atmospheric fumes, sunlight, washing, perspiration, and dry cleaning.

corduroy, a cut-pile fabric woven with either narrow or wide wales, or without wales.

crepes, fabrics with crinkled, pebbly, or puckered surfaces.

crocking, the rubbing off of dye from wet or dry fabric.

denim, inexpensive, strong, twilled cotton cloth, widely used in jeans.

denim seersucker, a denim weave with a seersucker ripple.

double-cloth, two separate cloths combined in weaving through the use of binding threads.

double knit, two thicknesses of fabric knitted together. Will not stretch, sag, or wrinkle.

drill, strong, twilled cotton cloth, used for sportswear and work clothing.

embossed, design pressed into fabric with hot, engraved rollers.

faille, fabric with flat, horizontal ribs.

flannel, plain or twill weave with a slightly napped surface.

flocked, very short fibers attached to a printed-on adhesive base to give a suede or pile effect, solid or in designs.

gabardine, a firmly woven, twill-weave fabric with relatively smooth surface.

georgette, heavy sheer crepe.

gingham, woven cotton fabric or blend in a medium weight fabric.

homespun, coarse linen or cotton fabric.

jersey, plain fabric knitted in tubular form.

lawn, sheer, plain cotton weave, made of fine yarns often in a high thread count.

melton, coating with face napped carefully, to show the weave clearly.

organdy, sheer, crisp, plain cotton weave made of fine yarns.

organza, transparent, crisp, silk organdy.

ottoman, heavyweight fabric with pronounced crosswise ribs.

pongee, plain-woven, light- or medium-weight fabric.

poplin, fabrics with a fine rib running crosswise.

sailcloth, heavy, strong canvas weave.

satin, a fabric with yarns floating along the surface, to provide a lustrous face.

seersucker, lightweight cotton fabric with crinkled stripes.

shantung, a rough, nubbed surface caused by slubs and knots in the yarn.

vat dye, indicates superior dye; fastness to light and washing.

voile, lightweight, sheer, plain weave, with a crisp, airy feel.

winter cottons, dark cotton fabrics in standard weaves; well-designed, crease-resistant; often finished to "handle" like wool or linen; have become fashion-

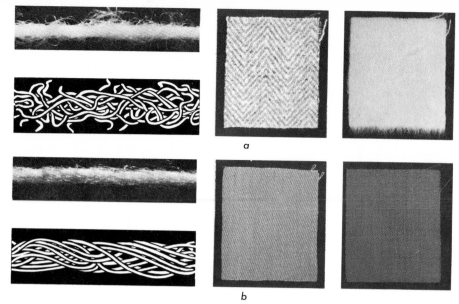

a

b

Figure 7-19. Woolen yarns have both long and short fibers intermingled—carded only. Woolen fabrics, as this herringbone tweed, and fleece cloth, have fuzzy, napped surfaces, *a*.

Worsted yarns have only long fibers in smooth formation—carded and then combed. Worsted fabrics show the weave distinctly, with little or no surface fuzz. Examples shown are gabardine and crepe, *b*.

able through good designing and tailoring by French, Italian, and American dress designers. Fuller, Thomas, Herbert Meyer, and Hope Skillman cottons are synonymous with quality and style.

woolen, wool fabric made of woolen yarns loosely twisted of shorter, carded fibers. These soft, fuzzy, fluffy yarns produce such fabrics as tweed, suede cloth, broadcloth, and Shetland-type woolens. Felting, shrinking, or napping in finishing often result in a barely discernible weave. Heavily napped fabrics may have weak foundations. A weakness of napped woolens is wearing-off of the nap along edges where rubbing occurs, as at the lower edge of the sleeve. This type of fabric may also pill (Fig. 7-19, *a*).

worsted (wŏos'tid), wool fabric made from worsted yarns—long fibers combed parallel before spinning into smooth, tightly twisted yarns that feel wiry, firm, and hard. Fabrics made of worsted yarns are firm and compact, with distinctly visible weaves, as in gabardine and crêpe. They tailor well and hold their press but may develop a shine in wearing or in poor pressing (Fig. 7-19, *b*).

yarn, a strand of fibers laid or twisted together.

yarn count, total number of warp and filling yarns per square inch. Yarn count is usually expressed in two numbers, as 86 (warp) x 76 (filling). In percale, "80-square" means 80 yarns in each direction. In sheeting, "Type 140" refers to a total of 140 yarns per inch. The higher the yarn count in a given class of fabrics, as gingham, the finer the yarn. Other things being equal, a better balance between warp and filling yarns indicates greater durability. Cotton broadcloth is an example of fabric with unbalanced yarn count, having a much higher warp count. Being weaker in the filling, it tends to split more easily than madras, oxford, or percale.

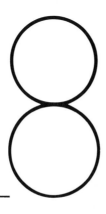

Sewing Equipment

A few well-chosen tools and equipment are essential for the home dressmaker. Basic equipment assumes good lighting and a full-length mirror, along with a sewing machine, pressing equipment, and a cutting table or folding cutting board. A work center with adequate storage is an advantage (Fig. 8-1).

Cutting Tools

For cutting, choose medium-sized shears, 7 to 8 inches long, that will be used for no other purpose. *Bent-handled shears* are preferred because they do not lift the fabric so far off the table during the cutting process (Fig. 8-2). *Trimming scissors,* 4 to 6 inches long, are convenient for use at the machine for clipping threads,

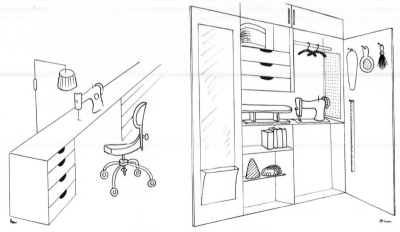

Figure 8-1. Home sewing center.

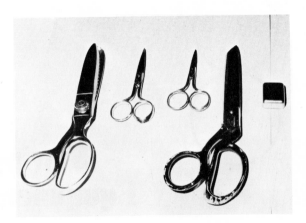

Figure 8-2. Bent-handle shears are an advantage in cutting fabric, and smaller scissors have many uses. The small object is a magnetic block for use as a gauge on the machine.

holding in the ease of a seam close to the presser foot, and for snipping slashes in the fitting room. Embroidery scissors, 3 to 4 inches long, are valuable for cutting the corners of piped buttonholes and in embroidery work. (Protection with a cork or case is advisable.) A lower-grade quality in scissors will be adequate for paper work. *Pinking* shears are not essential, but they give a decorative edge that protects raw edges that ordinarily ravel very little; however, they sometimes damage the garment and waste time. Zigzagging and other finishes are more popular. Pinking shears are not satisfactory for use in cutting out a garment for the reasons presented on p. 266.

Measuring Tools

An excellent selection of measuring tools would include a firm cloth *tape measure*, 60 inches in length, with numerals reading from either end, and stiff

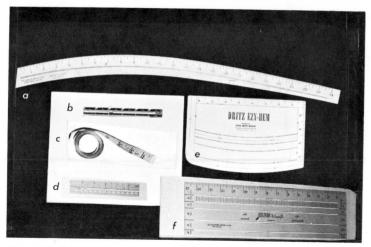

Figure 8-3. Measuring tools: *a*, curved ruler for "truing" curves; *b*, 6-inch metal gauge; *c*, firm, 60-inch tape measure; *d*, metric ruler; *e*, hem-width measurer; *f*, plastic ruler with slots for marking; *g*, yardstick with attached tape line.

enough to stand on edge when measuring curves (Fig. 8-3); a 36-inch *yardstick;* a short ruler; and a 6-inch adjustable *metal gauge.* Plastic *rulers* (see-through style with ruled guidelines) are helpful in marking buttonholes and for using mathematics in spacing. Several sheets of $\frac{1}{4}$-inch ruled paper, or cross-section paper (8 to 10 squares per inch), aid in making buttonholes. A curved measuring stick has many uses, especially in lines during pattern alteration. Adjustable *hem markers,* chalk or pins, are also useful items. A metal hem-measurer, curved to fit hem shapes, is a suggested guide for pressing and measuring hem widths.

Marking Aids

Dressmaker's tracing paper comes in several colors; use the lightest one possible for your fabric. Its use is described in Chapter 12. For marking cloth, use a *dressmaker's pencil* (Dixon's Best no. 352, white, orange, or light blue). In selecting *tailor's chalk,* avoid the wax type, which might stain.

A *tracing wheel* is needed—one that is not wobbly but firm, smooth, and sharp (that will not snag the fabric). A needlepoint type makes a fainter line, which is desirable on thinner fabrics; this wheel is less likely to tear the pattern (Fig. 8-4, *a*). A wheel with a serrated edge makes a good heavy line, for heavy, loosely woven fabrics; deep points are more effective on thicker fabrics. A smooth wheel is recommended for delicate fabrics such as velvet and knits subject to snagging, that might be damaged by other types of wheels.

Needles, Pins, Pincushion, and Thimble

Needles can be purchased in a variety of sizes and shapes (Fig. 8-5). *Betweens* are short, recommended for short fingers and dainty hand sewing, *a. Sharps* are

181

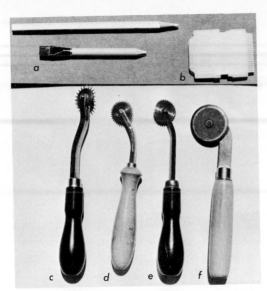

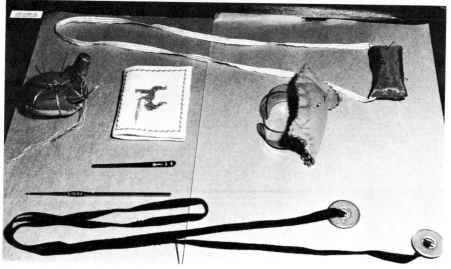

Figure 8-6. Types of pincushions; a needle-book, bodkin, crochet hook; plumbline of tape weighted at each end.

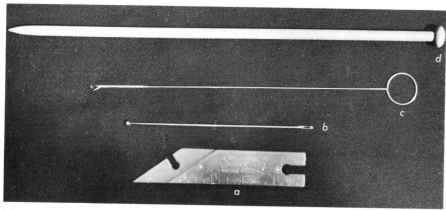

Figure 8-7. Turning tools: *a*, point turner; *b*, ball needle; *c*, long wire with hook; *d*, for turning belts and ties.

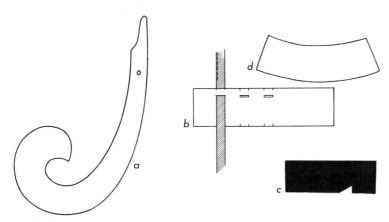

Figure 8-8. Guides for accuracy: *a*, Dietzen plastic curve for truing up curves; *b*, cardboard gauges—slits cut to stitch rows of braid without basting; *c*, use the distance from the end to the straight side of the notch for measuring; *d*, shape of hem for marking and pressing.

Figure 8-9. Plumb line: valuable for checking direction of lengthwise seams.

for turning bias cording in a knitted fabric, *b,* and a long wire with a hook can be used in turning other fabrics, *c.* For turning belts and long ties, use a $\frac{1}{4}$-inch *dowel stick,* smoothed to a slightly rounded point. A *tapestry needle, bodkin,* or *safety pin* also serves the purpose, but scissors will likely cause damage.

Guides for Accuracy

A Dietzen *plastic curve,* no. 17, is useful in pattern alteration and designing (Fig. 8-8, *a*). A device for stitching rows of braid or tape (as on a sailor collar) without basting is a cardboard with slits cut by a sharp knife at measured intervals, *b.* A *cardboard gauge* of the desired size, *c,* is sometimes easier to use than the adjustable metal one.

Special *gauges* for the sewing machine are available for the sewing kit. A plastic or *rubber mat,* about 4×6 inches, screwed to the bed of the machine in front of the presser foot, has $\frac{1}{4}$-inch grooves that serve as guides for the partially sighted seamstress. It guards the fingers and prevents the work from slipping. Another satisfactory guide is a magnetic bar to use instead of masking tape. It is movable without the use of a screw.

Plumb Lines

Plumb lines are valuable aids in checking the directions of seams and grain. A small board or flat, strong box, with one end of a string tied to it and the other to a weight, provides a line for judging the side seam (Fig. 8-9). Place the board high under the arm.

Another plumb line was shown in Figure 8-6. This can be placed around the neck and looped once at the CF or CB neckline to judge lines at these points. To judge lengthwise grain position in a sleeve from shoulder to elbow, have an assistant hold the line at the end of the shoulder.

Additional Equipment

A cording foot or *zipper foot* (adjustable type) will be needed for your brand and model of machine. A special foot is required for invisible zippers.

It is convenient to keep a small notebook, a pencil, and masking or cellophane tape in your sewing box. Other aids to include are a bodkin, crochet hook, emery bag, stiletto or awl, a needle-threader, extra needles, and bobbins.

In the absence of a regular wastebasket near the machine, you might use the upper machine drawer to catch clippings and waste. Or, to aid in neatness and organization, keep a paper or plastic bag taped to the right of the machine. Extra notions can be selected with the pattern and fabric.

The French-Model Waistline Tape

The French-model waistline tape (Fig. 8-10) is a device for checking the waistline measure in making waistbands, in fitting, in altering commercial-pattern waist measures, and in attaching inside tape to a waistline seam. Use $\frac{1}{2}$-inch twill tape or 1-inch grosgrain ribbon.

Cut it four inches longer than your waist measure. Turn one end under one inch and stitch firmly. Stitch $\frac{1}{4}$-inch tucks in each of the quarters for future adjustments. Fit the tape over your slip and turn the other end under so that the folds just meet at center front. Establish the location you prefer; make it as tight or loose as you like. Sew on a hook and eye. Locate and *mark* with machine stitches (underarm) the side seams according to a garment that fits you best, or according to a pleasing balance between front and back as viewed in the mirror, or according to seams on your dress form. In general, the front measures one to two inches longer than the back: for a 25-inch waist, the front is $13\frac{1}{4}$ inches and the back $11\frac{3}{4}$ inches, or $6\frac{5}{8}$ inches for half the front and $5\frac{7}{8}$ inches for half the back. (Mature women require about 13 inches for the back and 15 inches for the front.) This tape should be labeled—one for each customer or each member of the family, whenever waistline styles are in fashion.

Other equipment for special problems will be introduced in relevant chapters.

Machine Needles and Bobbins

Unfortunately, standardization of machine parts is nonexistent. Know the name and number of the model of your machine, the kind of needles and bobbins you need, and where to get them. Ball-point needles will be essential for quality performance on knit fabrics to avoid snagging.

For average-weight fabrics, use needles of medium size (no. 14 Singer). For finer fabrics, use finer needles (nos. 9 to 11 Singer). Follow the suggestions in your own machine booklet. See Table 7-6.

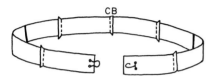

Figure 8-10 French-model waistline tape.

Pattern Testing and Alteration

Understanding your pattern is an essential first step in the procedures of checking it for size and making alterations, if indicated. Planning ahead to eliminate fitting problems or to keep them to a minimum promises many rewards.

Knowing Your Pattern

A quick overview can furnish needed facts regarding the types of information presented on the pattern envelope and guide sheet. At this point, you will be concerned especially with symbols and their meanings, as grainline markings, edges to be placed on a fold, and where alteration lines are placed (if included).

187

RECOGNIZING THE PARTS OF A PATTERN

Early in dressmaking, it is helpful to recognize at a glance where each pattern piece belongs in relation to the finished garment and the shapes of various pieces. Do you know the differences between the front and back of a blouse or dress as to length of shoulder seam, shapes of neck and armhole, and width at waistline and hipline? Learn to distinguish the front from the back of the sleeve (Fig. 9-1).

WHY ONLY HALF A PATTERN? Obviously, there are several reasons why most patterns come in halves rather than as whole patterns. The most important reasons are that the right and left halves are exactly alike if cut together, time is saved, and the resulting garment is more likely to be balanced.

In assymetric designs, where right and left sides are not alike, a whole right side and a whole left side of the pattern must be furnished. By consulting the directions, learn which pieces represent a whole pattern; which pieces require a pair, not duplicates; and which pieces represent a half, to be placed on a fold.

Pattern Preparation

The most important steps in preparing a pattern include the following:

1. If the pattern is wrinkled, press it with a slightly warm iron.
2. Extend the lengthwise grainlines on the larger pattern pieces, unless the pattern has quite long grainlines on it.

    The lengthwise grainline is necessary in each pattern piece as an aid in altering the pattern. This line may coincide with markings for the CF (center front) or CB (center back). It is more accurate to use CF and CB markings, if these are to be on the grainline, and ignore the other marking, which may not be printed exactly parallel to the CF or CB. This procedure saves time, as well (Fig. 9-2).
3. The crosswise grainline in the sleeve can be drawn in at the base of the sleeve cap.

    It is more accurate to first draw in this grainline from corner to corner (Fig. 9-3). Then fold this line over on itself from end to end. The resulting crease is on the lengthwise grainline and in the middle of the sleeve. Draw this corrected grainline through the entire length of the sleeve. Because printed grainlines are sometimes slightly misplaced on a pattern, this method insures accuracy.
4. Possibly mark the edges to be placed on a fold, or add any other identifying marks you wish to use.
5. Return to the envelope all sections of the pattern which are not needed for the view chosen.

DOES YOUR PATTERN REQUIRE ALTERATION?

Past experiences may have provided you with the necessary information as to type and amounts of alteration needed. If you do not have this knowledge at the present time, perhaps you will be able to accumulate it while you sew on this garment. It is a great advantage to know what variations from the pattern are required for your figure.

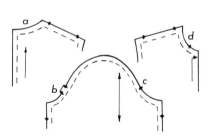

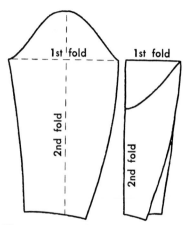

Figure 9-1. Distinguish between back and front necklines, and back and front sleeve-cap lines: *a,* back neckline; *b,* back sleeve cap; *c,* front sleeve cap; *d,* front neckline.

Figure 9-2. Identify CF, foldline, and grainline on your pattern. Use CF as the grainline in this type of pattern for an accurate placement.

Figure 9-3. Establish the crosswise grain at the base of the sleeve cap to check the accuracy of the lengthwise grain.

Testing the Pattern

Review the following alternatives, considering the simplicity of the procedure and the probable effectiveness for your situation.

1. *Proceed to alter your pattern and/or cut your garment, using past experience as a basis for judgment.*

This will be a satisfactory plan if you really learned the lessons of past experiences; if you are using the same brand of pattern on which you base your experiences; and if there have been no changes in your figure since you last used a pattern.

2. *Compare the pattern with a garment that fits you well.*

This is an easy method of checking certain measurements, especially lengthwise measurements, such as the length of a skirt, sleeve, or back bodice. Remember, the measurements of the new pattern must be compared with a garment of similar design.

3. *Try on a shell, or a test garment, that has been cut from a basic pattern.*

You may have tried on a shell when you were deciding which pattern size to buy. If you made careful notes regarding any changes indicated, you are ready to consider them at this time. If not, trying on a shell now is a simple step toward identifying and locating variations in your figure. Cutting and basting a test garment for yourself may be worth serious consideration if you have had problems in fitting. It would be of help to you now and also in the future, in case of weight or figure changes.

4. *Try the pattern on.*

If a shell is not available and your past experience in fitting suggests a figure difficulty (such as a sway back, a full bust, or round shoulders), it is a good idea to try the pattern on.

5. *Compare your measurements with those on the Body Measurements Chart.*

This is, in reality, a comparison of your body measurements with those of a person whose size corresponds with the standard measurements printed on the Body Measurements Chart. You have already compared your three circumference measurements (bust, waist, hip) with these measurements. In snug-fitting garments, you might reasonably expect to need an alteration to correct any differences. For example, if your bust measure is 1½ inches larger, and your waistline is 2 inches smaller. You may need to add to the bustline, and you will need to subtract from the waistline the amounts of these differences.

One difficulty in checking measurements is the possible margin of error. Only those trained in the science of anthropometry can be absolutely accurate in finding the exact spots on the body from which to begin and end the measurements. Besides, fashion designers change these locations for style reasons. For instance, shoulder widths were short in 1931, widened in 1933, leveled down in 1935, and widened more in 1937. Shoulder lines were very short in 1890, to balance the full gathered sleeves. The widened, drop-shoulder effect of a few years ago gave a casual air—like a shirt. In the late 1960 s, the emphasis on youth shortened shoulder seams, so that the sleeve cap set higher; the underarm curve was raised to make the wearer seem taller, trimmer, more slender, and girlish.

Keep in mind what you have learned from *experience*. Suppose that your partner takes your bust measure and reports it as 36 inches. You are positive that you are wearing well-fitting garments that were cut by unaltered size 12 patterns. What does this indicate? Tighten the tapeline to a snug measure; it probably will now register 34 inches, or be very close. Of course, if you are unable to reduce the measurement, it may mean that you are not a discriminating judge of fit in your garments—that you should alter the pattern for a larger bust.

Trying on a shell, a garment, or pattern may provide a better basis for determining the correctness of the pattern size than basing judgment solely on measurements, unless you are very careful in taking them.

6. *Compare your measurements with those of the pattern pieces.*

This plan may be tedious, time-consuming, and often disappointing in its results, depending on the problem. A satisfactory use might be in checking the length of a skirt; an unsatisfactory use might be checking the bodice length when blouson styles are in fashion. Comparing your body measurements with the standard body measurements is better; otherwise, you may not preserve this season's fashion-right look—which includes style and fashion ease.

YOUR DECISION

The decision as to your next step involves either

1. Proceeding without the further checking of your pattern (based on experience).
2. Checking and comparing measurements of (a) a well-fitting garment, (b) the Body Measurement Chart, or (c) your pattern.
3. Studying the fit of this size pattern or garment on your figure.

DID YOU CHOOSE MEASUREMENTS? When you were making the decision concerning the best pattern size for you, did you record measurements in addition to the three circumference body measurements plus the center back waist length? If so, refer back to Table 6-3, p. 123. Information available there may be helpful in testing your pattern.

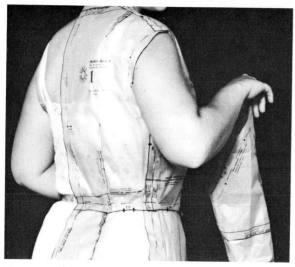

Figure 9-4. Lap edges of pattern, so that the pinned pattern seams will lie smoothly on the body as the pressed garment seams would lie, with pins on the outside of the pattern. The sleeve has been pinned in the same manner.

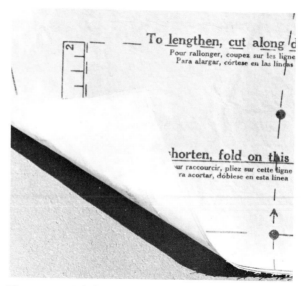

Figure 9-5. A lightweight, press-on interfacing fabric has been pressed to the back of the pattern for added strength when fitting problems are complicated.

DID YOU CHOOSE A FITTING? Note the pattern that has been prepared for fitting (Fig. 9-4). Seamlines are pinned with the edges lapped and seamlines coinciding. Pins are placed parallel to and on the seamlines, which permits the waistline seam to lie flat and smooth on the figure. Naturally, pins placed across the waistline would prevent the pattern from following the body contour. Placing the pins on the outside of the pattern is convenient for making changes.

Although the pattern would appear neater, it is unnecessary to take the time to trim all pattern margins away; in case they are not trimmed away, it will be necessary to slash through them at intervals on concave curves, as at the neck and armholes, in order that the line follow the body contour.

Your degree of anticipation of fitting problems might justify a variation in handling your pattern. You may want to try pressing pattern sections to a press-on type of interfacing fabric. This not only preserves the pattern, but gives it a "hand" more nearly like your fabric and costs less in time and money than making a test garment. The sections so treated could be limited to those primarily involved with your needs, such as the bodice front and back, in case your variation is a larger curve at the bustline (Fig. 9-5).

ASSEMBLING PATTERN SECTIONS

1. Pin in the pleats and darts, according to the marked lines. Instead of gathers, fold in soft, wide pleats. Omit pockets, collars, ties, and facings.
2. Pin the pattern together, seam line on seam line, matching notches and lapping one piece over another, to fit the right half of the figure. Place pins parallel with and on the seam line.
3. Pin the parts together step-by-step as suggested in the pattern guide sheet, beginning with smaller sections, until you have a front blouse and a back

191

blouse; then pin the shoulder and underarm seams to make a half blouse. To prevent tearing the pattern, place the first pin on the underarm seam about 2 inches below the armhole.

4. Pin the *sleeve* darts and seams, leaving 2 inches free below the armhole. Pin the sleeve in the upper armhole only, after the pattern has been placed on the figure.

5. Pin sections of the *skirt* together to make a half skirt front, then a half skirt back; then lap the front over the back at the side-hip seam to make a half skirt.

6. Pin the blouse and skirt together at the *waistline* (to a belt, if inset). The result will be half of a garment, reaching from the center back to center front for the right half only. If part of the garment is asymmetrical in design, a part of this, obviously, will not be pinned to another section.

7. Pin up the lower hemlines to give you a better idea of the proportions.

FITTING A TEST GARMENT   Fitting a test garment rather than the pattern provides more accurate information about how the design can be expected to fit in fabric. Use your pattern to cut the garment, then machine baste the seams.

CHECKING FIT IN PATTERN OR GARMENT   Here is the order of steps to be taken:

1. Arrange for assistance in checking the fit and making decisions.

2. Pin a tape, or tie a string, around your normal waistline and try on the paper pattern over foundation garments. Try on jacket and coat patterns over a dress or blouse. Compare the waistline of the pattern with your waistline. Anchor the center front and center back to your slip and the shoulder seam to your slip strap.

3. Examine the pattern in front of the mirror. Note the kind and amounts of change needed. If there seems to be a pronounced bulge, it may help you to see the cause of the difficulty if the skirt and bodice patterns are separated. Change darts and seams if necessary to correct the fit on the person. Mark the best places to make alterations.

4. Carefully remove the pattern, alter it accurately, and try it on again. Repeat these steps until the pattern seems satisfactory.

What to Look for at the Fitting

1. Look for possible changes needed in the length of
   a. Bodice.
   b. Skirt.
   c. Sleeve.

2. Examine the pattern for width. This examination should confirm what you already know about the width of the pattern at the bust, waist, and hip, so it may not need to be very extensive. You can determine the necessary changes by arithmetic. In case your measurements are the same as those

on the measurement chart, you may expect the pattern to be correct, or approximately correct, in width. You can expect to add or subtract width, according to the differences between your measurements and those given, in case the design is a basic type with minimum amounts of ease. This conclusion is made on the assumption that the measurements you took are accurate—snug. This ease, in excess of body measurements, must be preserved. If all of this extra size in the garment is needed to cover your larger body, the garment will be too tight to set well. This minimum ease, allowed for fit, is not to be confused with additional ease allowed for style features, such as gathers or a draped line.

    a. Does the pattern reach from CF to CB without displacement? You will be able to judge this more accurately in a test garment; the pattern will seem a bit small, as it does not lie as flat against the body as cloth does.

    b. Is the pattern correct through the shoulder and chest area for you and the present mode?

    c. Is the neckline correctly located?

    d. Is the width correct across the upper back shoulders?

  3. Look for evidences of larger body curves or hollows.

    a. Line.

      (1) Do seams set smooth and straight?

      (2) Is the waistline seam in the correct position; is the bodice too long in the back or too short in the front, or vice versa, indicating larger body curves or hollows above it?

    b. Balance.

      (1) Does the shoulder seam lie flat along the shoulder, or does it rise above the shoulder at the armhole and hug it at the neckline, indicating sloping shoulders; does it do the reverse, indicating square shoulders?

    c. Wrinkles.

      (1) Are diagonal wrinkles evident in the bodice, skirt, or sleeve, indicating larger body curves? Mark an X on your pattern at the point of any wrinkles.

      (2) Are other wrinkles present? Where?

IDENTIFYING ANY PROBLEMS

In checking your pattern or test garment for length, width, and any additional evidences of poor fit, were you able to identify any problems? In case you do not understand a condition you observed in your pattern or garment, take a quick look at the sketches shown on pages 220 to 239; you may be able to locate a situation that corresponds to your difficulty.

ALTERING THE PATTERN

Three sleeve patterns have been altered for length, following suggestions found in most pattern guide sheets and reference books. Study these sketches in an effort to recognize the methods used and the standards attained (Fig. 9-6).

TECHNIQUES EMPLOYED	STANDARDS

1. Patterns were shortened by
  a. Pleats made at right angles to the lengthwise grainline and kept even in width, *a*.
  b. Cutting pattern into two parts and lapping edges evenly, *b*.
2. Patterns were lengthened by cutting the pattern perpendicular to the lengthwise grainline and spreading the two edges apart evenly, *c*. Changes were made within the patterns between points of articulation—between joints where the body moves.
3. Where an edge was lengthened or shortened, corresponding edges were altered to match.
4. Transitional lines were drawn to correct the lines broken by pleats or slashes across slanting or curved edges.
	A. Original grainlines are preserved. (Grainlines remain straight where tucks and spreads are made perpendicular to them and kept even in width.)
	B. Patterns are kept in proportion and balance. (Changes were made in *a* and *c*, both above and below the elbow on the assumption that the two sections of the arm grew proportionately. A check would determine whether equal amounts are needed in the two locations.)
	C. Change is created where needed and is not obvious. (Change made between points of articulation kept the elbow dart in its normal position.)
	D. Designer's lines are preserved. (The designer's carefully cut, curved pattern edges, darts, and notches remain undisturbed, permitting the altered pattern edges to fit together perfectly—following the drawing of transitional lines to straighten and/or smooth them.)

5. Construction details are avoided, if possible, in making changes.	E. Necessary markings for construction and decorative details are undisturbed.

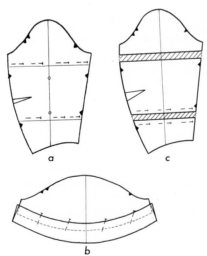

Figure 9-6. Methods for changing pattern length.

Changing Length in Other Patterns

The techniques for changing bodice and skirt lengths are the same as those for altering sleeve patterns—preserving the original grainline, altering adjoining edges to match, and making changes within the pattern where needed to preserve the designer's lines. In basic bodice designs the darts will often be crossed by the slashed line or pleat. This will require transitional lines to correct the darts and seamlines (Fig. 9-7).

To Lengthen

1. Draw a line across the bodice front pattern, perpendicular to the lengthwise grainline, between the lower edge and the bustline. Draw a line on the back in a corresponding position.
2. Draw two parallel lines on a piece of paper with the distance between them equal to the desired spread of the pattern.
3. Slash on the marked alteration line of the bodices and securely fasten each edge along the marked inset with pins or tape.
4. Draw transitional lines from the point to the wide ends of the dart; relocate the point, if necessary.
5. Use the same techniques for the skirt, making the change somewhere between the hipline and lower edge.

To Shorten The process for shortening a pattern involves the same principles used in lengthening (Fig. 9-8).

1. Draw two parallel lines across the bodice front pattern, perpendicular to the lengthwise grainline, between the lower edge of the pattern and the bustline, with the space between the lines equal to the amount the pattern is to be shortened.
2. Take your choice of these two methods: fold a pleat, or slash and lap the pattern edges.
   a. Fold a pleat: fold on one of the marked lines, bring the fold to the second line and fasten it with pins or tape.
   b. Slash the pattern on one of the marked lines, lapping the edges bring the slashed line to the second line. Fasten it with pins or tape.
   These techniques require approximately the same amount of time and give accurate results if carefully done.
3. Draw transitional lines from point to ends of dart, on side seam from bustline to lower edge of pattern, and on skirt side seams.
4. Make corresponding changes on the back bodice.
5. Use the same techniques for the skirt, making the changes somewhere between the hipline and lower edge, or use an alternative plan, discussed in the next paragraph.

Where Designer's Lines Are Less Important

Some situations suggest simple alternatives to changing length within the pattern. These apply to changes at hemlines where there are no complicated designer's curves to be preserved, and where a perfect cutting line may not be essential—especially on skirt edges, which often require new hem markings in fitting (Fig. 9-9).

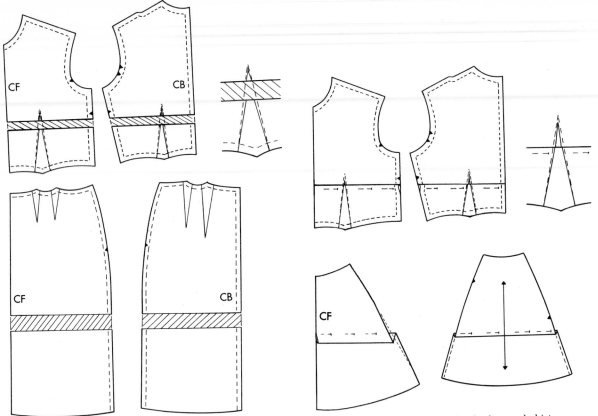

Figure 9-7. Lengthening bodice and skirt.

Figure 9-8. Shortening bodice and skirt.

Compare sleeves *a* and *b*. Altering *a* within the pattern, as shown, is the simplest and most satisfactory way of changing it, with its slanting seamlines. Its hem would not fit the sleeve if length were taken off or added at the lower edge. Where a pattern is irregular in shape, safer and quicker results are obtained by making the change within the pattern.

The lines in sleeve *b*, with the sides apparently perpendicular to the lower edge, would present no problem in having length removed or added at the lower edge.

The skirt pattern, *c*, might be lengthened by adding extra paper at its edge; a faster method for adding length to a skirt is to hold a gauge just ahead of the scissors when cutting the fabric. As a safeguard, and reminder that additional length is to be added, place pins at the corners (in the path of your cutting line) when you make the pattern placement, *d*. It is questionable whether method *e*, for shortening, could be done as quickly as folding a pleat within the pattern.

CHANGING WIDTH   Since your pattern was selected to conform as nearly as possible to your measurements in width, necessary changes should have been minimized. However, for those measurements that did not conform to the standard, you may be involved with some alterations. As you study these commonly recommended alterations for width, watch for any new techniques or standards.

196

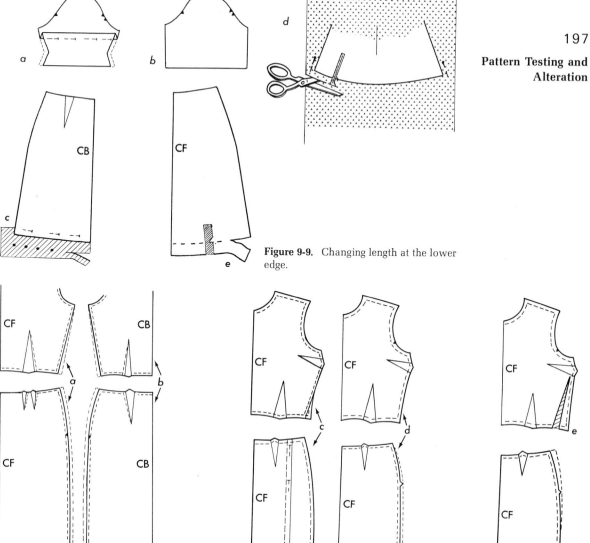

Figure 9-9. Changing length at the lower edge.

Figure 9-10. Changing width—when changes are slight.

SLIGHT ALTERATIONS

1. In increasing or reducing width, where needed alterations are slight, changes can be made at seams without altering designer's lines perceptibly (Fig. 9-10).

2. To increase width, mark new lines on pattern margins if space is available; on paper pinned along edges; or plan to add the increases when cutting the garment. An extra ¼ to ½ inch can be added at side seams, at waist or hip. In *a*, it would be advisable to make the change in a transitional line from armhole to waistline at side seams.

3. To decrease waistline and hipline, re-mark the cutting line, plan to baste

a deeper seam when the construction process is started, or fold a pleat in pattern, c.

4. To increase the hipline without changing the waist measurement, alteration d can be used successfully, provided the addition needed at the hipline does not exceed ¼ inch (1 inch total change on the four seam allowances of this two-gore skirt. More change is possible, if the side hipline is decidedly curved.) If this amount of curve is too much, plan to add equal amounts at waist and hip and increase the size of the darts. To stitch the dart ⅛ inch wider at the waistline (to remove the ¼ inch added to this half of the skirt front) can hardly make a perceptible change in appearance. For greater amounts, an extra dart can be added.

5. To reduce the waistline without changing the hip measurement, distribute the excess width among the darts, or add new darts.

6. To increase the waist measure without changing the hipline, technique e or f can be used.

More Extensive Changes

Patterns may require pleats or slashing and lapping to reduce width, or slashing and spreading to increase size—the same or similar techniques that were used in lengthening the pattern (Fig. 9-11).

WIDENING THE SHOULDER

Changes affecting width in small areas of the pattern are accomplished by slashing only as far as necessary to change that part.

In case the shoulder width is too narrow, length must be added to the shoulder seam without making changes in other areas of the pattern (Fig. 9-12). Why is the slash in a extended to the armhole seam? The pattern would not lie flat otherwise, b. Why does the slash not continue through the seam allowance at a'? Such a procedure would increase the length of the armhole seam, an undesirable procedure, as the sleeve would not then fit the armhole. Length is needed only in the shoulder seam.

Under what circumstances would patterns be slashed as a, b, or c in Figure 9-13? This would depend on how far below the shoulder the change is needed. Pattern b would obviously provide extra width across the shoulder to a greater depth than c. Note the locations of transitional lines on a, b, and c shoulder seams.

NARROWING THE SHOULDER

Where the pattern is too wide across the chest and shoulders, one is confronted with the problem of preserving at least a part of the shoulder extension (Fig. 9-14). You will note that the normal curve of the armhole has a bias extension near the shoulder. This is easily seen in b, cut by an unaltered pattern. The shoulder lines in c and d were shortened by the technique demonstrated in e. Although a part of the extension remains in c, it has all been removed in d, resulting in a pinched-in look across the shoulders. Use of the technique shown in e is satisfactory, in case some extension remains.

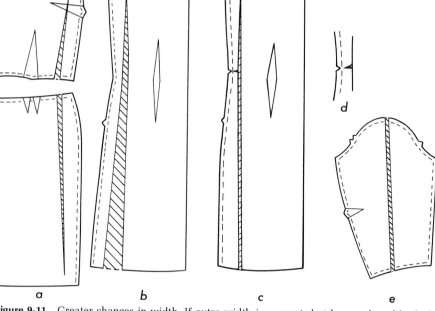

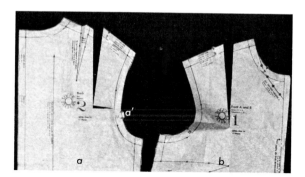

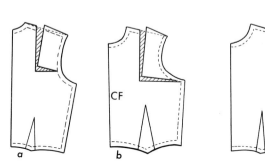

Figure 9-11. Greater changes in width. If extra width is unwanted at lower edge of *b*, slash from alteration line at waistline seam, *c* and *d*, and lap to keep added width even, *c*.

Figure 9-12. Changing width in localized areas only. Note that *b* does not lie flat on the table.

Figure 9-13. Widening the shoulder.

Alteration *f* is used where there is a shoulder dart. This change will narrow the garment to a greater extent from the lower armhole level all the way to the top of the shoulder, but this may be an advantage in such cases. Widening a long dart is generally a successful process, as the point is still sufficiently narrow to present no problem in construction. If the needed change does not exceed ⅜ inch, it is safe to widen on each side of the dart lines; if the change is greater, remove all of the excess width on the armhole side of dart, to avoid making a perceptible change in the width of the front panel. Care would be required to avoid making

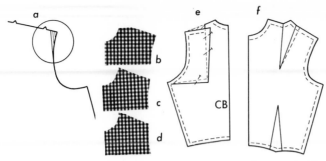

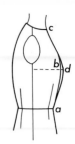

Figure 9-14. Alter pattern for narrow shoulders to leave grain like *b*, or *c*, rather than *d*, which gives a pinched appearance at the shoulder.

Figure 9-15. Which line is longer, *adc* or *abc*?

a dart that is too large for the person's figure. Although this plan works well with a long front dart, it cannot be used with the short dart on the back shoulder. In that case it might be possible to ease the extra length along the back shoulder seam. A change of design in the front to a dart tuck or gathers might be considered.

If the pattern has seams entering the shoulder, as in a princess style, the width of the side section can be decreased to reduce the shoulder length. Make the change at the seamline extending to the bustline, to be inconspicuous. The center section or panel, where the change would be more conspicuous, thus remains unchanged.

Other suggestions for handling this problem in extreme cases include (1) adding a shoulder dart; (2) cutting the garment by an unaltered pattern, or altering it to leave a sufficient amount of extension, and trying to ease the fabric along the seam, using seam binding as a stay and pressing to shrink the ease; or (3) using a firm-bodied underlining in the shoulder area and supporting the end of the shoulder seam by a thin shoulder pad. The latter solution might be an advantage, also, in improving the individual's proportions.

What happens if this problem is left for correction in fitting? If the front armhole is deepened at the top of the shoulder, the result is similar to *b* and *a*—the extension may be removed in the deepened seam.

Altering for Body Curves

Body areas for which alterations may be needed include these seven basic curves:

1. Bust.
2. Round or "wing" shoulders—protruding shoulder blades.
3. Square shoulders.
4. Abdomen.
5. Back hip or seat (derrière).
6. Side hip.
7. Large upper arm.

200

Do larger body curves require more length? More width? Both length and width? Note the front silhouette lines in Figure 9-15. Is *adc* a longer line than *abc*? If a tape line were placed across the front of the body, underarm seam to underarm seam, would the line be longer over point *d* than over point *b*? Obviously, a figure with the silhouette line, *adc,* will require more length and more width of fabric to cover the large curve.

Our earlier problems were concerned with the techniques of adding either length or width to a pattern. How can both be added in the area where extra fabric is needed?

LARGER BODY CURVES

BUST AND ROUND SHOULDERS What differences do you note in the alterations used in Figure 9-16 and those that have been considered earlier for changing length and width? Earlier, slashes avoided darts, where possible. Here, the pattern has been slashed through the darts and spread to allow both length and width. The slashes have been located to add this extra area of fabric exactly where needed—in *a, b,* and *c* for a larger bust curve, and in *d* and *e* for larger shoulder blades. Why was the pattern slashed through the darts? To answer that question, observe the side seam of *a.* It needed no alteration, so its length has not been changed; the dart will be stitched on its original seamlines. Because the spread has widened the dart, it will be larger than the original, in order to cover the larger curve of the body. The same is true of the waistline dart. Placing the spread within the darts, retains the original length of the underarm and waistline seams, leaving them undisturbed and providing fabric where it was needed within the pattern. This plan will work well when the darts are fairly long and the amount to be added to the width is limited. If the amount is extensive it will be necessary to add an extra dart, dividing the width between the two, *b.* Pattern *b,* which required a greater spread than *a,* has been slashed in a nearby position in order to add a second dart; keeping these shorter underarm darts narrower insures darts that set smoothly at their points.

In pattern *c,* the slash extends through the shoulder and waistline darts to provide extra length and width as successfully as in *a* and *b.*

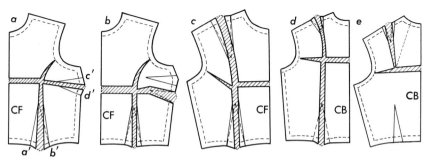

Figure 9-16. Alterations for larger body curves. Large bust, *a, b,* and *c*; round shoulders, *d* and *e.*

Back patterns, *d* and *e*, demonstrate the application of the same principle used in correcting the front—provide more length and width over the curve—in this case, round shoulders or protruding shoulder blades. The alteration in *e* would present a problem possibly in the increase in size of the back shoulder dart. To avoid this, the dart might be increased slightly in size, and the extra length eased along the shoulder line. Another possibility would be to slash on the dotted line at the neck and transfer most of the extra shoulder length into a neckline dart— some should be kept to ease in. Because this dart would be a little longer than the shoulder dart, it could be wider and still be stitched to a smooth point.

What is the reason for the added length at CF and CB on *a* to *e*? The same amount of added length is needed at the center of the garment as over the fullest part of the bust or shoulders, from shoulder to waistline; the garment floats over the hollow, although a bra would hug the body more closely and the length of the CF line would not be as long as a vertical line over the bust.

Which of the standards for an altered pattern, p. 194, apply to changing the pattern for larger bulges? You will note that Standards A, B, C and D apply in these cases.

CHARACTERISTICS OF PATTERNS ALTERED FOR LARGER BODY CURVES. (FIG. 9–16)

1. Patterns slashed lengthwise and crosswise over the fullest part of a body curve are separated to provide extra length and width to cover the body.
2. Patterns that require width at one side and not at the other are kept flat by slashing to the seamline on the opposite side (but not through the seamline. Pattern is folded to flatten the seam allowance).

What additional standard are you able to add to the list of standards for pattern alterations, after considering alterations for body curves? *The pattern lies flat (there are no wrinkles that you just mash down).*

SQUARE SHOULDERS If the body silhouette is more square, additional length will be needed to cover the longer curve across the top of the shoulder. More width may be needed also, depending on the roundness of the figure.

The three methods shown for achieving this condition vary slightly (Fig. 9-17). The slashes made in *a* permit the side section to be moved upward, lengthening the underarm seam and lifting the shoulder seam at its armhole end. This alteration will require the same change to be made on the back, with no change in the sleeve.

In *b* the result is the same, possibly, with one exception—it may not be as accurate, unless the pattern armhole is used as a guide for marking this new armhole and relocating the notches. Freehand drawing may not provide an exact designer's curve that will fit the body as well, or the sleeve, which needs no altering.

Some figures require additional length from the top of the shoulder to the armpit, especially the slightly heavier figure. For this type, *c* is a desirable method; naturally, the back must be altered in the same manner. The sleeve cap, *d*, will require the same amount of added length, to match the extra length in the back and front.

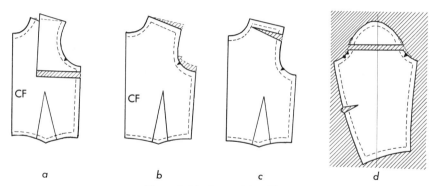

a   b   c   d

Figure 9-17. Square shoulders.

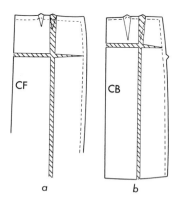

Figure 9-18. Larger abdomen and rear hip.   a   b

ABDOMEN AND REAR HIP It is easily seen that the principles and techniques in these situations are the same as those that applied to the larger bust and wing, or round shoulder, problems (Fig. 9-18). An extra dart in *a* keeps the finished waistline unchanged in length, and the grainline at center front straight.

In case the design already has two darts, a third one can be added, or slashes can be made through both darts, dividing the added width between them, *b*. With the shorter front darts, try ease and thin gathers along with the darts. The same alteration in the back would provide for a larger derrière.

SIDE HIP A more rounding curve at the side hip will require extra width and length, which can be added to the pattern edge if the amount needed is not extreme (see Figs. 9-10, *d* and 10-26). Draw a new line in the pattern margin or add extra paper. Starting at the position of greatest curve, add the amount needed and draw a line parallel to the edge of the pattern from this point to the lower edge of the skirt. Draw a new line from the hip point to the waistline, keeping it parallel or curving toward the original line to narrow the distance, possibly a maximum of $\frac{1}{4}$ inch, *b*. The waistline of the pattern may be used to mark the higher line at the side, gradually returning to the original line at the center of the patterns (apply the same change to CF and CB). Ease any extra length at the waistline between the last dart and the side seam; adjust it to the waistline stay.

ONE LARGER HIP Where only one hip is larger, apply the correction to one side only. Re-mark the dart on the side for the larger hip to keep the darts balanced on each side of the center front and even in length (see Fig. 10-26).

LARGER UPPER ARM Alterations for a larger upper arm may require a greater number of darts or more easing along the elbow position, and easing in the sleeve cap (Fig. 9-19). Because of this extra length in the cap, fabrics that can be eased readily are the most successful choices.

Altering Other Patterns

Application to other styles of patterns of the techniques used for larger body curves are presented in Figures 9-20, 9-21, and 9-22.

SMALLER BODY CURVES OR HOLLOWS

SMALL BUST AND SWAY BACK Note the similarities to the changes that were made for larger curves. They are the same, except that length and width have been subtracted rather than added (Fig. 9-23).

In *a*, the pattern has been slashed through the waistline dart and lapped to remove the width across the bust. This narrows the lower dart also, as it should, for a smaller curve. The amount of reduction in the underarm dart is removed at the lower edge.

The sway-back alteration—a hollow centered around the back waistline—requires shortening of both the bodice and skirt, *b*. Patterns can be slashed and lapped, or a dart can be used to remove the length at the center back with no change at the side seam. Transitional lines are drawn to straighten CB lines on both pieces, from upper to lower edges, and on the darts that were crossed by slashes, *b* and inset *c*.

HOLLOW CHEST In Figure 9-24, front and sleeve will require altering for a hollow chest, where the upper arm is thin and small, *a*. If the garment fits correctly at the armhole, the tuck or lapped edges will reduce to zero at the armhole seam, and no change will be required in the sleeve. Where the garment is too large around the neck, *b*, the pattern is slashed from the neckline to the point of the bust and

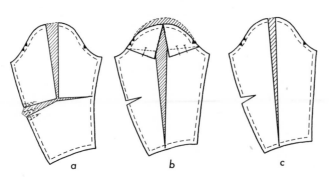

a *b* *c* **Figure 9-19.** Larger upper arm.

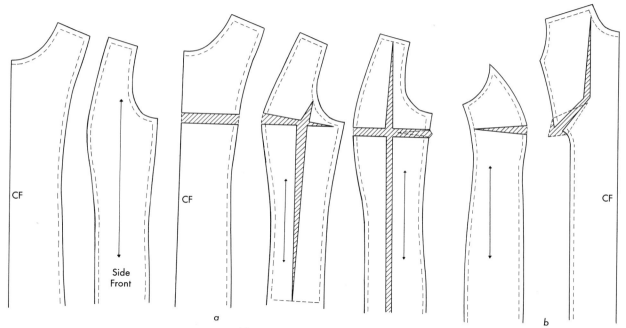

Figure 9-20. Princess pattern.

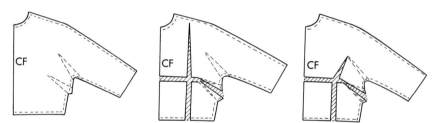

Figure 9-21. Kimono-sleeve pattern.

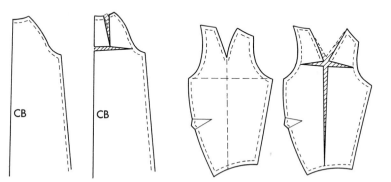

Figure 9-22. Raglan-sleeve pattern.

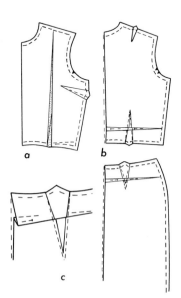

Figure 9-23. Small bust and sway back.

205

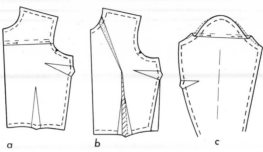

Figure 9-24. Hollow chest.

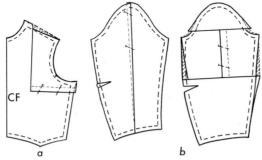

Figure 9-25. Sloping shoulders and thin arm.

through the waistline dart. Lap the edges at the neckline. This widens the dart. Unless this extra fullness is needed for a larger bust curve, reduce the lower dart to its original width, moving the dart line nearest the side seam. Then, remove the excess width at the side seam.

SLOPING SHOULDERS The alteration for sloping shoulders (Fig. 9-25), requires identical changes in back and front, with no change in the sleeve pattern. Because the underarm seam has been shortened, it might be necessary in some cases to add extra length in the lower part of the pattern. In situations where the seam is deepened at its armhole end, the sleeve cap would require shortening (Fig. 9-25, *b*) to make it fit the new armhole.

Testing and Altering the Pants Pattern

The basic techniques for altering pants patterns are the same as for other garments—changing length and width, and altering for larger or smaller body curves. Alterations in width may be more easily made than in skirts since there are four seams on which to make changes through waist and hips, whereas there are only two in some skirt designs.

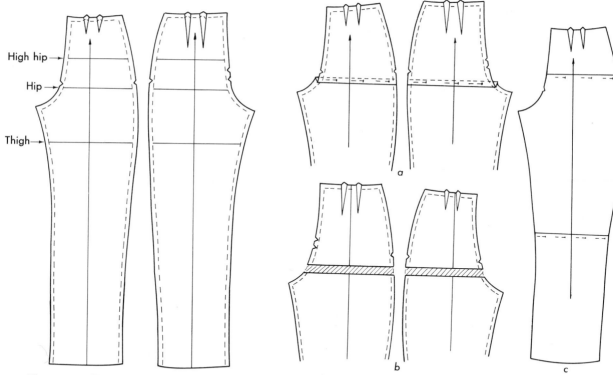

Figure 9-26. Pants—testing and altering.

Figure 9-27. Changing length.

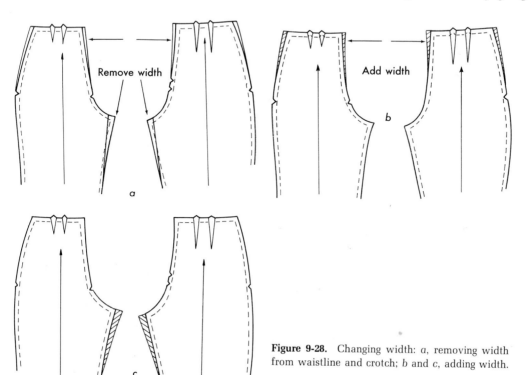

Figure 9-28. Changing width: *a*, removing width from waistline and crotch; *b* and *c*, adding width.

207

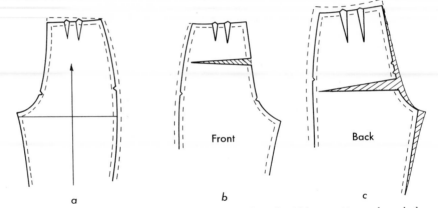

Figure 9-29. Altering for curves: *a*, providing length and width at pattern edges; *b*, larger abdomen; *c*, larger derrière.

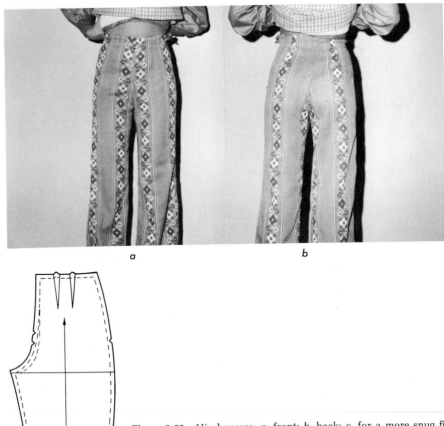

Figure 9-30. Hip-huggers: *a*, front; *b*, back; *c*, for a more snug fit in the seat, narrow the pattern in this area.

Compare your measurements with the pattern measurements at points where you measured (Fig. 9-26).

1. For average figure—length of crotch measured at side of body compared with side seam of pattern.
   Tuck, or cut and spread pattern to allow ¾ to 1 inch extra ease for standing and sitting comfort.
2. For large abdomen or derrière—length of your crotch measurement compared with the length of the crotch seam of pattern; measure the pattern with the tape line standing on its edge along the curved crotch seams at CF and CB.
   Tuck, or cut and spread pattern to allow 3 inches of extra ease. Add to the length of front or back crotch seams (or both, depending on the location of body curve), adding width at the center seam and tapering to nothing at the side seamline.
3. Your measurement at upper leg, compared with the combined width of front and back patterns at this same distance below crotch.
   Alter, if necessary, to provide 2½ inches of ease in width.
4. Your instep measurement compared with the width of pants leg at lower edge.
   Alter, if necessary, to provide 1 inch of extra width.
5. Your measurement at side of body compared with length of the pattern side seam.
   Check to see that there is sufficient extra length for the hem allowance.

In case your measurements vary greatly from the average, or if you have had difficulty in fitting trouser-type garments, it will be to your advantage to cut and fit a muslin test garment before cutting your garment.

Note the striking similarities between the alteration procedures for pants, as compared with other garments (Figs. 9-27, 9-28, and 9-29).

For hip-huggers, the fit is made more snug through the seat by deepening the curve in the center back seam (Fig. 9-30).

Introduction to Generalizations

The term generalization is used here to designate a general conclusion that has been reached through the study of a group of facts, ideas, and experiences leading to clarified concepts in dressmaking procedures. Some examples are assembled here in a cause-and-effect arrangement in order to emphasize relationships and to provide a simply stated conclusion which may be applied to the solving of new problems.

These examples of generalizations in clothing construction involve standards (satisfying results), which have been described in the left column, and present a goal or objective. In the right column, the cause, techniques, or procedures have been stated, by which the desired objective or result may be obtained.

These lists, provided at the ends of a number of the following chapters, are not intended as an all-inclusive body of generalizations, but present examples of some of the more basic ones. They are presented as a challenge to you to restate in your own words, and to expand the list in the light of your experiences and understanding. You may find exceptions; if not now, surely in the future as you meet new problems you will see the necessity of altering current-day procedures and developing flexibility in both thinking and communicating with others. Through reasoning, one's results may be forecast, one's failures explained. Successes may come through the ability to recognize the relationship between the old and the new.

Generalizations

Directions: Read each generalization across both columns, and note the relationships as pointed out in the headings.

EFFECT SOUGHT OR REASON WHY	THE CAUSE OR WHAT TO DO
1. To save time, effort, and expense in alteration,	select a pattern or ready-to-wear garment in a size that is correct in the shoulder and chest area.
2. To avoid damaging pattern or fabric before the lines are approved, when testing patterns or pinning for the first fitting,	do not turn under corners and curves, but lap and pin one section over the other, seamline on seamline (exception: slash the seam allowance of a high neckline).
3. To prevent the loss of necessary markings for construction and decorative details,	avoid disturbing locations of notches and construction guidelines.
4. To alter length or width where designer's lines are simple and fairly straight,	use a gauge to add on or cut off exact amounts from pattern edges.
5. To alter a pattern for length or width without changing the designer's lines, to keep pattern in proportion and balance, and edges fitting together,	make changes a. within the pattern: b. between points of articulation: c. perpendicular to lengthwise grain to change length and parallel to lengthwise grain to change width: d. on corresponding edges.
6. To make changes less obvious,	make small alterations in several places rather than make all the change in one or two places.
7. To change the length of a pattern, when the lower edge is quite uneven,	alter above that edge.
8. To change the length of a pattern at a hemline where the exact designer's line is relatively unimportant,	add to or cut off at the lower edge, if this technique is simpler.

EFFECT SOUGHT OR REASON WHY	THE CAUSE OR WHAT TO DO
9. To add width at one side of a pattern but not at the other,	keep the pattern flat by slashing to (but not through) the opposite seamline.
10. To confine the spread to a small area of a pattern,	slash only as far as needed, turn at right angles, and cut to the nearest silhouette seamline or corner.
11. When the lower edge of a basic-type pattern or test garment rises above or falls below a horizontal level, because of a larger body curve or hollow directly above,	alter the pattern, usually, for width and length at, or near, the curve or hollow.
12. To provide extra length and width in altering a pattern to cover a curve,	a. slash through the darts that point to the curve, if possible; b. make two slashes, one crosswise and one lengthwise, over the fullest part of the curve. The added space at the seamline is absorbed in darts or other forms of ease.
13. To remove excess length and width over a hollow,	fold darts or pleats in the pattern, or slash and lap the pattern over the hollow.

Fitting Patterns or Garments

A well-fitted garment adjusts naturally to the movements of the wearer, is comfortable, and presents a pleasing appearance in harmony with the figure.

Suggestions on fitting apply equally to fitting the pattern, the test garment, ready-to-wear, and the wide variety of garments of varying design made by the home sewer.

Five Clues to a Good Fit

Familiarity with the factors involved in fitting enables one to recognize well-fitted garments. There are five factors:

213

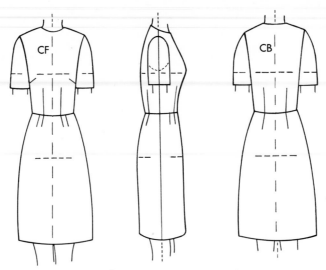

Figure 10-1. A well-fitted basic dress.

1. **Grain.** Lengthwise and crosswise yarns or threads in a woven fabric.
2. **Set.** Garment fits smoothly on the body, is free of wrinkles.
3. **Line.** Seamlines and the edges of the garment.
4. **Balance.** Garment sets evenly and hangs so that it extends the same distance from the body on one side as on the opposite side.
5. **Ease.** Sufficient looseness to make garment appear to be the right size and comfortable.

These five clues are interrelated. If the grain is not true, the garment may be off-balance, undesirable wrinkles appear, seamlines do not appear straight, and there is drawing or pulling at other points. Sometimes one clue is more apparent than the others; if you recognize only one and make the correction, all of the other undesirable characteristics may disappear. In a simple dress, not purposely cut on a bias or in some unusual style, it is easy to identify the evidences of good fit. Observe these evidences in Figure 10-1.

GRAIN

The lengthwise grain is perpendicular to the floor at the CF and CB, unless off-grain seams are present there. The crosswise yarns are parallel to the floor at the CF and CB on the bust- and hiplines. As the grain enters bias seams, or where it is near darts, its direction does not remain parallel to the floor (Fig. 10-2). The lengthwise grain in this cape hangs straight and stays close to the figure along the CF and to either side for a few inches (approximately in the space equal to the distance between the points of the breasts). The crosswise grain is approximately in a horizontal position in this area. The bias direction of the fabric sags, ripples, and swings away from the body. The grain on the right half of the garment should match that on the left half, except in the case of asymmetric draping. If the crosswise grain curves up or down where it should be parallel with the floor, it is *because of a larger curve or hollow on the body directly above the curve.* If you do not correct the grainline, wrinkles, sagging, or swinging away from the body elsewhere will result.

Sometimes the grainline is off because of failure to cut carefully.

SET

A well-fitted garment sets smoothly, without undesirable wrinkles. Graceful folds created by gathers or other design features are not to be confused with wrinkles—slanting triangles—which form where the garment is strained over some curve.

Creases due to poor pressing, and folds that are obviously due to posture or motion detract from the smooth appearance that is one of the characteristics of a well-fitted garment. These features are not to be mistaken as indicators of the need for fitting, unless they are caused by poor posture and no improvement can be made.

LINE

The basic *silhouette* seamlines—shoulder and side seams—follow the general silhouette of the body, outlining its shape. The shoulder seam is at the top of the shoulder. (It is wise to locate it ½ inch toward the back for a round-shouldered person.) The side seam appears continuous from the tip of the ear to the ankle, perpendicular to the floor and the circumference lines, and about halfway between the front and back of the figure when viewed from the side. The CF and CB of the garment coincide with the corresponding positions on the body.

Figure 10-2. Study the behavior of the grain. As it approaches the bias side seams, note the great amount of sagging. (Courtesy of The Wool Bureau, Inc.)

The *circumference* seamlines—neckline, armholes, and waistline—are smooth curves that follow the natural curves around the body. The neckline rises slightly in the back. The armhole is oval—neither round nor pointed—and does not bind or sag. It does not curve over too far into the back or front, or shoulder of the blouse, nor does it extend too far away from the natural joint out onto the arm. The waistline is parallel with the floor, or a slight bit lower in the back. Hemlines are true and parallel with the floor.

Design lines within the silhouette, such as pleats, darts, and seams, are graceful, direct, and smooth.

BALANCE

A symmetrical design hangs at equal distances from the body from right to left, and from front to back (except where a back fullness or flow of line is a part of the style). The neckline fits the neck snugly at all points. If the shoulder seam bulges more (or less) at the neck than it does at the armhole, it is out of balance.

EASE

The garment seems to be the right size—neither too loose nor too tight. It has enough ease for comfort, but not so much that drooping and sagging occur. Some of the evidences of improper amounts of ease are a shoulder seam that is too long; tightness and drawing across the sleeve cap; bagginess under the arms; waistline too high, tightness over the bust; narrowness across the shoulders; and cupping under the seat. The waistline seam should be as snug as the belt worn over it.

If a part of the garment is too loose, the adjoining section may feel too tight in proportion; sometimes it is better to tighten up the full section than loosen the (apparently) tight section. Experiment by pinning tucks until a comfortable proportion exists. Snug bathing suits and the tight styles of the 1880s can be as comfortable as looser styles because the snugness is balanced, and the seams are placed so that the garment follows body movements.

Ease is the difference between body measurements and the measurements of the garment at a given point as provided by the designer. The amounts of ease to allow when fitting should be adapted to the current fashion, style of the garment, your activity, your fabric, and your build.

Minimum amounts of ease vary somewhat with the design and are not to be followed literally, but they are helpful guides; they do not include style fullness such as unpressed pleats or shirring. Some suggested amounts were included in Table 6-3, p. 123.

General Suggestions for Fitting

In Chapter 16, you will find complete details regarding *when* to fit a garment and the preparations to be made for each of three fittings. In this chapter we will be concerned with *how* to fit.

FITTING A PATTERN

Suggestions for preparing a pattern for fitting have been given on p. 191.

FITTING A GARMENT

Pin or baste seams, as you consider advisable. You might expect a more accurate test with seams basted.

FITTING PROCEDURES

1. Have the whole garment ready. A skirt should be pinned to the bodice or band at the waistline before fitting to keep it located correctly and to avoid stretching; pins should be placed parallel to and on the seamline, because this enables the garment to lie smoothly over the body.
2. Wear the type of shoes and undergarments to be worn with the garment. Be careful not to stretch it. Adjust plackets and other openings, CF on CF and CB on CB. Have shoulder pads in place if they are in fashion. Have buttons, belts, and other accessories ready.
3. Fitting is done *right side out* so that the garment will be fitted to allow space for seam thicknesses underneath and give a better idea of its eventual appearance.
4. Before accepting a fitting as satisfactory, bend your arms, sit, and walk to be sure that the grainlines, seamlines, and hems return to their desired position without obvious adjusting.
5. Fit both sides to be sure that the correct size is maintained. Even though your right side is not the same shape as your left, try to make the two sides alike, if possible. If the differences are unusual, however, fit and finish the two halves independently.
6. *Do not overfit.* Do not find too many faults. Attend to the most obvious problems; the others probably will disappear.
7. To establish a new line, work on the right half only, use a tape to guide you, and place the pins parallel to and on the line being formed. This is safer than using a pencil or cutting on the figure. After removing the garment, place the right and left halves together for trimming so that both halves will be alike. It may be desirable to alter and replace the pattern for cutting.
8. In conducting a fitting, make a simple mental note, or write in the column provided on your plan-of-work sheet (p. 310), about lengthening or shortening a dart, raising or lowering its point, and releasing the side seams $\frac{1}{8}$ inch. If the garment is a great deal too tight, you might rip a short distance at the place most obviously tight to determine the amount of total let-out needed. Turn to the wrong side, and use your mathematics in deciding where to rebaste seams.

   If only a slight change is needed, or the fitting is more complicated, rip a small amount at the place to be changed and repin as a lapped seam, placing the pins at right angles to the overlap. Work first on the right and then on the left. Rebaste on the wrong side, or you may find it helpful to slip-baste the lapped seam on the right side (See slip stitch, pp. 289 and 462).

Rely on darts and eased-in areas instead of attempting to make all corrections on basic seams.

Because both width and length are required to cover a larger curve, letting out seams is not always enough; the area over the curve may need shifting up or down to provide length over the area; hence, ripping the entire seam may be required.

9. In *fitting*, note closely ease and wrinkles leading to points of strain. Note the balance and the amount of rise or fall crosswise in the grain, if this is visible, and in the lower line of a blouse, skirt, or sleeves to indicate the amount of adjusting needed above the bulge or hollow causing the trouble; remove the garment and rebaste the seam directly above the curved line in the amount indicated.

   It often helps to compare the measurements of your new dress with those of a dress that fits you satisfactorily.

10. What responsibilities do you, your partner, and the teacher have in your fittings? You have your garment assembled, with needed accessories or tools. Your partner pins your placket. She helps you recognize any problems and decide on possible causes and remedies. Then the instructor is consulted as to the validity of your analysis. Managing your fitting in this way develops thinking ability, broadens and deepens the experiences of both you and your partner as you help each other with fitting problems, and provides you and your instructor with a better basis for evaluating your progress.

11. A *dress form* adjusted and padded to your proportions and posture would afford an excellent opportunity for you to make small alterations (by pin-fitting) and to experiment in applying the basic methods presented in this chapter.

12. *Style* through fitting comes by being fashion-conscious and aware of the effect of short darts versus long ones; of carefully graduated curved darts versus ruler-straight darts, where this shape applies; soft ease versus too-snug seams in bodice, skirt, and sleeves; and direct versus wavering lines of stitching. Although your pattern was correctly altered, made in one texture it might not need changing; in another fabric many little changes may be indicated.

Blousing is created (in bodice or sleeve) by extra width or extra length, or a little of each. Thus, if one has a discriminating eye for style (shape) as well as for fashion, one needs patience for several "correction fittings" (p. 309). Ripping and repinning in the fitting room are almost a necessity.

Slavish following of seams and hems in the pattern may not yield the ultimate in satisfaction. Study fashion models to become more conscious of recent changes in silhouettes. How full are skirts, sleeves, and greatcoats? What lengths are skirts and jackets?

Solving a Fitting Problem

Judging the fit of your garment is similar to judging the fit of your pattern.

1. Recognize evidence of poor fit.
   a. Off-grain condition.
   b. Wrinkles.
   c. Lines out of place.
   d. Off-balance condition.
   e. Tightness or looseness.
2. Determine cause—body versus pattern proportions.
3. Decide on remedy.
4. Correct by neatest, simplest method.
5. Understand cause-and-effect relationship with a resulting generalization or principle to help you alter patterns and ready-mades in the future.
6. Understand how the pattern might have been altered to eliminate the need for fitting.

Examples of fitting problems and suggestions for possible solutions follow.

Analysis of Problem (Fig. 10-3)

EVIDENCES OF POOR FIT Set—horizontal folds or wrinkles are lying between the waistline and hipline, in both back and front.

CAUSE OF DIFFICULTY Large hips—skirt is too tight around hips, there is not enough ease here. Its narrowness prevents its slipping far enough down to take its position on the larger circumference at hip level and fit smoothly over the hips, a.

CORRECTION IN FITTING

1. Let out vertical seams in skirt (and bodice if tight at waistline), b.
2. If side seam flares slightly and hem is wide enough, the fit can be corrected by taking a deeper waistline seam to lift skirt and bring a larger circumference measurement over the full hips, c.

(If this garment were a ready-made, the problem of altering would involve the same question: Is there enough width in seam allowances and hem to make the necessary adjustments? Another question to be decided in considering such an alteration in a garment with side placket is this: Are you willing to reset the zipper? In a dress, you might push the zipper higher into the bodice without ripping the skirt.)

CORRECTION OF PATTERN Add width to silhouette seams in cutting; increase darts or ease in the excess at waistline, d. See p. 199 for other possibilities.

Analysis of Problem (Fig. 10-4)

EVIDENCES OF POOR FIT Set—crosswise folds, wrinkles, appear between waistline and hipline in the back only, a.

CAUSE OF DIFFICULTY Sway back—there is more length in garment than is needed to cover this hollow of the body. If the rear hip has enough prominence,

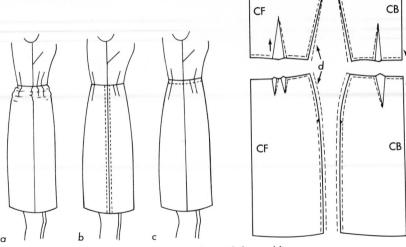

Figure 10-3. Analysis of the problem.

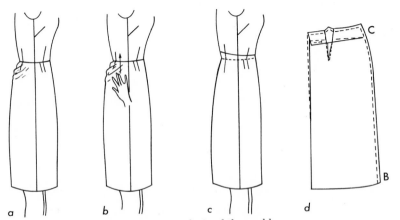

Figure 10-4. Analysis of the problem.

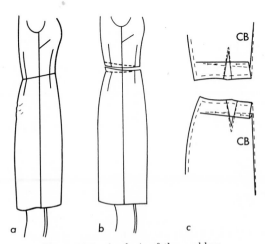

Figure 10-5. Analysis of the problem.

the side seam may hang in the correct position, with folds or wrinkles forming above the rear hip, *a*.

CORRECTION IN FITTING   Moving the hand across a wrinkle—at right angles to it—will smooth and push out the excess fabric width (at the wide end of the wrinkle) and indicate where to make a deeper seam, *b*. In this case, the waistline seam of the skirt will require deepening, *c*; darts, also, may need widening, to leave the length of the back waistline unchanged, or the excess length in waistline may be eased to make the hollow less conspicuous.

CORRECTION OF PATTERN   Fold a dart across the skirt back between waist- and hiplines to end at side seam—not to extend into the seam allowance (you can slash through seam allowance to the point of dart to flatten the pattern) *d*; correct CB to keep grainline straight; darts will require correction. It is unnecessary to take time to draw these lines on the pattern, since this can be taken care of in transferring the lines to the fabric. Trace the lines in their new locations. This alteration preserves the designer's line at the waistline, so that skirt will fit bodice, as planned.

ANALYSIS OF PROBLEM (FIG. 10-5)
EVIDENCES OF POOR FIT   Line—waistline drops below normal waist across the back; skirt sags at hemline on back; side seam hangs toward the front, *a*.
Balance—skirt is unbalanced at hem; it hangs nearer to the body at the back than at the front.

CAUSE OF DIFFICULTY   Sway back and/or flat rear hip—flat shoulder blades (overerect figure) might also be partly responsible for this difficulty.
As the back waistline is not in a normal position on the body, it is likely that the figure has a flatter shoulder-blade area than normal, causing the seam to sag as it crosses the hollow section of the back.

CORRECTION IN FITTING   The back waistline sags because of a hollow above the waistline and/or flat shoulder blades. There is more length than needed at center back. A hollow back, below the waistline and/or a flat rear hip, permits the skirt to sag in back, affecting the position of the side seam and the balance.
As in Figure 10-4, take a deeper seam across the back waistline, pushing the excess length out of the skirt. As the back bodice is too long, the same treatment will be needed to correct it, *b*. The darts will require deepening to make waistline seam correct in length, or ease it, as suggested on pp. 200 and 203.

CORRECTION OF PATTERN   Note the altered patterns, *c*. Review the correction for this case: Length has been removed from the back in both skirt and bodice—this side of the body was flatter or smaller.
Try to state the condition recognized in the preceding paragraph in general terms that might apply to other cases also. Did your statement embody the following idea?
To correct the balance, take a deeper seam above the side where the garment

hugs the figure, or let out the seam above the side where it swings away from the figure.

ANALYSIS OF PROBLEM (FIG. 10-6)

EVIDENCES OF POOR FIT   Set—wrinkles point to rear hip, *a*.

Line—side seam swings to back; skirt hikes at back hemline.

Balance—skirt is unbalanced at lower edge, hanging closer to body in front than in back.

CAUSE OF DIFFICULTY   Larger rear hip—large derrière.

CORRECTION IN FITTING

1. The technique shown in *b* might prove satisfactory in very mild cases, but this technique only partially corrects the difficulty.

2. If waistline is too large to be eased successfully after letting out side seams, deepen the dart in *a*, or add another dart, as in *c*.

3. Rip side seam, lift back above lower edge of front, let out seam on back, and ease back, in line with the fullest part of the hip, *c*. To shrink fullness out, press—pushing the side of iron toward seam, over the fullness. Cut off front skirt at hemline, to even line.

CORRECTION OF PATTERN   To alter pattern for a larger curve, *d*, slash in both directions, with slashes intersecting at the point of the wrinkles—the fullest part of the bulge. The slash bisects the dart and increases its size (divide into two darts, if one seems too large or add a new one).

ANALYSIS OF PROBLEM (FIG. 10-7)

EVIDENCES OF POOR FIT   Line—side seam swings toward front, *a*.

Balance—skirt is unbalanced at the hem—it hangs nearer to the body at the back than at the front.

CAUSE OF DIFFICULTY   Thick thigh—problem not sufficiently serious to show wrinkles.

CORRECTION IN FITTING   There are two alternatives:

1. If the difficulty is not great, the fit can be corrected by lifting the skirt at back waistline, with the greatest deepening of seam at the CB, decreasing in width gradually around to front darts, probably.

2. If the procedure preceding is not sufficient to correct the difficulty, then the side seam must be ripped and the correction made as in *b*. Pin-fit this seam to save time in determining the amount of change needed to permit the side seam to fall back into its correct position. Distribute the extra length of the front evenly along the rebasted line, or concentrate it beside any apparent bulge, such as the hip bone or thick thigh bulge.

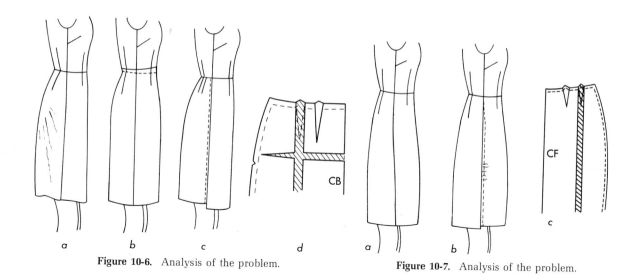

Figure 10-6. Analysis of the problem.

Figure 10-7. Analysis of the problem.

CORRECTION OF PATTERN Observe *c*.

ANALYSIS OF PROBLEM (FIG. 10-8)

EVIDENCES OF POOR FIT Grain—grainline across the chest is not parallel to floor—it is lower toward the sides of figure, *a*.

Set—wrinkles point toward the neckline end of shoulder seam.

CAUSE OF DIFFICULTY Sloping shoulders, or thick neck.

CORRECTION IN FITTING

1. Take deeper seams at armhole ends of shoulder seams, to raise the grainline into the correct position, *b*.

2. Let out the neckline ends of shoulder seams and the neckline seam to permit grainline across center to fall into the correct position, *c*.

3. In case a sleeve is to be used in this garment, thin shoulder pads to fill the hollow between the figure and the garment may be an advantage in that no pattern alteration is required and the season's fashion-right shoulder slope is preserved.

CORRECTION OF PATTERN An adjustment will be made on the back also; check pattern length to determine whether additional length will be needed at lower end of side seam, *d*.

ARRIVAL AT A CONCLUSION What did you learn from this problem that might be of help when correcting the grainline? Try to state what was done in terms so general that the application can be made to other cases. Did your statement involve the thought expressed in the following one?

223

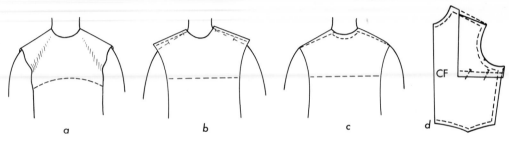

Figure 10-8. Analysis of the problem.

 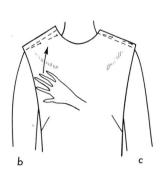 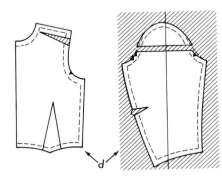

Figure 10-9. Analysis of the problem.

To correct the crosswise grainline, lift the sagging part by taking a deeper seam above it, or lower the rising part by letting out the seam above it.

ANALYSIS OF PROBLEM (FIG. 10-9)

EVIDENCES OF POOR FIT   Wrinkles—point to the armhole end of the shoulder seam.

Balance—garment stands away from the body at neck ends of shoulder seams and hugs it at the arm ends.

Ease—garment obviously is tight at armhole ends of shoulder seams, lacking sufficient ease here.

CAUSE OF DIFFICULTY   Square shoulders.

CORRECTION IN FITTING   The garment is tight at the arm end of the shoulder seam. This tightness can be released by letting out this end of the shoulder seam, c—in case there is adequate seam allowance. This will permit the neck end of the seam to drop into place and the wrinkle will disappear.

In case the shoulder seam is not wide enough to provide the needed ease, you have already learned another technique for removing a wrinkle: visualize a line across the wrinkle, at right angles to it, b; this line points to a seam that can be deepened to smooth out the wrinkle—the neck end of shoulder seam and the neckline seam.

CORRECTION OF PATTERN Pattern alteration, *d*, would have corrected the fit.

225

Fitting Patterns or Garments

ARRIVAL AT A CONCLUSION Review the correction for this case: arm ends of shoulder seams were let out—made less deep; neck ends of shoulder seams and neckline seam were taken up—made deeper.

Try to state the procedure described in the preceding paragraph in terms that would apply to other cases also. Did your statement embody the following idea?

To remove a wrinkle, let out the seam or seams near the point of the wrinkle or take a deeper seam on a construction line at right angles to the wrinkle.

ANALYSIS OF PROBLEM (FIG. 10-10)

EVIDENCES OF POOR FIT Grainline—rises above the curve of the bust, *a*.

Set—diagonal wrinkles point to the bust. Note the armhole bulge—especially undesirable in a sleeveless garment.

Line—the side seam slants toward the front; lower edge of bodice rises above the waistline in front.

Balance—the lower edge is off-balance, projecting away from the body in front and hugging it at the back.

Ease—garment appears tight over the bust. (This would be more evident in the fabric.)

CAUSE OF THE DIFFICULTY Larger bust.

CORRECTION IN FITTING General rules were stated for Figures 10-8 and 10-9 that might be useful in correcting grainlines and removing wrinkles. Test them on this problem.

1. To correct the grainline, let out the seam above the area where the grainline rises; use of this rule in *c*, permits the grainline to drop into a straight position, in case this added length is sufficient; if not enough, you may also need to deepen the seam above the area where the grainline drops—the arm ends.

2. To remove a wrinkle, take a deeper seam in a construction line at right angles to the wrinkle; smooth the wrinkle out by pushing it into a dart or seam—in this case the underarm dart. If there is no underarm dart, make one to lift the side seam level with CF at the waistline. Let out the side seams to give as much width as possible, increasing width of the front darts at waistline. Shorten all darts pointing toward the bust, to give width over the bulging figure.

To compare altered pattern, *d*, with fitted front: sizes of darts were increased, in each case; length was added over the bust in each case, although the amount that can be added in fitting is limited to what can be taken from seams.

CORRECTION OF PATTERN Altered pattern, *d*.

ANALYSIS OF PROBLEM (FIG. 10-11)

EVIDENCES OF POOR FIT Ease—there is too much width across the shoulder and chest, causing garment to drop off the end of shoulder, *a*.

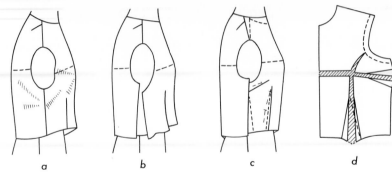

Figure 10-10. Analysis of the problem.

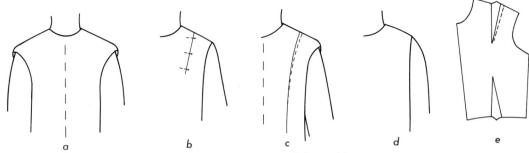

Figure 10-11. Analysis of the problem.

CAUSE OF DIFFICULTY   Narrow shoulders and chest.

CORRECTION IN FITTING   Try to find some way to narrow this garment without deepening the armhole seam near the top of the shoulder, if possible—deepen the shoulder darts, add new shoulder darts, or deepen any seams that enter the shoulder seam, c. For a professional appearance, it is important to retain the bias extension (Fig. 9-14a). If the armhole seam is stitched on a straight, vertical grainline here, d, the garment has a pinched-in appearance. Also, width has been removed on the side section rather than from the front panel section of this princess-line dress.

CORRECTION OF PATTERN   This alteration (Fig. 10-11, e) leaves the bias extension and does not disturb the panel width between the shoulder darts.

The disadvantage in using a pattern that is not correct in width through the shoulders is illustrated here. It is more satisfactory, and as easy, to alter for a larger bust and avoid complications involved in narrowing the shoulders.

Sleeve Problems

STANDARDS FOR A WELL-FITTED SLEEVE
Standards for a well-fitted, plain sleeve (Fig. 10-12) are as follows:

1. It does not slip off the shoulder too far for comfort or style.
2. The curve of the armhole is smooth and gradual.
3. The crosswise grain is parallel with the floor above the elbow.
4. The lengthwise grain hangs straight from the end of the shoulder to the elbow.
5. There are no diagonal wrinkles on top or crosswise folds underneath the armpit.
6. A short sleeve is balanced: it does not poke out farther from the front of the arm than the back; it does not hug the underarm or poke out on top (unless cut with a short cap, as a shirt sleeve).
7. It appears loose enough to fit the upper arm; the eased-in fullness is evenly distributed—not puffy or puckered.
8. It is not so snug across the top that the blouse appears eased onto the sleeve.
9. A tight-fitting sleeve has a dart or eased-in fullness to provide room at the elbow.
10. A long sleeve, though more snug in the lower half, should not be too tight around the lower part.
11. The seam does not twist. Hanging straight down, it ends on the thumb side of the arm.
12. The wristline stays over the prominent wristbone when the arm is bent.

ANALYSIS OF PROBLEM (FIG. 10-13)
EVIDENCES OF POOR FIT Grainline—crosswise grainline rises in bodice below arm end of shoulder and across sleeve, a.

Set—wrinkles radiate from shoulder and upper arm, pointing toward arm end of shoulder.

Line—lower edge of sleeve is lifted higher on the outside of sleeve, as compared with the underside, next to the body.

Balance—lower edge of sleeve is unbalanced—hugs inside of arm and swings away on outside; bodice hugs arm end of shoulder and stands above body at neck end.

Ease—bodice and sleeve appear tight at arm end of shoulder.

CAUSE OF DIFFICULTY Square shoulders.

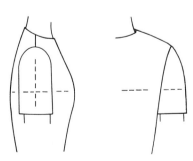

Figure 10-12. Standards for a well-fitted sleeve.

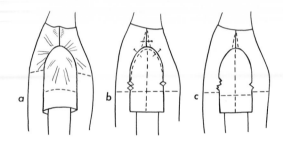

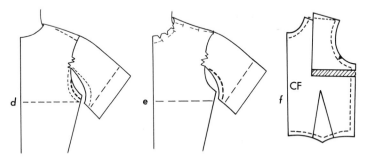

Figure 10-13. Analysis of the problem.

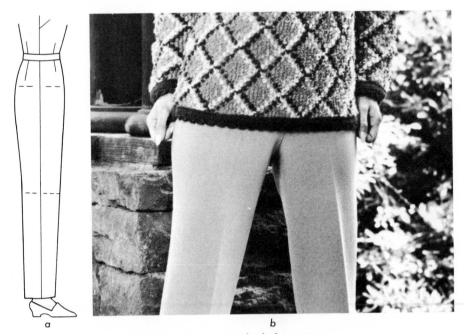

Figure 10-14. Standards for pants.

CORRECTION IN FITTING The aim is to provide length and width over knobby end of shoulder.

229

**Fitting Patterns or
Garments**

1. Release seams near the point of the wrinkles—arm end of shoulder seam and seam at top of sleeve cap—to relieve strain and wrinkles, *b*.
2. If shoulder seam is too narrow for releasing sufficiently, as in *c* and *d*, take a deeper seam at neck end and correct the neckline, *e*.
3. If the small amounts of release are insufficient to correct difficulty, additional length in armhole and sleeve cap can be provided by making a smaller seam at lower armhole, *d*, and a deeper seam at lower sleeve cap, *e*. In *c*, *d*, and *e* notches in sleeve are lifted above those in armhole.

CORRECTION OF PATTERN Altered pattern *f*.

Standards for Pants

1. The front creases, or lengthwise grainlines, and the side seams hang perpendicular to the floor (Fig. 10-14).
2. The pants fit smoothly across abdomen and seat areas.
3. There are no diagonal wrinkles—crosswise grain is kept level at hips and knees.
4. The crotch is high enough to prevent sagging of the seat, but low enough for comfort.
5. The legs are balanced and easy.
6. The waistline is at the normal location and does not glide downward in the back when the wearer is seated.

ANALYSIS OF PROBLEM (Fig. 10-15)
EVIDENCES OF POOR FIT

1. **Grainline.** The grainline rises in the front, from the abdomen area to the hemline, *a*.
2. **Set.** Wrinkles radiate from the abdomen area on a diagonal line into the back.
3. **Line.** The lower edge is lifted higher at the front than at the back.
4. **Balance.** The lower edge is unbalanced, it is closer to the ankle at the back than at the front; an unbalanced condition is also apparent in the seat area—the back hugs the figure at the base of the seat, whereas the front has excess fabric in the loose folds of the wrinkles.
5. **Ease.** The front appears tight over the "tummy," as the wrinkles are ending there—pointing to a tight area. Because the front is borrowing from the back, the latter is pulled tight against the body at the base of the seat.

CAUSE OF DIFFICULTY Larger abdomen.

CORRECTION IN FITTING Provide length and width in the front for the larger curve of the abdomen, *b*.

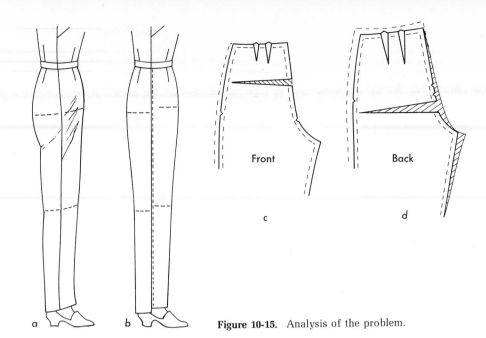

Figure 10-15. Analysis of the problem.

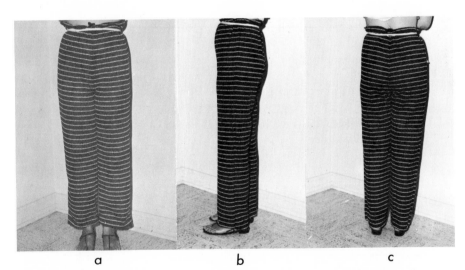

Figure 10-16. Analysis of the problem.

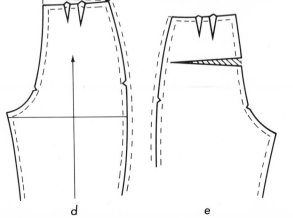

1. Rip the side seam and lift the front to straighten the crosswise grainline and remove the wrinkles; let out the side seam on the front and pin it into position, easing the excess front length in line with the abdomen. The waistline seam can be narrowed across the front, returning to the original width at the side seams.

2. Release the CF seam across the abdomen, if additional width is needed, changing only that part of the seam covering the tummy curve. To make a shallow seam in the stride curve might make the stride measurement too short.

CORRECTION OF PATTERN   Extra length over the abdomen can be added by method *c* or *d*.

ANALYSIS OF THE PROBLEM (FIG. 10-16)
EVIDENCES OF POOR FIT

1. **Grain.** Here is a situation where the grainline offers little assistance in judging fit; the grain runs parallel to the floor at the side seam, which was cut on the straight grain. As one would expect, the grainline drops at CF and CB as it approaches these slightly bias seams, but there is no standard to be used regarding the amount of drop, so this leads one to use another indicator.

2. **Set.** The garment sets smoothly across the front, *a*, but shows slight wrinkling below the back hip.

CAUSE OF DIFFICULTY   Larger abdomen and slightly wider crotch.

CORRECTION IN FITTING   Note the condition at the waistline (garment is to be finished with elastic, without a placket). Why is the fabric that extends above the waistline narrower across the front than at the sides? The answer is evident as one studies *b*. To cover a larger abdomen than the pattern was made for, extra length has been borrowed from the upper margin.

The slight folds below the rear hip, visible in both *b* and *c*, indicate the need for a little more width in the crotch. This will permit the pants to be lifted slightly higher at the CB, so that these wrinkles can be lifted out. It is well to remember that pants that hang very straight from the hipline may have a minimum of sitting room. This amount of break along the CB might not be considered objectionable.

CORRECTION OF THE PATTERN   Add length for the abdomen and add to the crotch width at the inside back leg seams (Figs. 10-15, *c* or *d*; 9-28, *c*; and 10-17).

ANALYSIS OF THE PROBLEM (FIG. 10-17)
EVIDENCES OF POOR FIT

1. **Set.** Wrinkles radiate from the crotch in the front, pointing upward, *a*, and are present below the seat, *b*. As these pants do not have a placket, the gathers at waistline are necessary.

2. **Ease.** The garment appears very strained and tight across the seat.

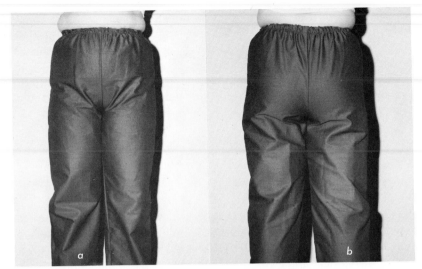

Figure 10-17. Analysis of the problem.

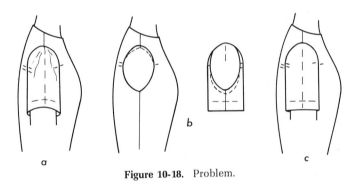

Figure 10-18. Problem.

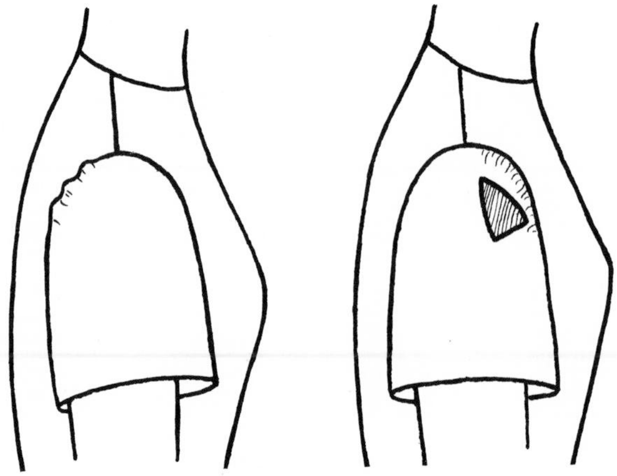

Figure 10-19. Problem.

Cause of Difficulty   Large hips and wide crotch—front to back.

233

Fitting Patterns or
Garments

Correction in Fitting   This garment was chosen in a size too small for the figure. Releasing the side seams on both front and back would probably correct the difficulty, provided there is a wide seam allowance. In case more crotch width is needed, release the inside leg seams.

Correction of the Pattern   Add width to the side seams, and crotch if necessary.

Test Your Understanding of Fitting Problems

Problem (Fig. 10-18)

1. What are the indications of poor fit in *a*?
2. What is the cause of the difficulty?
3. State a fundamental rule or generalization that might be used to remove the wrinkles.
4. Show how the technique suggested in no. 3 of the following list will apply to this case.

Suggested Answers or Solutions

1. *Wrinkles* point to top of sleeve cap, indicating lack of *ease;* lower edge of sleeve is out of *line,* with outside of sleeve at hem lifted above the edge next to the body.

2. Sleeve cap is too short; this might be owing to the design—shirt sleeves and bell sleeves are designed to fit in this manner, and blouse sleeves often are designed with shorter caps; in a blouse or dress with a normal set-in sleeve, this condition might result if sleeve is set too high on shoulder, as when bodice is too narrow across the shoulders. As there are no evidences of poor fit on the bodice, it can be assumed that the difficulty is not square shoulders.

3. To remove a wrinkle, let out a seam (or seams) near the point of the wrinkle, or take a deeper seam in a construction line that is located at right angles to the wrinkle.

4. Narrow the seam at the top of sleeve cap, *b* (and at upper armhole, if bodice appears narrow through the shoulders, *a*), and/or deepen the seam in the lower part of sleeve cap, *b*—these lines are at right angles to the wrinkle, though not quite so easily seen in the cylinder of sleeve. The hem now assumes its correct position, *c*.

Problem (Fig. 10-19)

1. Evidences of poor fit?
2. Cause?
3. The fundamental rule to be used?
4. How does No. 3 apply?

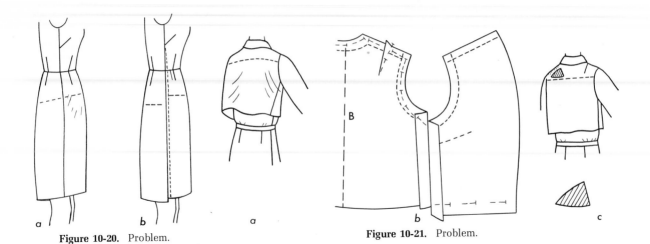

Figure 10-20. Problem.   **Figure 10-21.** Problem.

SUGGESTED ANSWERS OR SOLUTIONS

1. Sleeve off-balance, line at lower edge thrown out of position, a concentration of ease in upper back sleeve cap.

2. End of shoulder is knobby, larger at front, and flat at back.

3. To correct the balance, lift the side of garment that hugs the figure, and lower the section that swings away from the figure.

4. Rip the armhole seam (in the upper part—notches to notches) and lift the back notches on sleeve above those on the dress, shifting the sleeve around so that front notches on sleeve are below the front notches on garment, to balance the sleeve.

PROBLEM (FIG. 10-20)

1. What figure difficulty is apparent in *a*?
2. What is the relationship between *a* and *b*? Explain.

SUGGESTED ANSWERS OR SOLUTIONS

1. A large abdomen.

2. Wrinkles pointing to the abdomen indicate tightness there. A larger curve on the front of body is also indicated by the side seam, pulled out of place toward the front; the CF of skirt lifted higher than the CB at hem; and, by the lack of balance. Provision of extra length and width over the bulge would have permitted the skirt to set and hang correctly.

PROBLEM (FIG. 10-21)

Observe the fit of this ready-made garment on a prospective buyer.

1. List evidences of poor fit.
2. What causes the garment to fit as it does?

234

3. What steps would be necessary in altering this jacket?

4. Explain why the steps recommended in No. 3 might, or might not, be adequate to produce a well-fitted garment.

5. Would you recommend this as a wise purchase?

SUGGESTED ANSWERS OR SOLUTIONS

1. *Wrinkles* point to shoulder blades, indicating lack of *ease* here; side seam of jacket slants toward back.

2. The evidences of poor fit noted indicate the presence of a larger body bulge under the back of jacket—round shoulders or protruding shoulder blades.

3. Collar and sleeves would be ripped off the back and shoulder, and side seams would need to be opened. Changes might be made as indicated by the line of pins in *b*: add extra length across bulge by lifting back above front at lower armhole; mark a new armhole, letting out seams as much as possible to give added width; the greater slant from upper armhole on back to neckline provides for extra length over the bulge; extra length on shoulder line might go into a small dart or ease. Hem would require adjusting.

4. Because of the narrowness of finished neckline and shoulder seams and the shortness of the jacket, the correction would be questionable if the difficulty is very great. Its success would depend on whether the mark of the hem might be pressed out to give an invisible original hem line.

5. A time-consuming, questionable process. Would depend on individual situation.

PROBLEM (FIG. 10-22)

1. What evidences of poor fit do you see?
2. Explain their cause.
3. Correction?

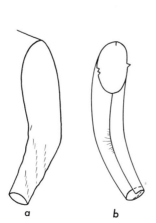

Figure 10-22. Problem.   **Figure 10-23.** Problem.

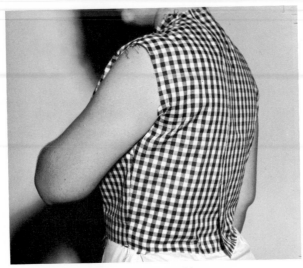

Figure 10-24. Problem.

1. Skirt is off-balance, swinging farther away from the body at front than at back. Side seam swings toward front. Front edge, at side seam, hangs nearer to floor than back edge. Back appears to be eased along side seam; front appears stretched.

2. The cause is incorrect basting of the side seam—the pattern was designed to match at edges. In failing to have lower, as well as upper, edges, matched, the side seam of front has been stretched, causing it to draw and pull toward the front. The back has been eased along this seam.

PROBLEM (FIG. 10-23)

1. What evidence of poor fit is present?
2. What is the cause?
3. How can it be corrected?

SUGGESTED ANSWERS OR SOLUTIONS:

1. The sleeve does not set smoothly—wrinkles are present, showing too much length along the front of sleeve in relation to the back.

2. There is not enough ease on the back of sleeve to provide for the curve of arm—not enough ease for the elbow. The wrinkles would become still more prominent when the elbow was bent more sharply.

3. To correct the fit, increase the size of the dart, or the amount of eased-in fullness at the elbow, on the back side of sleeve. This procedure will lift the back edge of sleeve above the front edge at the wrist, *b*.

PROBLEM (FIG. 10-24)

In what ways does this girl's figure vary from that of the model? Justify your decisions.

SUGGESTED ANSWERS OR SOLUTIONS   Did you diagnose round shoulders and a sway back as difficulties? Wrinkles pointing toward the shoulder blades indicate slight roundness here (which she was able to correct through better posture). Extra length across the back waistline results from sway or hollow back.

PROBLEM (FIG. 10-25)

1. Figures *a* and *b* show the same dress. Can you account for the differences in fit?

2. What could be done to improve the fit in *b*?

SUGGESTED ANSWERS OR SOLUTIONS   Obviously, the bust in *b* is too large for this dress, for it pulls tightly across the bust and wrinkles are pointing to this tight area.

To improve the fit, the underarm seam might be ripped and one or two darts made at the side seam to remove the extra length of fabric that is hanging in the wrinkles.

Actually, *a* and *b* show the *same girl in the same dress;* in *a* she is wearing her normal size bra, size 32 in an A cup; in *b* she wears a padded size 32 in a C cup.

For fittings, it is important to wear the undergarments you plan to wear with your garment.

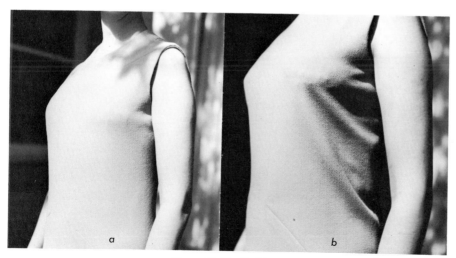

Figure 10-25.   Problem.

a   ← b →

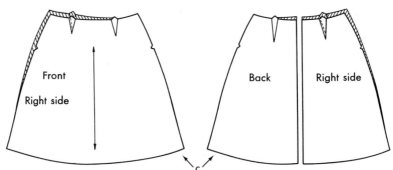

Figure 10-26. Problem.

PROBLEM (FIG. 10-26)

1. Do you see anything unusual about the fit of these skirts?
2. Explain the cause.
3. What corrections would you make?

SUGGESTED ANSWERS OR SOLUTIONS

1. Both skirts, *a* and *b*, hang farther from the body on the right side than on the left, displacing the CF or CB in each case. Why?

2. One would suspect a larger, fuller curve on the right side as being responsible for this condition.

3. Correction in fitting would be limited to the width of the side and waistline seams, if the change is to be made on the right side. A better plan would be to deepen the waistline seam around the left side; this would bring the left hem line to the level of the hemline on the right side and shift the CF and CB into their normal positions.

4. Pattern alterations are shown in *c*.

238

Figure 10-27. Problem.

PROBLEM (FIG. 10-27)
What can be done to correct a pleat that spreads too far apart at its lower edge?

SUGGESTIONS FOR CORRECTION   Rip the front band off, put the skirt on, and lift it at the CF until the pleat edges come together; pin the deepened seam to the band, and gradually reduce the waistline seam back to the normal width at the side seams.

PROBLEM (FIG. 10-28)
1. What are the evidences of poor fit?
2. How would you improve the fit?

SUGGESTED SOLUTIONS
1. There is excess width across the front, from waist to crotch line. Strain and tightness are indicated across the derrière, with the side seam pulled out of line toward the back. Much wrinkling is evident below the seat.
2. Try widening the seams on the front from crotch to waistline, on both front and side seams; let out these same seams on the back over the tight area. Release the inside leg seams to lengthen the back crotch seam; this should lift the garment at the seat and remove the wrinkles.
To provide a smoother line at the waist, darts and a placket are desirable for a person needing a great deal of width at the hip line.
These extensive fitting procedures can be eliminated by a relatively simple pattern alteration.

Figure 10-28. Problem.

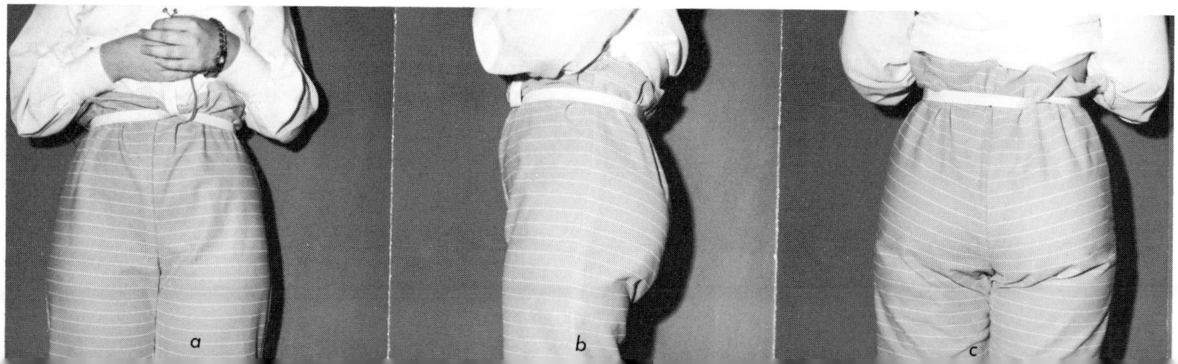

11

Fabric Preparation

What Is Grain?

The yarns in a fabric are referred to as *the grain* (Fig. 11-1). The lengthwise, or warp, yarns are parallel to the selvage and are designated as the lengthwise grain. A lengthwise stripe woven in the fabric is the lengthwise grain. A crosswise woven stripe is the crosswise grain. The direction of the yarn, therefore, determines the grain direction. By that definition, bias is not referred to as grain.

BIAS DIRECTIONS

Bias is a general term referring to any slanting line off the straight grain of the fabric. In Figure 11-1, observe the crosswise edge cut along a thread of the

241

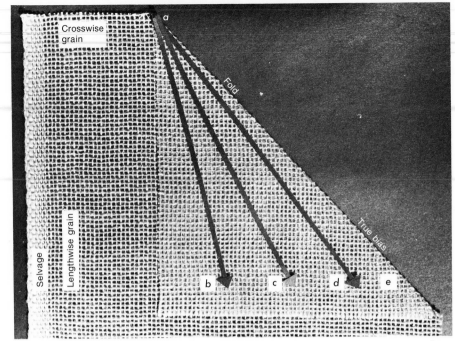

Figure 11-1. Lengthwise and crosswise grain; bias directions—varying degrees of garment bias, *a-b, a-c,* and *a-d;* true bias, *a-e.*

fabric. Observe this corner triangle; the crosswise thread at the upper end lies parallel to the selvage and lengthwise threads; also, you will note that the lengthwise thread at the lower edge of this triangle lies parallel with the crosswise threads. This foldline, lying halfway between the lengthwise and crosswise grainlines is *true bias.* All other degrees of bias are referred to as *garment bias,* illustrated in *b, c,* and *d* directions. The slanting line in the seam of a skirt is an example. Around the neckline and armhole, varying degrees of garment bias can be observed.

BIAS BEHAVIOR   In a woven fabric, the bias direction has more stretch than the grainline directions, with the true bias having the greatest amount.

LENGTHWISE GRAIN   The lengthwise grain is stronger and has less stretch than the crosswise grain. It behaves differently in other ways, also. The warp yarns tend to hang straighter. Except in unusual designs, the lengthwise direction of the cloth follows the length of the figure, hanging from neck to waist, from shoulder to elbow, and from waistline to bottom of skirt. Ruffles, pleats, and gathers fall in straight, flat lines or graceful folds—where the folds follow the lengthwise yarns. Folds following filling yarns tend to bulge in less graceful lines. Fabrics with heavy crosswise yarns or ribs (faille, ottoman) may set better if these heavy yarns hang lengthwise on the body. Designers sometimes change the grain directions to create different effects.

CROSSWISE GRAIN   The crosswise yarns are usually softer, less twisted, and have more stretch than the lengthwise yarns.

Figure 11-2. This skirt hangs unevenly because the grain condition is not the same in the two sections.

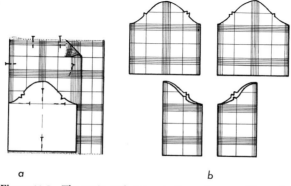

a   *b*

Figure 11-3. The grain and stripes in these sleeves will match and set smoothly.

HOW DOES GRAIN AFFECT A GARMENT?

Study the skirt shown (Fig. 11-2). Did you observe these conditions?

1. The center front of the skirt does not hang in a vertical line from waistline to hemline—it swings toward the model's right.

2. The fabric design is not the same on the two sides—the crosswise lines slant downward to a greater degree on one side.

CONCLUSIONS   The crosswise grain, obviously, was not at right angles to the lengthwise grain when the garment was cut, resulting in an uneven occurrence of crosswise stripes at the sides of the skirt, and a greater degree of bias in one side seam than in the other. Because of this, the grainline at the center front is pulled out of position.

In woven fabrics where yarns may shift somewhat, the right half must be cut to match the left, not only in shape but in grain. In fabrics where the position of yarns is fixed during the finishing process, the hang of the skirt may not be influenced to a great degree by the grain. In such situations, the design in the fabric becomes the main point for consideration.

Proper Condition of Grain

How do you know that the grainlines are in the proper relationship? A correct condition of the two grainlines can be observed in Figure 11-3, *a*, showing the selvages parallel to each other, the ends together, and both following the lines of a square table. This guarantees that the crosswise yarns are at right angles to the lengthwise yarns. These sleeves would be perfectly balanced as to pattern (plaid) in the fabric and grain, *b*.

Suppose you have purchased a solid-color fabric in which it is difficult to see the grain yarns. You place it on the table so that the selvages are lined up together along the side of the table. You note that the ends are lying exactly together along the ends of the table. Does this mean that the fabric is ready for the pattern placement? Does this indicate a right-angled condition of the grain? No, not unless the ends of the fabric are exactly on a crosswise thread. Only when the ends are on a grain yarn can you check the right-angled structure or know the *amount of change* needed, if any, to bring the fabric into this condition.

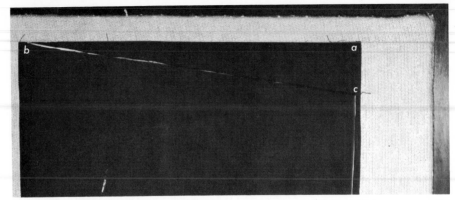

Figure 11-4. The end of this fabric, which is folded with selvages at the right, is on a crosswise thread. Why does it lie in the position *abc*?

Observe the fabric in Figure 11-4. When this was placed, folded in half on the table, the selvages were lying parallel to each other along the side of the table and the ends were together in position *ab*, as the salesperson had cut it. After the end was cut on a thread of the fabric, one corner was shorter, *c*. Why? The cloth was woven with lengthwise and crosswise yarns at right angles to each other, but in pressing and finishing, the crosswise grain was shifted out of line. This is a fault frequently observed.

It is possible, as demonstrated in Figure 11-4 to have the grain line of the pattern on the lengthwise grain of the fabric, and yet have the crosswise grain in an unsatisfactory condition.

STRAIGHTENING THE ENDS

Obviously, the first step to be taken when beginning work with a fabric is to learn whether the ends are on the grain yarn. If the fabric has been torn across the end, it is already on the grain, because it tears along a yarn thread. If the end has been cut, try to ravel the yarn all the way across. If it cannot be raveled off and it is coarse enough to be seen easily, cut exactly along a yarn. If you cannot ravel it all the way, pick up a filling yarn that appears to go all the way across and pull it gently as far as you can like a gathering thread. Do not try to pick it out with a pin or pull it out all the way, but cut as far as you can see the fine crinkly line it has made (Fig. 11-5). Then stop, crinkle the line as far as it will pull, and cut again. Continue pulling and cutting across the piece.

If it is not too wasteful and if the material is firm, you can tear across the end to straighten it. Clip through the selvage at one side; after drawing the yarn and cutting for a few inches, you might tear it the rest of the way. If the cloth

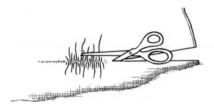

Figure 11-5. Cut ends straight with the grain. Do not pull out filling yarn all the way across—just cut along the crinkle to save time.

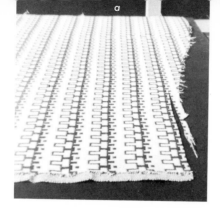
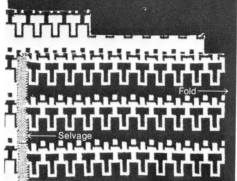
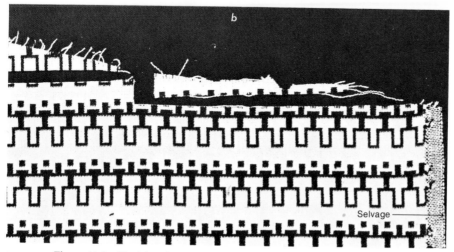

Figure 11-6. Straightening a very uneven end to avoid waste of fabric.

appears to shred or draw or split, stop tearing and pull a yarn the rest of the way. It is better to ask the salesperson when buying fabric either to tear it, to pull a yarn, or to make allowance for the waste.

MUCH UNEVENNESS   Where the end of the fabric is very uneven, it is unwise to cut away and possibly waste a wide strip of fabric (Fig. 11-6). In the woven pattern shown, the yarn can be followed easily in cutting. Start at the short corner and cut until the cutting line is possibly 1 inch deep into the fabric, *a*. Then snip off this segment by cutting on a lengthwise thread toward the uneven end. Repeat this procedure until the entire end is cut, *b*. When the fabric is folded in half, corresponding yarns must coincide, as they lie on top of and parallel with each other, *c*. This preserves more length part way across the fabric.

RESTORING THE RIGHT-ANGLED STRUCTURE

With both ends straight on the grain yarns, fold the fabric lengthwise, selvage on selvage, and check to see whether the ends and sides line up with the edges of the table. If you find the condition you observed in Figure 11-4, you know that the crosswise grainline is not at right angles to the lengthwise grain; in the finishing

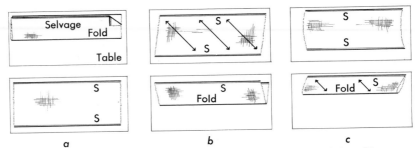

Figure 11-7. Stretch in the direction of the short corner on the true bias; left hand will be as far away from the long corner as the right hand is when placed at the short corner. Stretch the cloth *through its entire length.*

Figure 11-8. *a,* Lengthwise yarns or selvage should follow the side of the table; crosswise yarns should parallel the end of the table, whether open or folded. *b,* When torn ends do not follow the ends of the table, in a single layer or folded double, stretch entire length of cloth toward the short corner. *c,* Folded double in the factory, ends may appear as a curve; leave double to stretch.

Figure 11-9. Steps in straightening fabric: *a* and *b,* fabric as purchased; *c,* end on grain thread; *d,* stretching to restore lengthwise and crosswise grain threads to a right-angled condition; *e,* ready for pattern placement.

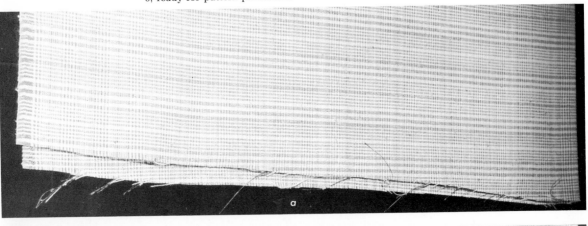

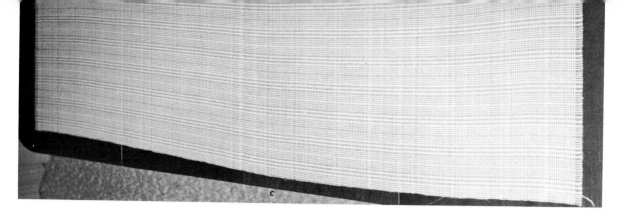

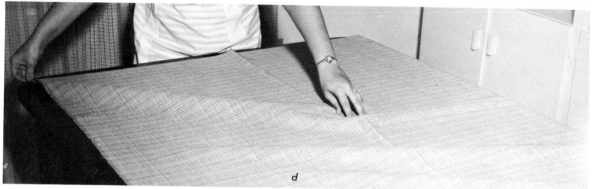

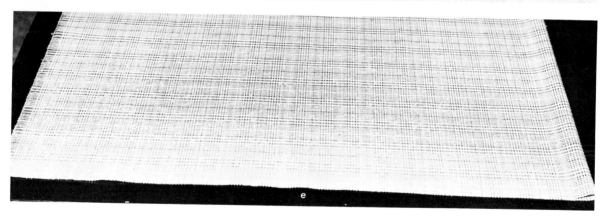

or pressing process the fabric was fed crookedly through rollers, which altered the right-angled structure. One corner appears short, and the opposite is long when spread out on the table (Figs. 11-7 and 11-8). Stretching diagonally from the short corner on the true bias throughout the length of the fabric may restore the grain to its proper condition. (If you pull from the long corner, the condition will be worsened. Why?) If you should pull too far, reverse the direction of pulling.

STEPS TO TAKE   Study Figure 11-9 and note, in order, the steps to be taken in changing fabric *a* to the right-angled structure shown in *e*—the plaid design was woven in.

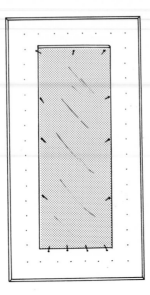

Figure 11-10. When the grain condition is difficult to correct, align the fabric and hold it in the right-angled position by pinning to a cutting board; steam-press and allow to dry before removing.

1. Unfold the fabric in order to determine which thread to follow in straightening the end, b.
2. Straighten each end by cutting along a stripe or tearing, c.
3. Determine the relationship of the lengthwise and crosswise yarns; they are obviously not at right angles to each other, because the end of the fabric is not parallel to the end of the table.
4. Restore the right-angled structure by stretching from the short corner on the true bias throughout the length of the cloth. Because the fabric is bowed at the center, and skewed or short on each corner, it should be folded and stretched on the double thickness, or handled from corner to center as shown in d. To stretch on the true bias, the distance from the end of the fabric at its center to the worker's left hand will equal the distance from the same point to the worker's right hand. The true-bias direction is the diagonal of any square section in the fabric.

STRAIGHTENING DIFFICULT FABRICS

In case the cloth is stubborn, clip the selvage at intervals or remove it. For a more flexible grain try steam pressing, followed immediately by the straightening process. Or, fold the fabric, selvage to selvage; pull the grain of the folded fabric into a right-angled position; pin it to a cutting board and steam-press it. Avoid creasing the center fold; pressing over a wet cheesecloth might be desirable, to provide additional moisture (Fig. 11-10).

Inexpensive fabrics and those treated for crease resistance are likely to be the most troublesome. Some fabrics cannot be pulled into shape by stretching or wetting them.

CREASE-RESISTANT FABRICS Many crease-resistant and glazed fabrics are set during the finishing processes, so that restoration of the right-angled structure may be an impossibility. With yarns fixed in such a manner, there is less need for straightening and less possibility that the two sides of the garment will set or hang differently, even though the fabric is off-grain. However, if the yarns are coarse enough to be visible, this defect is apparent; this is a special problem, also, in fabrics with designs such as plaids or large checks. You may not be able to match the pattern.

KNITS To straighten a knitted fabric that has rows of loops or courses visible on the wrong side, use tailor's chalk or baste along a row of loops across the width of the fabric. If the knit is in tubular form, cut along a lengthwise wale or rib near one of the folds.

When the wale is fine and difficult to see, it will be an advantage to mark it also with a line of basting. In a double-knit that appears the same on both sides, it may be helpful to mark several crosswise lines at right angles to the marked wale.

Washing knit fabrics before they are cut may be helpful in removing finishing chemicals, making the fabric easier to sew. Also, it is advisable to shrink them before cutting, in case they are to be washed. It is well to remember that knits tend to shrink more when machine-dried than when air-dried or drip-dried.

The techniques used for straightening woven fabrics can be used with knits. Fold, pin, and press the fabric into position, with the crosswise courses at right angles to the lengthwise wales.

BONDED FABRICS A desirable standard for bonded fabrics involves an on-grain woven or a straight knit, with identical conditions in the backing. The latter in tricot knit or in a loosely woven fabric, however, is not a great disadvantage if it is not off-grain to a great extent. The relationship of the two layers cannot be changed greatly because they are permanently bonded together.

MARKING EXTRA GRAINLINES AS GUIDES
Don't trust the original center crease in material as a guide for locating lengthwise grainlines. On twills, heavily napped woolens, printed crepes, jerseys, and lacy weaves, it is often confusing and time-consuming to locate the exact lengthwise or crosswise threads. Much time and trouble are saved by marking extra lines with chalk or basting them on the wrong side parallel with the selvage and parallel with the torn ends, 12 to 18 inches apart. This will be helpful also when working with plaids, crosswise stripes, or large floral patterns. Then, in intricate layouts, patterns can be correctly placed even where there is no selvage to follow.

RIGHT AND WRONG SIDES OF THE FABRIC Many fabrics come folded on the bolt wrong side out; cottons and linens generally are right side out. The identity of the right side is often in question. In case of doubt, look for imperfections, which usually are more noticeable on the wrong side. The wrong side of the selvage usually appears less finished. Smooth cotton fabrics are smoother or have less surface fuzz on the right side. On printed materials the brighter colors are on the right side; examine the selvage where the brighter side may be more easily seen—the pattern is often blurred on the wrong side.

When a twill weave is held up on the body, the twill will run down toward the right foot if the fabric is right side out. In gabardine, you will notice that the surface twill is different from the wrong side, so you would not be confused in this case. Some materials, such as gingham and broadcloth, have no apparent difference, which makes it easier to cut or piece during construction.

If it has been difficult to distinguish the right side, place chalk marks on the wrong side before placing the pattern and cutting.

CENTER CREASES Most fabrics come in such good condition that it is unnecessary to press them. Do not bother to press out center folds at this time unless they are off-grain and sharp. If the fabric has not been folded wrong side out, however, you may want to remove the center crease for ease in refolding. Press—do not iron—with the grain and on the wrong side. Experiment on a small corner to find the right amount of heat, moisture, and pressure to use without scorching, creating a shine, or changing the texture. Keep the selvages and ends straight.

PRESHRINKING FABRICS

If material has been Sanforized or you have a guaranteed residual shrinkage of 1 per cent or less, there is probably no question of a change in size sufficiently great for the garment to become unwearable—assuming the fabric will be handled as directed by the manufacturer. However, with the multiplicity of fabrics that often are used in a garment—the fashion fabric, underlining, interfacing, tape, and others—consideration should be given to the possibility of preshrinking any or all of the materials whose qualities you may question.

If you believe that your cloth should be shrunk, tear the ends or cut with the grain. Fold it neatly, right sides together. Soak it in a bathtub or large pan of hot water for thirty minutes to several hours. Drain off the water and squeeze out all you can without wringing. Hang it on a rod without completely unfolding it. Stretch the selvages and smooth the ends. Many fabrics can be left to dry and no pressing will be needed. Others are better ironed while they are still damp. Iron or press with the lengthwise yarns—still wrong side out and folded double—but avoid pressing in a crease. To make it grain perfect, pin the semidry cloth along the lines on a commercial cutting board, and press it to shape (Fig. 11-10).

If the grain was badly stretched before shrinking, all of that has been corrected if you have been careful to keep the ends and selvages matched during drying and if you have pressed without obvious stretching. Use your hands to smooth and straighten the fabric while it is drying on the rod and again on the press board. Do not press the center crease.

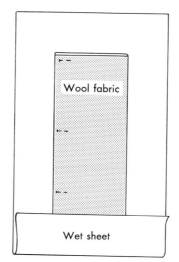

Figure 11-11. Fold ends and sides of wet sheet over wool fabric; fold grain lightly.

SPONGING WOOL CLOTH   Sponging partially shrinks wool cloth, removes wrinkles, and straightens the grain so that it is easier to cut and fit. Better pieces of cloth are already sponged, "London shrunk," or "ready for the needle" when sold in the retail store. Look on the selvage or label for these statements.

A reliable dry cleaner can preshrink wool fabric satisfactorily; select one who is aware of the importance of keeping the fabric grain in shape during this process.

Even though it takes time, you may prefer to shrink the fabric yourself. One method is to steam-press the folded fabric on the wrong side. Another method, more effective if the fabric has not been shrunk or if the grain is badly off the right-angled structure, is to place the fabric (folded right sides in with the torn ends as close together as possible and the selvages matched) on a wet sheet. Fold it together lightly and allow it to remain several hours but never until it is dry. With the torn ends and selvages together, smooth it out on a cutting board and let it dry on the flat surface. Press it before the fabric is completely dry (Fig. 11-11).

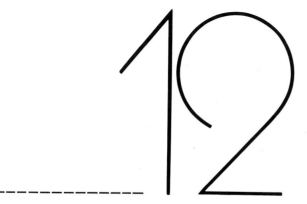

12

Cutting
and
Marking

Handling Fabrics

SOFT SLIPPERY FABRICS

Chiffon, and similar fabrics tend to slip and slide during pattern placement and cutting. Spreading the fabric on tissue paper and pinning the two together provide stability. Placing the fabric on a commercial cutting board, and pushing pins through the fabric and into the board, may provide additional assistance in keeping the grainline straight. Laying these fabrics out on a sheet may help to solve the slipping problem, but may not be as helpful as the tissue paper in the cutting process, as paper and fabric are cut together. Keep the left hand securely anchored on the fabric near the cutting line during this process. Mark the fabric lightly with chalk or with tailor's tacks.

KNITS

To prevent stretching a knitted fabric when making the pattern placement, keep it lying on a flat surface with none of it hanging off the table. (Use the floor, if necessary.) Allow it to relax as it is laid out smoothly.

For the more slippery knits—such as jersey, tricot, and Raschels—use tissue paper under the fabric. Pinning the fabric to the paper not only is helpful in keeping it straight, but prevents curling as the pieces are cut.

Because the lengthwise rib of a knit fabric is comparable to the lengthwise grain of woven fabrics, use the rib for placing the pattern pieces on the straight of the cloth. Avoid using a creased fold in the fabric unless it can be pressed out. Refold the fabric to place this crease away from the center of the garment. To further reduce curling, place pins close together at right angles to the pattern edge.

Because knits may have a slight nap or texture that may be undetectable, have all pieces lying in the same direction for cutting.

It is advisable to use ball-point pins to avoid snagging knits. Sharp scissors are needed for cutting.

Knits tend to curl less when the pattern is placed on the wrong side of the fabric, where the cut line is not in line with the wales.

The maximum stretch in knit fabrics is usually on the crosswise grain, rather than on the bias. Therefore, bindings that would be cut on the bias in woven fabric should be cut in the crosswise direction.

Underline knit fabrics in all areas where stretch is undesirable with a woven fabric to give stability. Where stretch is desirable, underline or line with a stretch fabric, or omit these fabrics.

STRETCH FABRICS

Smooth the fabric out and allow it to relax on a flat surface before cutting. Place the pattern as directed for "with nap" fabrics. Cut the garment in the direction of stretch in the fabric. Most garments, especially pants, require a fabric with lengthwise stretch. To cut on the crosswise stretch would result in an uncomfortable garment.

TWILLS

See if the fabric is reversible, and whether there is an up-and-down; identify the right side. Plan the twill to run in the same diagonal direction throughout the garment. There is no up-and-down in some twills. Bias seams at CF or CB always give the effect of mismatching, both in the diagonal line and in the dark and light effect; therefore, plan CF and CB on the fold or grain.

VELVET

Careful alteration of the pattern for velvet is most essential, as any alterations during construction will mar the pile. For cutting velvet, use the with-nap layout.

Velvet is cut with the nap running up for a richer, deeper color, or running down for a smoother, more lustrous appearance. To determine the direction, slide the hand along the surface; the smoother one indicates the nap direction. Draw a few arrows on the back to mark the nap direction.

Place the pattern on the wrong side, using sharp needles rather than pins to facilitate cutting and to avoid damage to the pile; the needles should be within the seam and dart allowances. Because the pile has a tendency to slip when the two layers are folded together, it is considered an advantage to cut one piece at a time. If the pattern must be placed on the fold, cut through one layer and then the other. Mark the fabric with tailor's tacks, using silk thread to avoid damage to the pile.

Velveteen and corduroy used in sport garments that will receive much wear are usually cut with the nap running downward. They do not require as much care in cutting as velvet.

Handle man-made furs as directed for pile fabrics. Place the pattern on one thickness of fabric, wrong side out; pin it carefully through the backing only; and tape the pattern to the fabric, or use weights to hold it in place. Use very sharp shears; with a long, heavy pile, cut through the backing only, using a single-edged razor blade, as for cutting fur.

BONDED OR LAMINATED FABRIC

Use fine pins when placing the pattern on the fabric, and tailor's tacks, or chalk, for marking, since tracing wheel marks do not show adequately. Do not overfit; this fabric should not be subjected to strain.

FELT

A nonwoven fabric without grain, felt lends itself to certain techniques that are not ordinarily possible in handling fabrics. Pattern pieces can be cut in any direction, and narrower seams are possible. Underlining increases its strength, which is normally weak.

VINYL FABRICS

To avoid damage to this fabric, do not use pins to attach the pattern—weights or tape should be used. Mark on the wrong side of cloth-backed vinyl with tailor's chalk or a smooth tracing wheel. Right-side marks can be made with a grease pencil and later wiped off. Use tape or paper clips to hold the layers together.

METALLIC FABRICS

Use care in pressing with steam—test on a swatch to determine whether steaming tarnishes the metal. Avoid pin marks, ripping, and permanent creasing.

BEADED FABRICS

An old pair of scissors should be used for cutting beaded fabrics because the blade will be dulled. Plan to line the garment, because the wrong side of a beaded fabric is very rough. To avoid bulk, use the lining fabric for the facings or finish the edges with a plain seam, joining the two fabrics without facings where possible.

Pattern Layouts for Cutting

Find the layout on your pattern guide sheet that corresponds to your pattern size, the style or view you have chosen, your fabric width, and the nap factors that affect the correct and economical placement of the pattern. To save time and avoid confusion, draw a pencil line around the layout to be followed.

The next decision to be made is whether to fold the fabric with the right or the wrong side out. Consider the merits of each plan.

RIGHT SIDE OUT   Where the fabric has a pattern that will be difficult to match, such as plaid, folding it right side out is an advantage. The design can be more clearly seen for matching.

WRONG SIDE OUT

1. This plan is an advantage where chalk marks and traced lines are to be placed on the wrong side.

2. It is simpler and possibly more accurate when marking with a tracing wheel. The cut pairs, such as the right and left fronts, do not have to be separated to insert carbon paper between them.

3. The right side, folded in, is protected from soil in handling.

4. The wrong side generally is smoother—an advantage in both cutting and marking, especially when working with velvet and fleecy fabrics.

FOLLOWING A LAYOUT

The pattern guide provides some very important information regarding layouts that are safe to use when the fabric has a nap or an up-and-down design. All pattern pieces will be placed in the same direction, with their lower edges nearer to one end of the fabric than to the other. To determine the direction of the nap, stroke the surface of the fabric lightly—the smoother direction indicates the direction of the nap.

Fleece fabrics are cut with the nap running downward. In fabrics with woven, knitted, or printed designs, the direction may be determined by the nature of the motifs, or by personal choice. For velvet, see p. 254.

Handling Patterned Fabrics

1. When preparing to use a plaid fabric, an important first step is to identify, without question, the type of plaid you have chosen. You probably determined when you made the selection whether the design was an even or uneven plaid.

2. Fabrics with unusually large figures, such as florals, can be held up to the body in an effort to visualize the most advantageous placement of the design units on the figure. Try to avoid cutting through these motifs where possible.

Figure 12-1. Using a wide-spaced plaid.

3. Place dominant stripes at the hemline when the hem follows the straight grain of the fabric; when the hemline is curved, as in an A-line skirt, a less prominent part of the design is desirable because the fabric pattern cannot follow the hem curve.

4. The center front of the pattern is placed on a dominant stripe, generally. This can vary with a wide motif or repeat, to result in a striking, unusual design (Fig. 12-1).

5. The center back is also placed on the center of a prominent stripe or unit of plaid, although not necessarily the most prominent one; this will depend on the size of the pattern in relation to the design and how it is to be matched at other points around the body. For example, if shoulder seams are matched, it may not be possible to use the same stripe at center back that was used at center front.

6. The design should match at center front and center back from neck to hem for all sections cut on a fold or a straight grain, including the collar and yokes.

7. The design should be continuous from back to front, matching at seams around the body (Fig. 12-2). Designs are easier to match through the lengths of the seams when shoulder darts are used, *b*.

Matching Stripes and Plaids

Techniques for placing the pattern so that the stripes will be matched are illustrated in Figure 12-3. As indicated in *a*, the design is not quite even in spacing or in color pattern—the colors of the narrow stripes on the crosswise are different

Figure 12-2. Match stripes and plaids at notches and hems if possible. Ignore matching notches above a bust dart, as this mismatched condition will be inconspicuous under the arm, and permit matching in the seam below this dart. Designs are easier to match when shoulder darts are used, rather than underarm, *b*.

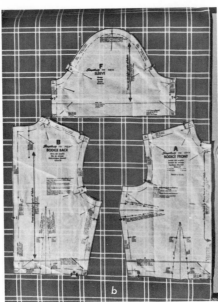

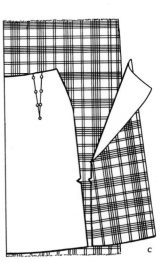

Figure 12-3. Before placing the pattern on a plaid, know which type you have—even or uneven. An even plaid is shown in *a*—stripes match in both directions when a corner is turned back. Patterns placed for matching below underarm dart, and at front armhole, with CF and CB on center of stripe, *b*.

from those in the lengthwise direction. Although the sleeve has been placed in the same direction as the bodice sections, this plaid is sufficiently even for it to be placed in either direction.

Note these conditions:

1. The center fronts of the bodice and back are placed on the middle of the stripe, with the CF placed on a fold.

2. The pattern is matched at the side seams up to the underarm dart; it, obviously, cannot be matched above, but the mismatch will not be conspicuous

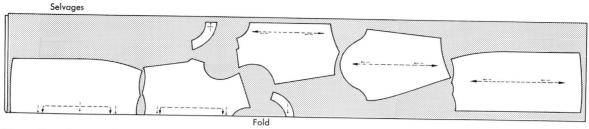

Selvages

Fold

Figure 12-4. Pattern placement for a fabric "without nap"—pattern pieces may face either direction.

in this location. To match this seam, the notches on back and front edges were placed in the same relation to the crosswise stripe. *Care must be taken to be sure these points match at the seamlines.* Lines drawn through the notches, as shown, are valuable aids in determining the exact points for matching.

3. The sleeve has been placed so that the stripe at the front notch on the sleeve cap matches the stripe at the front armhole notch. The notches in the back may not match, as in this case. When both cannot match, it seems preferable to match the front, as the back probably is less noticeable.

In *c*, the plaid has been matched at notches and lower edges; the lower part of the seam naturally is more conspicuous.

TRIAL PLACEMENT—PLAN I

Whether you follow the pattern layout or not, always make a trial placement of the pattern pieces before cutting any, to be sure of having enough cloth. A trial placement involves these steps.

1. Spread the cloth as instructed in the guide sheet (Fig. 12-4). In this case, the fabric is folded in half. Keep ends and sides of the cloth exactly parallel with the edges of the table during pinning and cutting. If there is a shortage of table space, begin at one end and leave the excess fabric on a chair at the other end of the table. Fold up the end with the pattern placed on it as you proceed with the placement. (Try to avoid this condition, if possible.)

2. You note that this layout for Plan I requires a fabric without nap, as all pieces are not turned in the same direction. If the fabric you are working with has a nap, look for a placement labeled "with nap."

3. Place the material on the table in the same relation to you as is shown in the layout.

4. Start at one end of the fabric; generally, a large piece will be placed first—in the layout for Plan I, a skirt placed on the fold is followed by the bodice front, also placed on the fold. Use a few pins at the fold lines to hold the pattern pieces in place—about three on the skirt and two on the bodice. No other pins are needed on these pieces at this point; in the event that there is not enough fabric for this placement, the pattern would need to be removed in order to explore another plan. In such a contingency, placing pins and then having to remove them wastes time and effort.

259

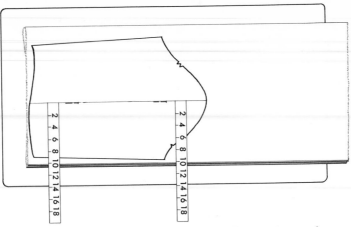

Figure 12-5. Measure from selvage to grainline of pattern in two places, near ends of pattern. Pin first on the grain at the widest point, taking a small stitch with pin so that the other end of the pattern can be pivoted into the correct position for pinning.

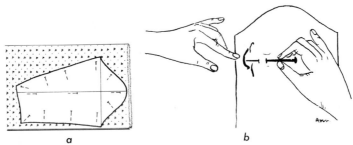

a   *b*

Figure 12-6. *a*, Pins correctly placed—on grainline first, then perpendicular to edges and diagonally at corners. *b*, To pin pattern to cloth, push up a small fold of fabric to catch pin point.

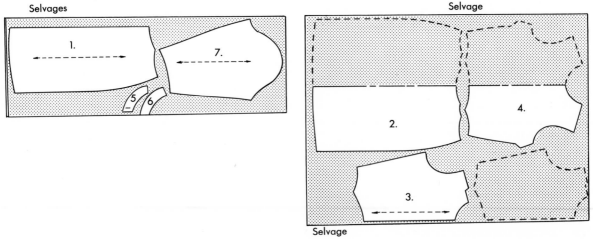

Figure 12-7. How does one proceed when the pattern guide sheet shows fabric cut in two parts?

5. The next three pieces have grainline markings within the pattern. How does the procedure for placing these patterns differ from placing a pattern on a fold? Review this technique in Figure 12-5. Measure and place pins on the measured grainlines.
6. Pin the front neck facing into position on the fold.

THE COMPLETED TRIAL PLACEMENT

1. The pattern pieces are placed accurately on the grain.
2. Pins are placed only on the grain lines—to save time in case shifts are found to be necessary.
3. Adequate space for the placement is assured.

FINAL PLACEMENT   Nothing remains to be done except to add additional pins along the edges of the pattern sections (Fig. 12-6, a).

After approving of the trial placement, place pins near the edges and corners at right angles to the edges, not parallel, except in satin (and then along the lengthwise grain, as already stated). Pins, normally placed perpendicular to the edge of the pattern, can be shifted slightly to make the stitch on the straight grain of the fabric. When pins are placed parallel with the edges of the pattern, a slight hump occurs at each pin location, making it more difficult to cut an accurate line. Avoid using many pins. Keep them back about one inch from the edge. Crepes, sheers, satin, and velvet may need two lines of pins, the extra ones outside the cutting line.

Hold the pattern and cloth down flat on the table as you pin. Lifting it up shifts the work. Pinning is simpler if you point the pin toward you instead of away from you. To keep work flat on the table when pinning, use both hands slightly extended to anchor the work to the table, b. Use the left index finger to push up a little tuck or fold of the cloth at the spot where the point of the pin is being pushed through to make a stitch. Thus, the two layers cannot shift out of position. This is a very important technique. It is used to pin the pattern to the cloth, two layers of cloth together, and a lapped seam or pleats in the construction of a garment.

Check your layout. Are all pieces accounted for? Are they placed correctly?

If you intended to add extra seam or hem allowances, check to see if you have left plenty of space. Pins placed at the corners to block cutting will remind you to add an extra allowance (see Fig. 9-9). Chalk marks are good reminders. Extra seam allowances are advisable if the pattern fits a little snugly; if the material ravels badly or is bulky; or if you anticipate the need for further fitting. Cut an extra seam allowance for zipper plackets.

LAYOUT—PLAN II

Pattern guide-sheet layouts frequently show situations where the fabric is folded for some pattern pieces and spread open for others, with these sections cut apart (Fig. 12-7). It obviously would be unsafe to place this skirt and sleeve and cut the fabric into two parts without being sure of having adequate yardage

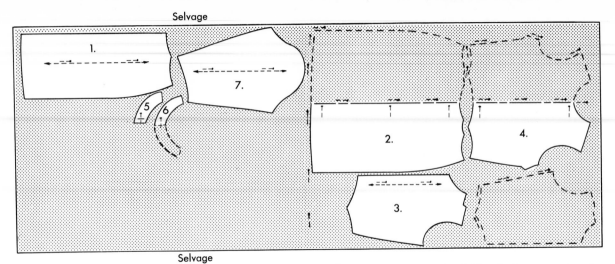

Figure 12-8. When some parts are to be cut on fabric folded in half and others are not, make the trial placement on the open fabric.

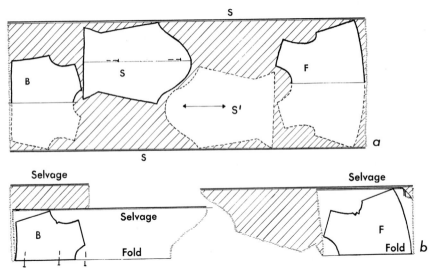

Figure 12-9. *a*, Broken lines indicate reserved spaces for duplicates, and mark the original placements of these patterns; *b*, final placements of bodice patterns after cutting sleeves.

for the remaining pieces. It is not intended that you cut the fabric before you are sure there is an adequate supply. Place a line of pins or chalk around the edges of patterns near this cut line, or mark the line with pins when you have reached that point in the placement.

A simple technique for avoiding such difficulties is to leave the fabric open for all the pieces during the trial placement (Fig. 12-8). To start at the left, all those pieces shown placed on folded fabric will be placed on one half the width of the fabric—the same amount they occupy in the sketch.

262

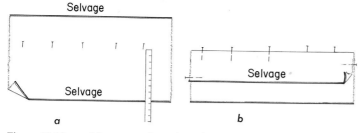

Figure 12-10. *a*, Measure and mark with pins to make an accurate lengthwise fold; or, *b*, estimate the width needed and check from fold to selvage.

What is the reason for having some pattern sections shaded and outlined with broken lines? Where a solid line outlines half a piece and a broken line outlines the other shaded half, this whole piece is to be cut on a fold. The parts outlined with broken lines indicate reserved spaces for underfolds for pattern sections *2* and *4*, and for one half of the back bodice. The technique for reserving this space is to place the pattern on the grain line, outline its shape with a few pins (chalk marks might be used if the fabric is wrong-side out), and then move the pattern to its second location.

Another example is seen in Figure 12-9, *a*. It is simpler to cut the sleeves first, since they do not require folded fabric. After sleeve *S* is cut, you have a choice of two procedures for cutting sleeve *S'*:

1. Leave sleeve *S* pinned to the pattern, turn the fabric over, place the pattern in *S'* position—fabric to fabric—check the grainline, add pins, and cut. This plan insures sleeves for right and left arms, because *like sides* of the fabric have been placed together. Both sleeves can be marked at the same time, in case there is an elbow dart or some other marking. *Should you forget to turn the fabric over, you will have duplicates—two sleeves for only one arm.*

2. Cut sleeve *S* and remove the pattern; turn the pattern over, place it in position *S'*, and cut the second sleeve. *Should you forget to turn the pattern over, you will have duplicates—not a pair for the two arms.*

Either of these techniques will provide a pair of sleeves, if you remember to turn something over—the *fabric* in *1*, or the *pattern* in *2*. The result in each will *always* be a pair.

The first may be a safer plan to follow, as it has a second safeguard: When the pattern, with the sleeve pinned on, is placed for cutting the second sleeve, you know you will have a pair if like sides of the fabric, either right or wrong sides, are facing each other.

To cut the bodices in Figure 12-9, *b*, fold the fabric on the proper grainlines to provide the width needed (Fig. 12-10).

TRIAL PLACEMENT FOR PLAN II (FIG. 12-8)

1. Place skirt back, sleeve, and both neck facings; pin them at the grainlines. The center front edge of the front neck facing will be placed on the fold line of the fabric.

2. Place skirt front pattern in shaded position, check grainline, and pin; then place a line of pins exactly on the CF pattern edge, *on the fabric but not on the pattern.*

3. Turn the pattern over, lining its edge with the pins that are marking the CF line, and pin it to the fabric.

4. Repeat step 3 for bodice front.

5. Place bodice back at the end of the fabric—beside the bodice front—pin grainline in position, and place a few pins to mark the space occupied by the pattern.

6. Remove back bodice pattern, turn it upside down in the solid-line position, measure it, and pin it on the grainline.

7. Cut the back bodice in the solid-line position and lay it aside.

8. As you are sure of the locations, it is now safe to cut across the fabric halfway through the width of the skirt at its lower edge, from *a* to *b*, so that is is possible to make an underfold; fold exactly on the CF line—the CF and the grainline of the fabric must coincide.

9. Check the grainline of fabric to be sure it is even. Place pins around the edges of skirt and cut. Lay it aside for marking later.

10. Follow step 9 for cutting front bodice. (This will be simplified if it is possible to use the same fold line as for skirt.)

11. Make the underfold for skirt *1* and the sleeve; check grainlines, and add pins around the edges, pinning through both thicknesses of fabric; cut.

12. To cut the other half of the back bodice, turn the fabric over; check to be sure it is straight on the table; place the pattern with fabric still pinned to it (this places like sides of fabric together for marking and insures a pair); check the grainline of the pattern; add pins around the edges; and cut.

STANDARD FOLDS FOR LAYOUTS

These folds are standard and arranged in order from easy to complex. Two of them were considered in Plans I and II.

1. Cloth folded lengthwise, selvage to selvage, generally wrong side out (Plan I). Pin through both layers in the trial layout as well as in the final placement. This is the easiest method because it saves time and table space; it may not save cloth.

2. Cloth opened out and folded crosswise, end to end, wrong side out. Pin through both layers in trial and final placements. This is often used for wider fabrics, wide circular skirts, and shirt, suit, coat, and pants patterns. It cannot be used on fabrics with a nap. Why?

3. Cloth open full width on the table wrong side up for a plan where part of the pattern is placed on the double fabric folded lengthwise, and part on cloth left open and cut in one layer (Plan II). Pin through one layer, placing the pattern on one half the width of the fabric for the double folded part. When it is acceptable, first cut the part on the single layer, then fold the cloth to cut the part folded lengthwise.

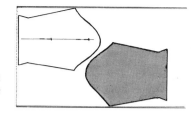

Figure 12-11. In some instances, there is an advantage in duplicate patterns, which may be cut in tissue or wrapping paper.

4. Cloth open full width on the table wrong side up for a plan where part of the pattern is placed on cloth to be folded lengthwise and part on cloth to be folded crosswise. Pin through one layer, using one half the area across the end to be folded crosswise. When satisfactory, first fold the crosswise part and cut; then fold the lengthwise part and cut.
5. Cloth open full width on the table right side up for intricate designs, asymmetric designs, bias cuts, or where the other types of layout do not work or appear wasteful. You may need duplicate patterns—cut an extra (Fig. 12-11). The safest plan is to keep patterns right side up, and place them on the right side of the fabric. This procedure gives assurance that a section designed for the right side of the body will fit that side.

PLACEMENTS FOR SPECIAL PROBLEMS

If no layout is furnished for the width of your material, or if you have insufficient yardage, you will need to rely on basic principles of pattern placement. This knowledge will be helpful because of the great variety of widths in today's markets.

The objectives in placing a pattern without a provided layout plan are as follows:

1. To produce all pieces cut correctly as to grain and design in cloth.
2. To have all scraps left over in a few large pieces rather than many small pieces.
3. To develop thrifty habits by saving yardage. This training also enables you to use remnants more cleverly.

If the Pattern Will Not Fit the Cloth

Where there is a definite shortage of fabric, never cut off-grain; grain controls the style and fit of the garment; decide which of the following alternatives would be wiser for you.

1. **Buy more fabric.** Is it available? Will it be worth the trip to the store and the cost? If so, which pieces should be saved for the new fabric so that the least yardage will be necessary? Buy the extra fabric before cutting any pieces to be sure it is available.
2. **Cut some pieces crosswise or on the bias.** Would a more or less satisfactory design be created? Will it wear as well? Yokes and bands often appear better crosswise, but sleeves seldom do.

3. **Piece certain sections.** Can the piecing be made invisible? Facings and linings can be pieced, but the pieced seam may make an imprint on the outer garment when pressed. Piecing under a decoration or pleat may help. Extra seams must be allowed on both edges of the new seam.

4. **Shorten pieces.** Check the pattern again on yourself to be certain that the style is not affected. Do not leave too skimpy a hem. In shortening a skirt, take off the same amount from each gore. Piecing along the side of a gore or across a sleeve is too obvious to be pleasing.

5. **Narrow some pieces.** Gathered sections can be made less full. Skirts can have some of the flare removed. Pleats can be narrowed or entirely omitted. Narrowing gores may permit closer dovetailing, hence length is saved.

6. **Supplement the material.** Use other material for facings, trimmings, or parts such as yokes, collars, bands, or pockets.

7. **Save on the seams.** Cut less-deep seam allowances on such pieces as belts, bands, and ruffles, but not on silhouette seams.

8. **Abandon the project.** Use another style of pattern entirely, or use the material for another article.

SUGGESTIONS FOR CUTTING

1. Keep the ends and sides of the material parallel with the table edges at all times.

2. Use bent shears to avoid lifting the fabric so far off the table that accuracy is decreased.

3. Cut in the direction of the grain, as nearly as possible.

4. Keep one hand flat on the pattern near the cutting line.

5. Cut with long, even strokes close to the edge of the pattern; never completely close the blades, since this is conducive to a choppy line.

6. Walk around the table as the larger pieces are cut; moving the pattern and fabric may shift the grain and require additional time for straightening.

7. If a hem or seam allowance is to be increased, hold a gauge just ahead of the scissors or mark the cutting line with chalk.

8. Cut notches outward with the point of the shears—not into the seam allowance to narrow and weaken it; two or three notches may be cut as one wide block (Fig. 12-12).

9. Do not use pinking shears to cut out a garment: this would result in an uneven edge that could not be used as an accurate sewing guide, especially on curves, as armholes, necklines, and collar edges; such thick shears lift the fabric off the table, shifting the pattern out of position; notches cannot be cut without picking up another pair of shears; many materials should have a finish other than pinking; many seams are trimmed to a narrower width later in the construction process, such as seams under facings and collars, thereby making the pinking of seams unnecessary. An exception might be the lengthwise seams in a many-gored skirt.

10. Cut any extra pieces that might be needed in finishing, such as bias strips, or sections for fabric buttonholes.

Figure 12-12. *a*, Cut notches out. A notch cut at point of sleeve cap that will join shoulder seam saves time in marking. *b*, A group of notches can be cut as one. On raveling fabrics, some dressmakers mark important notches (which will be used rather late in construction processes) with a line of basting, *a*. *b*, On firm, nonraveling fabrics, a short—⅛-inch—clip or slash can be used to mark ends of CF and CB or fold lines.

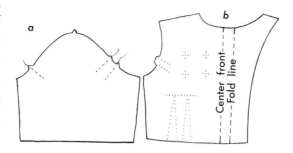

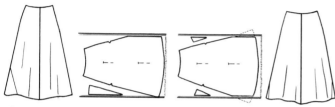

Figure 12-13. Two narrow piecings are less conspicuous than one wider one; they balance. Often the narrow ones disappear in hem or fold. All piecing should be on warp grain. Consider using a pattern with more gores or less circularity.

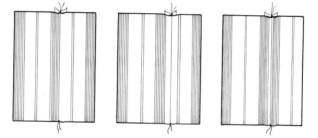

Figure 12-14. Piece along edge of a stripe, left; avoid piecing in a solid area, center; or mismatching the design, right.

11. Mark all pieces.

12. Stack together all units to be used together, such as sleeve facings with sleeves, all blouse sections, and all skirt sections.

PIECING

When the pattern extends beyond the width of the material, piecing may be necessary (Fig. 12-13). Make the piecing come on a lengthwise thread along the edge of a stripe, not in the stripe (Fig. 12-14). An easy method is first to turn under a seam's width on the edge to be pieced. Lap this over a scrap of the material to match the design, grain, nap, and face of the material. Pin it in place with the pins at right angles to the lap. Finish cutting the pattern. Use slip-basting stitches

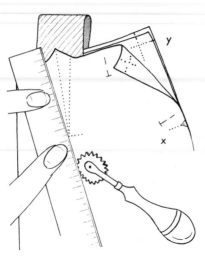

Figure 12-15. Dressmaker's carbon folded with colored sides facing is slipped between pattern and cloth, and table and cloth, so that colored sides will touch the wrong sides of the fabric. Run tracing wheel along ruler if lines are to be straight. Bisecting the dart aids construction. Mark termination points of darts and plackets. Ordinarily, it is unnecessary to mark seamlines; you can make a few short strokes as reminders at intersection, y, and at points that are to be slashed, as gussets and shawl collars.

¼ inch long in the fold. Turn to the wrong side to stitch along the basting, and press. Replace the pattern to check and trim off surplus if necessary.

MARKING Some of the symbols on the pattern that were necessary for proper placement may also be helpful in construction. In addition, other symbols clarifying the exact procedure in joining the pieces together will serve as invaluable aids. Those that should be transferred from pattern to fabric will depend much on the complication of the design, the fabric used, and your experience and ability in handling these or related projects. In an easily handled fabric in a casual garment of simple design, a speedy method of marking can be used with success. When constructing a complicated design in a fine fabric with the hope that it will rival the best that the ready-to-wear market has to offer, the anticipated techniques will be more involved.

METHODS OF MARKING

Methods of marking include the tracing wheel and dressmaker's carbon, tailor's chalk, dressmaker's pencil, tailor's tacks, and pins.

THE TRACING WHEEL AND DRESSMAKER'S CARBON

1. Use the tracing wheel and dressmaker's carbon on any firm fabric except sheers.

2. Lift the wheel frequently to avoid pushing up folds in the fabric.

3. Experiment with the fabric to learn how much pressure is needed.

4. Make each corner a true angle by tracing adjoining seams with separate strokes all the way to the end, one directly across the other (Fig. 12-15).

5. Trace straight dart lines beside a ruler; cross the termination point with a 1-inch stroke. Marking the middle of the dart makes folding easier.

6. Mark all termination points to indicate where the stitching is to stop, as at the ends of tucks, pleats, and placket lines. Trace the symbols with a line or an X.

7. Notches that were not cut out can be marked with the tracing wheel; use a line through the center of the notch, perpendicular to the seamline.

8. If there is no danger of the marking showing through to the right side, lines that are later to be marked by basting, such as CF, CB, buttonholes, or pockets, can be traced on the wrong side or on the underlining.

9. When an underlining is used, mark it only and not the fabric; an intricate design might be an exception.

10. When the fabric is folded wrong side out, cut a strip of dressmaker's carbon (tracing paper) 4 or 5 inches wide and fold it end to end with the colored sides in. (Two strips will be needed for a long line.) Insert the folded tracing paper with one side between the lower layer of fabric and the table and the other between the pattern and the upper layer of fabric.

11. When fabric is folded right side out, insert the folded paper between the two layers of fabric.

12. When only one layer of fabric is to be marked, use one thickness of paper, with colored side next to the wrong side of fabric.

13. Use the wheel without the carbon on very firm white fabric, or use white paper on white or pastel colored fabric. Use stronger colors on darker fabrics; be cautious in using dark blue.

14. Tracing regular seams is optional; time often can be saved by using a machine gauge when stitching. On very curved seams, traced lines may insure a greater degree of accuracy. Traced lines are invaluable on seamlines at the corners of yokes, collars, insets, and gussets where seam allowances are uneven in width and often extend out to a point.

TAILOR'S CHALK OR DRESSMAKER'S PENCIL A dressmaker's pencil, a block of tailor's chalk, or a piece of equipment to deposit chalk may be useful. These methods are satisfactory for any type of fabric except sheers, where they might show through the fabric. A pencil mark can be substituted for a notch if made on the wrong side. A convenient method for transferring a mark, such as a button location, to double layers with tailor's chalk is to place a block of chalk on the table under the fabric to be marked. Then mark the top layer with a dressmaker's pencil, pressing firmly. This technique marks both layers at the same time.

Another method for using these materials is to force pins through the pattern and both layers of fabric. On the side opposite the pattern, mark a dot with tailor's chalk or pencil where the pin penetrates the cloth. Then, hold the pins on the marked side and gently tear the pattern from under each pinhead; chalk the fabric at the pinheads.

PINS Marking with pins may be desirable on fabrics easily marred by a tracing wheel or pencil, or to speed up the process of marking (Fig. 12-16). This method

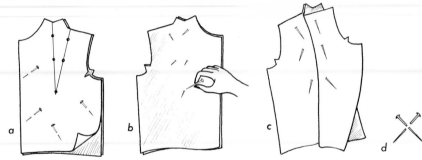

Figure 12-16. Marking with pins.

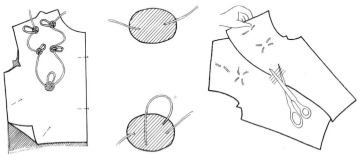

Figure 12-17. Tailor's tacks.

is useful only on details to be completed early in the construction process. The method is not so desirable where many features are involved.

Begin by inserting pin (do not take up a stitch) through the center of each marking and through both layers of cloth, *a*. Carefully lift off the pattern. To mark the other layer, turn the two layers over and insert another pin on the opposite side exactly where the first pin came through, *b*. Gently pull them apart, *c*. If the fabric is a loose weave, or if you do not plan to use the pieces at once, complete the processes with a tiny stitch by each pin left as it is, placing another pin across it for security, *d*.

TAILOR'S TACKS   This method can be used on any type of fabric. However, it is especially appropriate on soft fabrics where traced lines or chalk marks would be lost; on sheer fabrics because chalk marks might show through to the right side; and where markings are needed on the right side.

Tailor's tacks mark the right and the left sides and the right and the wrong sides at the same time (Fig. 12-17). They are fairly permanent and visible from both sides. Use a long double thread, preferably darning cotton, so that it will not slip out easily. At intervals along a marked line, such as a dart or pleat, take a small stitch or two quite loosely through the pattern and both layers of fabric. Leave long loops between the stitches. After all the lines are tacked cut the threads or loops between the stitches and remove the pattern, tearing it carefully at each stitch. Pull the two pieces apart gently to avoid pulling out the threads. Cut the threads between the two layers, leaving two or four little threads at each location.

Although tailor's tacks are time-consuming to make and may not provide marking as accurate as a traced line (if the stitches are spread too far apart), there are situations in which their use is justified. With such fabrics as delicate pastels, soft sheers, velvets, and extremely bulky materials, this type of marking is the best choice.

UNEVEN BASTING ON RIGHT SIDE

It may be desirable to bring to the right side certain lines that have been marked with a tracing wheel on the wrong side. Some of these markings will be essential and some will be optional, depending on the garment and fabric used.

Center front, center back, and *fold lines* along an opening in the garment can be marked in this manner. Where the pattern was placed on a fold, the center line would be basted along the fold. Probably the fastest way to mark CF and the fold line is to first trace the lines on the wrong side beside a yardstick, and baste along the traced line.

An alternative plan in a simple garment of firm fabric might involve bringing the CF line to the right side with pins; a few pins parallel to and on the traced line in preparation for fitting, or the use of tiny safety pins placed at button and buttonhole locations may be sufficient. Does the CB require marking throughout its length, or would short markings—an inch or two in length at the neckline and waistline—be adequate? If you anticipate fitting problems, or if you are working with difficult fabrics in more complicated designs, the entire line of basting will be essential.

Grainline markings are desirable for some pieces, such as the lengthwise grain in sleeves, the crosswise grain at the base of the sleeve cap, and the crosswise grainlines at the bust- or chest-, and hiplines. Lines basted in these positions can serve two purposes when underlinings are used: marking the grain and attaching the two layers of fabric together. (Suggestions for this process are considered in Chapter 17.)

The need for marking grainlines is eliminated when working with fabrics where the grainline is visible. A valuable ability to develop is grain consciousness, although, as was observed in Chapter 10, other factors are equally important and as easily used in judging the fit of a garment. Therefore, for many garments, the basting of grainlines can be considered optional. If the correct size has been chosen, the pattern has been altered with judgment, and the garment cut grain perfect, the need for grain-marking is relatively small. Obviously, when complicated fitting problems are anticipated, the need for grain-marking is increased.

OTHER WAYS OF MARKING

On materials that do not ravel badly, a ⅛-inch *slash* or *snip* may serve well for marking the ends of CF or CB lines (blouse, skirt, facings, collars, yokes) cut on a *fold* and the ends of fold lines along closings. For materials that ravel, you might use a traced or pencil-marked line.

Some lines in a garment, such as fold lines along openings and pleats, can be marked by *pressing*. Pins placed at each end of the line, $\frac{1}{8}$-inch clips at the ends, or chalk dots are the only marks needed. Fold on the line indicated, and hold it taut on the ironing board. Check to see that grain thread is straight along the fold, if the yarns are visible. Press the fold. Press lightly, or not at all, through hemlines. For long lines in soft, fine fabrics, it may be an advantage to first mark the line on the wrong side with a tracing wheel, to serve as a guide throughout its length. Where the lines to be pressed are not on a straight grain, care must be taken to avoid stretching. Pressing in this case would be questionable.

Generalizations

Directions: Read each generalization across both columns, and note the relationships as pointed out in the headings.

EFFECT SOUGHT OR REASON WHY	THE CAUSE OR WHAT TO DO
1. To keep grains of fabric at right angles to each other so that garment will fit well and stay that way,	a. prepare the fabric by cutting or tearing it along crosswise ends of cloth; then if the cloth is not a true rectangle, pull it diagonally on its true bias throughout its length, in direction of short corners only, or dampen and press it straight; b. have grainline of pattern on grainline of fabric; c. pin or hold the fabric pieces together to baste them for fitting or to stitch so that notches and intersecting seams match.
2. To insure an adequate amount of cloth,	make a trial placement of all pattern pieces before cutting any.
3. To insure cutting a garment that is grain-perfect, with resulting good fit,	have patterns in both trial and permanent placements pinned so that grain marking of each piece coincides with grainline of cloth.
4. To facilitate marking and simplify assembling of garment at CF and CB seams, when cutting two layers at once,	have material folded wrong side out before placing the pattern.
5. To insure cutting mates and to simplify marking, when duplicates must be cut separately from one layer of cloth,	leave the pattern pinned to (wrong side of) first layer; place right sides of fabric together with pattern on top; cut second layer.
6. To secure a straight-line effect and to increase durability,	because of the law of gravity, cut the part that is to hang straight down on the heavier grain (usually the warp).

7. Inversely, to accent a rounded, bulgy effect,

cut the part that is to hang down at right angles to the stiffer threads.

8. To secure a rippled or flared effect,

cut the area or line that is to flare on the bias.

9. To make a pleasing, orderly design,

stripes, plaids, and other motifs should match or balance.

Using the Sewing Machine

Standards for Stitching

Good stitching in any article has the following characteristics:

1. It has no tangles.
2. It begins and finishes exactly at the ends of seams, not a quarter-inch or so from the edge.
3. It has a length of stitch proportioned to the texture of the fabric.
4. It has the same size of stitch wherever visible.
5. It has elastic tension that locks upper and lower threads between layers of fabric.
6. It has no skipped or broken spots in seams or in topstitching.

7. It follows the intended line smoothly and accurately.

8. Where retraced, it appears as one line of stitching.

9. It shows no patching in topstitching.

10. It is not tied at the ends of seams that are to be crossed with another line of stitching; and it is not cut off close at the ends until crossed with another line of stitching.

11. It has tied ends at darts, dart-tucks, tucks, or pleats left about a quarter-inch long instead of being clipped short.

12. It has understitching on the seam side of facings about $\frac{1}{16}$ inch from the edge, catching the enclosed seams to the facing but not to the topside of the garment.

THREADING THE MACHINE   Directions for filling the bobbin and threading the machine are to be found in the booklet furnished with the brand and model of your machine. In general, the following information will be useful.

The *spool thread* follows in sequence from right to left, under and through the guides and regulators. The *needle* is set with its grooved side on the same side as the last thread carrier—the thread is then led along the groove to the eye.

ADJUSTING LENGTH OF STITCH   The length of stitch should be adjusted to the *weight or texture of the material, as well as to the intended use.* The general average on such fabrics as broadcloth is 14 to 16 stitches per inch. Slightly shorter stitches are used where there is strain and for topstitching finer fabrics; longer stitches are used for inside or enclosed seams; and extra-long stitches are used for basting.

1. For average-weight fabrics use medium (No. 14) needles; for fine sewing, especially on silk and nylon, use fine (No. 9 or No. 11) needles.

2. For machine basting, use a long stitch—6 to 8 per inch.

3. For staystitching use a standard stitch, 12 to 16 per inch.

4. For heavy coatings, use 8 to 12 per inch; suiting, silks, and rayons, 10 to 14; silk sheers, 10 to 16; rayon and nylon sheers, 9 to 12; pile, 10 to 14; organdy, 14 to 18; sailcloth, 8 to 10; wool or acetate jersey, 7 to 10.

RECOGNIZING AND REGULATING TENSION   Learning to recognize standard tension and to analyze poor tension promptly is necessary for efficient sewing. When you are sure of the trouble, it is easier to make the proper adjustment. You can learn to identify good and poor tension by either its *appearance* or its *performance* (Fig. 13-1).

In a perfect or balanced tension, *b,* the stitches are slightly oval, pinched in at the ends, and evenly shaped or regular. The stitches look alike on either side of the work both as to shape and tightness.

When the *upper tension is too tight, a,* the spool thread lies flat or *floats on the upper side,* and the work draws or puckers. More of the bobbin thread shows

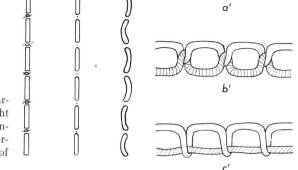

Figure 13-1. Right-side appearance of machine stitches: *a*, tight upper thread; *b*, balanced tensions; *c*, loose upper thread. Corresponding cross sections of stitches, *a′*, *b′*, *c′*.

between the stitches on the upper side than in a perfect tension. It has been pulled up that way by the too-tight spool thread.

When the *upper tension is too loose, c,* the stitches on the upper side look fat, bulgy, loose, sometimes looped, sometimes staggered in a sort of wavy line, and *none of the bobbin thread shows on the surface.*

It is easier to recognize tension by performance than by appearance. Stitch over two layers of cloth on the bias (Fig. 13-2). Then stretch the cloth firmly between your fingers and thumb. In a balanced tension neither thread breaks with moderate stretching, but under greater stress both will break. If the *upper thread breaks,* the *upper tension is tighter than the lower.* If the *lower thread breaks,* the upper tension is looser than the lower (the lower is too tight).

Another good way to recognize a perfect tension is to stitch and pivot for a square corner. If the corner draws a little or does not make a perfect right angle, the tension needs adjusting; if the stitch seems to draw or jump across the corner on the top side, the upper tension is too tight; if this effect shows up on the wrong side, the upper tension is too loose.

Study the instruction book for your machine and make adjustments as directed. After making a slight change to increase or decrease the tension, as indicated by its performance, stitch another sample on a double layer of bias and test it again. Keep adjusting and testing until a sample of balanced, perfect stitching is obtained.

REGULATING PRESSURE ON THE PRESSER FOOT   The pressure exerted on the fabric by the pressure foot is responsible for the smooth, even feeding of the fabric. Greater pressure is needed for adequate control on thick, spongy fabrics. Lighter pressure is required for sheer fabrics. Learn the pressures needed for various weights and textures of fabrics and how adjustments are to be made on your machine.

SELECTION OF THREAD   Information relative to types and sizes of thread suitable for use on various fabrics has been presented on p. 173. Special threads are available for use with man-made fibers and for knits, to provide qualities in harmony with their fiber content and stretchability.

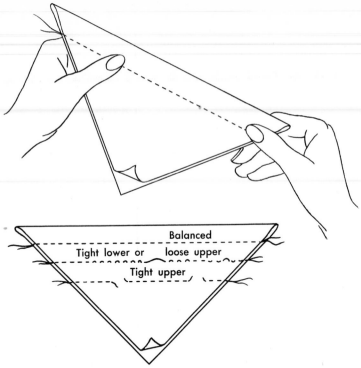

Figure 13-2. Test tension by stitching on a double layer of bias and stretching. The tighter thread will break.

Machine Control

Electric sewing machines may be operated with either foot or knee control. Begin by turning the balance wheel with the right hand to position the needle, then gradually press on the control. (Beginners are advised to practice with the machine unthreaded.) Keep the right hand on the balance wheel for a slow start and a gradual ending. Coordinate the power control with the right-hand control of the balance wheel. To begin work with precision, the left hand must do the guiding when the right hand is on the balance wheel.

EFFICIENT TECHNIQUES

Before beginning, pull up bobbin thread; left hand holds needle thread, right hand turns band wheel until needle takes *one* stitch down into feed and up. Pull needle thread until bobbin thread comes up (Fig. 13-3, *a*).

Keep bulk of work at left to avoid crowding under the arm of the machine, *b*.

In beginning and ending, to have complete control, stitch slowly with right hand on balance wheel and left hand on work.

In beginning, before lowering the presser foot, have take-up at highest point and position just the point of the needle in the fabric about $\frac{1}{16}$ inch from edge so that the feed has something to catch into, *b*. Be sure threads are *under* the presser foot—either straight back or diagonally back. It helps to hold them back a while after starting on slippery fabrics.

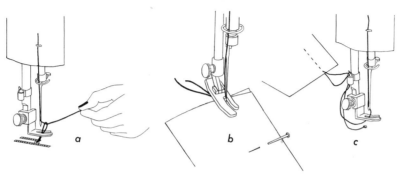

Figure 13-3. To begin sewing, pull bobbin thread up by holding the spool thread and lay threads back of presser foot. To end sewing, stop with needle up and pull work back. To cut off thread ends, scissors are preferred to the cutter, *c*.

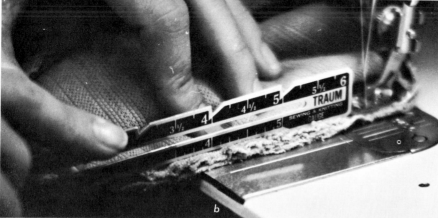

Figure 13-4. *a*, Controlling fullness in stitching is simplified by use of a tool to distribute and hold the fullness firmly along the edge of the seam allowance, *b*.

In ending, stop machine before running off the cloth to avoid tangling in the bobbin case and damaging the feed or presser foot.

In ending, stop with needle and take-up at highest point to avoid unthreading the machine when beginning to sew again; *always leave two or three inches of thread to prevent unthreading, c.* Pull the work straight back with threads under the presser foot to have enough in position to begin the next line of stitching. This habit lessens danger of bending or breaking the needle. At ends of seams, clip with small scissors to leave ½ to 1 inch dangling. Longer dangles get caught in other sewing; if cut off completely, stitching will ravel back. Tying or retracing ends of seams wastes time and may tighten or pucker the work.

Keep work well up on the machine; avoiding this dragging weight means that you have better control of the fabric while stitching.

If the top layer of the fabric tends to pile up, with extra length just ahead of the presser foot, the pressure on the presser bar needs adjustment. With pile fabrics, the adjustment of length between the two layers of cloth may be better-controlled if the layers are kept separated—lift the top layer slightly ahead of the presser foot—to avoid interlocking of the fabric yarns. A special "walking" presser foot is available for control of this problem.

If it is necessary to stop midway in a line of stitching, stop with the needle down to avoid disturbing the evenness of the stitching—a skipped stitch, or a looped thread.

The expert arches her fingers (Fig. 13-4) like a good piano player or typist. The left hand anchors cloth, and the right hand guides fabric into the feed and along the guide or gauge. For difficult basting, ease-stitching, or unusual shapes, stitch more slowly and bring the left fingertips closer to the presser foot.

Gauges and Guidelines

Following a gauge assures accuracy and speed without great effort. The metal screw is common equipment with machines (Fig. 13-5, *a*). Different seam widths marked on the throat plate or bed of the machine are a distinct advantage. If your machine does not have this type of gauge, or an alternative arrangement, a gauge can be improvised by the use of a strip of masking tape placed parallel with the presser foot, with its edge ½ inch from the needle hole to mark the location for staystitching. Draw a line on the tape ⅝ inch from the needle hole to mark the standard seam width, or, place a second piece of tape—in color—on the masking tape, *b*.

With practice, one learns where to focus the eyes in order to estimate spaces or margins for stitching straight lines or smooth curves. The widths of the toes of the presser foot can be a practical help in this direction, *c, d,* and *e*. In stitching along a fold, focus the eyes on the foldline and the needle, or on the line of stitching in relation to the fold, *f*. Also, line up the exact position of the presser foot in relation to the fold.

Special gauges for welt seams or topstitching are available. The quilter (Fig. 13-6) is often included in standard equipment. A magnetic metal bar or block is also a handy guide easily moved.

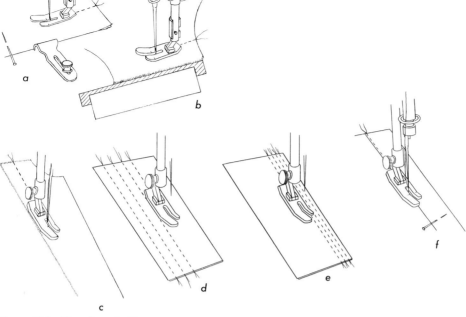

Figure 13-5. Use of a suitable gauge increases efficiency and speed: *a*, metal gauge attached with thumb screw; *b*, guidelines marked on the bed of the machine or masking tape; *c*, *d*, *e*, *f*, measuring with presser foot or focusing eyes on relationship between presser foot, needle, and edges or lines on the fabric.

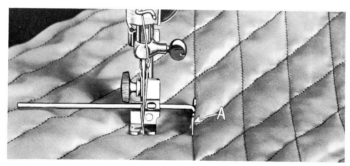

Figure 13-6. Quilter attachment with a gauge useful for tucks, topstitching, and welt seams. (Courtesy of Singer Manufacturing Company.)

A plastic or rubber gauge with ridges on it is helpful to hold slippery fabrics firm; it is especially useful for the blind or the partially sighted.

To stitch around a square or a circumference, begin some distance away from a corner or a weak point (such as an intersecting seam), so that retracing or tying a knot will not weaken, tangle, or be conspicuous.

To correct an irregularity, be sure that endings are on the seam side of the stitching, not the garment side, to avoid evidences on the outside of garment, *b*. Keep the two lines parallel and as close together as possible if the seam is to be pressed open (Fig. 13-7. *a*).

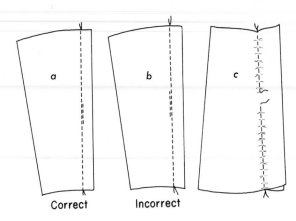

Correct   Incorrect

Figure 13-7. To correct an irregular line of stitching by patching, make the beginnings and endings on the seam side of the line as close to the intended line as possible. No knots are necessary when retracing overlaps the old stitching. If seam puckers, break stitches, smooth, and patch.

Puckering of fabrics may be due to faulty threading, too-tight tension, or too-short stitches, especially on bias seams, *c*. Break the stitch in several places; rip and restitch. Try a piece of lightweight paper next to the feed dog. Distortion of grain is decreased by using finer needles (size No. 9 or No. 11), synthetic or silk thread, a loosely wound bobbin, stitching slowly to keep the needle cool. A piece of masking tape over the needle hole makes a smaller hole, which prevents fabrics from being drawn down into it.

Stretchy knits and bias should be fed loosely into the machine to insure elasticity.

PIVOTING

Pivoting is a technique for changing direction in stitching. Although the machine instruction book will explain how to do reverse stitching, there are times when it is an advantage to turn the work and reverse the direction, rather than to stitch backward. Better control of the location of the line of stitching may be possible as one stitches forward.

To pivot, stop the sewing at a termination point with the needle down in the cloth, lift the presser foot, turn the cloth into the desired position, lower the presser foot, and stitch in the new direction (Fig. 13-8).

MACHINE ATTACHMENTS

Familiarity with one's tools—their advantages and their limitations—is essential for good work in sewing, as it is in any craft. Without it you cannot plan a piece of work that shows fine workmanship or that is original in design.

A few hours are not too much to spend in mastering an attachment for the sewing machine. Attend a demonstration to see how it is done; then, with the direction book and some practice materials, sit down to try it yourself. Be sure that the machine itself is working perfectly. Discover the use of adjustable parts. Never run the machine with the attachment unless some fabric is in place; the teeth of such pieces as the ruffler and buttonholer may become damaged.

Generally, the attachment is limited to a few size changes or none. For instance,

Figure 13-8. Pivoting is a technique for turning corners. Stop with needle down in the exact corner before lifting the presser foot to turn the cloth.

a tucker may provide adjustments for several different tuck widths, whereas only one width of binding may be obtainable.

MACHINE TROUBLES

The instruction book for your machine is your first source of information when troubles develop. Difficulties often arise because of failure to use the machine as directed. Therefore, a careful check of suggested procedures for the processes being attempted may disclose the reason for the difficulty. Look in the instruction book for a section providing helpful pointers on how to deal with these difficulties.

Threads tangling at the beginning of the stitching or down in the bobbin case may be caused by

1. Failure to have the bobbin thread drawn up through the hole in the throat plate before starting to sew.

2. Failure to have both threads pulled back and under the presser foot.

3. Failure to keep the machine oiled and free of lint.

If the machine is jammed or locked, first remove your work without damaging it. With scissors or a pin, pick out the tangles and lint in bobbin case. Oil parts that seem dry. If it still sticks, put your left index finger and thumb into bobbin case and slightly wiggle it and lift up on it; with your right hand, work the balance wheel back and forth to dislodge the caught thread. Complete the cleaning.

PURCHASING A MACHINE

When planning to buy a sewing machine, give careful consideration to the types available in relation to your needs and inclinations. Experience in the school laboratory or elsewhere will be extremely helpful in making a decision. Study as many sources of information as possible before making a decision.[1]

[1]*Buying Your Home Sewing Machine,* Home and Garden Bulletin No. 38 (Washington, D.C.: U.S. Department of Agriculture, 1969).

14

Hand Sewing Skills

Hand Sewing

Hand basting is less used today because machine basting is easier and less time-consuming. However, hand basting is often required on difficult fabrics such as crepe, chiffon, and velvet; on irregularly shaped pieces, pleats, lapped seams, and circular hems; and in basting underlinings, flat on the table. *Hand hemming* is used almost entirely on better quality dresses and coats, especially on soft, delicate fabrics.

Using one's hands as experts do is often the clue to a better product, to speed, and to actual enjoyment of the art of sewing. Holding the hands in a relaxed but purposeful position,[1] holding the work lightly, and *using a thimble* will be most

[1]Note the hands of talented musicians, typists, surgeons, electricians, cooks. Also, see Figure 13-4.

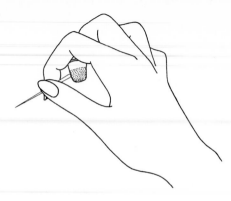

Figure 14-1. The advantage in using a thimble for hand sewing is the development of speed, when it is used correctly.

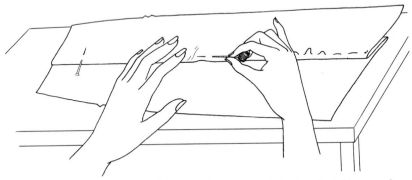

Figure 14-2. Position I. Use both hands to anchor work flat on the table in such processes as pinning a seam, or placing pattern on fabric. Push up a small fold slightly ahead of the point of the pin or needle, or use a curved needle (see p. 260).

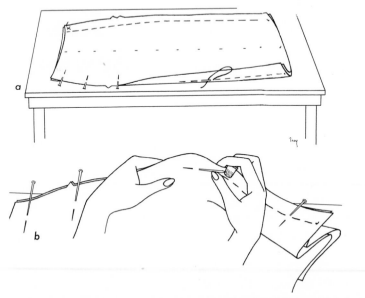

Figure 14-3. Position II. Seams were previously pinned flat on table to prevent stretching. Hold the work with the edge up in the hands and the bulk down on the table or in the lap out of the way.

helpful in developing both accuracy and speed in hand sewing (Fig. 14-1). Skill is acquired by concentration and practice, repeated at first on simple problems. Later, one will gain speed, often accompanied by some rhythm such as music.

BASIC HAND TECHNIQUES

Directions and illustrations here and elsewhere usually assume a right-handed worker. If you are left-handed, reverse the directions as to where to begin. For the illustrations, use a mirror or tracing reversal (See Fig. 14-4).

1. The bulk of the work is placed down or toward the worker with only the edge up in the hands to increase speed, to avoid crushing the work, and cramping the hand.

2. Most stitches progress from *right to left,* but the catch stitch is worked from left to right. Some decorative stitches progress vertically from the top down toward the worker. After getting started at the right place, turn narrow edges across your forefinger, always keeping the smaller amount of fabric in your hand. The left-handed worker should reverse, progressing left to right.

3. In general, the needle slants toward your left shoulder if you are right-handed (to the right, if you are left-handed). Study the illustrations or watch a demonstrator for variations of this rule. If the needle is fine (about size 10), you can pick up very tiny stitches. Pointing a needle away from oneself is awkward and tiring; it results in poor work and loss of time.

4. Begin and end hand sewing on some wrong-side construction, invisible on the outside.

5. Cultivate the habit of not pulling the thread up tight. If some stitches are tight, go back and stretch the sewing or use the point of the needle to loosen them. The looseness keeps the sewing soft, elastic, inconspicuous, and professional-looking. A too-tight thread will pucker the work and break in laundering and wearing.

STANDARD POSITIONS OF WORK

POSITION I Keep work flat on the table (Fig. 14-2) for pleats, folds, lapped seams, long seams, and hems that slip or stretch easily; for baste-marking lines, catch-stitching, basting underlinings or interfacings in place, and pinning patterns to cloth.

Both hands are extended, lightly curved, to *anchor* layers on the table and to keep fabric free from wrinkles. Work from right to left. The left index finger pushes up a little tuck or fold of cloth directly in front of the needle, while the needle in the right hand pushes through the fold one stitch at a time. Do not pull all the thread through but wait until you have taken several such stitches. The little fingers and the left thumb serve as weights to keep the work from slipping.

POSITION II Hold the work up off the table, horizontal in both hands, (Fig. 14-3) for running stitches—basting *short* plain seams, narrow hems, the first turn of a lapped seam; for gathering by hand and easing in fullness. Make stitches $\frac{1}{8}$ to $\frac{1}{4}$ inch long for basting and $\frac{1}{16}$ inch long for gathers. This is the most fundamental of all hand skills. The material is in a horizontal position between the thumb

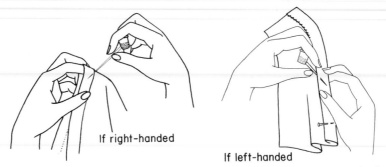

If right-handed

If left-handed

Figure 14-4. Position III. Hold the work vertically across the forefinger for hemming.

and forefinger of each hand. The hands are loosely curved. Work from right to left. Take one stitch at the beginning to hold the needle in place until your right hand is correctly located. With a definite wrist motion, shake or weave the needle up and down through the cloth. The left hand should aid also by bending or wiggling the cloth up and down at the point of the needle. After the needle is full of small stitches, pull the fabric back on the thread but leave the needle in place for the next stitch.

At first, practice to get the shaking or wiggling movement rather than to get uniformity in the length of the stitches. After practice you will be able to secure very fine ones. Notice how cupped and curved both hands are and that the side of the thimble rather than the end is used to push the needle. For small stitches, keep the thumb and index fingers of both hands close to the point of the needle—the farther apart you keep the thumbs and index fingers the longer your stitches will be.

POSITION III Hold the work across the forefinger (Fig. 14-4). Use this position for hemming, slip-basting, and many decorative stitches.

POSITION IV Hold the work horizontally—pinched firmly between the thumb and forefinger (Fig. 14-5). Use this position for overcasting, buttonholing, and running-hemming.

HAND BASTING

Wise planning, staystitching, the use of pins, and more expert handling of the machine can eliminate much hand basting. Learn all the ways of saving time, but remember that there are places where quality of work counts more. The ability to baste with ease in the minimum amount of time can be a valuable asset on some occasions.

Stitches used in basting are *running* (Fig. 14-6, *a* and *b*); *diagonal* or tailor's basting, *c*; and *slip*, *d* (using the slip-hemming stitch).

Lapped seams, pleats, eased-in seams, and decorative details are places where even the most experienced worker relies on good basting, especially if the material is difficult to handle.

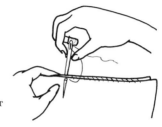

Figure 14-5. Position IV. The work is held horizontally for overcasting and overhanding.

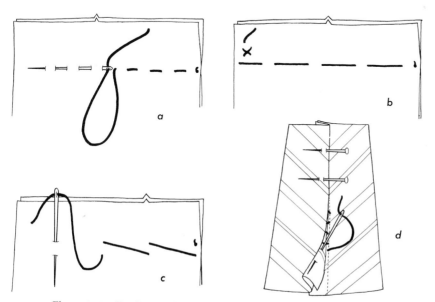

Figure 14-6. Basting stitches: *a,* even; *b,* uneven; *c,* diagonal; *d,* slip.

White thread is safest for basting on white and pastel colored fabrics. Dark colored threads often crock, leaving a colored dot where each stitch penetrated the fabric.

Basting with the grain keeps the fabric or piece in shape and reduces raveling. Have stitches firm enough to keep material secure but not puckered. Slightly stretch the basting before fastening the end. As a general rule, do not take back stitches in basting; they interfere with elasticity and a smooth set. Sometimes a back stitch may be necessary at intersecting seams to prevent them from slipping during machine work.

Place basting slightly to one side of the machine-stitching line to avoid the need for picking out those basting threads that get caught in the machine stitches. To end basting, a cross stitch in the seam allowance, *b,* is secure and easily removed. Cutting basting thread off too close to the work may result in its ripping during the fitting process. (Do not bite it!)

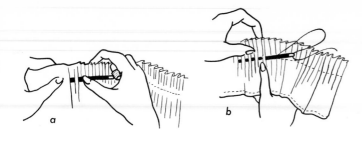

Figure 14-7. To gather, shake needle through cloth, with both thumbs in front of needle and cloth, both index fingers behind, all close together. Keep point of needle, *a*, near end of left index finger. Arrange a bunch of gathers on needle in fine pleats by pulling vertically before pulling needle through, *b*. Several rows make hand shirring more effective.

GATHERING

Hand gathering is done with $\frac{1}{16}$- to $\frac{1}{8}$-inch running stitches (Figs. 14-7, *a*, and 14-9, *a*). To condense excessive fullness into a small space, take long ($\frac{1}{2}$- to $\frac{3}{4}$-inch) stitches underneath and short stitches on the right side. For ordinary gathers or ease, shake the needle and cloth between the thumb and fingers of one hand (Fig. 14-7, *a*). With the other hand, firmly pull the gathers to set in little pleats along the needle, *b*. Then pull the needle out and repeat the procedure. Hand gathers around the top of a full skirt are easier to make if a long double thread or heavy-duty thread is used.

For *shirring* (Fig. 14-8), make two or more rows $\frac{1}{8}$ to $\frac{1}{4}$ inch apart. Draw up all the end threads together to produce the desired fullness and wind them in a figure-eight around a pin.

For *uniform gathers* (machine or hand) avoid stitching over seams. After seams are stitched, begin the gathering at the seam line, with seam allowance lifted out of the way. Gathering stitches should be sewn through one layer only. The gathers are then pinned to a band or other seam. Match notches, seamlines, ends, intersecting points, and centers to insure correct distribution. Place pins at right angles to the easing or gathering line (Fig. 14-9). It is wiser not to tie the ends of gathers until after fitting.

If you have used hand gathering, you should probably hand baste with small stitches. If you used machine gathering, you probably can stitch without basting, unless fitting is involved.

EASING-IN BY HAND

The back of the shoulder seam is usually longer than the front and so must be eased in. The back of a tight-fitting sleeve at the elbow, if not darted, is eased onto the front to allow for bending the elbow. Your pattern usually tells you where easing-in occurs. Whenever a pinned seam comes out unevenly, examine it carefully to see whether you have stretched one side or whether there is a part to be eased in.

Keep the full side uppermost, under your thumb (under your control!) (Fig. 14-10, *a*). Match the notches and then any intersecting seams or lines. Insert pins about one inch apart—perpendicular to the seamline—to distribute the fullness evenly. Use short stitches, $\frac{1}{8}$ inch or less. You are really gathering through two thicknesses. Use your *left thumb to mash down the fullness* on top until it disappears on the needle. It helps to cup the work over your left hand so that the eased-in portion arches above the plainer layer. Slightly stretch the seam and basting thread before fastening it off with a cross stitch and leave one inch or so of thread for "give" in fitting.

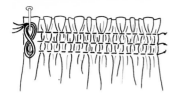

Figure 14-8. Shirring (several parallel rows of gathers)—pull all three threads at the same time; wind around a pin in a figure eight; then with both hands, arrange neatly.

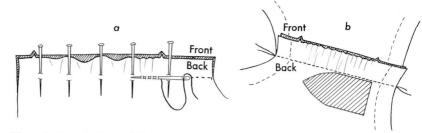

Figure 14-9. *a*, Easing-in fullness at shoulder seam by hand. *b*, After stitching, shrink out the ease by using the side of the iron with steam.

Figure 14-10. Tying an ordinary knot may not be new to you, but these steps may help you to teach a beginner some day!

After fitting, stitch and press with the grain. Press the piece over a tailor's ham with the seam turned away from the full side. Use the side of the iron parallel with the seam, *b*. Use some moisture to help shrink out the fullness. (See Chapter 15.)

Buttonholing and Embroidering

Buttonholing and blanket stitching are variations of the basic sewing stitches described in this chapter and in Chapters 24 and 28. Compare these with Figures 24-14 and 28-4.

OVERHANDING AND OVERCASTING

Overhanding (or whipping, now an out-moded term) applies to binding two edges together with an over-and-over, but shallow, stitch. (See Figures 14-5 and 27-20, *a* and *b*.) Overcasting follows the same procedure but is spaced rather loosely with stitches about $\frac{1}{4}$ inch apart. It is used as a seam finish to prevent fraying, but has been largely replaced by pinking, zigzagging, or leaving the edge raw (Fig. 19-7).

PINS The simplest process can often be made easier and shorter and give a more professional result. The art of pinning two layers flat on a table without their slipping requires deftness from both hands. Use the little fingers to anchor the work or brace it against slipping; the left index finger pushes a slight fold toward the point of the pin and is not moved until the right hand has pushed the pin forward and the fold is smoothed out (See Fig. 12-6, *b*).

KNOTS Steps for tying knots in basting thread are shown in Figure 14-10. See Figure 18-5 for the steps in tying a square knot.

291

Pressing

In dressmaking, pressing is as important as stitching. In the dress factory, the presser is a highly paid technician.

If a professional look is to be achieved, each construction line must be adequately pressed before another seam is stitched across it.

Pressing can shrink or stretch a fabric at will; it can mold flat cloth over rounded pads to make it fit the curves of the body. Poor pressing stretches necklines, seams, and bias out of shape. In good pressing we strive to retain the original texture and finish of the cloth: if the fabric is crepey, we try to keep it that way; if it is fuzzy and dull, we must not flatten the nap, rub it the wrong way, or let it develop a shine. We do not like to see on the outside of the garment any marks or imprints of seams and darts. Overpressing results in a homemade look.

Creasing folds with an iron, in bands, belts, straight hems, and pleats, may form guidelines to do away with some marking and basting; however, care must be taken in using this technique on sharp curves, bias edges, or crepes, as it is easy to stretch them out of shape.

Pressing Equipment

An adjustable ironing board is essential for comfort and efficiency. In addition, a tailor's *press board* (Fig. 15-1, *b*) placed on a table, although not essential, is helpful for pressing short seams and small details. The table prevents the garment from stretching during pressing. The narrow end is just right for shrinking the sleeve-cap seam. A thick, soft padding on the ironing board gives more successful results, especially in pressing heat-sensitive fibers.

One of the most important pressing jobs is that of molding the garment around the sleeve cap and darts to preserve the natural curves of the body. A sleeve roll—cloth cut in the shape of a sleeve and stuffed, *d*—works as well as, if not better than, a sleeve board (1½ to 4 inches by 18 inches). The tailor's "ham" is valuable for this purpose, *e*.

The *point presser, a,* is popular for pressing seams open in lapel and collar points (11 by 4 by ¾ inches on a base 12 by 5 by 1 inches); use it uncovered. The curved end of the point presser is useful in pressing seams open on the ends of round collars and other curves. A rolling pin slit lengthwise and covered is useful

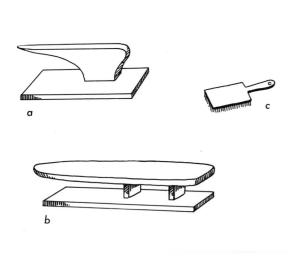

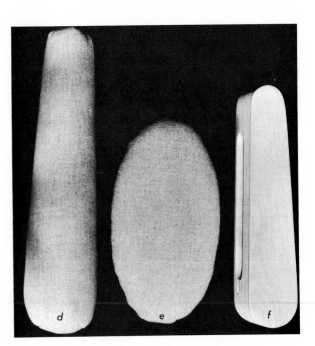

Figure 15-1. Equipment for pressing.

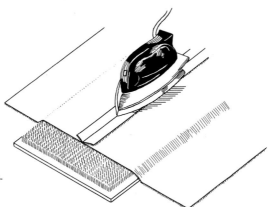

Figure 15-2. Needle board for pressing pile fabrics, especially velvets.

to press the seams without leaving imprints on the right side. Tailors like uncovered hardwood—such as a yardstick or a broom handle with one side flattened to prevent rolling—for flat seams; they prefer to press right side down against the hardwood, but right side up over a well-padded surface.

Tailors use a beater, *f*, to flatten seams, pleats, coat fronts, and collar edges for sharper lines; it is made of heavy hardwood, beveled and grooved for easier handling. A firm brush, *c*, can be used to preserve a soft texture.

A needle board is used for pressing pile fabrics (Fig. 15-2).

Cheesecloth, organdy, unsized muslin, cotton marquisette curtain fabric, or chemically treated cloths make good *press cloths* to protect the garment from overheating, scorching, or developing a shine. Be sure to remove any sizing. With the dry iron, and often with the steam iron, extra moisture is needed. Wet cheesecloth is ideal, for the moisture spreads more evenly and the nap tends to cling to the fibers of the fabric being pressed; when raised, the press cloth draws them up with the steam, thereby avoiding the hard, flat look. A strip about 9 by 24 inches is easier to handle than a large square. Keep the edge near the edge of the iron so that you can lift it frequently and peek under. Organdy and the transparent press cloths have the advantage of see-through property. On textured fabrics use a strip or scrap of the same material for a press cloth, as woolen on woolen, or a woolen on a twill, crepe, or rib- or rough-surfaced fabric. Avoid new unbleached muslin, because the natural oil or sizing in it scorches quickly, sticks to the iron, and soils your work. Bleached muslin, when new, has starch or sizing in it, which also soils the iron. If you do not have a steam iron, two press cloths are desirable—one damp, one dry. With a steam iron, use a dry press cloth on the right side of fabrics (unless cotton or linen) to protect against shine or scorch.

Tissue paper or heavier paper *slipped under* darts, seams, and hems being pressed on the wrong side prevents imprints from showing on the outside. However, its use is unnecessary on ordinary fabrics, if you learn to handle the iron correctly: touch the seam lightly with the edge of the iron, after steaming it well.

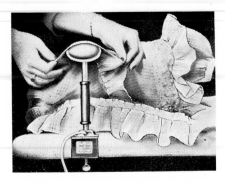

Figure 15-3. Electric puff iron. (Courtesy of Vin-Max Co.)

Keeping the press board cool and dry aids in professional press jobs. Move the work to different areas on the press board. A perforated type of ironing board minimizes this problem.

A *steam iron* that can be used dry will spray extra moisture. An electric *puff iron* (egg size) is ideal for ruffles and puffed sleeves (Fig. 15-3). *Home pressers*, with pressure plates similar to those in a commercial plant, are now available. An electric hand steamer is a useful appliance, especially for travelers.

USING AN IRON

1. Do not let the iron cord drag over your work.

2. To avoid scorching the ironing board cover, tilt the iron back on its heel when not in use.

3. If starch or sizing is stuck to the iron, let it cool; then scour it with soap and nonscratching scouring powder or baking soda.

4. Turn off the iron when it is not in use.

5. It is safer to use distilled water in a steam iron.

REMOVING DEEP WRINKLES AND CORRECTING GRAIN   Fabrics of garments that are wrinkled, puffy, warped, or stretched off-grain can be restored to their original straight shape and smoothness by care in pressing. First arrange and pin the material on the press board or commercial cutting board, straight as to grain and wrong side up. Cover it with a damp cloth, or dampen the press board, and cover the fabric with a dry press cloth. Lower and lift the iron to produce steam in the cloth. Rearrange the fabric to straighten the grain where needed. If it is badly wrinkled, apply extra steam and pressure. Work with the grain, but do not push the iron about. Too much pressure produces a shine. Lifting the press cloth frequently causes the steam to rise, lifting with it the fuzz of the fabric. Decide if more or less moisture and pressure are required. Such steaming will shrink a puffed, stretched area back into shape. Allow the fabric to dry on a table or on the cutting board.

1. Regulate the iron temperature as directed on the permanent care label, or on the dial setting for the fabric. If you are unsure about fiber content, begin by testing with a low-temperature setting.

2. If you are working on thin fabrics or doing slow work, as in shrinking or pressing gathers, keep the iron temperature slightly lower than for heavier fabrics.

3. Linen and cotton require considerable moisture for eliminating wrinkles and should be pressed until dry for a smooth finish.

4. Wool requires moisture in pressing to prevent damage to the fibers—dry heat makes them brittle.

5. Thick materials need more pressure; use the beater to create sharp flat edges. The procedure in steam pressing is to apply the steam, lift the iron, use the beater, hold it firmly for a second or two, and lift. Too much pressure can develop a shine; too little does not flatten enough.

6. In general, the thermoplastic, man-made fibers are heat sensitive—they tend to melt and glaze; therefore temperatures must be watched carefully. These fabrics often press better dry; use a soft pressing pad to help prevent glazing.

7. Thermoplastics, except permanent press fabrics, can be heat-set, so care must be taken to avoid creasing before the garment is properly fitted.

8. Use the tip or edge of the iron on seams; hold the iron above the fabric and apply it lightly to easily damaged textures.

9. Press with the grain.

10. Avoid pressing over bastings or pins.

11. Press embroidery, braid, buttons, and such rough textures from the wrong side over a soft pad, as over several layers of a Turkish towel.

12. Press collars, lapels, cuffs, belts, and pockets first on the wrong side, then finish them on the right side very lightly over a press cloth. First press firmly along the edges to maintain a true silhouette. Work from the outer edges toward the inside.

13. Avoid pressing lengthwise creases in sleeves or lapels. To avoid a crease, let the fold of the sleeve hang off the board while you press the rest of the sleeve—if a sleeve board or tailor's roll is unavailable.

14. Remove any stains or soil before pressing, as heat would probably set the stain.

15. Press curved areas of the garment over a curved or rounded pad; if none is available, improvise with a folded towel over the curved end of the ironing board.

16. To reduce the shine on worsteds, sponge them with a cloth slightly dampened in a weak solution of two tablespoons of vinegar to a quart of water, or one tablespoon of ammonia to a quart of water. There also are commercial preparations to remove shine. Steam-press the fabric and keep raising the press cloth to raise the nap of the wool. Brush it briskly. Hang the garment up to air and dry. A wool press cloth or firm cheesecloth helps to pull up the nap. If the nap has been worn down, rub it gently with very fine sandpaper or a suede brush. Use the same techniques on any fabric where the shine is the result of overpressing.

Figure 15-4. Lift both iron and press cloth up and down so steam can escape. Use a tailor's ham to mold curves; press from wide end toward point; place iron lightly on fullness surrounding point of dart, to shrink and smooth the fabric.

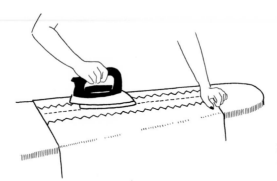

Figure 15-5. Hold straight line (as seams, belts, yoke edges) firmly directly ahead of iron.

Pressing During Construction

DARTS

A dart is used to fit flat cloth to a curve on the body. Preserve the curve or bulge by pressing the dart over a tailor's ham, but arrange the dart in a straight line (Fig. 15-4).

Press from the wide end to the point. Observe the fullness at the point of the dart and set the iron in different positions over the curved ham to remove the slight bubble of fullness.

Underarm darts and elbow darts are pressed downward on the wrong side. Vertical darts such as those in the top of the skirt or at the shoulder or neck of the blouse are pressed on the wrong side toward CF or CB.

Press the fold of the dart flat separately on the wrong side before pressing it to one side of the garment. Then turn to the right side and press along the stitching line of the dart—over a press cloth—so it appears as open and flat as a seam. Turn back to the wrong side to remove any imprint by pressing under the dart. Add more steam if necessary.

Wide darts may be trimmed to ⅝-inch width, but not slit to the end (Fig. 18-3). Press them open. Curved darts and darts that taper at both ends, such as the darts in a jacket, should be clipped at the widest part before pressing to keep them from drawing (Fig. 18-2). Dart-tucks are not pressed beyond the stitching line so that fullness will fall softly.

Press each seam or any line of construction before crossing it with another line of stitching. Lengthwise seams must be pressed before the circumferences they enter are stitched, if they are to lie flat and smooth.

Have the seam perfectly straight on the board before steam-pressing. Use one hand to hold the seam firmly and straight ahead of the iron (Fig. 15-5); avoid stretching it out of shape. Press with the grain—not against it. Check the straightness of your line with a yardstick (especially with long seams).

Press a seam first from the wrong side and later touch it up on the right side to give a perfectly pressed look.

The first step in pressing a seam is to press it flat on the wrong side and then press it open, even though it will be closed later. Seams to be pressed together in the same direction, such as facings or enclosed seams, are more perfect if pressed open first and then pressed together in the direction they are to lie. The first pressing should be dry, the second with moisture. (The *exception* to this rule is seams that join facings to the garment and that are to be understitched. They can be handled successfully in light- and medium-weight fabrics without first pressing them open.)

Plain seams used in piecings and joinings of bias strips should be pressed open. The enclosed seam of straight facings and straight French seams are more quickly manipulated if they are pressed open before turning. Lapped seams and seams at the back edges of pleats should not be pressed open. Armhole seams are not pressed open. Sheers look better if the seams are pressed to one side—the seam shows through the cloth and its width appears out of proportion for the lightweight fabric. If very sheer, the narrower French seam is desirable.

If gore seams are to be closed in sheer fabrics, front gore seams are pressed toward the CF, back gore seams toward the CB. *Seams with much fullness on one side are turned to the direction of the plain side.* For example, with a plain shoulder seam, press to the front, but with a shoulder having shirrings at the front, press to the back. Observe your guide sheet for special cases where the designer's plan may indicate a different treatment. Try to recognize the reason for the variation.

In pressing curved seams, as in princess-style garments, have your scissors handy at the pressboard to slash the concave (inside) curves. (See Fig. 18-2.) Press such curved seams over a ham. A few short clips are better than one long one; wait until the last fitting before cutting too many. Convex curves may require notching.

A good technique for a lapped seam is to lay the press cloth over it only about $\frac{1}{4}$ inch past the stitching line. Press without allowing the pressure of the iron to rest on the raw edges. Another method is to keep the raw edge of the lapped seam off the edge of the ironing board.

Pleats

Pin and/or baste the pleats in place, keeping basting stitches a short distance back from the fold of pleat ($\frac{1}{4}$ inch) so that it can be pressed without pressing over the basting. After the first fitting, stitch as far as planned from the bottom up, if the pleat is to be stitched in place. Clip the bastings along the stitching but not below; remove. Steam-press only the stitched part of the pleating until it is smooth and flat, ready to be attached to the belt or yoke.

After the second fitting, the lower hemline is established. Remove enough of the pleat bastings at the lower edge to permit putting in the hem. Finish the hem and press. Clip the seams at the back edge of pleats where they enter the hem (Fig. 26-5).

Pin the pleats and grain straight on the ironing board (Fig. 15-6). Steam press first on the right, then the wrong, side. Press the hem just lightly enough to crease mark. After the fitting and hemming, press again across the hem. (Skirts pleated all the way around may be hemmed before pressing—all fitting being done at waist or hipline.) Then start at the top and set the iron down evenly along each pleat. Keep lifting the iron and the press cloth. If the pleats are not creasing sharply enough, increase the dampness, the pressure (use the beater), and perhaps the heat. Remove bastings before the work is dry. Slip a strip of paper under each pleat. Cover with the cloth and press. Turn to the wrong side and press the back edges of folds with the paper strips in place. Turn back to the right side to touch up where needed; press all pleats dry except in wool—let them dry neatly on a hanger or flat on a table. Pressing each fold of the pleat, on both outside and inside edges, will sharpen them. (Basting, by machine or hand, along the back edges of pleats, especially through the hem, will be a great advantage.)

You may be able to lay in pleats in some materials without basting. To do so, place the skirt section to be pleated right side up over the ironing board. Fold a pleat in by folding on one line of markings and bringing to the next line. Pin the fabric to the board at both top and bottom, stretching it slightly taut. Check all the pleats for even spacing. Place pins along the side of the board to prevent the weight of the skirt from dragging the pleats and pulling them out of line. Steam

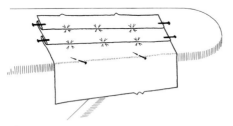

Figure 15-6. To press pleats, pin ends to board and along sides so that weight will not drag article off.

Figure 15-7. Use side of iron parallel with seam to shrink out fullness. Point iron into seam to preserve fullness.

press by lifting the iron up and down evenly along (not across) the pleats. Lift it frequently to see that the pleats are not disturbed. Slip a piece of paper under each pleat and press again to remove print marks.

GATHERS

Gathers are pressed by holding them firmly at the stitching line with your left hand as you nose the point of the iron into them (Fig. 15-7). Reduce the heat for such slow work, or you are likely to scorch the fabric.

EASED FULLNESS

To shrink out ease or fullness, hold the side of the iron parallel to the stitched line, beginning a few inches away from it. Then move the iron across the fullness, bringing it all the way to the seamline to flatten and shrink the fabric (Fig. 15-7). Examples of areas that may require such treatment are a back shoulder seam that has no dart; the sleeve cap, elbow fullness, and extra fullness in the hem of a circular skirt.

THE WAISTLINE

Waistline seams are pressed away from the fuller side, and if they are inside curves, they should be clipped. Arrange the seam in a curved position right side up on the board or a ham. Press to avoid imprints. Use the side of the iron parallel with stitching.

Inset belts may be pressed right side up over a ham or point presser, or the edge of the inset may be placed along the very edge of the ironing board. Place the edge of a press cloth on the edge of a lapped seam. Do not press hard. Use the side of the iron parallel with the side of the belt, so that it barely touches the stitching and fold of the lapped seam and entirely escapes pressing the gathers or the raw edges of the seam underneath. Hold the belt firmly straight ahead of the iron to establish a straight line.

THE SLEEVE

To give a fashion-right look, press the sleeves lightly on a sleeve board or pad, without a center crease. The current fashion or the style you desire will dictate the direction for pressing the armhole seam after it is stitched in. If a puffed or

Figure 15-8. *a*, Touch up outside of armhole seam lightly. *b*, Use press cloth or slipcover on iron for top pressing. If today's style calls for a slight roll at top of sleeve cap, do not press flat but just enough so that seam does not look un-finished.

a   *b*

stand-up silhouette is in vogue (as the empire look with puffed sleeves), leave the armhole seam unpressed. If the gathered sleeve is to fall naturally in line with the shoulder seam, clip it at the notches and at intervals above (on the garment side only) and press the seam toward the body in the upper half. In pressing, hold a pad in your hand inside the sleeve cap and give a final pat or two on the right side, but do not try to plaster the seam flat (Fig. 15-8).

Shaping Bias Strips

When bias is used as a binding or facing, it can be stretched or eased in readily. The extra fullness, where eased in, can be shrunken or steamed out until the fullness disappears. A bias strip can be steamed and molded or shaped into a semicircle so that it can be more easily fitted around curves (Fig. 15-9). To do so, slightly dampen the strip. Do not have the iron as hot as you normally would for this fabric, because in working more slowly you might scorch it. With your free hand, shape the strip (without stretching) into a curve. Use the side of the iron parallel with the edge of the strip. Gently push the side of the iron toward the inner circle where the rippled fullness is. The steam will shrink out the fullness until there are no pleats left. Do not stretch the outer edge of the circle. If you have curved it too much, it can easily be stretched out when it is basted to the garment.

Note that such shaping widens the strip. Where you shrink in less fullness, it will be narrower. Use a gauge to trim the strip to the desired width. Such strips have great decorative possibilities. (See Chapter 20.)

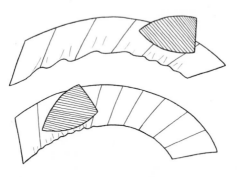

Figure 15-9. Molding bias strip into a circular shape for use as a trim or facing on curves. Use left hand to distribute fullness evenly as side of iron shrinks inside curve.

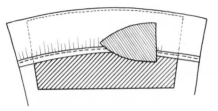

Figure 15-10. Shrink out fullness, with iron parallel to eased line. Press lower edge from bottom of skirt toward top, with the grain—*not around* the skirt, and not over bastings. Keep paper between hem and skirt so that skirt will not be shrunk also and to avoid imprints on the right side. Keep lower edge a soft roll rather than too flat.

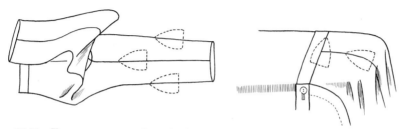

Figure 15-11. To press creases, place the legs on the board so that inner and outer seams match. The front crease stops just below the waist dart; back creases stop in line with the bottom of the crotch. Remove wrinkles around the seat and crotch on a pressing ham or over the end of the ironing board.

COLLARS

Use a curved pressing board or the curved end of the ironing board in pressing open the seam at the outer edge of a collar or other curved seam. If understitching is to be used, pressing the seam open can be eliminated in light- or medium-weight fabrics, where finger-pressing can serve adequately to hold the fabric in position for understitching—after the seam has been graded, or blended. The edge can then be pressed in a sharp crease without basting. Place the collar, or other part, on the ironing board, wrong side up. Adjust a few inches at a time—three or four—and press with the side of the iron parallel with the seam.

For pressing the seam open in ties (or string belts), use a wooden dowel stick or ruler slipped into the tie.

HEMS

After the hem at the bottom of the skirt has been marked, turned, and pinned (or basted) midway between the folded edge and the raw edge, the fullness, if any, at the top of the hem must be removed by easing (Figs. 15-10 and 26-1).

With a little practice, you may be able to shrink out fullness without an ease or gathering thread. Use the side of the iron to do this, and then trim the hem to an even width. When applying seam tape, this fullness can be controlled by easing the garment to the tape.

Fashion may decree whether the lower edge of the hem should be pressed, too, but avoid a sharp crease in silks, rayons, or sheers. To press these, use less moisture. In pressing the lower fold of a hem, press not around the hem but from the lower fold up to the hemming line, with more pressure on the fold line and less on the sewing.

PANTS

To press pants, first turn to the wrong side and press seams, hems, plackets, and pockets. Remove wrinkles around the seat and crotch on the rounded cushion or over the end of the board. Press cuffs, if any, with a piece of paper slipped

Figure 15-12. *a*, Iron a gathered ruffle along the hem first, position 1. Then point the iron into gathers, position 2. *b*, Arrange a circular ruffle on board in circular shape. Iron smooth with a diagonal or circular motion with the grain.

under them. Press the legs by folding on the board so that inner and outer seams match (Fig. 15-11). Place one leg flat on the board, inner leg up, and have the other leg folded back. Crease up as far as the crotch or as style demands. If a crease is to be used, it should continue, at least, to the lower edge of the jacket. Study current designs to determine whether creases are desirable.

THE FINAL PRESSING

Do not treat the dress just being finished as if it were a laundering problem. If your dress has been correctly pressed during the construction process, kept on a hanger, and carefully handled, it will not need much pressing at the end. Avoid too much dampening and overpressing, or the dress will look washed and ironed. Most cottons can be pressed directly on the right side; dark colors and textured materials should be pressed on the wrong side.

Press seams, darts, facings, and pleats on the wrong side first and in the direction they were turned during construction and in earlier pressing.

Press double thicknesses such as collars and belts on the wrong side first until they are smooth but not dry. Then finish them right side out.

Follow this order of work for the final pressing (and for ironing after laundering):

1. Press interior parts, such as pockets, facings, seams, linings, and shoulder pads.
2. Press dangling parts, such as sleeves and sashes.
3. Press ruffles and gathers before the parts they trim (Figs. 15-7 and 15-12).
4. Press yokes and shoulder seams before the lower blouse.
5. Press the top parts of long garments before the lower parts: blouse before skirt, skirt top before lower part of skirt.
6. The collar is usually last because its position next to the face is so important.
7. Hang the garment on a well-padded hanger to dry completely, without crowding.

Generalizations

Directions: Read across both columns to note the relationships between the parts of a generalization, as pointed out in the headings.

EFFECT SOUGHT OR REASON WHY	THE CAUSE OR WHAT TO DO
1. To preserve gathers in pressing,	nose the point of the iron up to seam.
2. To shrink out fullness,	keep the side of the iron parallel with the stitching in the seam.

16

Unit Construction and Fitting

The purpose of this chapter is to consider the integration of *construction processes* with *fittings*.

Information that usually is missing on a pattern guide sheet is when to *fit* a garment. Therefore, a plan of work is needed to include fittings. If the total procedure is outlined, one has a more unified idea of how to accomplish the goal. Knowing *how* each part is to be completed gives a better idea of *when* a given detail must be stitched in relation to other details. The steps in making a garment involve the reasons why a certain process should come before or after another one; what causes each effect or result; and when to fit the garment to achieve the

307

best results with minimum effort. It is desirable to save time, but not at the sacrifice of a good-looking, professionally finished garment. The best way to save time and achieve the desired results is to be sure of the fit of the garment before you start stitching it.

Definition of Terms

Silhouette seams (fitting or basic seams) outline the figure; they include the shoulder seams, underarm seams of the blouse, sleeve seams, and the side seams of the skirt. Most fittings are confined to these seams, although occasionally it is necessary to work with other seams, pleats, or darts.

Lengthwise seams are any seams perpendicular, or nearly perpendicular, to the floor. They may be silhouette, divisional, or design lines within the basic pieces.

Crosswise seams are those more or less parallel to the floor that enter a lengthwise seam or an armhole. Diagonal lines are usually treated the same way as crosswise seams.

Circumference seams encircle a part of the body at the neckline, armholes, waistline, cuff line, lower hemline, and circumference belt or yoke lines. Sometimes they are broken at openings or enter lengthwise closings.

Basic garment units are skirt front, skirt back, blouse front, blouse back, and a pair of sleeves.

To finish a seam (or dart) after fitting and stitching means to remove bastings, if any, and tie thread ends of a dart but not of a seam; to trim, slash, notch, pink, or overcast as needed; and to press. A seam or line of stitching (dart, pleat) is finished before it is crossed with another line of stitching.

To designate a seam with accuracy, call it either by its basic name, such as shoulder seam or skirt side seam, or name the two pieces it joins together, such as "the seam joining the center front panel and the side front gore."

Abbreviations used are F—front, B—back, CF—center front, CB—center back, R—right, L—left.

When to Fit

At each fitting, it is an advantage to check the four main units (bodice, sleeves, and skirt) in their relationship to each other. Each affects the other in balance and proportion, in both style and fit.

Two main fittings are adequate for the great majority of garments, with a third one needed mainly for more difficult fabrics and circularity in design. Such planning can greatly simplify garment construction and fitting and shorten the time involved (Fig. 16-1).

The purpose of the first fitting is to approve the width in the garment. Concentration is on the lengthwise and crosswise seams, with a tentative check on length, *a*.

The purpose of the second fitting is to check on length in the garment. This involves the location and the set of circumference seams (solid lines) and edges (dotted lines), *b*.

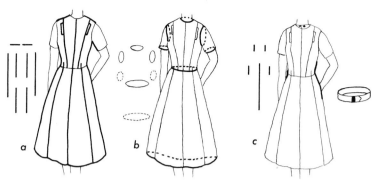

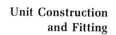

Figure 16-1. Heavy lines indicate construction lines to be emphasized in the three major divisions of work.

The purpose of the third fitting is to approve circumference edges: hems in crepes, chiffons, and other such fabrics; hems in circular designs; and any other details, trims, or accessories, *c*.

Supplementary fittings may occur at any step to approve a detail. Time can often be saved by checking a part of a garment to make a decision regarding such details as the length or location of a dart (not recommended for underarm darts pointing to the bust), gathers, lines of a shoulder yoke, locations of buttonholes, or length of a released pleat in a skirt. With this checking, many details in a unit can be stitched while flat, before it is attached to another unit. For example, hold the bodice front in position on the body (or pin the shoulder seams and slip it on body) to approve the locations of buttonholes. To prevent gaping be sure one is located at, or very near, the fullest part of the bust. Fabric buttonholes can now be made before joining the bodice front to the back bodice.

CORRECTION FITTING

When extensive changes are to be made in a garment following a fitting, rebaste (or pin-baste) it and try it on again. This process will be referred to as a *correction* fitting. One is still involved with the first fitting, so long as work continues toward the approval of lengthwise and crosswise seams.

All of the work involved in the fitting of circumference seams will be referred to as the second fitting.

PIN FITTING

For pin fittings, pins are placed perpendicular to the edges of pleats, hems, and side plackets when pinned on the figure. Pins are placed parallel to and on seamlines to insure proper fit around the curves of the body. Where used as a substitute for basting or stitching, pin basting naturally belongs where stitching would have been placed, and in the same direction.

FINAL PREPARATIONS FOR FITTING

Assemble all the materials needed—tools, notions, and accessories. A belt, *c*, will help the waistline effect if the design is to be belted. The neck seamline can be slashed before trying on the garment (Fig. 16-2).

Figure 16-2. Note neckline and shoulder area in this sleeveless blouse, prepared for first fitting. Tightness and wrinkles are evident in *a*, relieved in *b* by slashing neckline seam allowance almost to staystitching. (In case of question concerning fit, your partner can slash it after the garment is on.)

Take paper and pencil to the fitting room for recording the alterations needed; if a mimeographed plan or work sheet is available, take it and record any information in the designated column (Plan of Work Chart, pp. 316–17). Filing the information obtained at fittings will be valuable when another pattern is to be altered.

Unit Construction

An advantageous procedure in garment construction is to *complete a separate unit as far as possible* before joining it to another. This procedure involves less handling of the garment, tends to keep like processes of work together, and saves time and motion. For example, the order of the first steps to be taken in handling the bodice front (Fig. 16-3) follow.

1. Remove top pin near the neckline at CF, and staystitch necklines of both bodice sections (*a*). (If you are not familiar with staystitching, read pp. 326–27 before proceeding.)
2. Baste the CF seam (or stitch it if no fitting is anticipated on this line) in case pins should slip out while staystitching is in progress.
3. Staystitch shoulders, armholes, placket line, and corresponding edge (*b*).
4. Baste all darts.

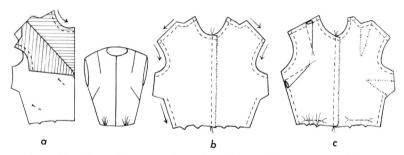

Figure 16-3. *a*, Two fronts kept pinned together while neck is staystitched. *b*, CF seamed before separating right and left fronts; staystitching completed before darts. *c*, Staystitching not needed where gathers or ease lines are to be used.

5. Add ease lines at waistline. This finishes the steps to be taken before the unit is joined to another—in this case, the back bodice.

Detailed information for the construction of each unit is illustrated and explained in the pattern guide sheet. How far does one continue with the various processes shown before stopping for a fitting? Answers to this question may be found in the following example.

INTEGRATING CONSTRUCTION PROCESSES WITH FITTINGS

The dress shown in Figure 16-4 is composed of these basic units:

1. Bodice back.
2. Bodice front (left and right).
3. Skirt back (two sections).
4. Skirt front.
5. Sleeves (left and right).
6. Collar.

Figure 16-4. Integrated construction and fitting.

STEPS IN CONSTRUCTION

BODICE BACK

1. Staystitch neckline, shoulder, armholes, sections of waistline seam (if quite bias), placket line on left and corresponding line on right (without stay stitching, right side can be expected to sag out of proportion to the left side, which has been staystitched and anchored to zipper tape).
2. Baste darts at neckline and waistline.
3. Go to another unit.

BODICE RIGHT FRONT

1. Pin interfacing into position and attach it along CF line.
2. Staystitch neckline, shoulder, armhole, sections of waistline seam if quite bias, placket line on left side and corresponding line on right side. The staystitching will attach the interfacing to the front neckline.
3. Baste darts at side seam and waistline.
4. Finish edge of front facing.
5. Go to another unit.

BODICE LEFT FRONT   Repeat procedure used for right front.

SKIRT BACK

1. Pin skirt sections together for basting (or stitching in case fitting this seam is not anticipated), leaving two or three inches free near the waistline.
2. Staystitch bias sections of waistline seam, placket line on left side, and corresponding line on right side.
3. Baste darts at waistline.
4. Go to another unit.

SKIRT FRONT

1. Fold and pin (or baste) pleats in position, with material kept flat on table.
2. Staystitch bias sections of waistline seam, placket line on left side, and corresponding line on right side.
3. Stitch across pleats at waistline.
4. Go to another unit.

SLEEVE—LEFT

1. Staystitch below notches in sleeve cap.
2. Ease-stitch (regular stitch length with unbalanced tension) from notch to notch across the top of sleeve cap in one line (for quick control of ease in later construction).
3. Machine-stitch the elbow dart (if no fitting at elbow is anticipated).
4. Put sleeve aside to be pressed later with the dart in the right sleeve.

SLEEVE—RIGHT   Repeat steps 1, 2, and 3 under Sleeve (Left).

PRESS Press elbow darts in both sleeves.

STITCH Lengthwise seams in both sleeves can be stitched.

COLLAR Construction at this point is optional. If one wishes to check the shape or size of the collar at the first fitting, pin interfacing into position and staystitch it to one layer of the collar.

The First Fitting

The plan presented here assumes a somewhat limited experience in clothing construction; the organization suggested provides the opportunity for checking fit at the proper time for the best results. With the experience and knowledge gained in fitting oneself, much less time and effort will be needed for fitting subsequent garments, barring figure changes. Taking these points into consideration, one can advance the processes in cases where no fitting problems are anticipated. In such situations, pinning or permanent stitching can be substituted for regular basting.

A speedy, workable plan for the first fitting suggests *basting* lengthwise and crosswise seams—those seams that require earlier construction—and *pinning* circumference seams, those that will not require precision fitting until later in the construction process (Fig. 16-5).

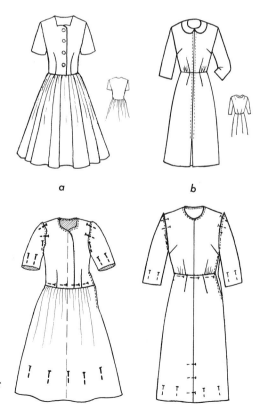

a   *b*

Figure 16-5. Typical dresses prepared for the first fittings.

Casual garments such as shirts, tent dresses, lounging clothes, and other garments that do not require close, careful fitting can be pin-basted for regular fittings. An exception would be the armhole seams for a normal set-in sleeve. A high standard of work, achieving evenly distributed ease in the cap and an even line of stitching around the armhole, generally requires basting, a prerequisite for approval of the fit of the sleeve.

The collar is not needed for the first fitting, unless one wishes to check collar proportions.

Facings are not involved, generally, although a front facing may be attached and clean-finished along with staystitching and the first basting processes.

AT THE FIRST FITTING

1. Approve location and fit of darts, pleats, tucks, and gathers.
2. Approve lengthwise, crosswise (shoulder seams, bodice yoke), and diagonal seams as to location, direction, and evenness.
3. Check and approve width in the garment, and correctness of fit.
4. Approve location of neck seamline; approve collar dimensions, in case these are being questioned.
5. Check the length of sections within the garment in cases where length affects the width. (Example: Length of the bodice affects location of the waistline seam, which may raise or lower the skirt from its normal position. Width in the skirt cannot be judged accurately unless this circumference seam—the waistline—is in approximately the correct position on the body.) In some difficult fabrics with drape and sag, it may be desirable to baste the waistline seam also for this fitting, but for most fabrics a careful pin fitting with seam allowances overlapped is adequate and time-saving.
6. Tentatively approve the locations of all other circumference seams, such as armholes and a skirt yoke line that extends completely around the body.

FOLLOWING THE FIRST FITTING
BODICE

1. Remove pins to separate sleeves and skirt from bodice; release hems.
2. Rip two or three inches of basting across underarm darts.
3. Permanently stitch underarm, waistline and neckline darts, and shoulder seams. Remove basting threads, except on underarm seams.
4. Make parts as collar, cuffs, and facings, that will be attached to circumference seams or edges.
5. Put bodice aside for pressing with sleeves and skirt.

SLEEVES

1. Stitch lengthwise seams in sleeves. (As no fitting of elbow darts was anticipated, they have already been stitched and pressed.)

2. Remove basting threads from seams.
3. Put sleeves aside for pressing with bodice and skirt.

SKIRT   Permanently stitch back darts, center-back seams, and side seams. Remove basting threads.

PRESSING
1. Press all darts in bodice.
2. Press all seams in bodice, sleeves, and skirt, except the underarm seams in bodice.

BODICE

1. Stitch the side seams of bodice (as underarm bodice darts have now been stitched and pressed).
2. Remove basting threads.
3. Put bodice aside for pressing, along with collar.

COLLAR

1. Attach interfacing to collar with staystitching (if not done earlier).
2. Stitch under collar to upper collar; grade and understitch.

PRESS   Press underarm seams in bodice.

Assemble for Second Fitting

SLEEVES (LEFT AND RIGHT)

1. Adjust ease lines at top of caps (see p. 396).
2. Press out fullness from seam allowances in upper caps. (See Fig. 22-2, *d*.)

BODICE

1. Stitch collar to bodice (if no fitting problems are anticipated).
2. Baste sleeves into armholes.
3. Baste waistline seam.
4. Leave circumference edges hanging for ease in marking hemlines.

AT SECOND FITTING

1. Approve circumference seams.
   a. Neckline: attachment of the collar (may be finished already).
   b. Armholes: the fit of the sleeves.
   c. Waistline: smoothness of seam and the fit of the skirt.
2. Mark positions of hemlines in sleeves and skirt (after armhole and waistline seams have been approved).

FOLLOWING SECOND FITTING

1. Stitch armhole and waistline seams; finish and press.
2. Make side placket (a lengthwise line that crosses a circumference line).
3. Hem sleeves (if line is not questioned).
4. Hem skirt (in case there is no question about the marked hemline).

AT THIRD FITTING

Check the pinned or basted skirt hem—in case of question regarding the marked hemline.

COMPLETION OF GARMENT

1. Make hems (if third fitting was necessary).

Plan of Work Chart (for Fig. 16-6)

Staystitch: 1. 2. 3.	4. 5. 6.	7. 8. 9.
What lines, if any, can be safely stitched before fitting? 1. 2.	3. 4.	

Prepare for First Fitting		First Fitting (Alterations Needed?)	Stitch and Press Following First Fitting	
Baste (Darts, tucks, etc. L'wise & C'wise seams) 1. 2. 3. 4. 5. 6. 7.	Pin: (Circumference, Seams & Edges)	(List here)	1st Trip to Machine: 1. 2. 3. 4. 2nd Trip to Machine: 1. 2. 3. 4. (Use back of sheet if additional trips are needed for your design)	Press: 1. 2. 3. 4. Press: 1. 2. 3. 4.
Prepare for Second Fitting		Second Fitting (Alterations Needed?)	Stitch and Press Following Second Fitting	
Baste: (Circumference Seams) 1. 2. 3. 4. 5.	(Mark skirt and sleeve hems after waistline and sleeves are approved.)		1st Trip to Machine: 1. 2. 3. 4.	Press: 1. 2. 3. 4.
Prepare for Third Fitting		Third Fitting (Check hem)	Steps to Complete Garment:	

2. Make machine buttonholes.
3. Sew buttons on.
4. Tack facings to seams, darts, or underlining.
5. Finish any other details, such as belt-carriers.
6. Provide a belt.
7. Press the completed garment.

Plan of Work

The preceding concepts of good planning are incorporated in a concise plan of work chart. This chart clarifies the minimum number of trips to the machine, ironing board, and fitting room. To fill in such a mimeographed chart gives a quick overview of the relationship between the steps in construction, fitting, and pressing.

Plan of Work Chart (Cont'd)

Staystitch:	1. *Necklines – front & back.* 2. *Shoulder seams – front + back.* 3. *Armholes – front + back.*	4. *Waistline of bodice.* 5. *Waistline of skirt.* 6. *Attach interfacing to collar.*	7. *Lower half of sleeve caps.* 8. *Lower edge of sleeves.* 9. *Neck facings.*
What lines, if any, can be safely stitched before fitting?	1. *Center - back seam of skirt.* 2. *Pleat at front of skirt.*	3. 4.	

Prepare for First Fitting		First Fitting (Alterations Needed?)	Stitch and Press Following First Fitting
Baste (Darts, tucks, etc. L'wise & C'wise seams)	Pin: (Circumference, Seams & Edges)	(List here)	1st Trip to Machine: Press:
1. *Darts – bodice front.* 2. *Darts - bodice back.* 3. *Shoulder seams.* 4. *Side seams – bodice.* 5. *Side seams - skirt.* 6. *Elbow darts.* 7. *Sleeve seams.*	*Collar to bodice (optional)* *Sleeves to bodice.* *Waistline.* *Skirt hem.*		1. *Darts in bodice.* 1. *All darts.* 2. *Darts in sleeves.* 2. *Side seams.* 3. *Side seams - bodice + facing.* 3. *Buttonholes.* 4. *Fabric buttonholes in belt.* 4. *Collar seam.* 5. *Join facing to collar.* 2nd Trip to Machine: Press: *shoulder seams –* 1. *bodice + facing.* 1. *Shoulder seams.* 2. *Sleeve seams.* 2. *Sleeve seams.* 3. *Facing to belt.* 3. *Belt seams.* 4. *3rd trip* *Finish edge of neck f.* 4. (Use back of sheet if additional trips are needed for your design)
Prepare for Second Fitting		Second Fitting (Alterations Needed?)	Stitch and Press Following Second Fitting
Baste: (Circumference Seams) 1. *Collar to neckline.* 2. *Sleeves in armholes.* 3. *Waistline* 4. 5.	(Mark skirt and sleeve hems after waistline and sleeves are approved.)		1st Trip to Machine: Press: 1. *Armhole seams.* 1. *Armhole seams.* 2. *Facings to sleeves.* 2. *Waistlines.* 3. *Waistline seam.* 3. *Waistline.* 4. *make placket.* 2nd trip to machine: 4. *placket* *3rd trip to machine:* *Neckline.* *attach collar + neck facing*
Prepare for Third Fitting		Third Fitting (Check hem)	Steps to Complete Garment:
Baste fold of hem *Pin upper edge of hem*			*Make hem* *Finish all details*

Figure 16-6. Underlinings are attached to the garment sections by hand basting at CF, pleat lines, through the centers of darts and all seams that do not require staystitching. Other edges are staystitched.

The preceding filled-in form illustrates the plan of work for the design shown in Figure 16-6. The garment sections were staystitched; the underlining was attached by hand basting and staystitching. Basic units have been assembled.

This organization of work provides for unit construction: after staystitching a unit, proceed to the steps listed for that unit under Prepare for First Fitting. These units, such as bodice front and back, are then joined to make the larger unit (Fig. 16-7). These units, assembled for first and second fittings are shown in Figure 16-8. A carefully made plan of work means that every construction line can be fitted (if fitting is necessary), pressed, and finished before a seam is stitched across it.

318

Figure 16-7. Six units have been assembled to form the four basic sections of the garment—bodice, skirt, and left and right sleeves—by basting darts and both lengthwise and crosswise seams: *a*, front view; *b*, back view; *c*, belt.

The best results are never obtained by stitching a line across an unpressed one.

This organization also provides a simple plan for having sections with like processes ready for attention at the same time.

Summary of Steps Involving Construction with Fittings

PREPARE EACH UNIT

1. Staystitch; this may involve attachment of underlining and/or interfacing and making fabric buttonholes.
2. Baste or pin-baste (permanently stitch, where fit is certain) any fullness that must be controlled before *seams* can be basted or pinned—darts, tucks, pleats, and gathers.

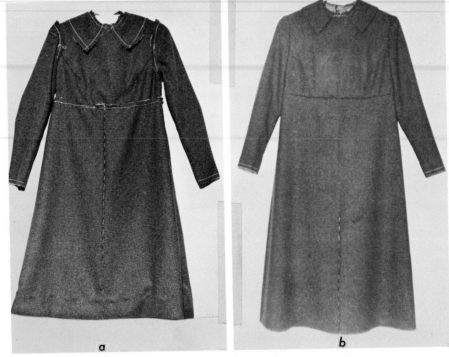

Figure 16-8. *a,* Ready for first fitting; *b,* for second.

PREPARE FOR FIRST FITTING

1. Baste crosswise and lengthwise seams (stitch permanently where fit is not questioned, and no other construction lines will be crossed).
2. Pin circumference seams—collar to neckline (optional); sleeves to bodice; skirt to bodice.
3. Pin circumference edges—all hems.

HAVE FIRST FITTING

FOLLOWING FIRST FITTING Stitch, finish, and press all construction approved at first fitting (may include making and attaching collar before basting sleeves and skirt to bodice).

PREPARE FOR SECOND FITTING

1. Baste circumference seams.
2. Leave circumference edges hanging for ease in marking hemlines.

HAVE SECOND FITTING

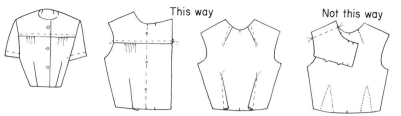

Figure 16-9. Complete front unit before beginning back unit (before joining yoke front to back unit).

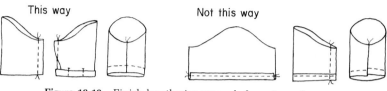

Figure 16-10. Finish lengthwise seams before circumferences.

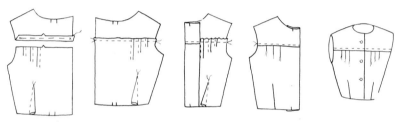

Figure 16-11. Finish lengthwise closings after crosswise seams.

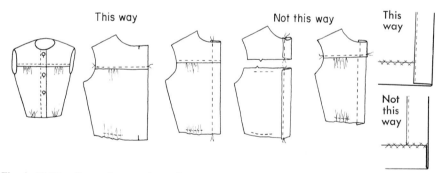

Figure 16-12. Crosswise or circumference seams must be completed before making the lengthwise closing—either a folded hem or a faced edge.

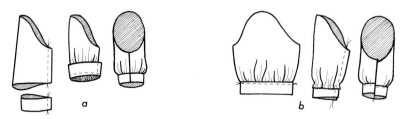

Figure 16-13. *a,* Dressmaker method of attaching cuff band *b,* Factory method usually leaves irregular edges.

PREPARE FOR THIRD FITTING

1. Mark, pin, or baste positions for hemlines which were established at the second fitting (to preserve them through next step in construction).
2. Stitch, finish, and press all *seams* approved at second fitting.
3. Construct lines which cross circumference seams, as placket.

HAVE THIRD FITTING   Approve hemlines (if there is a question regarding evenness).

COMPLETION OF GARMENT

1. Make hems.
2. Finish all details.
3. Press completed garment.

Evaluation

Observation of the sketches in Figures 16-9 through 16-13 will demonstrate and clarify reasons for some of the procedures presented earlier. How do these correlate with the generalizations that follow?

Generalizations

Directions: Read each generalization across both columns; note the relationships between the parts, as pointed out in the headings.

EFFECT SOUGHT OR REASON WHY	THE CAUSE OR WHAT TO DO
1. To save time, energy, and resources, to save confusion and error, and to create a satisfactory product,	organize work by a. doing like jobs in a group. b. handling work as little as possible. c. completing one unit before going to another.
2. To save time, with a well-sized and well-fitted pattern,	details such as darts within the front and back of blouse and skirt may be stitched to complete units before basting and fitting silhouette seams.
3. To keep the edges or ends smooth and unfrayed and to simplify fitting and adjustments,	*finish* lengthwise seams (darts and pleats) before beginning circumference lines.
4. To have the closing a durable, smooth, continuous lengthwise line with no seams showing at edges,	lengthwise closings should be made after the circumference and crosswise seams are finished.
5. To insure a satisfactory garment when finished and to save time,	all units (pinned or basted) should be tried on and fitted before stitching.

6. To secure a pleasing appearance in the garment with a minimum number of basic fittings,

check for
a. **width** at first fitting (details and silhouette seams basted, and circumferences pinned),
b. **length** at second fitting (circumferences basted),
c. **closings,** final circumference edges, other details at third fitting.

7. To be sure that each basic fitting is satisfactory,

have supplementary fittings to check corrections before proceeding with stitching or the next basic fitting.

17

Supporting and Preserving Shape

Consideration was given in Chapter 7 to the selection of supporting fabrics in harmony with the fabric and the design of the pattern.

Techniques for the use of these supporting fabrics and for the preservation of shape in the garment during construction are of basic concern in successful dressmaking. The latter will be considered first in this presentation, because methods for preserving shape apply to the handling of both fashion and supporting fabrics, which are often assembled together.

Preserving Shape During Construction

STAYSTITCHING

The first step to be taken in beginning the construction of a garment is to staystitch.

Staystitching is a line of regular stitching—correct length of stitch and tension for sewing the fabric—which is placed on certain off-grain edges to prevent their stretching during the construction processes. For staystitching, a matching color of thread is used and the stitching is made through a single thickness of fabric, unless the garment is interfaced or underlined along this edge; in this case, the staystitching may be made not only through the fabric, but through one or two supporting fabrics as well.

Staystitching is used in the following instances:

1. Slanted crosswise or lengthwise seams where bias occurs: as shoulder and yoke seams, and along off-grain seams over body curves, as bust and back shoulder, in princess styles.
2. Circumference seams: neckline, armholes, and off-grain parts of waistline—because these bias edges will be handled during several processes prior to stitching the seams.
3. Bias plackets and their corresponding edges—*regular lengthwise seams are not staystitched.*

Some bias edges are not staystitched. Observe the kimono sleeves in the soft crepe fabric shown in Figure 17-1. Because of the cut of this type of sleeve, deep folds of fabric will form at the ends of the shoulders, with some folds hanging along the sleeves, as well. Careful examination reveals a greater number of folds in *a*. Why? Both sleeves have been basted for a fitting, under identical condi-

Figure 17-1. Free-hanging lengthwise seams should *not* be staystitched. *a*, Basted seam with staystitching is tight and drawn; *b*, without staystitching, is freer to stretch and sag with the surrounding area. Pressing will improve *b*.

tions—the same length of stitch, the same tension, and in the same direction, from neckline to lower edges. The only difference in the two sleeves is that sleeve *a* was staystitched along this bias line, all the way from neckline to lower edge; sleeve *b* was staystitched from neckline to end of shoulder only.

The bias seam that hangs more or less free from the body stretches somewhat and sags with the surrounding area when it is not staystitched. When staystitched, the seam is less flexible and draws. Identical results can be observed in any free-hanging bias seam in skirt, dress, or coat. For this reason, lengthwise lines are not staystitched, except for bias placket and corresponding lines. Staystitching is used to prevent stretching—it is needed, for instance, at the shoulder seams, which support the weight of the garment and, it is hoped, will set smoothly and retain their shape during the life of the garment.

If your garment is underlined, you either stitch or hand-baste the two layers together. If you stitch them, be sure the tension is not too tight. If the seam draws, stretch it to break the stitching and patch the broken places. Naturally, this applies, also, to the stitching of the seam, which will be done later in the construction process. It is obvious that staystitching—whose purpose is to fix and hold the shape exactly as cut—is not needed or wanted along such free-hanging lines, if no underlining is to be used. When all parts of the garment are allowed to sag according to their nature, the garment sets properly, and the excess length resulting from sagging is removed when the skirt is evened at its lower edge.

DIRECTION OF STAYSTITCHING   The most important point to consider in staystitching is the direction in which the stitching is made. Less stretching occurs when the stitching is done in the direction of the grain—the direction in which the grain yarns along the edge are pointing (Fig. 17-2). Determining the grain direction is

Figure 17-2. The grain yarns along a cut edge point in the direction of the grain. Note the shoulder—the threads pointing toward the armhole; the direction for staystitching is from neckline to armhole.

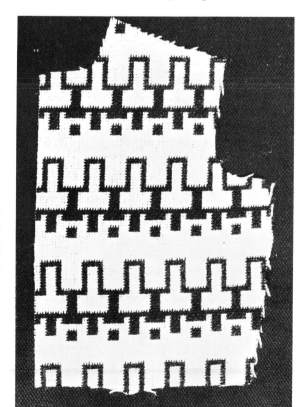

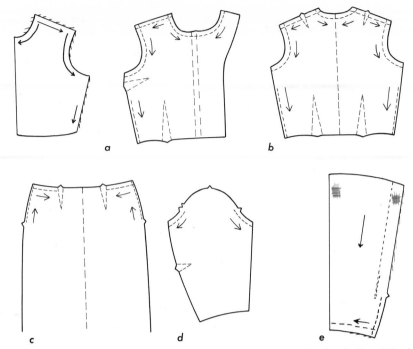

Figure 17-3. Staystitch $\frac{1}{16}$ to $\frac{1}{8}$ inch inside the seamline, except for the placket. It is placed $\frac{1}{4}$ inch from the cut edge to keep it back from the edge of the closing. In stitching seams that have not been staystitched, use directional stitching; retrace at placket end, *e*.

easily done by stroking or simply observing the raw edge. The grain yarns, like pointers, will always indicate the direction of the grain.

Stitching in the direction that the grain yarns point is called directional stitching. Staystitching, therefore, is an example of directional stitching (Fig. 17-3). In stitching seams that have not been staystitched, use directional stitching. Seams that have been staystitched can be stitched in either direction; stretching has already been controlled by the staystitching.

Staystitching in Relation to Seamline Because staystitching is not removed, it is located in the seam allowance where it will not show in the finished garment. It is placed $\frac{1}{16}$ to $\frac{1}{8}$ inch from the seamline at the neckline, shoulder, armhole and waistline, and $\frac{1}{4}$ inch from the edge along the bias placket and corresponding lines. ("Corresponding line" refers to the line on the other half of the garment, such as the seamline on the right hip. This bias seam, with only one line of stitching, can hardly be expected to support the weight of the skirt without stretching as adequately as the left side—staystitched and anchored to the zipper tape.)

Providing Body and Reinforcement

Body and reinforcement can be supplied by any of the four classes of fabrics discussed earlier—underlining, interfacing, lining, and interlining. The first of these to be used in the construction of the garment is the underlining, if one is being used.

PROCEDURE FOR UNDERLINING

1. Place the garment section on the table, wrong side up, and spread the underlining on it, with the side showing construction markings up. Check to see that center line and grainlines coincide with the grain of the fabric (Fig. 17-4, a).
2. Pin-baste the fabrics together along the center, either with pins placed closely together and parallel to lengthwise grainline; tailor's basting, a; or regular basting, b. (Place pins perpendicular to CF for regular basting.)
3. Fold the garment from center toward side and smooth the excess width in the lining toward the side seam. Pin along the edges of pattern from top to bottom, placing pins perpendicular to the seamlines, c.
4. Trim off the excess underlining fabric at the seams, so that the edges of the garment fabric and underlining are even.

Figure 17-4. Attaching underlining to garment.

5. Repeat this process for the other side.

6. If there are darts in the section, unfold and hand-baste the two layers of fabric together through the center of the darts, from the point toward the edge, in order to push any excess width toward the edge. Start the basting line two or three stitches in front of the dart's point, to hold this area firmly and keep the knot in the thread away from the point of the dart, *b* and *d*.

7. Hand-baste the fabric edges together, placing stitches slightly to the garment side of the seam, so that they will not be caught in the stitching lines. Diagonal or tailor's basting gives a more stable line than regular basting, *d*. (If the fabric is not difficult to handle, basting might be eliminated.)

8. Remove pins. The section is now ready for staystitching.

INTERFACING

Interfacings are attached to the wrong side of the garment with some possible variations.

Where an underlining or backing fabric is used, the interfacing is placed in position after the underlining is attached. Or, it may be attached to the underlining before the latter is applied to the garment section (Fig. 17-5).

ATTACHING INTERFACING TO THE GARMENT Along a closing of the garment, the interfacing can be attached to the garment side or to the facing side. Two advantages in attaching it to the garment side are having it in the proper position for making fabric buttonholes and providing cushioning in the seam—where the facing is cut as a separate piece. It is a satisfactory process for any weight of fabric (Fig. 17-6).

Pin the interfacing fabric into position next to the wrong side of the garment section to which it belongs; if an underlining is being used, the interfacing will be placed in position after the underlining is attached.

1. After clipping off upper corner of interfacing, pin it into position, lining center front and fold lines.

2. Baste on center line to hold the two pieces of fabric together.

3. Fasten interfacing along fold line with running-hemming, herringbone, or machine stitches hidden on the facing (Fig. 17-7).

4. Staystitch all lines that require this treatment.

5. Mark for fabric buttonholes, if they are to be used; they may be made at this time if desired—hold garment section to the body to approve locations. Because the edges have been protected by staystitching, it is safe to handle the fabric.

ATTACHING INTERFACING TO FACING The technique here is similar to the preceding plan, except for the edge finishing (Fig. 17-7). Placing the interfacing on the facing of the garment is more satisfactory for light- and medium-weight fabrics, if a clean finished edge is desired. This stitching may anchor the edge of the interfacing securely in the stitched edge, although it adds some bulk (Fig. 17-7).

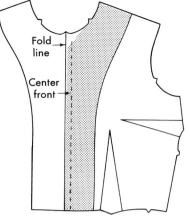

Figure 17-5. Back neckline interfacing may be attached to underlining before the latter is placed on the garment section.

Figure 17-6. Attaching interfacing to garment side of front closing. Clip off upper corner to remove bulk from seam.

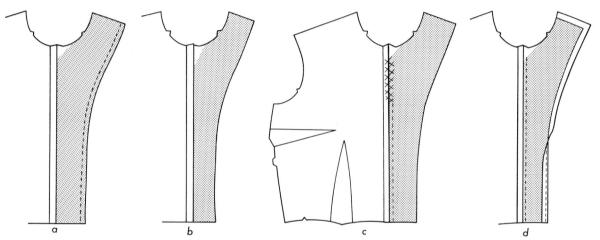

Figure 17-7. Interfacing attached to front facing: *a,* edges machine-stitched together; *b,* facing faced with interfacing fabric—enclosed seam along outer edge; *c,* interfacing attached along fold line with hand stitches, or with machine stitching on facing; *d,* clean-finished edge, with interfacing caught in turned-and-stitched edge.

INTERFACING A COLLARLESS NECKLINE

There are a number of methods for attaching the interfacing to the neckline, the choice of which might depend on the fabric and personal preference.

Consider these alternative methods:

1. Trim off shoulder seam allowances, and staystitch front facing to front neckline and back facing to back. Use herringbone stitch to fasten shoulder lines to garment slightly short of shoulder seams (Fig. 17-8, *a*).

2. Staystitch neck, shoulder, and other necessary lines in bodice, without the interfacing. Later in the construction process, after shoulder seams are fitted, stitched, and pressed, prepare the interfacing and attach it to the neckline $\frac{1}{2}$ inch from the edge.

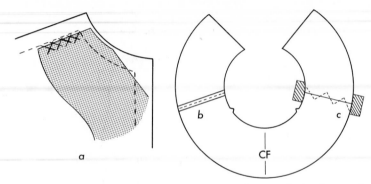

Figure 17-8. Interfacing for collarless neckline shows three methods of removing bulk at seams: *a*, hand stitching shoulder of interfacing to wrong side of garment; *b*, seam allowances lapped, stitched, and trimmed; *c*, seam allowances removed, edges held together with machine stitching.

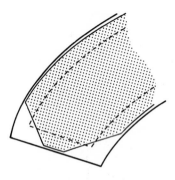

Figure 17-9. Interfacing staystitched to collar.

PREPARE THE NECK FACING Lap the shoulder seams, and pin them for stitching with seamline on seamline. Stitch one or two lines near shoulder seam; and trim seam allowances close to stitching, *b*. Or, remove seam allowances, place a strip of paper under the seamline, and stitch across it in a zigzag line, *c*; tear paper away.

INTERFACING A COLLAR
Follow these steps in applying the interfacing:

1. Trim interfacing diagonally at the corners and pin it to the wrong side of the collar. If the collar has a seam at its outer edge, prepare the interfacing as shown in Figure 17-9.
2. Staystitch the two edges together $3/8$ inch from the edge.

THE LINING
A lining, cut and marked in the same manner as the garment, is constructed separately. However, it should be altered and constructed along with the garment. See methods for attaching, pp. 480–81.

Generalizations

Directions: Read across both columns to note the relationships between the parts of a generalization, as pointed out in the headings.

EFFECT SOUGHT OR REASON WHY	THE CAUSE OR WHAT TO DO
1. To preserve shape, improve the appearance, and add durability to a garment,	a. choose supporting fabrics to give desired firmness or body, without changing the inherent nature of the outer fabric; b. equalize potential shrinkage in all fabrics to be used together; c. consider possible stretching of each layer of fabric used (free-hanging sections, as skirts, may be best kept separate).
2. To preserve grain and bias lines in a well-tailored garment,	stay-stitch a. with the grain; b. $\frac{1}{16}''$ from the seamline, within the seam allowance; c. on shoulder seams; d. on circumference seams (where bias); e. on bias placket lines (both right and left sides); f. on shaped details that are bias, as yokes, insets.
3. To create a free-flowing drape in a gored skirt,	allow the gores, pinned or loosely basted, to stretch before stitching; therefore, never staystitch these bias or other lengthwise lines.
4. To determine the directions for stitching to preserve the grain—directional stitching—	note the direction in which loose yarns along the edge are pointing, and stitch in this direction (the right and left halves must be stitched separately).

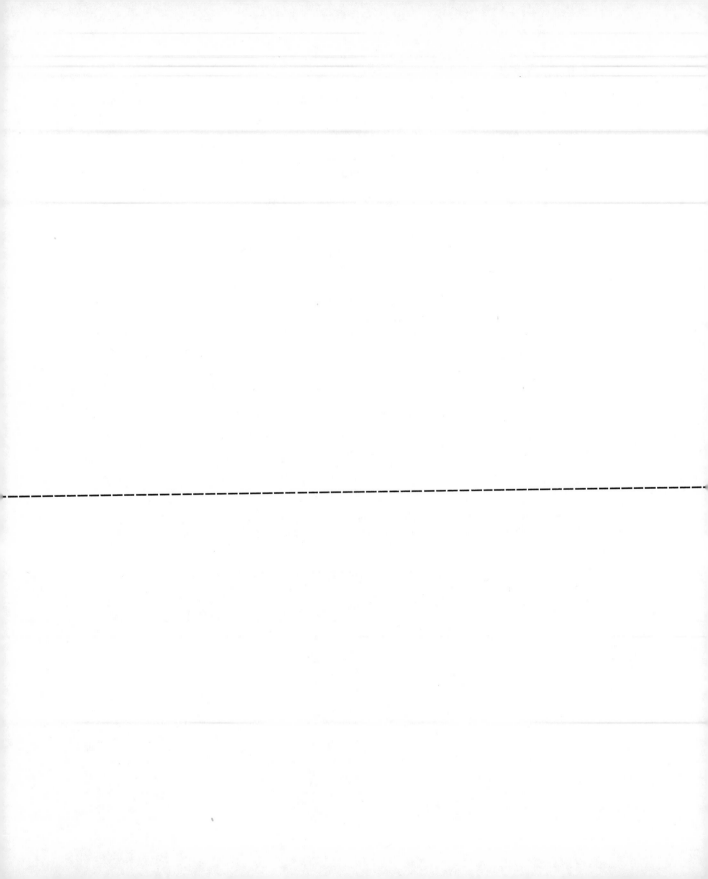

Darts, Tucks, Pleats, and Gathers

How does one account for the great similarity in the placement of structural lines and details in garments? What are the basic underlying goals to be reached in constructing a garment?

Two goals are apparent:

Shaping the fabric to body curves.

Controlling the design fullness for comfort and appearance.

Shaping Fabric to Body Curves

DARTS

A dart is made by stitching a line that tapers to a point along a fold; its purpose is to fit the fabric to a curve of the body. Its point will be located near the largest part of a body curve.

Consider the following problems:

1. Note darts *a* and *b* in Figure 18-1. Which is better? Why?

Dart *a* is a waistline dart and *b* an underarm dart, both pointing toward the fullest part of the bust. The garment is made of a woven fabric. Examination of the fabric's condition around the points of the two darts reveals smoothness at the point of *b*, indicating a dart stitched gradually to a thin point. This is evidenced also by the grain yarns of the fabric. Dart *a* shows a very different condition. The dart is thick near its point, resulting in a bubble or pucker in this area; study of the fabric grain indicates the lack of gradual tapering; note the large number of grain yarns that have been taken into the dart only a short distance from its point, causing the bubble.

2. Compare darts *a'* and *b'*, showing a wrong-side view of the stitched darts. What relationships are evident? The width of dart *a'*, near its point, is much greater than the width of dart *b'*, leading up to its point.

3. Study of the relationships between darts *a* and *a'*, and *b* and *b'*, clarifies the reasons for the unsatisfactory qualities of darts that are too wide near their points. The method of stitching shown in *a'* was responsible for the bubble at the point of *a* in the dress; the method used in stitching *b'* can be credited with the smooth point of *b* in the dress.

4. If you were stitching dart *b'*, would you be more likely to stitch a smooth, thin point if you started at the wide end, or at the point? The tapered point probably could be more easily achieved if approached from the wide end.

As our standard is a tapered point in the final stitching, in machine basting—and later in stitching—begin at the wide end and stitch toward the point, stitching slightly inside the traced line on the fold side. To insure a smooth point, have the last ½ inch of stitching almost parallel with the fold, *b'*.

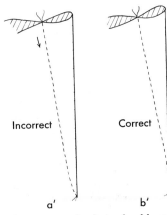

Figure 18-1. A dart should set smoothly at its point. What causes a pucker at the point of *a*?

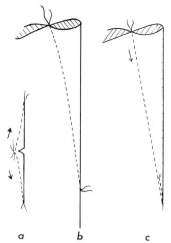

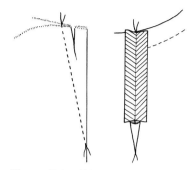

Figure 18-2. *a*, Double dart, slashed at waistline to fit the curve; *b*, curved dart; *c*, incorrect point treatment shows a thick, retraced point.

Figure 18-3. Trim a wide dart to seam width and press open, pressing the short end as a box pleat.

5. Why was the double dart (Fig. 18-2, *a*) slashed at its mid-point?

This slash is necessary to give a smooth fit over the curve of the body at the waistline.

A single dart may be curved, as on a side hipline where there is no side seam, *b*.

6. Dart *c* was retraced near its point, as you will note. Will this technique result in a pleasing point? Compare this with Figure 18-1, *b'*.

Retracing the point of a dart is undesirable and unnecessary, since this is not a point of strain; it is the opposite—a bit of ease that must be kept as small and flexible as possible for a smooth fit over a body curve. Retracing adds thickness and stiffness and accents the point.

7. Think of two reasons for finishing a dart as shown in Figure 18-3.

In a bulky fabric, the dart is narrowed, at least to the standard seam width; it may be narrower, depending on fabric and location, as under a lining. A box-pleat effect is pressed near the point to maintain the appearance (throughout the length of the dart) of a smooth, pressed-open seam—as judged from the right side of the garment.

After thinking through the preceding questions, you probably have set some standards for a well-made dart.

Standards for Darts

1. A dart appears on the right side as a plain seam, well pressed and lying smoothly without a pucker or bubble at its point. (Exception: Darts are sometimes stitched on the right side of the garment to give a decorative effect.)

2. To achieve the standard listed in No. 1, the point of a dart must be very thin.

3. The stitching at the point never rips or unravels.

4. Double darts crossing the waistline of a garment—with points at both ends—are slashed, if necessary, to make them lie flat in the curve of the body.

5. To make them set better in heavier fabrics, wide darts are trimmed to the seam width and pressed open to form a box pleat near the point, in order to give a smooth line.

MAKING A DART

Narrow darts are sometimes marked on the pattern by a single line. Fold along this line and stitch as directed, usually $\frac{1}{4}$ inch from the wide end to the point (Fig. 18-4, *a* and *b*).

Wider darts are marked on the fabric by two traced lines. If you marked the bisecting line in the dart, fold on this line. Run a pin through the opposite markings on the two lines, and take a small stitch with the pin, *b*. Pin first at the point of the dart, then at the wide end, keeping both sides smooth. Place a pin or two between. Pins are placed at right angles to the fold, heads up. Examine your work as you proceed to see that there are no wrinkles on either side. If you have had a pin fitting for shoulder darts, or you have learned from experience that these do not require changes, they can be stitched before the garment is assembled. It is seldom safe to stitch other darts (pointing to the bust- or hipline) without a fitting.

The thread ends are tied in a square knot and left $\frac{1}{4}$ to $\frac{1}{2}$ inch long (Fig. 18-5). Remove the bastings, trim to a narrower width, if necessary, and press before stitching a seam across the wide end of any dart.

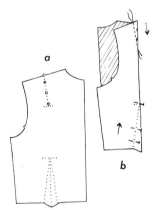

Figure 18-4. Darts properly traced at termination points: *a*, a single line at neck or shoulder for folding a narrow dart; *b*, a bisecting line in a wider dart as an aid for folding. Insert pins at right angles to stitching line, taking a small stitch with pin.

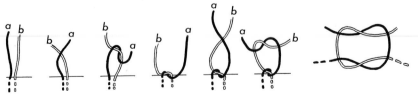

Figure 18-5. Steps in tying a square knot.

TUCKS A *tuck* is a fold of fabric, with a line of stitching through the two thicknesses of fabric parallel with the fold. If the stitching does not continue throughout its length, it is referred to as a released tuck. These are short tucks—releasing fullness into the garment may involve the fundamental dart. Tucks that are stitched throughout their length do not involve this dart and are used solely for design interest. Tucks are made on either the right or wrong sides—they are more decorative when placed on the right side.

Tucks may be spaced at varying distances, in which case careful attention is needed to achieve a pleasing proportion. *Blind tucks* are made wider than the space between the tucks, so that the line of stitching is covered by the edge of the next tuck.

Pin tucks are very narrow.

Standards for good tucking demand even widths and spaces with good stitching. Fold along the line of pins or tailor's tacks, usually on the grain, and pin at right angles across the fold of two thicknesses. (Do not make a pleat, which is three layers deep.) Use a gauge to insure even spaces (Fig. 18-6). Baste, if necessary, so that machine stitching will not coincide. Set the gauge or a tucking attachment to insure even stitching.

Pressing tucks as each one is stitched is conducive to accuracy.

1. First, stitch the tuck nearest the center.
2. Press the fold on the side that will be folded underneath.
3. Then, press the tuck from the wrong side of the fabric in the direction it is to lie, being careful to flatten it well at the seam. A little fold pressed in here can interfere with the evenness of the space between this tuck and the next one.
4. Press lightly, possibly with press cloth, on the right side; place a strip of paper underneath the tuck, if there is a possibility of imprint.

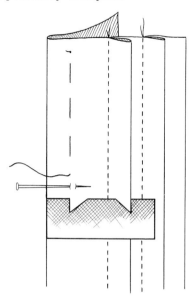

Figure 18-6. Use a gauge to fold tucks accurately.

Figure 18-7. Retrace the lower end of a dart tuck, since there is likely to be some strain in the garment at this point.

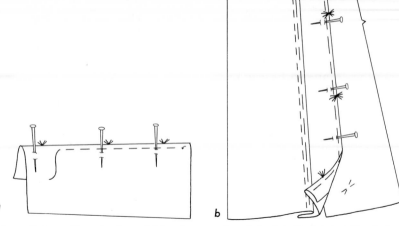

Figure 18-8. *a*, Pin or baste, or fold and press, edge of pleat. *b*, Pin into position before stitching seam at back edge of pleat.

Repeat these processes as each tuck is made. This procedure makes it easy to check each tuck for straightness before proceeding to the next.

Dᴀʀᴛ-Tᴜᴄᴋs   Dart-tucks are made the same as darts, except they are not stitched completely to the point; thus, they leave a fold of soft, unpressed fullness. What ending will be the most satisfactory for the stitching at the released point (Fig. 18-7)? As the dart-tuck fits the body smoothly, throughout its stitched length, there will be some strain at the end of this line, so retracing is better than tying threads; or, one can turn a square corner at the end of the line of stitching, stitch to the fold, and tie the threads at that point.

Pʟᴇᴀᴛs   For neat pleats, two lines of basting or pinning are required for each pleat, one to form a straight fold and the other to hold the fold in place (Fig. 18-8).

Crease along the foldline and pin at right angles to the fold. Baste ⅛ inch back from the fold, which would be like a tuck basted through two thicknesses. (On firm materials, which crease readily, this basting can be omitted.) Lap this fold over to the second line. Pin it in place at right angles. Check to see that the spacing is even and matches the other spacings as planned. Baste flat on the table through the three layers (Fig. 14-2). Keep the bastings slightly loose to prevent marks when steaming. Clip and remove the basting as you press before making a hard crease. Baste the entire length, except for unpressed pleats, which are basted only as far as they are to be stitched. Complete the basting of each pleat before pinning the next one.

If the under (or back) fold falls on a seam, baste or stitch the seam *after* the upper fold is basted. In this way any inaccuracy is pushed out into the seam.

Eᴀsᴇ
Ease stitching is used where the extra fullness to be added is slight. Just push

340

more fabric into the feed. If this does not add sufficient ease, rip out the work; with *looser tension and a standard-length stitch,* restitch the part to be eased and draw it up to fit. Lengthening the machine stitch may give you a thread that can be pulled, but it will give you larger pleats that are difficult to shrink out. Some lengthening may be necessary on thick, bulky fabrics. Keeping stitches short is a special advantage in easing firm, closely woven fabrics. You will encounter this problem over the bust of the side sections of princess styles, a back shoulder and sleeve that have no darts, scoop necklines, sleeve caps, and the waistlines of a skirt or bodice.

Ease usually involves the fundamental dart, with the extra length in the seam merely eased, rather than stitched into a dart form.

GATHERS Gathers are small, unpressed folds or pleats that can be made by drawing one of the threads in a line of machine stitching, by using an attachment that performs this function, or by using elasticized thread. The size of the pleats is controlled by the length of stitches used.

It is quite probable that gathered sections generally contain the fundamental dart. For example, a full-gathered skirt will contain, at its upper edge, a sufficient length of fabric for the wide ends of any darts that might, in a fitted skirt, begin here and end in points nearer the hipline. In addition to these unstitched fundamental darts, extra fullness is provided. This is referred to as *design fullness.* The designer makes ingenious use of design fullness in locating both the structural lines and the decorative design in the pattern, often in combination.

If the tensions of the two threads of machine stitching are fairly loose and unbalanced, the tighter of the threads can be pulled to create gathers. This principle can be used to advantage when easing or gathering without a machine attachment. Simply pull the tighter thread and adjust the fullness. Here are three simple ways to stitch for gathering.

1. *Loosen the lower thread* by inserting the bobbin correctly but failing to pull the thread through the slots of the bobbin case. Stitch with the wrong side of the fabric up where the gathers are desired. Pull the tighter spool thread. Test your machine to see if this is a practical method for your model.

2. *Loosen the upper thread* by changing the tension. Stitch with the right side of the fabric up. Pull the tighter bobbin thread for gathers. Both methods are effective on the sleeve cap, especially on close weaves, because the stitch is short and ease is better controlled. For very full gathers at the top of a skirt, use heavy-duty thread.

3. *Lengthen the stitch* with or without changing the tension. This method provides larger bits of ease resulting in coarser gathers.

POINTS ON GATHERING
1. The thread to be pulled should be extra strong.
2. The one to be pulled is the tighter in tension.
3. The side with the loose tension thread looks better and should be on the outside of the garment when gathering threads are to be left, as in shirring.

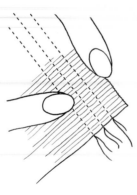

Figure 18-9. Two or three rows of machine gathers, made with loose tension, are pulled up together and arranged in neat, pleat-like folds. Short stitches yield fine gathers; longer stitches result in coarse gathers. Pull the tighter threads.

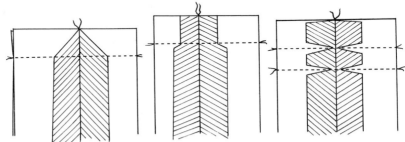

Figure 18-10. Trim bulky seams before stitching across them at waistline. Use method at right before gathering across a seam. (It is often better to stop stitching at each seam, flipping the edges out of the way to begin again.)

4. Two or three rows of gathering $\frac{1}{8}$ to $\frac{1}{4}$ inch apart look and set better than one. Have one row on the traced seamline. One row may be satisfactory for the skilled person.

5. Pull the tight threads of all rows simultaneously, until gathered section fits the adjoining seam.

6. Adjust the shirring by holding the gathers firmly under your left thumb and pulling the fabric down with the right hand until it sets in neat little pleats (Fig. 18-9).

7. Pull both thread ends through to the wrong side—do not tie them until you are sure they fit the place planned—then tie them but do not cut them off too close.

8. A stitch slightly longer than usual helps the gathers to slip more smoothly, but they appear as slightly larger pleats.

9. In stitching across seams, have them pressed flat, preferably open, and clipped (Fig. 18-10). If fabric is heavy, stop the stitching at the seamline and start again on the other side of seam.

10. Gathers set better stitched along the softer filling threads (across the heavier warp).

SHIRRING   Shirring consists of a group of gathered lines (Fig. 14-8).

ELASTICIZED GATHERING OR SHIRRING   Use elastic thread on the bobbin to produce a flexible, snug-fitting effect in the garment. Wind elastic thread on the bobbin by hand, stretching it slightly. Use about six or seven stitches per inch and make a test sample to determine whether the machine works freely without loosening the tension.

Stitch on the right side of the fabric, holding it taut with one hand in front of the presser foot and the other hand behind it. For shirring, it will be necessary to stretch all of the previously stitched lines as you sew. Tie knots in the thread ends, and be sure they are well secured when they are stitched in the seam that crosses their ends. Extra security can be provided by folding $\frac{1}{4}$-inch of the seam allowance over the ends and stitching across the enclosed knots.

A Generalization

1. To taper a dart to a fine point, following the body curve,	stitch from the wide end to the point, swinging the last inch in a slight curve toward the fold.

Seams and Edge Finishes

Assembling Garment Sections

The choice of a seam to be used will depend on the type and weight of the fabric and the current fashion relative to decorative structural lines. Plain and enclosed seams occur repeatedly on any garment, even though more decorative seams may be at the forefront of fashion, and included among those on the garment.

BASTING

Although basting on the machine saves much time, some more delicate fabrics require hand basting, such as velvet and chiffon. On long, plain seams, machine basting works successfully if the fabric is not marked or damaged by the stitched line. If basting is done on the seamline, you will need to decide at the fitting on which side of the basting to stitch. Stitched in the same place, basting stitches would be difficult to remove.

A useful trick in assembling a *many-gored* skirt is to baste *from hip up to waist only*. Have a fitting, and hang the skirt so the bias folds and seams will stretch before permanent seaming.

For basting or stitching seams that have not been staystitched, use *directional stitching*. After a line is staystitched, it can be seamed either with or against the grain.

PLAIN SEAM The plain seam is simple to make; it is inconspicuous, pliable, and adaptable to a wide variety of uses.

To obtain a satisfactory seam, place right sides of the fabric together, match and pin it at the notches, at the ends where seamlines intersect, and in between as needed (Fig. 19-1, *a*). The important point is to match the intersecting seamlines or hemlines rather than only the raw edges. That way, the intersecting seamlines, as well as edges at seamlines, will form a continuous line, *b*. If one side appears longer than the other, as the back does in this case, the extra length will need to be eased in to make the edges fit. How to ease in is described on pp. 280 and 290; and by hand in Figure 14-9.

Variations of the plain seam are shown with topstitching (Fig. 19-2). The single topstitched seam, *a*, has both seam allowances pressed in the same direction, with topstitching parallel to the seam. The width of the space between the two lines of stitching would vary with the weight of the fabric and the garment design. The double topstitched variation, *b*, is the same, except that the seam was pressed open and topstitching placed on each side. See the directions for topstitching, p. 352.

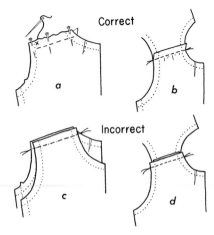

Figure 19-1. *a*, Plain seam, hand-basted at shoulder; *b*, machine basted to retain ease, with intersecting seams perfectly matched; *c*, failure to match intersecting seams results in displaced circumference lines in *d*.

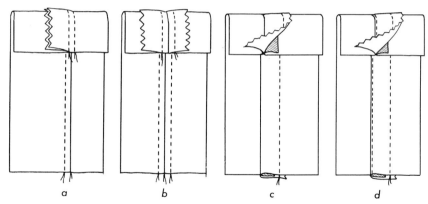

Figure 19-2. *a* and *b*, Topstitched seams—single and double; *c* and *d*, welt seams—single and double.

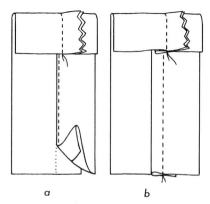

Figure 19-3. *a*, Lapped seam; *b*, tucked seam.

WELT SEAM The welt seam (Fig. 19-2, *c*), similar to the topstitched seam but wider, is used chiefly on heavy coats. It is stitched first as a plain seam on the wrong side. One edge is trimmed off to the width the seam is to be stitched on the outside, such as ⅜ inch wide. The two raw edges are pressed to one side, with the narrow one enclosed under the wider one. On the outside, it is stitched slightly beyond the narrow raw edge underneath so that the stitching will not catch it. Try the quilting foot or a gauge (Fig. 13-6) as a guide.

A double welt seam, *d,* is made by stitching another line along the fold on the outside close to the original stitching inside. It appears somewhat like a stitched fell on the right side, but has a raw edge exposed on the wrong side and, of course, is not bulky.

LAPPED SEAM For a lapped seam, the edge of one side is folded on the seamline and placed on the right side of the other edge. The stitching line is placed near the edge (Fig. 19-3, *a*).

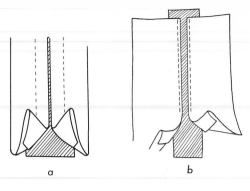

Figure 19-4. *a*, Slot seams—edges together; *b*, spread apart.

TUCK SEAM   To make a tuck seam, fold one edge of the fabric as for a tuck. Lap this edge over the other edge so that the fold will coincide with the seamline on the other side. Stitch through the three layers of fabric to form a tuck the desired width, *b*. A standard width seam is allowed—the minimum width should be at least $\frac{1}{4}$ inch.

SLOT SEAM   Hand-baste a plain seam and press it open. Place an underlay the width of the two seam allowances on the wrong side. Topstitch it at equal distances from the basted seam and then remove the basting thread (Fig. 19-4, *a*).

Variations of this seam can have space left between the two sections of the seam to provide a wider and possibly contrasting "slot," *b*. This seam is a variation of a lapped seam, whereas *a* is a variation of a tuck seam.

CURVED SEAMS   Before stitching a curved seam, as princess lines over the bust or shoulder blade curves, both edges would be staystitched $\frac{1}{8}$ inch from the

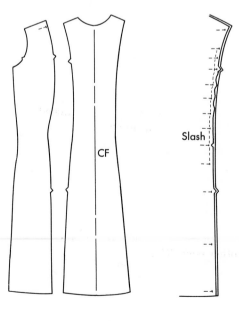

Figure 19-5. The curved seam in this princess design requires slashing at the waistline to fit the straighter CF section, and easing along the bustline.

seamlines. As the two edges are pinned together, clip the seam allowance on the inward, concave curve almost to the staystitching to make it lie smoothly (Fig. 19-5). Baste-stitch the seam with the slashed side up for greater accuracy in placing seamlines together. When the seam is pressed open, notch the outward, convex curve sufficiently to make it lie flat.

FRENCH SEAM A French seam appears as a plain seam on the right side of the garment; on the wrong side it is clearly a seam enclosed in a seam (Fig. 19-6). Because it consists of four layers of cloth, it is suitable only for sheer fabrics. For straight, short seams in transparent fabrics, such as organdy or batiste, it is neat, without ravelings. It cannot be used on curves such as yokes and armholes.

A well-made French seam is narrow—$\frac{1}{8}$ to $\frac{3}{16}$ inch wide—even in width, free of whiskers or ravels on the right side, and finished on the original seamline.

To make a French seam, place the wrong sides together, pin or baste on the seamline and approve the fit of the garment—the seams will be on the right side. Stitch $\frac{3}{16}$ inch from the seamline, nearer the raw edge; crease the seam open and then to one side. Trim the seam to within $\frac{1}{8}$ inch of the stitching line. Turn the garment to the wrong side and work the first seam out to the edge, to be enclosed in the second seam. Baste or pin the seam and stitch it on the original seamline, producing a seam $\frac{1}{8}$ to $\frac{3}{16}$ inch wide, *a*. This second stitching can be done by hand, with fine running stitches and an occasional back stitch for strength. A poorly made seam shows a channel along its edge (on the wrong side of the garment) because it was not pressed open or worked out properly before turning.

MOCK FRENCH SEAMS A *mock French seam* (Fig. 19-6, *b*) is made where the enclosed finish is desired but where a French seam would interfere with the fitting—such as at the armhole. To make it, first stitch and press a plain seam on

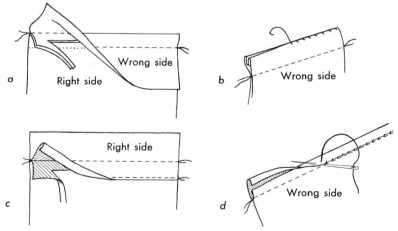

Figure 19-6. *a*, French seam; *b*, mock French seam; *c*, stitched fell; *d*, standing fell or self-bound seam.

the planned seam line on the wrong side of the garment. Trim it to a width of ¼ to ⅜ inch. Turn the two raw edges together toward the inside and finish them with tiny, running, overhand stitches or machine stitching close to the folded edges.

FELL SEAM The stitched fell is used on shirts, pajamas, and work or sport clothes. It is made right side out and has two rows of stitching showing on the right side with only one line of stitching showing on the wrong side (Fig. 19-6, c).

A good stitched fell has two lines of stitching on the right side evenly spaced about ¼ inch apart; it is matched in length, tension, and color of thread; the first line of stitching is on the original (marked or traced and fitted) seamline, so the garment fits as designed; there are no wrinkles on the underside; the edge stitching is on the right side close to the fold, so that a tuck cannot be pressed back in ironing; and the lap is in the correct direction.

The plain side folds over the fuller eased-in part of the seam—the blouse over the sleeve, the yoke over the blouse. At the CF of trousers, lap left over right for boys and right over left for girls. The side seams of trousers, skirts, blouses, and sleeves should have the back trimmed to make the front lap over the back in order to make the seam continuous with a placket lap, if any.

To secure a good stitched fell, follow these steps. Pin the right side out near the seamline allowed by the pattern and corrected by a fitting. Stitch on the exact seam line on the side that will be up when the seam is completed. Press it in the proper direction. Trim the under layer of the seam to within ⅛ inch of the stitching and the upper layer to ⅜ inch wide. Turn the wide edge under ⅛ inch to make a smooth fold ¼ inch wide or less. Keep one hand underneath as you baste this fold down flat to the garment covering the ⅛-inch edge. Stitch about 1/16 inch from the edge.

A *hemmed* or "*standing*" *fell* is made in a similar manner, but the first stitching is on the wrong side and the last step is done by hand-hemming the fold to the original stitching line, *d*.

An *imitation stitched fell* is used to replace the tedious work of a flat-fell seam. Simply press a plain seam to one side; turn it to the right side and stitch ¼ inch from the first seam through three layers.

REVERSED SEAM Where a hem or facing is turned back to the right side of the garment for decoration, it is necessary to reverse the seam. Stitch a plain seam on the wrong side to a point about ¼ inch beyond the point to be covered with the hem or facing. Clip the seam to the stitching, then turn the seam right side out and stitch the rest of it as a plain seam on the outside of the garment (Figs. 21-8 and 26-5).

ENCLOSED SEAM A plain seam, used to join double layers, as in a collar, when turned inside is called an enclosed seam. These seams are the hidden seams in a finished garment—inside the collar, cuffs, belts, bindings, and hems or under the facings.

Enclosed seams will be considered in Chapter 21.

Seams—Special Situations

STRETCHY OR SHIFTY FABRICS Place tissue paper under the fabric and stitch through the fabric and paper, for fabrics such as stretch single knits, chiffon, and thin crepes.

NAPPED OR PILE FABRICS Stitch in the direction of the nap. Where one fabric is unnapped, keep this layer up—next to the presser foot—to reduce slippage. Hand-baste delicate fabrics, such as velvet, with silk thread before stitching.

BIAS EDGES

When stitching a bias edge to a straight edge, have the pins fairly close together and place the bias next to the feed; the straight side lying on top tends to control the slight ease in the under layer. If both sides are bias and the seam will hang free, as a skirt seam, it is advisable to stretch the seam slightly when stitching. This will prevent tightness and drawing after the garment area around it has sagged. This line can also be stitched against the grain. A bias skirt seam, however, would be staystitched from hip- to waistline, as stretching there would be undesirable.

ONE SIDE FULL OR BULKY When one side is gathered or pleated, keep that side up, in order to be able to adjust the fullness and folds. Authorities disagree about stitching the armhole curve: a smoother curve is obtained when stitched with the garment side up, but one is less likely to catch a tiny pleat or pucker when the fuller sleeve side is up. If the basting is done by machine, the problem can be solved simply by basting on the sleeve side and stitching on the garment side. See Figure 13-4 for use of the hands for controlling ease when stitching.

TOPSTITCHING

Topstitching on seams and garment edges adds structural decoration in effective ways. Variations in color, type of thread, and stitches used add additional interest.

The line can be stitched with the thread that is being used in the construction of the garment. A more decorative effect is gained by the use of the buttonhole twist, in either a matching or contrasting color or value.

Topstitching can be done during construction or after the garment is finished, depending on its nature and location. For seams, in general, the stitching will be done during construction. The plain seams, single and doublestitched, are examples. This can be true also for multiple stitched lines on collars, cuffs, or lapels. On heavier fabrics, the decorative lines can be stitched through the fashion fabric and underlining or interfacing, but not through the cuff or collar facing. Careful planning is needed in order to avoid stitching through too much bulk and across seamlines of varying thicknesses.

Obviously, the fit of the garment should be approved before the seams are topstitched.

How to Topstitch

1. Adjust the machine to 6 to 8 stitches per inch; use a size 16 needle.
2. Use buttonhole twist on both spool and bobbin—wind it on bobbin by hand.
3. Test a sample to determine whether the machine feeds smoothly; if not, the tension needs adjusting.
4. Stitch on the top side; use a guide for stitching, such as quilting foot, tape, basting line, or other appropriate technique.
5. On heavy fabrics, it is more effective to stitch two lines close together.
6. Leave thread ends about two inches in length, thread into a needle and carry to wrong side where they can be woven in and out of a seam allowance or possibly tied to another thread.

Hand Stitches

A couture touch can be added by hand stitches such as the prickstitch, pickstitch, or saddlestitch. The principle use of prickstitch is in attaching the zipper to the seam; pickstitch and saddlestitch function as decorative stitches only and are usually applied after the garment is finished. See pages 430, 471, and 488.

Edge Finishes

Finishing fabric edges presents the same or similar conditions wherever they may occur in the garment—on a seam allowance, a facing, or a skirt hem.

Finishes are optional on many fabrics; a firm fabric requires no finishing. Seam finishes can provide extra support and durability for many fabrics, they can prevent raveling, and they present a more attractive appearance if the garment is not to be lined.

Hand Overcasting—Machine Overedging   On fabrics that ravel badly, hand overcasting is a durable finish that reacts well in laundering (Fig. 19-7, *a* and *b*). If facilities are available for zigzagging or overedging by machine, *c,* time can be

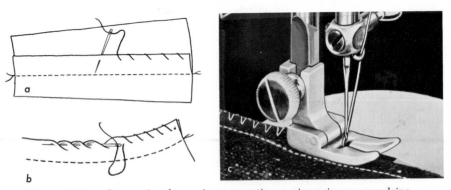

Figure 19-7.   *a,* Overcasting; *b,* running overcasting; *c,* zigzagging or overedging.

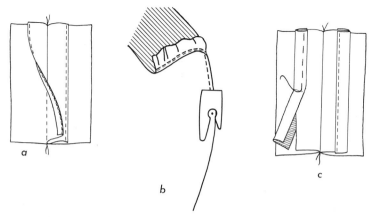

Figure 19-8. *a*, Plain seam, with edges turned and stitched; *b*, technique for clean-finishing; *c*, edges bound.

saved—although there may be instances where the softer finish provided by hand stitches will be preferable.

MACHINE-STITCHING   A machine-stitched line, ¼ inch from the seam edge, can serve adequately. Overcasting can be added in raveling fabrics, or the edge can be finished with pinking where there is little raveling and this more decorative finish is desired. Even though the points may fray somewhat, the slightly fringed edge may prevent long yarns from raveling farther. If used, pinking is more suited to dry-cleaning processes. It is undesirable for sheer fabrics, where the finish shows through.

TURNED EDGES OR A CLEAN FINISH

Seams with their edges turned under and stitched present a neat appearance and are durable (Fig. 19-8, *a*). Because of their bulk, they are more suitable for light-or medium-weight fabrics. They are unsatisfactory for sharply curved seams. Their principal uses are on unlined jackets and coats.

To make this finish, press the seam open, turn each raw edge under ¼ inch, and stitch ¹⁄₁₆ inch from the fold—with the grain where possible. Off-grain edges are easier to control when they are first staystitched on the line where the fabric is to be turned, *b*. With the slightly full seam allowance next to the machine, the fullness is kept under control by the upper layer as the edge is stitched.

BOUND EDGES

Bound edges on seams (Fig. 19-8, *c*) are used on unlined jackets and coats where the fabric is bulky and inclined to fray. Use bias binding if the seams are curved. To eliminate bulk, select a thin binding, but keep it suitable for the fabric—such as cotton binding on a washable cotton. Be sure the binding has been fully shrunk.

Probably the easiest technique for applying the binding smoothly to a heavier fabric is to stitch one side of the bias binding, unfolded, to the wrong side of the seam. Then you can bring the binding over and stitch it on the upper side. On lighter-weight fabrics, good results can be obtained by placing commercially folded binding over the seam-allowance edge, with the narrower fold on top, and stitching near the edge on the top side. Also, see the Hong Kong finish, p. 474.

Straight edges can be bound with woven seam binding, and for a more decorative edge finish, stretch lace can be used on either straight or curved edges.

Generalizations

Directions: Read each generalization across both columns; note the relationships between the parts, as pointed out in the headings.

EFFECT SOUGHT OR REASON WHY	THE CAUSE OR WHAT TO DO
1. To keep fabric flat and smooth when pinning a pattern in place, when pinning for basting or stitching, and for outside fitting of a basted seam,	place pins at right angles to the edge in the most advantageous position for cutting or stitching.
2. In pinning (rather than basting) a seam for fitting and to establish guidelines,	place pins parallel to and on the proposed seam lines.
3. To pin or baste two edges together, one of which is fuller than the other, in order to see the fullness and control it,	hold the full or bias side next to you.
4. To obtain a flat line and avoid pressing a small tuck or crease along a plain seam,	press it open, whether it is to be finished open or closed, unless it is to be understitched (understitched seams can be controlled without pressing them open).
5. To create a flat smooth seam or dart without a tuck or wrinkle, to save time (and to avoid damaging garment in trimming),	finish completely (by removing basting, trimming, pressing) one line of sewing before crossing it with another.
6. To keep enclosed seams flat and smooth,	trim to $\frac{1}{4}''$, or $\frac{1}{8}''$ in firm fabrics to be understitched; or exact width of welt seam. (Pinking is superfluous and spoils a good line.)
7. Double layers are easier to iron and stay in proper place,	if they are topstitched or understitched.
8. To reduce the effect of excessive width in seams of lightweight or sheer fabrics,	seams are usually pressed together.

9. To reduce the bulk in seams and wide darts of heavy fabrics and avoid imprints,

press them open; or if turned in the same direction, grade or blend edges by trimming one $\frac{1}{16}''$ to $\frac{1}{8}''$ narrower, with the wider one next to the outside of the garment.

10. To reduce the bulk when one side of the seam is full (gathered or pleated),

press seams together away from the fuller, bulkier side.

11. To make a placket in a seam lap front over back, to fill in hollow at front of shoulder, or to follow grain in pressing closed seams and darts,

usually press silhouette seams to the front; vertical darts and seams within a section toward the center front or back; horizontal darts and seams within a section down, because of their natural weight (law of gravity).

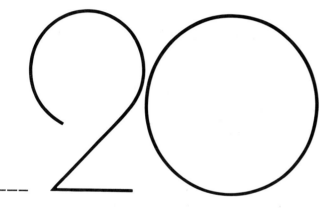

20

Bias— Cutting and Using

Bias is a general term referring to any slanting line off the straight grain of the fabric. Cloth has the most stretch possible when it is cut obliquely on an angle of 45 degrees, exactly halfway between the lengthwise and the crosswise grains. This is *true bias* (Fig. 20-1, *a*).

Functions of Bias

Observe the differences in *b* and *c*. If you want to use a strip of fabric around a curve, which is better? Why? Because of the nature of true bias, it can be stretched along the outside, convex curve and eased along the other edge—the inside, concave curve—to make it lie flat and smooth.

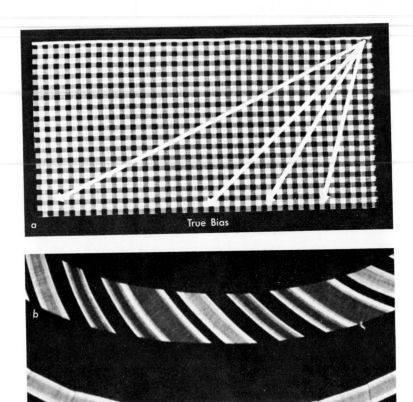

Figure 20-1. Which position in a is true bias? b, A true-bias strip is easily shaped into a curve; c, only slight shaping is possible on the grain of firmly woven fabric. Note the pleats needed to achieve this degree of curve.

CUTTING BIAS STRIPS

How can one be sure of finding the true-bias location in a piece of fabric? One plan is shown in Figure 20-2. Warp and filling grains must be at right angles to each other and the fabric should have body or firmness; this technique would be difficult in soft sheers and crepes. Measure along the side of the strip and mark the point that makes this line equal to the width of the fabric. Using a yardstick, draw a dotted or dashed line connecting this point with the corner.

Another plan is to fold a corner of the cloth in the manner shown in Figure 20-3, a. Does this fold line mark a 45-degree angle? There is evidence that it does. Now analyze what was done to achieve this condition and try to state this in your own words. Did your statement involve the following idea? Fold the fabric so that the lengthwise yarns lie parallel to, or coincide with, the crosswise yarns.

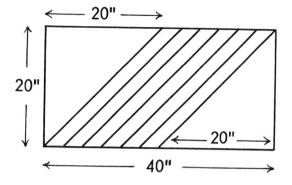

Figure 20-2. One method of finding the true-bias position and marking fabric for cutting bias strips.

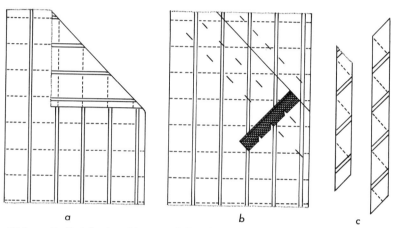

Figure 20-3. *a*, To find the true bias, match lengthwise grain to crosswise. *b*, Measure accurately at several intervals, beginning at bias fold. Trim ends of bias strips on warp grain.

With this information and understanding, you are in a position to cut a true-bias strip from any fabric, as long as you can identify the location of its two sets of yarns—you must be able to see both warp and filling.

It is obvious that the grain lines must be at right angles to each other, so you will have checked on this condition, previously. If it is difficult or impossible to see the grain lines in your fabric, mark the lines with pins, or with chalk, on the wrong side, by measuring from the end or selvage of the fabric.

Hand-press the fold gently to avoid stretching it out of shape. Using an iron is hazardous. If the fabric is stretchy, the best results may not be obtained by trying to cut along the fold; open the fabric and follow the crease mark. Time is saved if the fabric is left double, so that two strips can be cut at the same time.

If you want bias strips, mark a line on the crease with chalk or with a tracing wheel, *b*. With a gauge, make marks for as many lines as will be needed. Cut them with the smoothest possible strokes. Then trim off both ends of each strip along a warp yarn. Ravel one yarn across the end to test it, *c*.

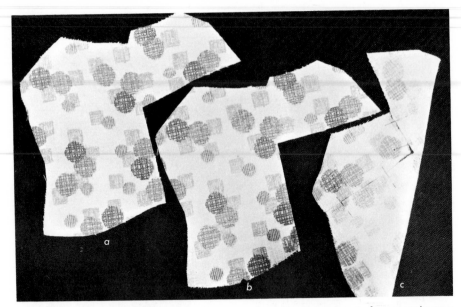

Figure 20-4. To find the true bias position on an irregular scrap, *a*, cut along a grain yarn to straighten an edge, *b*. This grainline can now be placed parallel with the other grainline (length or crosswise) to provide a fold on the true bias, *c*.

If the fabric is stretchy and delicate, pin it on a tracing board. Have true-bias lines drawn on a piece of paper. Pin this pattern straight on the cloth. Run a tracing wheel lightly on the lines to mark the strips for cutting.

If you want to use the creased bias line as a guideline for placing the center of a blouse or sleeve or the grainline of a gore to be cut on the bias, it is safer to use chalk or uneven basting to mark it.

Often in cutting a garment, you have only an irregular scrap of fabric left from which to cut bias strips. How can you identify a true-bias line in such a fabric as *a* (Fig. 20-4)? In case you are absolutely sure that checks are perfect squares, you might cut along a line of them diagonally from corner to corner. However, in case the fabric is designed in some other pattern, or is a solid-color fabric, you will need to cut along a thread somewhere to straighten an edge of this irregular scrap, *b*, so that you are able to see this grain thread (warp or filling) as you bring it into a position parallel with the other grainline, *c*.

JOINING BIAS STRIPS

Study the joinings in the bias strips, *c* through x (Fig. 20-5). What standards have been reached in strip *e*? What errors were made in strip *f* to x'?

A well-made bias strip is uniform in width. All its seams are flat; almost invisible; and slanting in the same direction—along warp yarns or crosswise yarns in filling ribs—to give a flatter joining.

Common errors are seams stitched straight across the bias strip that are

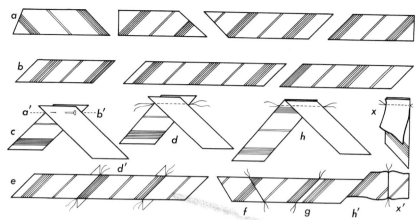

Figure 20-5. *a*, Incorrectly cut bias strips; the first is not true bias, others not trimmed at ends; *b*, all cut correctly, ready to join; *c*, correctly pinned to test matching; *d*, correctly stitched on seamline from intersecting corners so that finished edges of strip will be continuous; *e*, design line matched; *f*, no attempt to match design—difficult on crosswise grain; *g*, unmatched; *h*, raw edges were matched but not on seamline; result is a jog in strip; *x*, another incorrect method, results in a wavy crosswise seam, *x′*.

stretched, wide, and bulky; jogs in the strip that are caused by matching the raw edges of the seam rather than the seamlines; seams on the crosswise grain, which usually stretch more than those on the firmer lengthwise grain; disregarded patterns, *f* to *x′*.

TECHNIQUES FOR JOINING BIAS STRIPS

1. Have both ends of each strip cut on a lengthwise yarn (Fig. 20-5). Plan for ¼-inch seam allowances.
2. Place the ends with right sides together, seamline on seamline. Slip one strip beyond the other about ¼ inch. The strips will be at right angles to each other, *c*.
3. Pin on seamline for testing (for beginners). Basting is not needed. Open up to see if all seams are on the wrong side. Check them to see if the strips are matched; cut off a little if necessary to produce a perfect match.
4. At the machine, remove the first pin and insert the needle at the exact beginning of the seam before lowering the presser foot.
5. Stitch exactly on the seamline—¼ inch from the raw edge and from angle to angle (*a′* to *b′*).
6. Stitch all the seams, then press them open.

CONTINUOUS BIAS STRIP

Mark all lines on the true bias (Fig. 20-6, *a*). With right sides together, join the ends with the width of one strip projecting beyond the edge at each side. Stitch

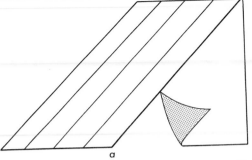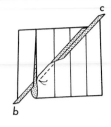

Figure 20-6. Continuous bias strip.

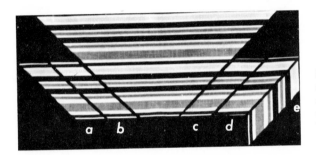

Figure 20-7. Alternating and nonalternating bias. Explain effect of a whole skirt front cut with CF on a true bias. Would not right side seam set differently from left? Why?

a ¼-inch seam and press it open. Begin cutting at one end, *b*, and continue around the cylinder to *c*.

ALTERNATING AND NONALTERNATING BIAS Study Figure 20-7 in relation to the following questions.

1. What is the difference between alternating and nonalternating bias?
2. If the two nonalternating strips, *a* and *b*, were joined at their ends, would the strip be straight and the stripes continue in the same direction?
3. Would *c* and *d* form a straight strip if sewed together at the ends?
4. Could *d* and *e* be sewed together to form a straight strip?

You have found that the two bias strips, *a* and *b*, cut parallel to each other along a bias line in the fabric will form a straight, continuous strip when sewed together. The strips, *c* and *d*, also cut along a bias line, can be joined to form a straight strip. You probably noticed that strip *e*, cut from the left side, will not join *d*, cut from the side at right, to form a straight strip; they would form a right angle. These two, joined along the sides of the strips, give still a different pattern. This is *alternating bias*. Both bias strips and the various treatments of alternating bias can be used to provide decorative effects in clothing.

Using Bias Strips

Bias strips are used for bindings, facings, cording, and other decorative trimmings (Fig. 20-8). Because of its elasticity and pliability, the bias strip can be applied to curves, provided it is not finished too wide. A facing of firm fabric at the normal neckline, for instance, can, probably, be finished no wider than $\frac{5}{8}$ to $\frac{3}{4}$ inch, for a flat, smooth finish. A loose, flexible weave might possibly be as much as 1 inch wide.

For application as a facing on a curve, it is possible to shape the bias strip with an iron (Fig. 15-9).

Figure 20-8. Bias can be joined to form interesting patterns. (Courtesy of Margaret's, *a*.)

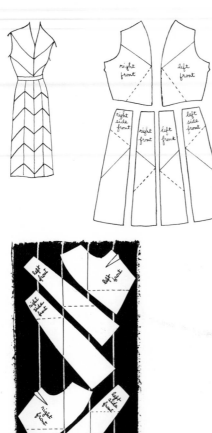

Figure 20-9. To take advantage of stripes, grainlines on a pattern may be shifted to the true bias.

SHIFTING GRAINLINES Grainlines on a pattern can be shifted to the true bias location to provide a different design in stripes (Fig. 20-9). Cut and label left and right parts of the pattern. Fold creases on the true bias and label them to lie on stripes. This method insures mates, with stripes matching at the seams.

Generalizations

What understandings have you reached in your study of this subject? Try to state them. Do your statements involve the following ideas?

1. *True bias*—the most pliable section in a fabric—occurs at the fold made when lengthwise and crosswise grainlines are laid parallel to each other.

2. A true-bias strip can be shaped into a smooth curve.

3. Seams in bias strips tend to be less conspicuous and less stretchable when joined on the firmer, heavier yarns (usually warp) or along a striking design line.

4. Strips of bias cut parallel to each other—nonalternating bias—form a straight line when joined together.

5. Strips cut along bias folds at right angles to each other—alternating—form a right angle when joined together.

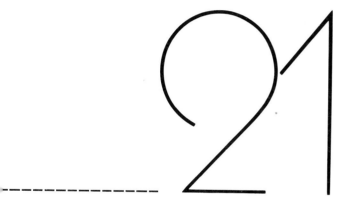

Facings, Bindings, and Collars

Facings

A *facing* is a piece of fabric that is attached along an edge, then turned to lie flat on the cloth, and visible from one side only. It may lie on either the right or wrong side, but it is more often placed on the wrong side of garments. It may be turned to the right side for a decorative effect.

A shaped, or fitted, facing is cut in the shape of the garment area on which it is to lie.

Straight strips and bias strips of fabric may also be used to face edges.

PROBLEM

Consider the lines shown in Figure 21-1. Which types of facings are suitable

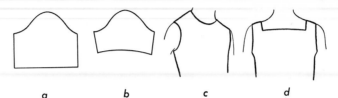

a   b   c   d

Figure 21-1. Type of facing depends on shape to be faced.

for these designs—straight, bias, or fitted? If you are not already familiar with the properties of bias strips, look back to Chapter 20 for assistance in arriving at your decisions.

DISCUSSION OF PROBLEM

a: Either a straight or bias strip would be suitable for facing this sleeve, with the lower edge a perfectly straight line and the sides at right angles to it. A straight facing, in this case, would be synonymous with a shaped, or fitted, facing.

b: This curved line would require either a bias or fitted facing. Naturally, a straight one would not fit this curved line.

c: Fitted facings would be more suitable for both neckline and armholes, although bias strips could be used. Why is a bias strip less desirable? Bias strips *cannot* be made to lie flat along lines as curved as these, unless they are kept rather narrow—probably no wider than ¾ inch. This width would not give a pleasing proportion; the bias facing would not stay in place without being hand-stitched to the garment and this line would show, even if stitches were made quite invisible, resulting in a nonprofessional appearance.

d: This neckline would require a shaped facing; it would be less bulky if front and back facings were each cut in one piece, to face both neckline and armhole. Shoulder and underarm seams in facing would match those in dress.

STANDARDS FOR FACINGS

1. A facing, whether shaped, straight, or bias, should lie flat, smooth, and free of wrinkles.
2. Enclosed seams are trimmed to remove bulk to a maximum of ¼ inch in width. One side may be graded to ⅛ inch, if the fabric is fairly firm or if understitching is to be used.
3. Seams on curves will require slashing, notching, or narrow trimming to make them lie flat.
4. An inside facing does not show along the edge, on the right side of the garment; conversely, with an outside or decorative facing, none of the garment shows along the edge—understitching is an advantage.
5. A facing is even in width, unless unusual in design.
6. Seams of shaped facings match garment seams.
7. Seams of bias facings are, preferably, on warp threads and are located inconspicuously.

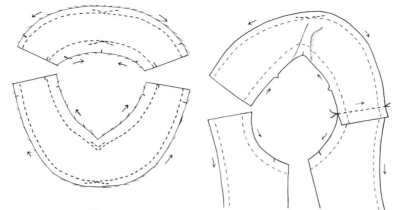

Figure 21-2. Staystitch before making seams.

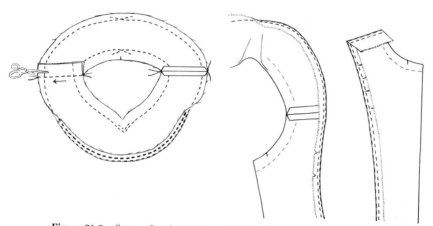

Figure 21-3. Seams finished before finishing free edges of facings.

8. No hand stitching is visible on the right side; shaped or fitted facings can be tacked to seams or darts crossed to hold them in position.

PRELIMINARY PREPARATION

Staystitching is optional on neckline seams of facings and is not required on the shoulder seams because they are so short (Fig. 21-2). Staystitching fixes the neckline of the dress; it will not stretch regardless of whether the facing seam is stayed. However, there is a slight advantage in staystitching the facing—the two go together easier, but the slight extra ease in the unstayed facing is easily handled.

For ease in handling, the outer free edge of facings should be *finished before* the facing is applied to the garment (Fig. 21-3).

The choice of a finish will be influenced by several factors, including fabric, design, and intended use. Simple finishes might include a zigzag or overedged finish by machine; staystitching with the edge left raw in nonraveling fabric or finished with overcasting, or pinking, if desired; the facing faced—with a lighter weight fabric, if bulk is a problem; or edgestitching or a binding where these finishes are not too bulky. (See Chapter 19).

In case the garment is to be lined, it is unnecessary to finish the facing edge, as the lining will cover it.

After a facing is attached and the seam has been properly finished, the line may be either *topstitched* or understitched to help prevent the facing from rolling out and showing along the outer edge.

ENCLOSED SEAMS   Enclosed seams were identified earlier as the hidden seams in a garment—invisible inside a collar, cuff, pocket flap, bound edge, or hem—visible only when a loose facing is lifted.

Because this seam receives little strain, is less subject to wear due to friction, and should not contain excess bulk, it can be trimmed narrower than other seams, especially if it is to be further stabilized by machine stitching along the garment edge. Special treatments are needed in handling this type of seam, depending on its location in the garment, the shape (whether straight, curved, or angular), and the direction in which it will be turned in the finished garment. Consideration will be given to these various conditions in succeeding pages.

GRADING SEAMS   An enclosed seam is graded to remove bulk. If it is to remain pressed open in the finished garment, as the shoulder seams in a neck facing, the seam is first pressed open and then each side is trimmed to $\frac{1}{4}$ inch.

If the layers in the seam are to be pressed in one direction, lying together in the finished garment, it is desirable to trim them to different widths. Usually the edge lying next to the garment is trimmed to $\frac{1}{4}$ inch, the edge lying next to the facing to $\frac{1}{8}$ inch, and the interfacing to $\frac{1}{16}$ inch (Fig. 21-4, b).

UNDERSTITCHING   Understitching is a line of stitching placed near the seamline that attaches a facing to the garment. It is placed on the facing through three thicknesses of fabric—the facing and the two thicknesses of the graded, enclosed seam.

Understitching helps to prevent the facing from showing at the outer edge after it has been attached, c and c′. It is used most often on faced edges of collars and necklines with or without collars, where topstitching is not desired.

The enclosed seam, usually, is not pressed before trimming but must be handled properly on curves and corners (see next section). Finger-press the graded seams toward the facing side, with right side of garment up and seams under the facing; hold the work flat, as you stitch about $\frac{1}{16}$ inch from the seam, on the facing side—not catching the garment or the collar. It is possible to stitch around inside corners continuously, as on a square neck, but not around an outside corner. (See also Figures 21-7, d; 21-10, d, e, f; and 21-11, d.)

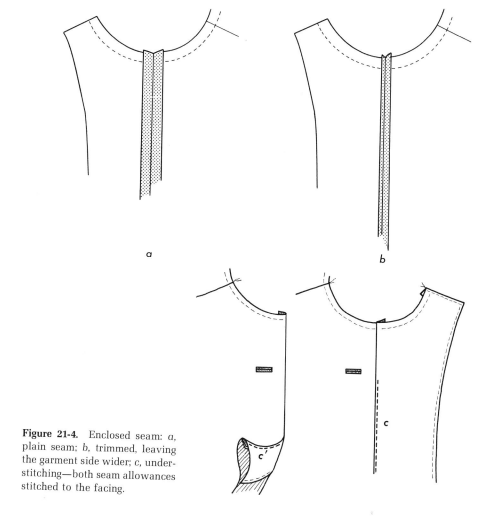

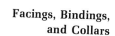

Figure 21-4. Enclosed seam: *a*, plain seam; *b*, trimmed, leaving the garment side wider; *c*, understitching—both seam allowances stitched to the facing.

CURVED SEAMS   Seams stitched in a curve require special treatment to make them lie flat without unnecessary bulk, when they are turned back on the garment (Fig. 21-5).

The dotted line in *a* shows the original location of the seam allowance along this concave curve. Which line would be longer, *cd* or *ef*? Slashing is necessary for *c–d* to take the position of *ef*.

In *b*, it is evident that the convex curve in this seam allowance must lie on a smaller area when it is turned back on the garment, except at the corner that requires slashing. To remove excess bulk, the fabric folds in the seam allowance are snipped off. Care should be taken in cutting, to keep $1/8$ to $3/16$ inch away from the seam or fold line, in this lapped seam. Cut away only the part projecting above the garment; the removal of a larger notch than that is likely to result in angles along the seamline.

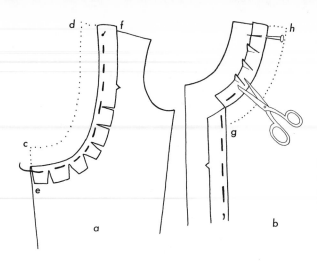

Figure 21-5. The seam allowance in *a* required slashing to permit the concave curve, *cd*, to turn back and lie in position *ef*. The convex curve, *gh*, shows fullness in the seam allowance when turned back on a smaller area.

If these were enclosed seams, the proper procedure would involve trimming and then slashing, *a*; and then trimming, *b*, and checking to determine whether enough bulk has been removed. It is evident that when the seam in *b* has been trimmed to $\frac{1}{8}$ to $\frac{3}{16}$ inch, the excess fullness has probably been removed.

HANDLING CORNERS
Study Figure 21-6 and try to answer the following questions:

1. Explain the relationship between *a* and *b*.
2. Why are the corners of *a* slashed and those of *d* trimmed?
3. Why are *c* and *d* trimmed differently?

Check your answers by the following explanations:

1. The seam allowance in *a* is shown turned back on the garment in *b*. Because it must lie on a larger area in the *b* position, slashing to the corners is required to allow sufficient spreading for it to flatten completely.
2. Although the seam allowance in *a* is to lie on a larger area, that in *d* will lie on a smaller area after turning. Therefore, its corners are trimmed to remove bulk, preventing overlapping of the seams.
3. Because of the difference in angles at the ends of the two belts, the corners are trimmed differently, but with the same end in view—trim seams sufficiently to prevent overlapping inside the belts.

HANDLING CURVES
Again, studying Fig. 21-6, try to answer the following questions:

1. What is the relationship between *a* and *e*?
2. What procedure shown is common to both *a* and *e*? Why?
3. Try to state the reason for the procedure observed in question 2 as a generalization that fits both cases.
4. Considering *d* and *f*, what do these have in common?
5. State, in general terms, the procedure that fits these cases.

Compare your answers with these:

1. Facings are being attached to both *a* and *e*; *a* has inside corners and *e* has an inside curve.

2. Seam allowances in both *a* and *e* have been slashed.

3. When seam allowances with inside corners and inside curves are to be turned back on larger areas, they must be slashed to allow for spreading.

4. Numbers *d* and *f* have outside corners and outside curves; these seam allowances are to be turned back on smaller areas.

5. When seam allowances on outside corners and outside curves are to be turned back on smaller areas, clip off corners and wedges to remove bulk and make them lie flat.

SHAPED NECK FACING—INSIDE FINISH

A shaped neck facing for a collarless garment is easier to apply than a bias facing and is less conspicuous. Shaped facings are cut separately for the front and the back by patterns that come with the garment pattern. The facings should match the garment as to shape and grain. If the shoulder seam and neckline of the garment were altered during fitting, make the same alterations on the facing.

Your pattern guide sheet usually follows the steps illustrated in Figure 21-7:

a: Staystitch ¼ inch from the outer free edge with the grain.

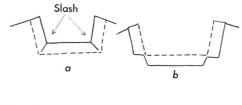

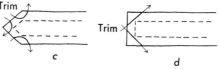

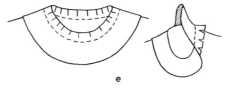

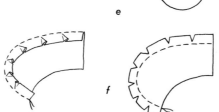

Figure 21-6. Enclosed seams should first be trimmed to ⅛ to ¼ inch before slashing inside corners, *a*, and curves, *e*. Wedges are clipped off outward corners, *c* and *d*, and possibly from outward curves, *f*. If the seam is to be understitched in light-to medium-weight fabrics, *grading* it to slightly narrower widths, as ⅛ to 3/16 inch, may eliminate the need for clipping wedges, resulting in a less bulky, yet durable edge.

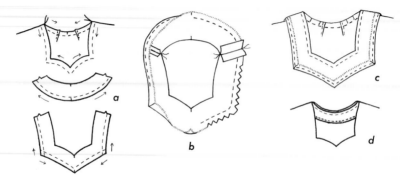

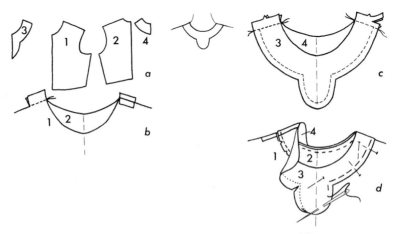

Figure 21-7. Shaped facing—inside finish.

Figure 21-8. Steps for decorative facing at neckline.

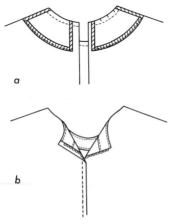

Figure 21-9. Preparing facing for back zipper placket.

b: Stitch the shoulder seams in a plain seam slightly deeper than the seamline planned, so that the facing will be slightly smaller than the area it faces. Press it open and trim it to $\frac{1}{4}$ inch. Finish the outer or free edge of the facing.

c: Pin the facing with the right side facing the right side of the garment. Stitch it on the neckline seam. Trim it to $\frac{1}{4}$-inch, grade bulky seams, clip inside curves or corners, and turn it. (Clips may be made before stitching to straighten curve.)

d: Understitch the facing to the neckline seam. Press lightly so that no imprints are made on the right side; tack the free edge (previously edge-stitched) to any seams, darts, or folds, so that no stitches can be seen on the right side. On underlined garments, the facing may be completely hand-hemmed around outer edge, if desired, with stitches catching underlining but not the fabric.

Many ready-mades are designed with deeper neckline facings, so that no tacking is necessary. Naturally, the extra depth adds bulk and warmth.

Shaped Facing—Outside Finish

An outside, shaped facing (Fig. 21-8) is similar to an inside facing with the following exceptions: The shoulder seams of the facing are made slightly narrower than those on the garment to fit the outside—not the inside—of the garment. It is highly important that shape and grain match exactly, *a.*

Reverse the shoulder seams of the garment at a point just under the finished facing, *b.* (See Fig. 26-5.) Leave the shoulder seam wide on the wrong side of the garment. Press the seam on the outside of the garment, *b,* and trim it to $\frac{1}{4}$ inch. Staystitch free edges of facings on seam line and trim them to leave $\frac{3}{16}$ inch to turn under. Stitch the shoulder seam of the facings as planned; press open, *c;* and trim to $\frac{1}{4}$ inch.

Place the right side of the facing to the wrong side of the garment, so that it will be right side out when finished. Trim it to $\frac{1}{4}$ inch, grade seams, and clip curves. After turning, understitch it so that none of the garment shows at the outer edge, *d.*

Pin the facing down at intervals so centers, seams, and grains all match. Examine the free edge to see that proportions and the design planned are satisfactory and that right and left sides match. Clip inside curves and corners, and miter (if necessary) outward-turning corners and curves, as for a lapped seam; turn edge under.

Machine-stitch or slip-stitch a decorative edge, depending on the design, fabric, or effect desired.

Preparing Neck Facing for Back Zipper Application

The garment neckline has been interfaced and the facing has been completed, with inner edge finished appropriately for your fabric.

Before placing the finished facing on the neckline, press its ends back on the wrong side (Fig. 21-9). The end that is to be attached to the lapped side of the placket is turned under $1\frac{1}{8}$ inches; the other end is turned under $\frac{1}{2}$ inch, *a.* Trim the seams on each side to $\frac{1}{4}$-inch, and stitch the facing to neckline. Turn the facing to wrong side, grade the neckline seam and understitch it, ending understitching

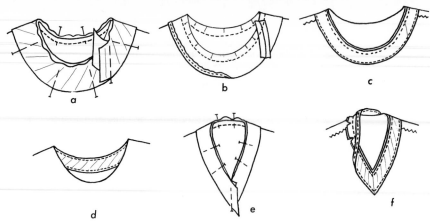

Figure 21-10. Steps for bias facing of necklines.

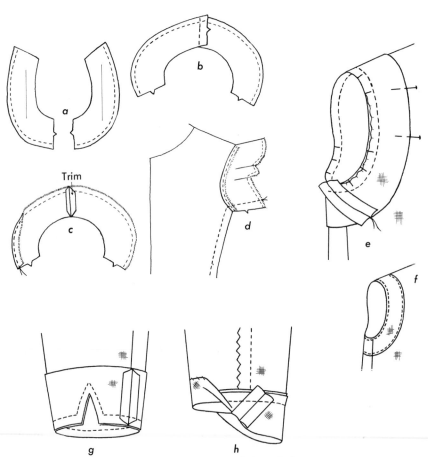

Figure 21-11. Facing armhole and sleeve.

at back fold lines of the facing. Tie any threads on the inside. Turn and press the neckline seam allowances—which extend beyond the ends of the facing—to the inside of the garment, *b*.

Bias Neck Facings

How does one adjust a bias strip to the curve of a neckline? Study *a* in Figure 21-10.

Bias facings are applied by *easing* the bias strip around a *concave curve* so that it lies flat along its outer edge, without cupping. It is more easily done if the $\frac{5}{8}$-inch seam allowance is cut to a $\frac{1}{4}$-inch width before pinning. Because it is staystitched, and has been approved in fitting, it is safe to trim the seam. Plan for the seam of the strip to fall near the shoulder, to be $\frac{1}{4}$ inch wide, and on the grain; this means overlapping $\frac{1}{2}$ inch as you pin, *b*. This short seam must be completed, stitched, pressed open, and trimmed before stitching around the neckline, *c*.

Bias facings are applied to an outward, *convex* curve by slightly *stretching* the edge to be attached, because the outer finished line is longer than the inner one.

Faced Armholes and Sleeves

Traditional bias and shaped facings are shown on sleeveless armholes in Figure 21-11. When using this method, make the facing seam a little deeper, so that it will not be too bulky and wrinkle under the outside area. When stitching the circumference seam, make the shoulder and lengthwise seams match exactly.

Facings fit better when their sections are cut on the same grain as the garment sections, which places shoulder and underarm seams in the facing as in the garment. Today, the pattern companies often cut the armhole facing in one piece, without the shoulder seam. The advantage is the elimination of a slight bulk and one step in construction. With less stable, washable fabrics, better results may be obtained by adding the seamline and restoring the grain to correspond to that in the garment. The one-piece facing can be expected to give more satisfactory results when its inner edge is tacked only to seams and darts, not to the underlining, as it does not lie as smoothly when cut in this manner.

A short-cut for attaching an armhole facing (Fig. 21-11, *d*) works satisfactorily. It involves approval of the armhole location at the first fitting and attachment of the facing after the shoulder seam is finished and before the side seam is stitched. The seam will be pressed open and the facing part of it trimmed to $\frac{1}{4}$ inch. The edge finish is neater, in this case, if it is turned and stitched after the facing is attached. This method may be used for a short sleeve, where careful fitting is not required (Fig. 22-10).

Facing a Skirt

If there is not a sufficient hem allowance, use a *bias facing* for a curved edge. Occasionally, an outside facing is used for decorative purposes.

Cut *bias* strips 2 to 3 inches wide. Join the ends along lengthwise threads with a $\frac{1}{4}$-inch seam pressed open, until strip is a little longer than needed. Press and shrink out the fullness by using the side of the iron to convert the strip into a semicircular shape. It is easier to shrink out the fullness now than after it is on the skirt, although it can be done as in a regular hem.

Rip out the old hem, brush out lint (which may soil the crease), and steam-press thoroughly with the grain. Hang and trim evenly.

With right sides facing, pin the bias strip around the skirt. Let the end of the strip overlap the beginning about $\frac{1}{2}$-inch; cut off the ends along warp yarns, and stitch together in a $\frac{1}{4}$-inch seam. Press open. This seam should be as neat and flat as any other. (*Lengthwise seams should be finished before stitching circumferences across them.*)

Stitch around the bottom of the skirt. Trim the seam if it is wider than $\frac{1}{4}$-inch; grade. Turn the facing to the inside of the skirt and understitch. If the fabric is bulky, the seam can be pressed open for a flat, smooth finish, and understitching omitted. With this plan, the seam will be pulled farther to the wrong side—the width of the enclosed seam, $\frac{1}{8}$ to $\frac{1}{4}$ inch.

Finish raw edge with any suitable finish, being sure to see that seam at lower edge is pulled slightly to the wrong side—$\frac{1}{16}$ to $\frac{1}{8}$ inch—to hide the facing. Avoid overpressing, which shows imprints.

Bindings

A *binding* is attached along a garment edge in a plain seam and shows as an extension on both right and wrong sides (Fig. 21-12). The finished width depends on fashion, texture and weight of the fabric, and the purpose of the binding.

STANDARDS FOR BINDINGS

1. A binding can be cut on the straight grain or on the bias.
2. It is even in width.
3. It should lie flat and smooth, without ripples.
4. Seams of bias bindings are, preferably, on warp yarns and are located inconspicuously.
5. No hand stitches are visible on the right side; stitches are fastened along the line of stitching, in the seam allowance, rather than in the garment.
6. A well-made binding finished by machine on the right side will have even stitching, either on the binding or on the garment, in the groove very close to the binding.

BINDING A CONCAVE CURVE

With an awareness of the characteristics of well-made bindings, the next step is to determine how these standards can be reached.

Thinking through the following questions, based on Figure 21-12, may assist you in expanding your understanding of bias bindings.

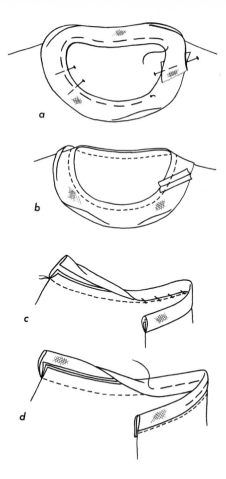

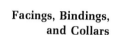

Figure 21-12. Steps for bias binding of necklines.

1. Where will the finished garment edge be located, as indicated in *b* and *c*?

The finished edge of a binding is also the finished edge of the garment. Therefore, you will need to study your guide sheet to determine whether the seam
allowance is to be removed before attaching the binding.

2. Should the bias strip be eased or stretched at the seamline in *b*? Why? (If
you cannot answer these questions, see p. 357 for information on the nature
of bias.) In which case would you expect to get a more perfect binding: if the inner
edge (not the seam edge) lies flat on the bodice when the seam is stitched; if the
inner edge rolls up off the bodice when the seam is stitched?

The finished edge will be shorter than the seamline; therefore, the binding
should be stretched where it is stitched so that it will not be too long and loose
at its shorter folded edge. For this reason, its inner edge will be expected to curl
and roll upward as it is being attached.

3. According to recognized standards, joining bias strips on the lengthwise
grain is considered preferable. Why?

The point is made in Chapter 20 that joining bias strips on the lengthwise,
or most prominent, grainline—where there is less stretch in the fabric—results in
a flatter, neater seam.

4. How is binding standard No. 5 achieved, *c*?

Binding standard 5—no visible stitches on the right side of a hand-hemmed binding—is achieved by catching the stitches in the seam allowance along the line of stitching, but not on the garment side of the seam.

ATTACHING THE BINDING For a *plain binding,* use a bias strip that is twice the desired width of the finished binding plus two seam allowances. Pin and baste the strip around the neck with right sides matched and the seamline of the bias on the seamline of the garment. Stretch the binding at points of greatest inward curve (Fig. 21-12, *b*); the bias will appear slightly cupped. Overlap the ends of the bias strip ½ inch (near the shoulder seam). Cut ends on the warp thread and stitch the standard ¼-inch seam used in a bias strip; press it open, *b.* Then stitch around the circumference on the seamline. Remove the basting but do not press now. Turn under the raw edge of the bias ³⁄₁₆ inch and fold it over the seam on the wrong side. For an invisible hand finish, using a few pins for pinning it into position is an advantage, to determine whether the ease is distributed without ripples; basting is unnecessary. Hem the fold to (but not below) the line of stitching with hemming stitches, *c.* Vertical hemming stitches, with the needle carried into and under the seam allowance, provide a firm, inconspicuous stitch without floating threads. Avoid stretching the binding with your thumb, or you will pull wrinkles in your work. Press up to the binding, but do not press the binding itself too flat.

FRENCH BINDING For a French binding, where a thicker roll is desired, use a 1¼-inch bias strip doubled lengthwise, *d.* Baste the two raw edges to match the raw edge of the neck, stretching it on the concave curve. Stitch the seam slightly narrower than the desired finished width of the binding (stitch a wider seam but trim narrower).

Turn the folded edge of the bias over once to the wrong side and hem it down by hand to the stitching, or work from the right side and baste through the middle of the binding. Right side up, machine stitch in the little groove just off the binding on the garment itself.

BINDING A CONVEX CURVE

The convex, outward curve (Fig. 21-13) is frequently encountered in dressmaking, in the silhouette edge of a collar and in the lower front edge of a jacket.

To attach a bias binding to this type of curve, will you stretch or ease the binding at the seam line? Why?

In this case, the finished edge of the binding will be longer than the line on which it is stitched. It will, therefore, require easing around the curve to provide extra length at the fold line. Otherwise, it will be attached in the same manner as that described above.

BINDING CORNERS

For binding an *outside* corner, there may be an advantage in first trimming the seam allowances to the width of a standard enclosed seam—¼ inch—before beginning this construction, if a narrow binding is desired (Fig. 21-14, *a*).

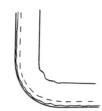

Figure 21-13. Ease a binding on a convex curve—first step.

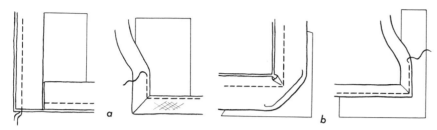

Figure 21-14. *a*, Binding outside corners; *b*, binding inside corners.

With the binding strip pinned or basted in position, stitch along one side to within the width of the seam allowance and tie thread ends. Fold the binding as shown; start at the edge and stitch along the other side across the fold of binding strip. Turn binding to wrong side, folding a mitered corner. Finish the binding by hand-hemming on the wrong side, or stitch from the right side, either on top of the binding or on the fabric as close as you can get to the binding. With the latter method, be sure the binding is wide enough on the wrong side to be caught in the line of stitching.

For binding an *inside* corner, stitch along one side and beyond the corner, the width of the seam allowance (Fig. 21-14, *b*), and turn the fabric into position for stitching along the other side. Form the miter as the strip is turned to the wrong side. Finish the binding by hand-hemming on the wrong side or stitch from the top side, on the binding, or on the fabric as close as you can get to the binding. With the latter method, be sure the binding is wide enough on the wrong side to be caught in the line of stitching.

Collar Styles

Collars are generally described according to their outer shape or silhouette, such as Peter Pan, sailor, or notched; but also as to the roll or flatness, as cowl, mandarin, or convertible (Fig. 21-15). As a dressmaker, one considers the method of construction or application, such as band, shirt, shawl, convertible, or nonconvertible. A sailor collar may roll or lie flat; it may be attached by the shawl method, or with a bias or shaped facing. Any style may hug the neck or stand away, depending on the shape of the neckline. The neckline is often hollowed out to give a comfortable, cool effect or to provide room for a necklace or scarf.

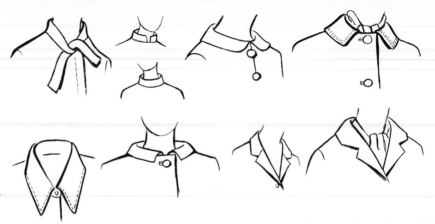

Figure 21-15. Collar styles—left to right, upper row: tie; mandarin and bias binding folded; flat Peter Pan; rolled collar; lower row: shirt, rolled, convertible; shawl collar.

Figure 21-16. Which of these collars are well made, which are poorly made? Collars *b* and *c* are obviously poorly made.

STANDARDS FOR FLAT AND ROLLED COLLARS

Study these photographs of collars (Fig. 21-16). Which are well made? Which are poorly made? The characteristics of a well-made collar include the following:

1. The collar sets smoothly.
2. It is balanced from side to side—ends are in the same relationship at CF and CB, to left and right sides.
3. The outside edge of the collar lies flat, or almost flat against the garment; its corners or edges do not roll upward.

4. The collar facing is not visible along the edge.

5. The points in notched lapels are sharp and regular in line.

Collar Construction

FACED OR LINED COLLARS

The under collar (facing or lining) in dresses and blouses is usually *cut* like the upper collar as to size, shape, and grain. (In tailoring the under collar is often placed on the true bias.) If the interfacing is placed underneath the upper collar, it cushions the collar, making a less noticeable imprint, because it gives an extra layer between seam allowances. This method has a special advantage with light-weight fabrics. For medium and lightweight materials, interfacings of the same material minimize shrinkage problems. It sometimes helps to cut the interfacing on the bias. Watch for new types of interfacing materials—there may be a new one any season.

In the construction, attach the interfacing to the collar when you staystitch. To prevent the under collar from showing along the edge of the finished collar, it is necessary to have the upper collar slightly larger than the under collar. How do you accomplish this? (Sometimes your pattern provides a slightly larger upper collar pattern in suit and coat patterns.) If you have cut both upper and under collars by the same pattern, you cannot stitch the two collar sections together on normal seam lines and expect the facing to stay concealed. You may do one of two things:

1. Make the upper collar larger than the under collar by stitching a narrower seam on the upper collar. This is accomplished by slipping the raw edge of the upper collar back inside the raw edge of the under collar (Fig. 21-17, *a*). This difference is determined by the thickness of your fabric: on medium-weight flannel, $\frac{1}{8}$ inch should be sufficient; more than this amount would be needed on heavy fabrics and slightly less on thin ones.

2. Make the under collar smaller by trimming off a small amount from the outer edge. Disadvantages of this plan are that cutting the edge away from the pattern's perfect silhouette may result in a less accurate line; in cutting the edge away you may have lost notches or other markings; extra time has been used and material unnecessarily handled; and you may confuse the upper and lower collars and may accidentally cut the edge off the upper collar instead of the under collar.

By either of these methods you have a larger upper collar. Match and pin centers, ends, notches, and then several places in between to ease in fullness; baste if necessary, and stitch on the seam line, *a*. With practice you can learn to control the ease without basting.

In *finishing the silhouette seam*, first trim the interfacing as close as possible to the seam—$\frac{1}{16}$ inch; trim the other edges preparatory to understitching to $\frac{1}{8}$ to $\frac{3}{16}$ inch in width (on fine or medium-weight firm weaves, as broadcloth, $\frac{1}{8}$ inch is adequate); on heavier fabrics, edges may be blended or graded to make the seam next to the upper collar wider, probably not over $\frac{1}{4}$ inch, the maximum standard for enclosed seams.

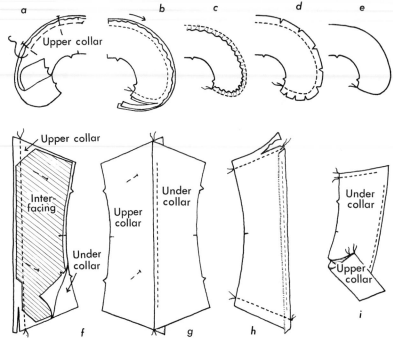

Figure 21-17. Making collars—round and pointed.

If the collar is round with a sharp curve, it may be difficult to understitch on the machine. In this case, you could either topstitch or understitch by hand. With this problem in a rather thick fabric, you will need to remove any wedges. Crease the trimmed seam to one side to determine how much extra fullness needs to be removed (Fig. 21-17, c); trim off the little darts thus formed, d. (See also Fig. 21-6.)

Turn the collar to the right side, e. Hold the seam as flat as possible and understitch it. Press lightly from the outer edge toward the neckline—*not around* the edge of the collar.

THE POINTED COLLAR

After pinning the interfacing in place on the wrong side of the upper part of a pointed collar (Fig. 21-17, f), match the right side of the facing (lining) to the right side of the collar. Stitch across the longer seam, f. Trim the interfacing seam to $\frac{1}{16}$ inch, the other part of the seam to $\frac{1}{8}$ to $\frac{3}{16}$ inch. Turn it right side out, g, and, *without pressing*, use your fingers to hold the fabric smooth as you understitch (stitching facing to seam), beginning and stopping one inch from the ends. Press it right side out so that the understitched facing is concealed underneath. Then turn the wrong side out again to fold the ends for stitching, h. Fold them so that the crease just pressed in is reversed and exactly at the end of the seam at the point of the collar. Pin it so that the end of the upper collar is pushed back from the edge of the undercollar to prevent the undercollar from showing along the edge of the finished collar.

To stitch, insert the machine needle exactly on the reversed fold at the point of the collar. A knot tied at this reversed crease insures a more accurate and less stiff point than retracing. (Starting at the neckline seam means that the reversed crease may be displaced, resulting in an unshapely point.) Stitch, trim, and turn; understitch the ends a short distance (if practical, perhaps by hand), *i;* press.

Attaching Collars—General Techniques

Steps that apply to all types of collars are as follows:

Prepare the garment neckline and the facing—if a facing is to be used—as for a faced neckline. (See p. 373.) The collar will be inserted between them.

Pin the collar in place—matching the centers and notches, and being sure that ends of collar are placed exactly according to the marks indicated on your pattern.

Slash necklines of garment and collar (if curved) to straighten the seam allowance, for accurate measuring along seam gauge for stitching. Note how this line straightens out, after slashing (Fig. 21-18). For a normal neckline curve, slashes will be required about every $\frac{1}{2}$ inch. Make the slashes about $\frac{3}{8}$ inch into the edge, or a bit farther if the line is not straight. However, *never slash through the staystitching,* as this is what prevents stretching of the neckline during the construction.

Baste or pin-baste collar into position, stitching on the garment side. (This step may be omitted, but basting at this stage eliminates the necessity for handling and adjusting several layers at one time for the final stitching.) However, pin-baste the collar first, then the facing on top of it is a satisfactory plan, especially with an easily handled fabric.

Stitch, trim, and grade the seam, and understitch wherever possible. On a collar to be worn open, stop understitching far enough back that it will not show.

Attaching a Collar With Shaped Facing This method is the simplest way of attaching a collar. It has the advantage of the seam turning down toward the

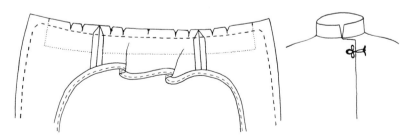

Figure 21-18. Attaching collar with a shaped facing—continuous front and back—dressmaker's method.

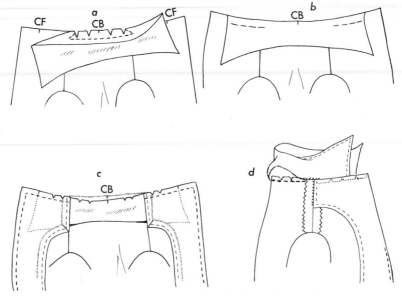

Figure 21-19. Collar applied with front facing only.

bodice so that a rolled collar and a standing collar like the Chinese style set better. Its disadvantage lies in the thickness of the seam. (Your guide sheet may show a different method because of the style.)

Follow the steps just presented under "General Techniques." In step 2, remember to place the wrong side of the collar to the right side of the garment.

Between steps 4 and 5, insert this one: Place the completed facing on the collar (Fig. 21-18) before stitching on the garment side.

ATTACHING COLLAR WITH FRONT FACING ONLY Have the free edge and shoulder seam of facing clean-finished. Complete the collar except for neckline seams. Slash staystitched seams in necklines of blouse, collar, and facings, almost to the staystitching, so they can be matched together to make a straight line for stitching.

Attach back of undercollar to back of blouse from shoulder seam to shoulder seam, right sides facing (Fig. 21-19), through two layers, *a*. Baste CF's of collar ends to CF's of blouse on neckline seam from CF to shoulder through three layers, *b*.

Pin and/or baste the facings over the collar fronts, matching corners, centers, and shoulder seams, *c*. Machine-stitch from bottom of blouse up to corner of lapel, pivot (with diagonal stitch or two) and stitch along neckline to shoulder seam (through blouse, collar of two or three layers, and facing) on both the right and left halves.

Finish by trimming, slashing, and grading seams. Turn the facing to wrong side and understitch to its seam wherever it is needed to keep it from rolling free at outer edges and where it will not show from right side.

Clip the neckline seam of blouse and collar at the shoulder points to enable the seam to be turned up into the collar, as a band. Hand-hem invisibly to cover the original seam stitching on both the neck and the shoulder seams of facing.

Attaching a collar without the back facing is more intricate and is probably shown in detail in your pattern guide sheet.

ATTACHING COLLAR WITH BIAS FACING Complete the collar (Fig. 21-20) and baste-stitch, or pin-baste, the two neckline seams together; slash curves almost to the staystitching. Slash garment neckline to its staystitching, and pin or baste them together, matching CB, CF, and notches. Trim to ¼ inch to match bias strip. Ease bias around neckline, *b* (as was done in Fig. 21-10). Complete by hand, *g*, or machine, as desired.

This method is used less today, because the process is simpler with a shaped facing. A bias facing is softer and cooler; it is used frequently on children's clothes, lingerie, and blouses. The last hemming, *g*, may be done by machine for durability in laundering.

BIAS ROLLED COLLAR

Straight collars, such as the mandarin and the "smoke-ring" type—a wide bias strip—may be attached as bindings.

The curved neckline should first be slashed almost to the staystitching until it smoothes out into a straight line (Fig. 21-21). For the tie collar, *b*, sew right side of band to right side of garment. If the band folds over, like a convertible collar place right side of band to wrong side of garment. Trim seam to ¼ inch and hem by hand, so that no stitches are visible on the right side of garment.

A STANDING SHIRT COLLAR

A standing shirt collar is made of two parts: the collar proper and the band that supports it, called the "stand" (Fig. 21-21). Matching centers throughout is vital for correct neck size.

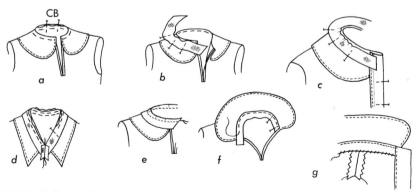

Figure 21-20. Collar applied with bias facing. Basting in *f* may be replaced by understitching, and hand hemming in *g* by machine stitching.

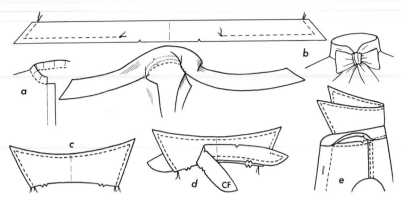

Figure 21-21. *a* and *b*, Collar applied as a band. *c*, *d*, and *e*, Standing shirt collar. Band, CF, is called the "stand."

Stitch upper and under collars together, trim, and turn. Press with seam out at very edge. Stitch ¼ inch from edge, *c*.

Insert the collar between inner and outer band sections, *d*. Stitch on the seamline and trim to ⅜-inch width. Turn right side out and press.

Pin, baste, and stitch the inner stand to the inside of the shirt. Turn the free edge of the outer stand down over the seam and stitch it, *e*, on outside of garment.

This collar is used on many shirt-style garments—for both girls and boys.

SHAWL COLLAR

The shawl collar is cut as part of the blouse front. It is simple to make if you staystitch shoulder and neck seams accurately, pivoting corners.

In addition to the regular staystitching, *reinforce* on the traced seamline, around the *inside corner* where the front shoulder and collar seams meet. *Do not slash* all the way into the corner until after a fitting and shoulder seams have been stitched (Fig. 21-22).

Stitch CB seam of the collar, press open, and trim to ¼ inch; trim off interfacing to 1/16 inch. Prepare facing with CB seam slightly narrower. The upper layer in the finished garment should be slightly larger than the under layer; clean-finish the free edges.

Pin the blouse front and back shoulder seams together, CB, matching the armhole ends of seams and the end of the front slash with the exact point where the back neckline intersects the back shoulder seam.

Slash the inside corner and the curved back neck seam so that it will straighten out, *c*. Match corners and centers to stitch back neckline across the ends of slashes.

Press shoulder seams open and the neck seam up. Apply facing as usual.

This entire process can be done successfully without basting, by care in staystitching, slashing, and pinning seamline on seamline at all points. Basting can be a liability, as extra handling may cause greater raveling of the narrow seam

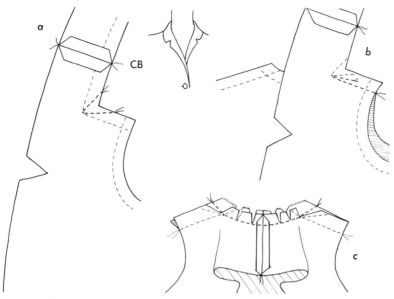

Figure 21-22. Attaching shawl collar (cut in one with lapel).

allowances at the corners. A faced reinforcement here would be an advantage on some fabrics (see p. 392).

TAILORED COLLAR FOR HEAVY FABRIC

For a tailored collar in a heavy, bulky fabric, as wide-wale corduroy, it is wise to use two separate neckline seams; by this method, no more than two layers of fabric are joined in a seam.

With the right sides facing, pin the neckline of the *undercollar* to match the neckline of the garment at CF and CB, notches, and corners of the lapel or the ends of the collar. Slash all curves to the staystitching until the necklines match and are straight for stitching. Baste or stitch the neckline as a plain seam (Fig. 21-23, *a*). If the location of the neckline was approved at the first fitting, stitch it, stopping at CF line or seam position at collar ends. *Do not stitch across seam allowances at the ends of the collar.* Tie threads.

With right sides facing, pin the neckline of the *upper collar* to the neckline seams of facings—matching notches, shoulder seam positions, and the seam positions at the ends of the upper collar. As in stitching the undercollar to the neckline, *do not stitch across seam allowances at the ends of the upper collar.* Remember to stitch the neckline seam less deep, if necessary, to preserve the easy roll of the upper collar. This line will be continuous if there is a back facing. (Be sure the shoulder seams of the neck facing have been pressed open and trimmed to $\frac{1}{4}$ inch to remove bulk.) If no back facing was provided, you will stitch on the

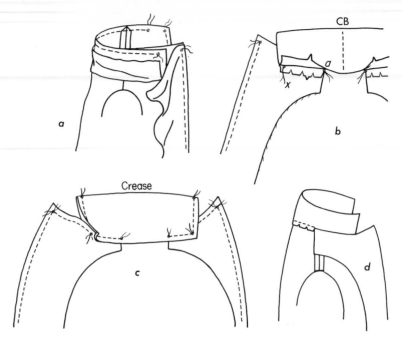

Figure 21-23. The notched collar for a tailored coat. Seam at outer edge of collar, if one, has been stitched and finished, leaving ends open. In *a*, undercollar stitched to neckline, ending at seamlines at front edges of collar; front facings attached at CF. *b*, Uppercollar stitched to facings. *c*, Ends of collar and upper edges for lapels closed to seamlines. Because no seam allowances have been stitched down, there is no drawing, resulting in a smooth notch after seams are pressed open and trimmed. In *d*, back neckline basted loosely.

neckline seam of each front facing from shoulder seam to seam at end of collar, *a* to *x*. Tie thread ends.

CLOSE ENDS OF COLLAR   The last step is to close the ends of the collar and the ends of the neckline seam to form the notches where collar joins lapel. For a well-formed notch with seams hidden under edges of the garment, pay close attention to the following details.

As in joining collar sections, slip the edge back on the section that is to show on the right side of the finished garment. (This provides enough length on the top side to permit it to roll over the edge and thus hide the seam.)

Be sure to start your stitching exactly on the wrong-side-out crease that you have already pressed along the edges of front facings and the collar. (This technique permanently places the seam under the garment edge at the corner.) Make one or two stitches diagonally across the corner and continue stitching along the seamline at the end of the collar. (This will give a better-shaped, less bulky corner.)

Stitch to the tied threads at the end of the line of stitching at the neckline, lifting seam allowances so they will not be caught in stitching, *c*. Skill in this technique results in a clean-cut notch that needs no slashing to make it set properly, because you did not stitch over any seam allowances.

FINISH NECKLINE SEAMS   Clip the neck curve of the garment seam and press it open. Use the point presser to open the seam at the point of the collar, or press it on a wooden dowel. Trim the seams to $\frac{1}{4}$ inch (leave them a little wider on heavy, raveling coat fabrics). Turn the collar and facing right side out. Work out the corners of the collar and lapels neatly with a blunt-pointed stick. With the underside of the collar up, roll the enclosed seam and press the edges of the notched lapel so the seam is back from the edge.

Using heavy-duty, silk, nylon, or Dacron thread, baste the neckline seams together, with the upper collar seam lying on the undercollar seam (both seams pressed open), *d*.

YOKES AND INSETS

A *yoke* may be attached to the adjoining section by either a plain seam or a lapped seam. Lapped seams appear a little more tailored and are easier to make if the yoke has curves, corners, or points. The other section should first have darts or pleats stitched and pressed. If one desires to stitch a half inch or so back from the edge of the yoke to give a tucked effect, the overlap must first be faced and underlap extended to match.

The stitching that shows on a lapped seam can be made so close to the edge that it is practically invisible if fine stitches and fine matching thread are used; hence, it is no longer regarded as a seam confined to tailored dresses, but is used on sheers and soft dresses as well.

The *seam around a square corner* can be a plain seam throughout, or a plain seam in the lengthwise direction and a lapped seam in the horizontal direction to make a semiyoke effect (Fig. 21-24, *a*). In skirts and epaulet sleeves, it is easy if you do not try to do it in one continuous stitching, but stitch the two sides separately.

Considering *b*, formulate answers to these questions:

1. What is the reason for staystitching around the corner of the front section?
2. How close to the corner should the slash extend?
3. Why does the front section appear straight across the corner, after being placed in position on the side section?
4. What is *the one* condition that must be met to achieve perfect results in stitching a plain seam around a corner?

To make a continuous plain seam, *b*, first staystitch around the inside corners for reinforcement, then slash almost to the stitched corner, until the seam straightens out to fit the adjoining section. Basting is *not* helpful; it may cause raveling. Match beginnings and notches; pin and stitch to the exact corner where you pivot and proceed. The slashed section must be on top so you can be sure to keep the seamline of the slashed section exactly on the seamline of the other

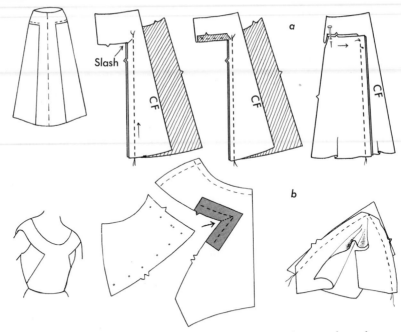

Figure 21-24. Yoke with panel adjoining skirt gore; *a*, yoke seam lapped, gore seam plain, *b*, supporting fabric staystitched around inside corner before slashing, for a continuous plain seam.

as you stitch around the corner. This technique presupposes perfection in cutting and in matching raw edges and the pivotal corner. If there is no danger of their showing, traced markings on seamlines are advisable here because this is the test: Can you stitch seamline to seamline throughout the length of this line? If so, it will fit perfectly.

After you have had experience with this type of problem and are sure you will not need to rip, you can strengthen this corner by shortening the stitches. Or, after stitching the seam exactly where you want it, retrace the line—about one inch from the corner in each direction—with very short stitches.

Another means of reinforcing is to face the corner with a matching-color, firm, lightweight fabric, such as organdy, crepe, Undercurrent, Poly-SiBonne, or a featherweight press-on fabric.

Generalizations

Directions: Read each generalization across both columns, and note the relationships as pointed out in the headings.

EFFECT SOUGHT OR REASON WHY	THE CAUSE OR WHAT TO DO
1. To understitch a facing that has a corner,	first stitch the longer side only and understitch it before seaming the shorter side.

2. To avoid wrinkles on the outside of a garment finished with an inside facing,

be sure that facing matches shape and grain of garment and that the upper or outer surface is slightly larger.

3. To keep seams at inside corners and curves (concave) smooth and as planned in shape and size,

because the inside lines of concentric circles or similar shapes are smaller than the outside, slash them before turning under or back.

4. To be safe,

it is wise not to slash until after staystitching and fitting, if possible.

5. To make outward turning corners and curves (convex) in seams lie flat without bulk or pleats when pressed to one side,

trim seams, then remove wedges and clip off corners.

6. To obtain a smooth, unpuckered bias binding,

ease strip around convex curves—slightly stretch it on concave curves.

7. To obtain a smooth, unpuckered bias facing,

stretch strip around convex curves—ease it around concave curves.

8. To join an inside corner or curve to another piece in a plain seam, to preserve the true shape and prevent puckers,

slash to the staystitching at intervals until the two edges fit or form a straight line for stitching.

Sleeves

Standards for a Set-in Sleeve

The standards for a well-fitted set-in sleeve are listed on pp. 226–27.

Setting a Plain Sleeve

Use a pattern of the correct size. Do not try to use the sleeve pattern of one company in the armhole of a pattern of another company, or a size 14 sleeve pattern in a size 12 blouse. Check the pattern to see that two inches or more of ease in width are provided at the base of the sleeve cap, depending on current fashion.

Such firmly woven materials as taffeta, chintz, polished cotton, and broadcloth are almost impossible to ease smoothly into a standard armhole. They should be

395

reserved for puffed, kimono, raglan, shirt, or sleeveless styles. Woolens, linens, and spongy fabrics are ideal for easing and shrinking.

Cut both sleeves with the grainlines of the pattern exactly on the grainlines of the fabric. Have notches and the highest point of the sleeve cap marked. Have the sleeve cap ease-stitched (Fig. 22-1). All seams—lengthwise and crosswise—that enter the circumference armholes should already have been finished and pressed.

PREPARING THE SLEEVE

Measure the length of the upper sleeve cap from notch to notch. To measure accurately on a curve, stand a stiff tape measure or flexible ruler on edge to follow the seamline.

Fasten ease-threads in the sleeve cap at one end.

Draw up ease to make upper sleeve cap $\frac{1}{4}$ inch longer than the measured upper armhole. Fasten threads (Fig. 22-2, *a*).

Distribute ease to give an even appearance. Very little ease is needed across the top, but more is needed where the sleeve is bias. An even distribution of this ease, so that no bubbles appear on the sleeve side along the ease line, will insure a smoothly set sleeve with a minimum of effort. Hang the sleeve cap (top section) over the tips of your fingers as you judge the distribution of ease. If any bubbles are present, they will be preserved if basted, *b*. Continue shifting the ease until it appears even, as *c*, before proceeding to the next step. In this technique, you can see why a short machine stitch with a loose tension can serve you better than a lengthened machine stitch. The short ease-stitch breaks the fullness into very tiny bits, whereas long stitches result in small tucks, which are more difficult to ease in smoothly.

With the sleeve cap wrong side up over the end of the pressboard or rounded cushion, shrink the fullness from the seam allowance, *d*. Do not let the iron touch the sleeve beyond the seam allowance. Rotate the side of the tip of the iron a little at a time until most of the ease disappears. If you have pressed a pleat in, dampen and remove it.

BASTING SLEEVES IN ARMHOLES

With the sleeve and garment right side out, hold a sleeve next to the bodice to be sure that notches will match. Hold the two edges together at the underarm seams, and turn the bodice wrong side out, still holding the underarm edges together. Do not turn the sleeve wrong side out. Holding the sleeve side of the seam facing you, pin a plain seam, matching notches, and the shoulder and under-arm seams of the sleeve to the bodice (Fig. 22-2, *e*). Remember to place pins at right angles to the seam, taking a very small stitch at the seamline, with heads toward the edge. You may need to place one or two additional pins in each quarter. Experts avoid using more than ten pins altogether.

With the sleeve toward you, baste by hand or by machine, depending on the fabric. Basting stitches should be placed very close to the ease-stitching on the seam allowance side.

Warning! Do not stitch sleeves in until after the second fitting.

Figure 22-1. One ease line—placed on sleeve cap seamline between notches—will give adequate control of ease if you use regular length stitches with loose tension to divide the fullness into very small bits.

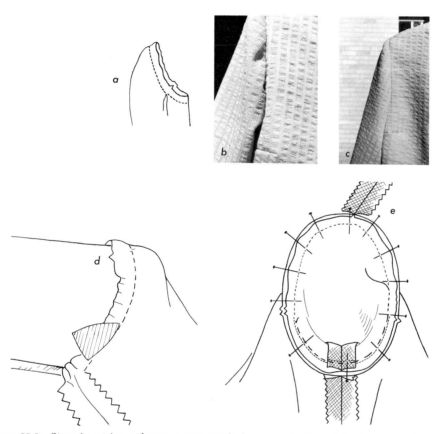

Figure 22-2. Steps in setting a sleeve: *a*, ease stitch drawn up to fit armhole, in preparation for second fitting; *b* and *c*, distribute ease evenly; *d*, shrink ease from seam allowance; *e*, hand baste or machine baste for second fitting—on sleeve side.

STITCHING ARMHOLES

When the circumference fitting (regular second fitting) results in both sleeves hanging free of wrinkles with grainlines straight, machine-stitch as close to the basting line as possible but not on it. At the second fitting, decide on which side of the basting to stitch.

You basted the sleeve with the full side toward you, because it was easier to control the fullness. Now, if you stitch with the garment side up, you can stitch

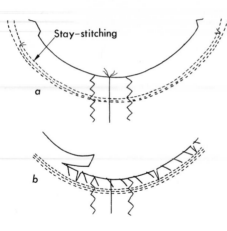

Stay-stitching

a

b

Figure 22-3. *a*, In stitching armhole seam, retrace the lower section, notch to notch, for durability—$\frac{1}{16}$ to $\frac{1}{8}$ inch from stitching, on seam allowance side; *b*, trim to $\frac{3}{8}$ inch for a more roomy, comfortable armhole (may slash or trim to $\frac{1}{4}$ inch in lower part for additional roominess in firm fabrics); overcast if fabric ravels.

a truer curve. A second line of stitching is desirable in the lower half of the armhole for reinforcement. A convenient plan is to start at a notch and stitch around the lower half, along the upper half, and through the lower half a second time. Place this stitching $\frac{1}{16}$ to $\frac{1}{8}$ inch inside the first stitching, on the seam allowance side (Fig. 22-3, *a*).

FINISHING THE ARMHOLES

Correct your stitching for possible irregularities or little pleats of the eased-in fullness caught in the seam. Remove bastings. Trim the seam to $\frac{3}{8}$-inch width for a roomier, more comfortable armhole. The raw edges may be left unfinished if the fabric will not ravel, or they may be overcasted or zigzagged. Binding and French seams are now out-of-date because they interfere with a smooth set or press.

Press the seam in the direction suggested in your pattern. Currently a standard plain sleeve is usually pressed with the seam toward the sleeve, where it adds to the padded effect. If the seam is pressed toward the garment, as it is in gathered caps to give a real set-in appearance, the upper half of the armhole, but not the sleeve cap seam, will need clipping where it curves. For this reason the second row of machine stitching is a safety device. (For details of pressing, see p. 301.)

Fashions are sometimes given firmness and smooth shape by a thin shoulder pad. If your shoulders are sloping, you can preserve the season's fashion-right look by using a pad to hold the garment in position. If used, pads are placed in position

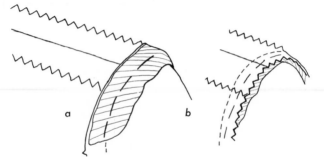

a   *b*

Figure 22-4. *a*, Bias fold basted into sleeve cap adds a soft roll for smart smoothness; *b*, seam and roll pressed very lightly into sleeve cap. Lingerie straps add to comfort and proper set on shoulders.

under the garment and pins are placed on the right side of the garment. After fitting, baste the pad to the shoulder seam loosely. Tack the pad also at the point where it meets the armhole seam. Do not let these stitches show on the outside of the garment; keep them loose, but have the ends secure.

To soften and smooth the top of the cap, cut a bias strip of self-material or outing flannel about 1½ to 2 inches wide and 7 inches long (Fig. 22-4). Fold it lengthwise or use it singly. Baste it smoothly, with its raw edge or edges matching the raw edges of the sleeve cap; let it taper off about one inch above the notches; then press all the layers lightly down toward the sleeve. Because this is a matter of fashion, study your pattern instruction sheet or observe good ready-to-wear. This tailoring detail is often the difference between a less expensive and a more expensive garment.

The addition of this bias strip fills in the slight space between the armhole seam and the sleeve. The amount or lack of ease in the cap will determine whether this strip should be used.

Finally, on the blouse, make lingerie guards (Fig. 27-11, *b*) on both shoulder seams, or pads to keep your bra and slip straps from sliding off the shoulders, to anchor the shoulder seam at the right place.

KIMONO SLEEVES   The kimono or unmounted sleeve cut in one with the blouse should be fitted more loosely than a plain set-in sleeve. The longer the kimono sleeve, the looser it should be. The underarm concave curve must be clipped to prevent puckering when it is turned and pressed. The seam can be reinforced by using blanket or buttonhole stitches around the slashes. A double row of machine stitching also helps. A seam tape stitched along this curve is a satisfactory reinforcement (Fig. 22-5).

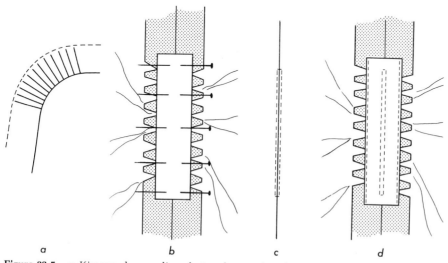

a   *b*   *c*   *d*

Figure 22-5.   *a*, Kimono sleeves clipped at underarm; *b* and *c*, reinforced with seam binding or bias strip and topstitched; *d*, edges of tape stitched to seam allowances.

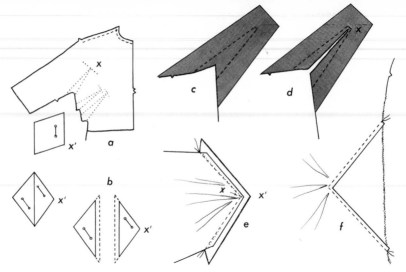

Figure 22-6. Gusset for kimono-type sleeve.

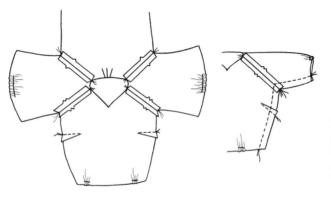

Figure 22-7. Simplified method of making raglan-sleeve styles for short sleeves or a child's coat.

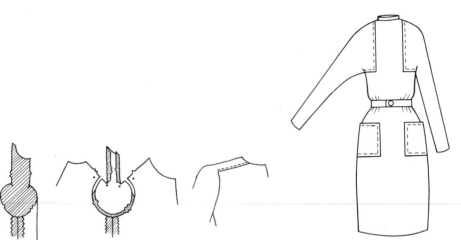

Figure 22-8. One method of constructing epaulet-sleeve styles.

Figure 22-9. Dolman sleeve.

Gussets prevent underarms of kimono-style sleeves from drawing and tearing out. Trace the line and the termination point as for any dart (Fig. 22-6, *a*). An easy way to put in a gusset is shown. Note that the gusset pattern, a diamond shape, was cut into two triangles. Be sure to add a seam allowance where you cut it. This technique gives greater bulk than the diamond-shaped gusset. Note that underarm seams of the gusset are bias and the corners that reinforce the blouse are on the grain.

You may prefer to follow your pattern instruction sheet and use the regular gusset. Any method requires careful staystitching, slashing, and matching seamline to seamline around the corners.

RAGLAN SLEEVES Raglan sleeves can be set in as regular set-in sleeves, or the slanting seams can be joined to the body of the blouse before making the underarm seam (Fig. 22-7), in which case the sleeve and body seams are made as one continuous seam similar to the underarm curve of a kimono blouse. It will need clipping on curves to relieve puckers and, possibly, retracing for durability. In bulky fabrics, it sets much better under the arm, where the regular set-in sleeve method is used.

EPAULET SLEEVES Follow your guide sheet for details for making epaulet sleeves. The following procedure is simple:

Stitch the sleeve seam and the underarm blouse seam and finish them separately. Stitch the circumference as a plain seam *before* the lapped shoulder seam. Then prepare the strap part of the epaulet as a lapped seam after first clipping exactly at the corners (Fig. 22-8). Compare with Figure 21-24.

DOLMAN SLEEVES Dolman sleeves are a variation of kimono sleeves. They can be set in by the methods suggested for set-in, epaulet, or raglan sleeves (Fig. 22-9). This lapped seam is simpler to construct than a plain seam, because of the corner.

SHIRT SLEEVES Shirt sleeves are short in the cap and therefore easier to set than the standard sleeve. This design lends itself particularly well to drip-dry fabrics that do not ease readily, to casual styles, and to our desire to speed up processes. They are usually joined to the armholes before making the underarm seam (Fig. 22-10). Use the seam of your choice. Then stitch the sleeve and blouse underarm seams continuously. Follow your guide sheet, observe ready-to-wear, or consult Figure 19-6 for the stitched fell.

SHORT SLEEVES A short sleeve is not just a long sleeve cut off and hemmed. If the long sleeve is extra wide or cut straight down (Fig. 22-11, *a*), it can be adjusted by folding it up at the lower edge. But if the sleeve seam slopes toward the bottom, it cannot be hemmed without puckering, *b*. To secure the correct allowance for the hem, fold the sleeve pattern up first, *a*, and then cut the slanting sides so it will open out, *c*, to make a smooth hem.

Sleeves with shaped lower edges, *d*, need to be faced.

The hem of a sleeve should be made after the lengthwise seam is finished and usually after the sleeve is set in the armhole. Then the hang and set of its lower

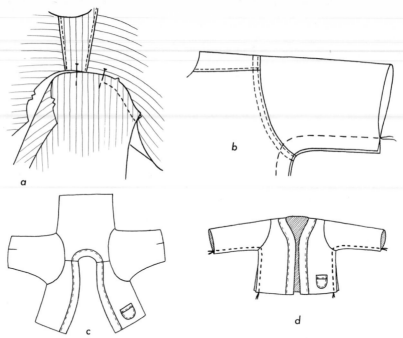

Figure 22-10. Shirt sleeves are set in before making underarm seams.

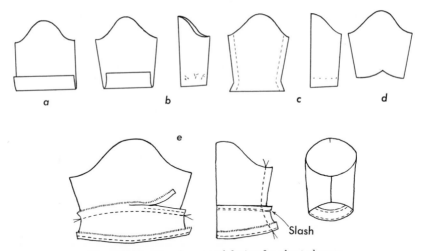

Figure 22-11. Plan hems and facing for short sleeves.

edge can be determined and adjusted, if necessary. It is made like any other hem, but since it is a circumference line, you will need to be careful to match seams and grainline when folding it up. Turn it right side out when machine-stitching so that it will lie smoothly under the presser foot as you work inside the tube. Very short sleeves, especially circular cuts, are more professional in appearance if lined throughout.

A shaped facing for the lower edge of the sleeve traditionally has its lengthwise seam stitched and pressed before it is applied. If you are sure of the fit at the lower

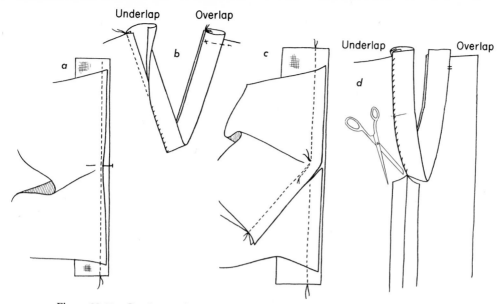

Figure 22-12. Continuous-bound plackets: *a* and *b* in a slash: *c* and *d* in a seam.

edge, it is easier in modern dressmaking to complete the crosswise stitchings—trim the seam and understitch—before closing the basic (sleeve) lengthwise seam, *e*. After closing the lengthwise seam, turn and edge-stitch the facing for a flatter finish across the lengthwise seam. The main precaution in this short cut is to match circumferences precisely. A smoother job that sets better results if the under-stitching and clean-finishing are done in a circle, after the lengthwise seam is finished. In tacking the clean-finished edge, make stitches tiny, far apart, and loose. On a sleeveless blouse this tacking may be needed only at seams. See Hems (Chap. 26) for further details.

Plackets Suitable for Sleeves

Continuous-Bound Placket

The continuous-bound placket is used in slashes and in seams concealed in gathers or under a pleat. It is standard on bishop and peasant styles of sleeves.

To make a *placket in a slash,* cut a strip lengthwise, not bias, about one inch longer than twice the length of the opening and $1\frac{1}{4}$ to $1\frac{1}{2}$ inches wide. Crease $\frac{1}{4}$-inch seams and a center fold to form a guide in stitching and finishing.

Open out and pin the center crosswise crease to the end of the slash, right sides together (Fig. 22-12, *a*). Slip the end of the slash back $\frac{1}{4}$ inch from the edge of the strip. One pin at the end of the slash is really enough. At the machine, work with the strip next to the feed and the garment up. Stitch to make a $\frac{1}{4}$-inch seam on the strip, which requires you to stitch to a point at the end of the slash. Stop there with your needle down. Raise the presser foot and fold the garment back out of your way to pivot and to avoid catching a pleat or pucker. Lower the presser foot and stitch on to the end.

Turn the strip over on itself as a binding and hem it by hand along the machine-stitching—not to the garment. Press the band back on the overlap section

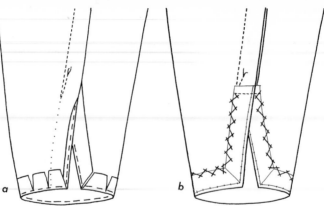

Figure 22-13. Taped wrist finish with placket.

and pin or tack it at the seam, *b,* until ready to use. Let the band extend from the other side to form the underlap.

To make the continuous-bound *placket in a seam,* pin the strip with right sides and seamlines matching the seams of the opening. Start stitching at the top and end at the bottom of the opening on one side so that the stitching meets the stitching of the seam below. Stitch with the strip underneath and the garment on top; retrace your ending.

For the other side of the opening, begin at the top and stitch down again to the bottom to meet exactly the stitching of the seam below; then retrace it. Thus, three seams meet at the same point—the end of the placket opening, *c.*

To complete the binding, clip the garment seam at this pivotal point, *d.* (To do so weakens the seam and destroys all possibility of future alterations, and that is why this style of placket is not so frequently used.) Finish the binding by hand hemming.

It is possible to finish the preceding two plackets on the machine, if you first apply the strip to the wrong side of the garment, so that the stitching, made from the right side, will be more nearly perfect.

Taped Wrist Finish

The taped wrist finish or placket is used chiefly on long fitted sleeves of silk or wool (Fig. 22-13).

To begin, staystitch the lower sleeve edge and the seamline of the front opening. Fold the seam back to the wrong side; miter the square corner; slash the seam wherever it is curved to make it lie smooth and flat, *a.* Allow the back to extend as an underlap, folding under, not on the marked seamline, but $\frac{1}{4}$ to $\frac{3}{8}$ inch in front of it nearer the raw edge.

Pin and baste the seam tape about $\frac{1}{8}$ inch back from the edge of the basted foldlines, *b.* Ease the tape on concave curves and miter it at corners. Leave $\frac{1}{2}$ inch extra at each end of the opening for a crosswise seam in the tape. Hem the outer edge of the tape to the sleeve by hand with vertical-hemming stitches, so they will not catch through and show on the outside of the sleeve.

Tack the inner edge of the tape to the sleeve and across the ends of the tape to fasten overlap to underlap. Press well and finish with two or three small fasteners or loops close to the edge. If the lengthwise seam of the sleeve is pressed to the front instead of open, this placket will not need any clipping.

Standard Shirt-Sleeve Placket

Make a shirt-sleeve placket before the sleeve seam so that work can be kept flat. The slash for the opening is usually one inch in back of the center of the sleeve on the grain (Fig. 22-14, *a*).

To fit a slash 6 inches long, cut a straight strip 13 inches long and $2\frac{1}{2}$ inches wide for the continuous binding, *b*. Place the right side of the strip to the wrong side of the sleeve and stitch in a $\frac{1}{8}$-inch seam from the bottom to the top of the slit—first on the front and then on the back of the opening. Sew a small dart ($\frac{1}{2}$ inch long and $\frac{1}{8}$ inch wide, tapering to nothing) on the sleeve at the end of the placket slash.

Work with the sleeve right side up, *b*. Fold the front part of the sleeve back on itself out of the way, *c*. Fold the strip over on the under or back opening of sleeve as an outside facing. But the strip is too wide for such a facing, so slash it from bottom of opening to end of opening to make it $\frac{7}{8}$ inch wide. Slit it across at the top $\frac{1}{8}$ inch, so that the facing can be turned under $\frac{1}{8}$ inch, leaving a facing $\frac{3}{4}$ inch wide. Baste and stitch this facing down on the right side of the sleeve—to become the underlap, *d*.

Drop the sleeve front down in place and pull the facing, attached to the front of the opening, out on the right side, *e*. Crease a turn-under of $\frac{1}{8}$ to $\frac{1}{4}$ inch on free edge of the strip and bring it over to the seam. Pin and baste it in place as a binding to cover first stitching, *f*. Leaving $1\frac{1}{4}$ inches above the end of the opening, cut away the rest of the strip at point x. From this $1\frac{1}{4}$ inches, cut the pointed end of the overlap, leaving a seam to be turned under. Baste the point down in position, *g*.

To stitch the overlap, turn back the under part of the sleeve, B, out of the way, *h*; stitch up one side, straight across just at the fold of the strip, and down the other side. To stitch the point, *i*, pull the under part, B, down again in position. Stitch across $\frac{1}{8}$ inch above the other crosswise line and around the point at the lower edge. Trim any excess placket endings off even with the sleeve before attaching the cuff.

Cuffs and Cuff Bands

Cuffs for sleeves are made and attached in much the same manner as collars, attached in this case with a bias facing (Fig. 22-15).

Examination of the sketches in Figure 22-16 reveals that cuff bands are, technically, bindings. The same techniques are used for attaching them as those described for attaching collars (Fig. 21-21, *a* and *b*).

A cuff band, open at the ends, *e* and *f*, is necessary where there is a placket opening. Fit the band first to your wrist, allowing for seams, overlap, and fasteners. Close each end of the band by stitching a plain seam and tying knots at both ends because of the considerable strain in construction. Trim to $\frac{1}{4}$ inch and snip off

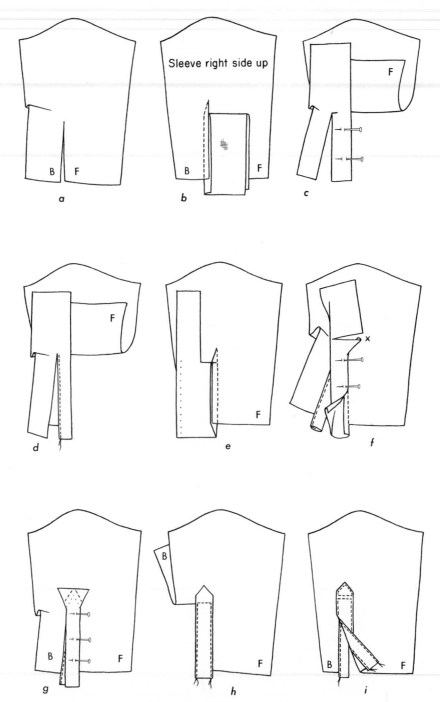

Figure 22-14. Shirt-sleeve placket.

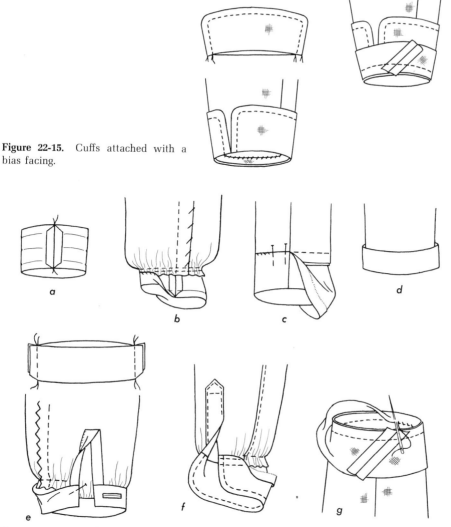

Figure 22-15. Cuffs attached with a bias facing.

Figure 22-16. *a* to *d*, Steps in applying band, closed style. *e* and *f*, Applying open band. *g*, Applying binding.

a corner of the ends. Turn and press the middle crease and the seamlines of the raw edges. Pin the right side of one raw edge to the right side of the sleeve, seamline on seamline. Pin the ends of the bands exactly flush with the placket overlap and underlap. Arrange pleats or gathers to suit the style. Pin and stitch exactly on the seamline, with gathers up. Begin and end beyond the end of the band over on the seam of the underlayer of the band (Fig. 23-2) or retrace or tie endings. Remove

Figure 22-17. Removing fullness from sleeve cap.

basting, trim to $\frac{1}{4}$ inch, and pin the seam of the underband up to the machine stitching on the wrong side and hem by hand—invisible on the right side, *b*. The sleeve, *g*, is finished with a narrow bias binding.

408

REMOVING FULLNESS FROM THE SLEEVE CAP   Should you wish to use a fabric that does not ease-in well, you might consider changing the set-in sleeve design. The basic problem, in this case, is to find ways of disposing of most of the extra length in the upper sleeve cap, which ordinarily has one to two inches. In Figure 22-17 examples are shown of sleeves that have had this excess fullness removed.

Sleeve *a* has a dart in the sleeve cap, approximately two inches in length, located to match the shoulder seam. Where the amount of fullness is excessive for a short dart, the designer can place a seam extending from the point of this dart throughout the length of the sleeve.

Another means of removing this fullness is shown in the cape sleeve in *b*. Rather than remove all of the excess, as in *a*, this design was made by pinning smaller darts at several carefully balanced positions in the upper sleeve-cap pattern. To make such a pattern flatten, it is necessary to slash from the lower edge of the sleeve to the points of these pinned-in darts. The spreads produce the extra width in *b*, resulting in a shorter, straighter line in the sleeve cap.

Sleeves *c* and *d* can be designed in a similar manner. Because they are shorter, they naturally are not as wide at their lower edges as *b*. Also, only part of the ease may have been removed in these cases. It is important to leave a minimum of ¼ to ½ inch to avoid a strained appearance in the cap.

23 Waistlines

A circumference seam around the body, located at the normal waistline, or fairly near (Empire and long waist), is being referred to as a waistline seam.

Any waistline finish should be smooth and flat.

Before basting the waistline seam, all lengthwise seams and details that enter this circumference must be completely finished and pressed.

The pinned waistline is tentatively approved at the first fitting; the basted waistline is carefully adjusted at the second fitting. It should be determined in relation to the band or belt to be worn with it and placed where it looks best on the body, consistent with present fashion.

Staystitching on curved seamlines, such as the waistline seams of a gored skirt, will prevent stretching in fitting and finishing. Usually the top of a plain skirt and the bottom of a close-fitting bodice are eased slightly at the waistline seam to

411

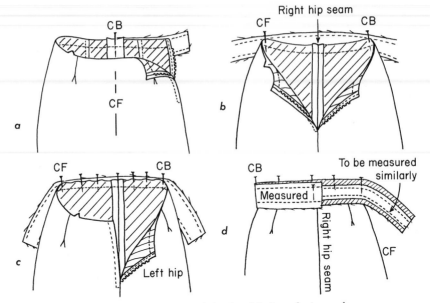

Figure 23-1. Steps in applying band before closing ends.

provide a soft, *unstretched* appearance just above and below the waistline. One inch (¼ inch on each quarter) extra in the bodice allows for ease over the normal rib cage. The same amount allowed on the skirt provides ease over the normal bulges of hip and abdomen.

Skirt Bands

A skirt is ready for a band when all seams entering the waistline are finished and pressed and the placket is completed.

Cut a skirt band three or four inches longer than the desired finished length. Cut it twice as wide as you want it finished, plus two seam allowances (or reduce one seam allowance to ¼ inch if you prefer an unturned selvage on the back).

Cut or tear a strip of preshrunk muslin, hair canvas, or self-material ¼ inch wider than half of the belt width. Crease the belt lengthwise through the center (if two seam allowances were added). Decide which is the outside of the band. Pin the interfacing to its wrong side. The extra ¼ inch of interfacing extends beyond the crease mark. Turn to the right side and stitch ⅛ inch from the crease on the back side of band, through one layer of fabric and one layer of muslin. Press it again to crease the muslin. The advantage of placing the interfacing next to the front side of the band is the same as for other uses—it cushions the seam, making it less conspicuous.

A press-on type of interfacing is very satisfactory on skirt bands. Remove all of the seam allowance and let the interfacing extend only to the fold at upper edge of band; press it into position on the wrong side of that part of the band that will show in the finished garment, for cushioning the seam.

METHOD I—APPLYING BAND BEFORE CLOSING ENDS

To fit a band on a skirt with a left-side opening, measure the creased and interfaced band along the waistline seam from the side placket to the CB with the band extending two inches beyond the placket (Fig. 23-1). Pin at CB, not at the placket end, *a*. Measure on the band one half of the desired finished waist measure and mark this point with a pin, *b*. Pin this CF point to CF of skirt. Distribute the ease from CF to CB and pin at the right side seam, *c*. Now fold the loose end of the front band over to make the left front of the band match the right front of the band in length, *d*. Mark it with a pin and pin it into position at the placket. Distribute ease between CF and the placket. Next take the loose end of the back and make the left back match the right back.

Check before fitting to be sure the right half will be exactly like the left half.

Baste the waistline seam as pinned.

Stop. Have your second fitting.

After the fitting, stitch the waistline seam (Fig. 23-2). Then finish the ends of the band. Close the ends so there is sufficient underlap—about a two-inch extension. In general, it is better design if the overlap finishes flush with the overlap of placket. Make a point at the end of the overlap if you prefer. (If a piped buttonhole is desired, make it before closing the front end.)

If no stitching is to show on the top, sew the right side of the band to the right side of the skirt in a plain seam (Fig. 23-3) and finish it by hand on the wrong side. Catch the hemming stitches only in the machine stitching or on the seam allowance nearby.

For a tailored effect use machine stitching and no hand hemming. Make a plain seam by stitching the right side of the fabric of the underband to the wrong side of the skirt, *b*. Then pin or baste the top band down to cover the seam stitching. Stitch around all four sides of the band, right side up. Do not begin and end at a corner.

For an easier process and less conspicuous stitching, stitch in the groove, on the skirt, as close to the band as possible.

Figure 23-2. Stitching and grading bulky seams. Inside view of band attached to skirt or sleeve so that end of closed band matches edge of placket. Stitching extends beyond weak point— a technique to save retracing and the weakness from tying a knot on the exact beginning or ending.

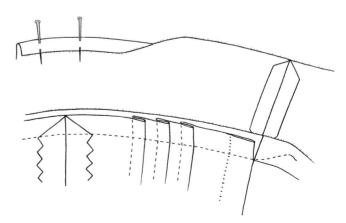

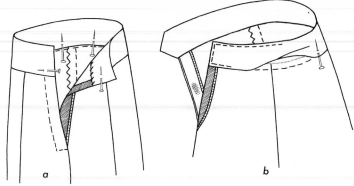

Figure 23-3. Skirt bands: *a*, finished inside by hand; *b*, finished outside with machine stitching.

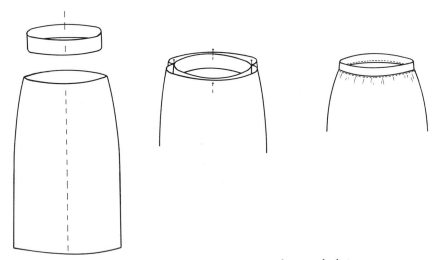

Figure 23-4. Applying band in knits without a placket.

METHOD II—APPLYING BAND AFTER CLOSING ENDS

Close ends of the band (Fig. 23-3) that has been previously fitted by comparison with a satisfactory skirt band you have or with the French-model waistline tape. Plan for the extension to be the underlap; mark CF, CB, and side seam points. (Using this method you begin at the left front instead of at the left back as in Method I.) Close the ends and attach them by matching CF, CB, and the seams. Stitch and finish as described in Method I. (See also Fig. 22-16, *f, g*.)

METHOD III—APPLYING BAND IN KNITS WITHOUT A PLACKET

Knit fabrics are frequently made into skirt designs without plackets. This type of skirt is not recommended for a person whose hips are more than 12 inches larger than the waist.

For a double-knit, the skirt should be 1½ inches larger than the hip measurement. The waistline of the skirt should be 1 to 2 inches larger than the waist measure, depending on the stretch in the fabric. The length of the waistband is cut across the ribs of the fabric for greater elasticity. No interfacing is used. Cut the waistband 2 inches longer than the waist measurement and join its end in a ½-inch seam.

A simple plan is to use elastic in a casing, formed by a hem, or in a band, with a very flexible and elastic line of stitching at the waistline. Elastic one inch in width is recommended. Cut it ½ inch longer than the waist measure, overlap its ends ½ inch, and stitch it securely.

STEPS FOR APPLYING BAND

1. Mark the quarter points of skirt waistline and the band with pins. With skirt wrong side out, place right side of band to right side of skirt and pin the two together at the quarter points (Fig. 23-4). Add additional pins if desired, pinning at the mid-points to distribute the fullness evenly.
2. Stitch the waistline seam, stretching both pieces if you are using a straight stitch. A stretch stitch is desirable, if available.
3. Match quarter marks on the circle of elastic to the quarter marks on the waistline seam; stretch the elastic to fit, and stitch its edge to the seam allowance near the previous line of stitching. Unless you are using a stretch stitch, stretch both elastic and skirt to insure sufficient length to slip over the hips.
4. Pull the waistband over the elastic and pin it in place, inserting the pins on the right side just below the seam line. Stitch very close to the band—in the groove—on the right side. Again, remember to stretch the fabric, to prevent a broken line of stitching when the garment is pulled over the hips.

If you consider an underlining desirable, a simple procedure is to finish it in firm fabric separately from the skirt, with a placket, and narrow facing or tape at its upper edge.

A more complicated technique can be used to attach both underlining and skirt to the band. Make several faced slashes in the underlining at the waistline, to permit stretching of the elastic in the waistband—four to six slashes would be needed; make them 3 to 4 inches long and face them with bias rayon or silk seam binding to give a flat, smooth finish under the skirt. Other techniques would be the same as for the skirt without an underlining.

STRETCHY KNITS   With the stretchier types of fabrics, such as sweater knits, the treatment described works well, except that the elastic may be cut 1 inch shorter than the waist measure. Because of greater stretch, the side seams can be shaped to narrow the waist somewhat. This same narrowing is desirable at the lower edge of the skirt, to prevent flare in the hem.

FINISHING SKIRT WITHOUT A BAND

If directions are not available on your guide sheet for this type of finish, plan to use seam tape, narrow grosgrain ribbon, a strip of fabric along selvage, narrow belting, or a bias facing. Any of these materials can be stitched along the seam line on the right side of the skirt and then folded to the wrong side to cover the seam allowance. Or, the seam allowance may be turned to the wrong side, and

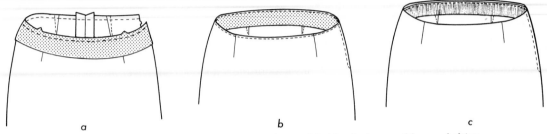

Figure 23-5. Finishing skirt without a band: *a* and *b*, bias facing; *c*, ribbon or belting.

the skirt topstitched to the ribbon or facing strip (Fig. 23-5). For a comfortable garment that sets well, slash the concave curve of the waistline and keep straight strips narrow—perhaps no wider than ½ inch. A bias facing may be wider, if desired. Clean-finish its lower edge and tack it to seams and darts. Make it of firm, smooth cotton or rayon fabric.

As skirts are designed with some extra width, to be eased onto the band to fit the slight body bulge below the waist, it is a good plan to tack narrow elastic under the tape or ribbon at intervals for a smooth set at the waistline. Two- or three-inch lengths would be adequate, with two in the front and two in the back.

Waistline Seam in a Dress

At the first fitting, the pinned waistline was checked, corrected (if necessary), and tentatively approved. The next step is to baste this seam for final approval at the second fitting.

A very simple method to use is the *plain seam,* because it is easy to baste, stitch, and finish. It is more difficult to change during fitting, however.

The *lapped seam* method is more satisfactory where the waistline is of an unusual shape. Careful, accurate fitting is easier with this seam (Fig. 23-6).

The direction in which you plan to turn the seam may influence your choice. You will turn the seam allowance away from the full, bulky part toward the flat, less bulky side; the waistline seam of a plain A-line skirt is turned down or lapped

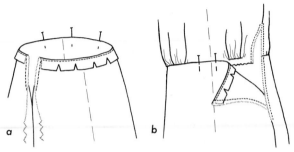

Figure 23-6. *a,* For lapped seam, turn staystitched seam to wrong side, pin and press, or baste; *b,* pin into position for basting to bodice.

416

over the full bodice on the outside (Fig. 23-7, *a*); a plain bodice of unusual shape laps over a skirt with fullness, *b*. When both bodice and skirt are bulky, a plain seam is needed. For instance, if there were no inset band and a plain seam were to be used in *c*, the seam should be pressed toward the bodice, since there are fewer gathers here. The bulging effect of the gathers would not be objectionable in this blouson design. However, a better plan is the inset band, as shown, permitting both bulky seams to be pressed toward the plain band.

Dress *d* can be joined with a plain seam or a lapped seam. In either case, it is necessary to clip the seam so that the center pleated section can turn toward the plain skirt, and the side-gathered sections can turn toward the plain areas of the bodice. In *e*, both seams will turn toward the plain midriff section.

INSET BANDS AND MIDRIFF SECTIONS

The inset band is a device to avoid sewing two bulky parts together in one seam. If the band or belt has underarm seams to match underarm seams in the garment, stitch these seams, and press them open. Do not trim them if you anticipate any alterations. The band can be applied with either a plain or a lapped seam. Remember that the circumference seams are made before the lengthwise closing.

An inset band, as *c*, will need the support of an interfacing fabric and, in addition, will generally be faced with either a self-fabric or an underlining fabric to hold the seam allowances in position and provide a smoother finish.

The wider midriff section, *e*, might be finished in the same manner as the narrower band, but might not require quite as firm support as the narrow band. It does not follow the body extremely closely, and the gathers are not as heavy as in *c*. A facing for section *e* might be optional.

REINFORCING WAISTLINE SEAMS

A waistline stay is essential to reinforce the waistline seam and maintain fit in the garment. A narrow strip of nonstretchable fabric is used for this purpose—ribbon seam binding, or a lengthwise strip of firmly woven, lightweight fabric, including selvage, is satisfactory.

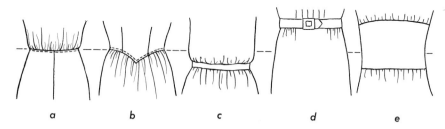

    a   *b*   *c*   *d*   *e*

Figure 23-7. Waistline finishes. Topstitching a lapped seam simplifies fitting. *a*, Lap the plain part over the fuller part. *b*, A lapped seam is necessary around an unusual shape. *c* and *d*, Plain seams are used where there is bulk on both sides, and *e*, where topstitching is not desired.

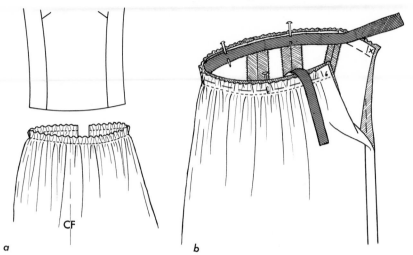

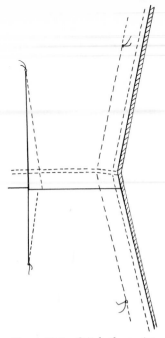

Figure 23-8. After bodice and skirt are basted together in a plain seam and fitted, pin tape to bodice waistline as in Plan a. Marking with pins, the CF, CB, and side-seam locations can be done by method 1 or method 2. (Place pins parallel to seam only if you plan to have a fitting before basting and stitching.)

Figure 23-9. Stitch the waistline seam less deep across the side seam allowances to permit these concave curves to lie smoothly after the zipper is attached.

There are two methods for applying this stay:

1. Apply it after the waistline seam has been basted, where no difficulties in fitting are expected (Fig. 23-8).
2. Apply the stay to the underside of the less full side (skirt or bodice) before basting the two sections together.

MEASURING THE STAY If you have a French-model waistline tape, simply measure off the distances on the stay and mark locations of CF, CB, and the two side-seam locations.

If you do not have a French-model tape, use the same technique as used in applying the skirt band.

STEPS IN MEASURING THE STAY

1. Measure the stay along the waistline seam from side seam to CB, allowing a small surplus ($\frac{1}{4}$ to $\frac{1}{2}$ inch), and pin it at CB.
2. Use one half of waist measure, and measure this distance from CB pin; mark spot with a pin. This is the CF of the stay.
3. Pin CF of stay to CF of garment.
4. Distribute the slight ease in the skirt between CF and CB evenly, pinning first at the mid-points of spaces (halfway between CF and CB then at the midpoints of the quarters, and on).

5. Fold the loose end of the back stay across the right back and mark the side seam location with a pin.
6. Pin the stay at side seam and distribute ease along left-back waistline seam.
7. Fold the tape hanging from the CF back over the right front, pin it at the side seams and distribute the ease along the left front.
8. Baste-stitch along the lower edge of the stay, slightly off the seamline on the seam allowance side.
9. Join the skirt and bodice together for fitting.

Treatments of Waistline Seam

To plan for a smooth fit, and to remove bulk where the waistline seam enters a side placket, consider these conditions:

1. Stitch the waistline seam $\frac{1}{8}$ to $\frac{1}{4}$ inch shallower through the seam allowances (depending on amount of curve) to allow the side seam edge to lie smoothly when it is turned under (Fig. 23-9). This is not a problem when the placket is located at CB, where the placket line is straight.
2. Before making the placket, to remove bulk at the seam, slash through the waistline seam allowance about one inch away from the side seam, on both front and back. Press ends of the waistline seam open (Fig. 24-3).
3. Trim off the ends of the waistline stay exactly at the side seamline; to eliminate bulk, the stay should not be extended across the seam allowance.
4. Stitch the upper edge of the waistline seam to the stay, to add stability and smoothness to the line.
5. In cases where there may be extra strain at the waistline seam, the stay may be left loose for the last one or two inches leading up to the placket on both sides. It can then be finished with a hook and eye to be fastened before closing the placket.

Applying a Stay Without a Waistline Seam

If there is no waistline seam, use seam binding or grosgrain ribbon for a stay that can be tacked to seams and darts.

Corded Seam

Prepare a cord covered as in Figure 27-15, *a*. Baste it in place on the outside of the bodice, raw edges matched, with the measured seam tape arranged on the wrong side of the bodice. Do not have the stitching of the prepared cord (or piping) close against the cord. Baste-stitch, also, back from the cord.

Baste the skirt in place, so that you can stitch on a line of gathers, this time against the cord so that previous stitchings will not show on the outside of the seam. Careful joining at the ends of the cord is required to avoid bumpy places.

24

Plackets and Buttonholes

When snug or semifitting styles are in fashion, plackets become necessary. These closings belong with the structural design, being kept relatively inconspicuous, as demonstrated especially by the invisible zipper.

The most common locations for plackets include the center back, center front, left-side seam, and wrist in a full-length, fitted sleeve.

A variety of materials and techniques are employed in constructing well-made closings. One's choice will depend on the type and design of the garment, the location of the placket, and the fabric.

421

Zipper Plackets

The wide use of zippers has greatly simplified placket construction (Fig. 24-1). Information relative to zipper types and their suitability for specific uses is included in Table 24-1.

METHODS FOR INSERTING ZIPPERS

There are three ways to insert zippers:

1. *Invisible application:* a centered application, appearing as a plain seam (Fig. 24-2; *a*).
2. *Lapped application:* one edge of the opening forms a lap that completely conceals the zipper. It has one line of stitching and is suitable for any garment, *b*.
3. *Centered or slot-seam application:* the two edges of the opening meet over the center of the zipper, *c*. It shows two lines of stitching; it is suitable for any garment, especially heavy fabrics because of the narrow overlaps. There is a tendency for the garment fabric to catch in the zipper teeth, and this is less evident with heavy fabric. It may not be as desirable as other types for a center closing because the zipper is not completely hidden. It is used for short applications especially, such as neck and sleeve plackets.

STANDARDS FOR ZIPPER PLACKETS

1. The zipper slides easily—the fabric is attached far enough from the teeth or coils to permit the free movement of the slide and yet hide most of the tape.
2. The placket is open to the end of the teeth.

Figure 24-1. Types of zippers: *a*, uncovered; *b*, covered; *c*, invisible.

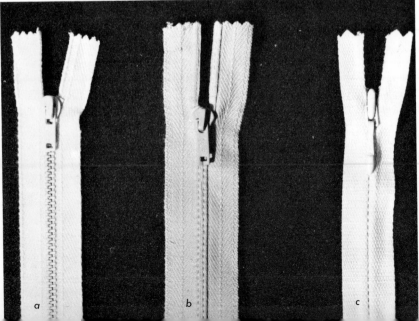

Table 24-1
THE SUITABILITY OF ZIPPER TYPES

TYPES OF ZIPPERS	USES	
Open at one end.	Necklines; skirt and pants plackets; center back or center front in blouses, tunics and dresses; side seam in sleeveless garments; short closings, as wrist or shoulder seam.	
Closed at both ends.	Dress side placket.	
Open or separating at both ends.	Overblouses, jackets, smocks, and coat dresses.	

OTHER CLASSIFICATIONS	CHARACTERISTICS	USES
Invisible	Appears as a seam —no stitching shows on the right side; requires a special presser foot.	Skirts, blouses, dresses, pants, and housecoats.
Regular	Attached to garment by lapped or centered slot application.	All types of garments and fabrics.
Metal teeth	Available in different weights.	A wide variety of uses: especially important for medium- and heavy-weight fabrics such as wool, vinyl, and fake fur.
Synthetic coils Nylon	Nylon coils can be damaged by heat— a press cloth is needed for protection; some can be purchased completely covered for protection and to hide the teeth.	For light- and medium-weight fabrics; especially in synthetic yarns.
Polyester	Polyester coils are heat resistant up to the temperature suitable for pressing cotton—above that, a press cloth is needed.	

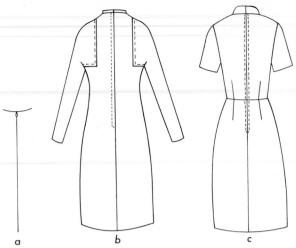

Figure 24-2. Application of zippers: *a,* invisible; *b,* lapped;
c, centered or slot seam.

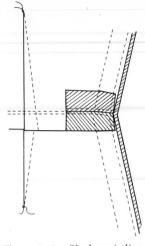

Figure 24-3. Slash waistline
seam about one inch from
side seam and press open to
reduce bulk.

3. Stitching lines across the closed ends of zippers are placed $\frac{1}{8}$ to $\frac{1}{4}$ inch from the zipper teeth.
4. The finished placket is flat and smooth, without puckers.
5. The wrong-side finish is free of any loose threads that might be caught in the zipper teeth.
6. If constructed by the lapped method, the zipper is hidden, about $\frac{1}{8}$ inch back of the edge of the overlap.

PREPARATION OF A GARMENT FOR ZIPPER APPLICATION

1. Have all the seams entering the placket line, finished and pressed. Check the width of the waistline seam allowance to be sure it was made narrower, to permit the placket to fit smoothly in the concave curve of a closely fitted garment. (See Fig. 23-9.) Slash the waistline seam about one inch from the underarm seam, back and front, and press it open to remove any bulk (Fig. 24-3).
2. Preshrink the zipper tape—if it is to be used in a washable garment—by soaking it in hot water for at least 10 minutes. Air dry and press the tape lightly.
3. It is easier to make a placket if the garment seam is $\frac{5}{8}$ to $\frac{3}{4}$ inch in width. If it is narrower than $\frac{5}{8}$ inch, extend the width with woven seam binding stitched flat, $\frac{1}{4}$ inch from the edge of the seam. A bias strip will be needed for a curved line, as for a princess style.
4. Check the length of the opening, which should be about $\frac{1}{2}$ inch longer than the length of the teeth or coils of the zipper. A slightly additional amount might be needed, depending on the fastener desired at the end of the placket, such as a hook or snap. The length of a zipper, as indicated on the wrapper, does not include the zipper tape.

5. Should the planned placket extend into a gathered skirt where there is no seam, it will be more satisfactory to apply the zipper to the bodice only and make a continuous bound placket in the slashed skirt. See p. 403.

INVISIBLE ZIPPER

The invisible zipper is applied in an open seam, before the seam is closed below it (Fig. 24-4).

1. Open the zipper. Steam press the back of zipper tape to flatten the coils. (Check the directions for your brand of zipper as to ironing temperature and use of a press cloth.)

2. Place opened zipper face down on right side of fabric with coils even with seamline and zipper tape on the seam allowance. The top stop is placed 1 inch below the upper edge of placket, *a*. If desired, zipper adhesive tape can be used to hold the zipper in place for stitching. Position the zipper foot with coil upright in the groove; stitch from the top of zipper to the slider; and retrace your stitches.

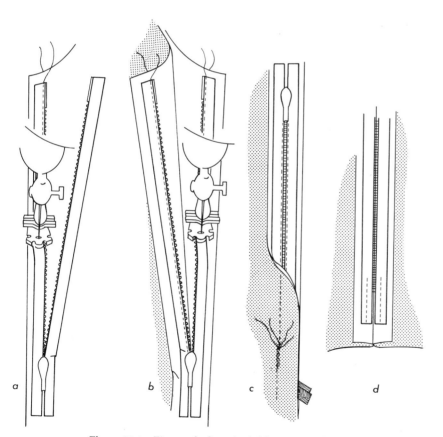

Figure 24-4. Zipper placket—invisible seam method.

3. With right sides of fabric together, place the second side of zipper face down on the other side of the placket. Align top edges and stitch as before, *b*.
4. Close zipper and pull ends of zipper tape aside, *c*. Stitch the seam below the zipper, beginning about $\frac{1}{4}$ to $\frac{1}{2}$ inch above the opening. Tie any threads at the upper end. (This line of stitching will involve an adjustment of the zipper foot.)
5. Machine stitch the ends of the zipper tape to the seam allowances, *d*.

TECHNIQUE FOR MATCHING FABRIC PATTERN   To *match* a fabric design when using the invisible method, sew the first side of the zipper and close it. With the unstitched side of zipper lying face down on the right side of fabric, use a dressmaker's pencil and mark lines on the tape at each stripe. In Step 2, match pencil markings with stripe when stitching. Anchor the zipper with zipper adhesive if fabric is difficult to handle.

Lapped Placket

CLOSED METHOD

This method is shown in directions that come with the zipper and in Figure 24-5.

For a side placket, have the garment seams staystitched $\frac{1}{4}$ inch from the edge, with the grain, on both right and left hips. See that the opening is $\frac{1}{2}$ inch longer than the metal part of the zipper, measuring from the circumference seamline to the end of the opening.

With this method, work on wrong side of garment. Machine-baste the opening on the seamline. Press open.

Open the zipper and place face down with the open end of the teeth $\frac{1}{4}$ inch below where the upper end of the placket will be finished. Pin upper end of zipper to the back seam only, never through the garment. Smooth the tape so that the teeth lie on the seamline. *Pin* the closed end of the zipper in position. The end of the metal should be $\frac{1}{4}$ inch above the closed end of the basted placket. These two pins are sufficient. With a zipper foot, stitch $\frac{1}{16}$ inch from the zipper teeth on the back seam allowance, stitching from lower end of the zipper tape to the top (directional stitching, with garment still wrong side out).

Close the zipper and turn it face up. Fold $\frac{1}{8}$ inch inside the back seam allowance and stitch close to the edge of the folded fabric. (This step completes attaching the zipper to the underlap.)

Spread the garment wrong side up, and turn the zipper face down, flat on the front side of the garment. Watch to see that the closed end of the placket is completely flat. Leaving a small tuck in the seam of the back below the metal, baste-stitch along the zipper tape on the front side. (With experience, or very careful work, you may eliminate basting, doing permanent stitching from the wrong side.)

Turn the garment right side out and stitch along the basted line on the overlap.

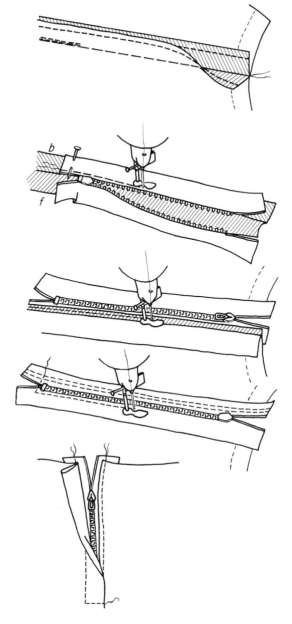

Figure 24-5. Zipper placket—closed-seam method.

OPEN METHOD

By this method, all work is done from the top side of the placket opening.

On the *underlap* (side seam of back of the skirt) make a fold ⅛ inch from the *back* seamline (Fig. 24-6). Pin this fold on the zipper tape right side up. The pull should be ¼ inch below the seamline of the belt at the top of the skirt, and the lower metal end ¼ inch above the closed end of the opening. (The opening was ½ inch longer than the zipper.) Begin at the bottom and use a zipper foot to stitch the entire length of tape 1⁄16 inch from the fold (or hem by hand).

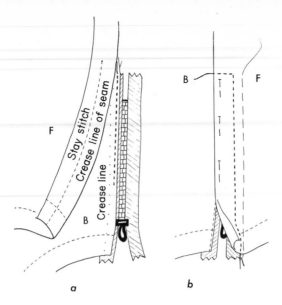

Figure 24-6. Zipper placket—open-seam method.

Prepare *overlap, b.* With the garment right side up, pin the *front,* folded on the seamline, in place over the zipper, original seamlines matched. Pin, baste, or overcast in place. Stitch on the right side to miss the metal zipper across the bottom and about ½ inch from the fold. Swing out a little at the top to leave room for the pull. Where machine work seems to pucker, use hand stitches—half-back or hand-picking stitches.

One-Inch Overlap

This wide overlap gives stability and definitely sets better on long seams, especially those that tend to pucker—as in pile fabrics, double knits, some synthetics, lace, crepe, chiffon, and fabrics bonded or permanent-finished. The hand finish gives a custom-made, couturier quality. In reaching from neck to a low waistline, the work can be kept flat and will be more easily handled in two separate pieces before attaching the skirt.

Overlap (right half of bodice) (Fig. 24-7): Cut $2\frac{1}{4}$ inches wider at center edge, plus $\frac{5}{8}$-inch seam allowance; press to the wrong side to make an overfold one-inch wide on the right side, leaving a $1\frac{1}{4}$-inch underfold on the wrong side, plus the seam allowance, *b.* The $\frac{1}{4}$ inch is the amount needed to bridge an ordinary zipper.

Underlap, c (left half of bodice), has seam allowance pressed to the wrong side with neck facing temporarily pulled up out of the way, *d.*

Neckline has been faced, *b* and *c;* overlap completed, *b;* underlap, with raw edge free at center of garment.

Have underlap seam allowance creased back to wrong side, *d.* Have overlap pressed to wrong side, *b,* so that crease is 1 inch from garment center on the outside and $1\frac{1}{4}$ inches plus seam allowance on the wrong side.

Place zipper face up with tape turned under at the top, *e.*

Pin top of zipper $\frac{1}{4}$ inch below neckline, *e.* Have center fold far enough from teeth to leave narrow channel for pull tab. Baste and hem by hand or by machine.

Pin the overlap in position as planned. Baste and sew it in place, *f*. Hand stitch with half-back stitches (Fig. 28-3). A fine needle and thread are used on fine fabrics as crepe and shantung or buttonhole twist on coarser, firmer weaves, as denim, crash, linen, gabardine.

Unlined garments to be laundered would probably have a machine-stitched overlap; if raw edges ravel, finish with overcasting. If garment is lined, sew the lining to edge of zipper tape with hemming or herringbone stitches. Complete facing; fasten with snap or hook and loop at neckline.

ZIPPER ABOVE A PLEAT

Handicapped people, and others as well, like a front closing with pleat free below the hipline, *g*.

If there is no crosswise seam, the fold below the lower end of the zipper may be left to hang free, as a pleat, in which case, the added amounts should be

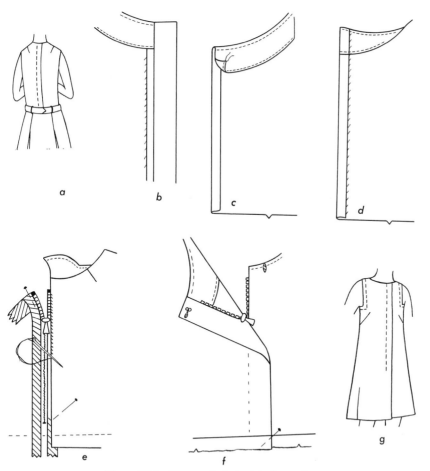

Figure 24-7. Zipper placket—1-inch overlap.

increased to 2 inches for the underlap and $4\frac{1}{4}$ inches for the overlap. Complete the zipper, and then make the seam at the back edge of the pleat.

CENTERED APPLICATION
SLOT-SEAM EFFECT Zippers may be applied to CF, CB, and underarm seams to give a *slot-seam effect*. (See Fig. 24-2, c.) If the seam is narrow, extend it with a tape. If a slash or seam opening is to be faced, complete the facing and press it. Baste-stitch to close the seam. Press it open. Pin the center of the zipper to the center of the seam on the wrong side, so the pull is $\frac{1}{4}$ inch below the upper end of the finished placket line. Stitch, right or wrong side up, whichever you think you can manage most accurately, $\frac{1}{4}$ inch from the center. An alternative plan is to overcast the finished opening together and set the zipper underneath. Stitch from the top side, by working from bottom up.

PLACKET OPEN AT BOTH ENDS Study your guide sheet for specific instructions on zipper application suitable for your design. In general, this application is centered, and two separate lines of stitching are needed.

OTHER PLACKETS
Methods for the construction of the continuous-bound, taped-wrist, and standard shirt-sleeve plackets will be found in Chapter 22.

HAND APPLICATION The application of a zipper by hand not only gives that extra couture touch, but works better on some fabrics than machine stitching. It is more desirable for delicate fabrics, pile, and stretch fabrics.

Use this method with either lapped or centered applications, constructed in the usual way up to the final top stitching. The hand stitch most suitable for this technique is the prickstitch. Suggestions for using it follow.

PRICKSTITCH This is a hand stitch used for inserting the zipper in a placket. The needle is brought up to the right side and is carried back to take a small stitch—about two threads. The needle is then brought up in position for the next stitch. The stitches are made through the fabric and the zipper tape. (See Fig. 28-3, b).

USING SPECIAL FABRICS
If *puckering* occurs—more probable with sheers and permanent press fabrics—hold the zipper and fabric taut between your fingers on either side of zipper foot, but allow the fabric to feed normally. Also, you may need to loosen tension and presser foot pressure and adjust stitch length.

If the zipper in a garment appears to *curl* after laundering, dampen the zipper tape on the wrong side and press.

For fabrics that *stretch*—single knits, sheers, and loosely woven fabrics—it is advisable to stabilize the seam before installing the zipper. Use seam binding or a strip of lightweight lining fabric on the straight grain, $\frac{1}{2}$ inch wide, and the length of the zipper. Center the strip on the seamline on the wrong side of the garment. Stitch it to the garment $\frac{1}{2}$ inch from the edge. Repeat this procedure for the other side.

Shortening a Zipper

If the length you need cannot be purchased, shorten a longer one. To shorten it at the bottom, baste or stitch the zipper in the garment. Make several overhand stitches across the metal, $\frac{1}{4}$-inch below the opening. Sew a large, straight metal eye above the hand stitches to form a new bottom stop. Cut off the excess zipper.

To shorten the zipper at the top, follow the plan as before, leaving 1 inch free at the top. Shorten and remove the necessary teeth. Bend a straight eye in half, slip it over the zipper tape, and sew it securely to provide the top stop.

Other Zipper Tips

1. Close zippers for laundering and dry cleaning.
2. If zippers become difficult to operate with wear, use beeswax, candlewax, or zipper lubricant.
3. For straight stitching, use the sewing guideline that is woven into some regular zipper tapes.
4. Sew both sides of your zipper in the same direction, if possible.
5. Avoid knots tied on the wrong side of the placket located near the zipper teeth, in case they should fray. A better technique is to carry the threads to the inner parts with a needle.

Buttonholes

Good designers believe in "buttons that button"—functional fasteners. Buttons are teamed with three classifications of buttonholes, determined largely by fabric and type of garment.

Fabric buttonholes lend an extra quality of fine tailoring to designs that incorporate buttons of medium to large size. Fabric buttonholes shorter than $\frac{3}{4}$ to 1 inch may appear out of proportion on many designs, because the minimum width of the lip is stabilized at about $\frac{1}{8}$ inch for durability. In a short buttonhole, when a part is hidden by the button, the remainder seems quite wide in proportion to the diameter of the button.

Machine-worked buttonholes seem to belong with casual, sport, and lounging types of garments. *Hand-worked buttonholes* may be a perfect choice for delicate, soft, fine fabrics and a couture touch. *Tailor's buttonholes* have acquired a new status with the added emphasis on pant suits, and the creativity offered in developing hand-sewing skills, including more sewing for men.

Seam buttonholes result when a seam is left unstitched the needed length for a buttonhole. When the seam is pressed open a slit remains, which substitutes very effectively for a buttonhole. Belts, ties, and straps, also, are pulled through such openings (Fig. 24-8).

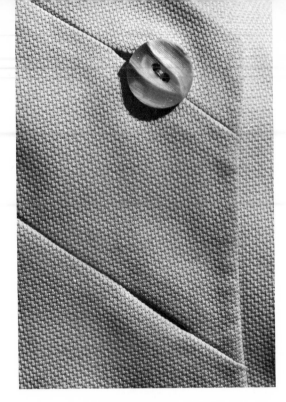

Figure 24-8. Buttonhole in a seam.

CHARACTERISTICS OF WELL-MADE BUTTONHOLES

1. Functional: The button slips through easily, without strain and excessive wear on the buttonhole.
2. Well-proportioned: Long and narrow, not too wide or bulky.
3. Well-planned spacing: Grain is observed; buttons rest on CF or CB, unless the design is unusual; all buttonholes in a series are the same size and shape.

FABRIC BUTTONHOLES In addition to the preceding characteristics of buttonholes in general, the following special standards apply to fabric buttonholes:

Flatness. The seam is pressed away from the lips, and excessive fabric is trimmed off, leaving ¼-inch enclosed seams, before finishing through the facing.

Neatness. The sides are equal in length; ends are equal in width; lips are even in width; corners are square, with no raveling or puckering; and no stitching is visible.

Durability. The corners are not cut too far; the ends are securely anchored; the hem or facing is neatly hand-stitched on the wrong side to cover raw edges.

PREPARATIONS FOR BUTTONHOLES

Location, size, and number of buttons, and preparation of the garment for buttonholes require careful planning.

Regardless of the type of buttonhole you plan to make, it is wise to select the buttons with your pattern and fabric—or at least near the beginning of the construction process. Design and buttons influence each other. Buttonholes cannot be started until the size of the button is known, because if the selection of the button is delayed until after a buttonhole is made, one then is limited in the choice of the button to one that will fit. This applies especially to the use of fabric buttonholes, which must be made early in the construction process. For any type of buttonhole, the minimum length is equal to the diameter plus the thickness of the button.

LOCATION OF BUTTONHOLES Most patterns have buttons centered on CF or CB lines, unless the design is unusual (Fig. 24-9). Buttonholes should be cut in the direction of pull—which is usually horizontal on dresses. Vertical buttonholes are used on shirt fronts and other garments where the strain is not great and the vertical buttonhole is more in harmony with the design. Buttonholes are usually placed on the grain. In some cases, *b*, good design might indicate a location on the bias, but the effect would still be interesting if these buttonholes were on the grain. Is *c* satisfactory? The margins are rather narrow. Obviously, *d* is wrong. A margin of pleasing proportions between the button and the edge of the garment can add much to the general attractiveness. Although markings establishing the amount of lap—when CF rests on CF of the other half of the garment—have been trans-

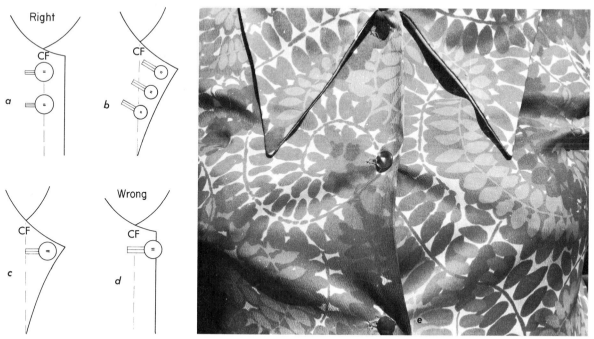

Figure 24-9. *a–d*, Location of buttonholes. A fastener is needed at a point of strian. A button placed at the bust line would have prevented this uneven line along the CF, and the wrinkles, *e*.

ferred from the pattern, it may be wise to check this proportion in relation to the size of button before proceeding further.

The right side laps over the left in women's garments, generally, both front and back; left over right for men's garments; front over back at the left hip for side plackets; and front over back at the wrist. Unusual designs sometimes disregard these general rules.

Check the marked locations of the buttonholes at the CF line. Is the top button located far enough below the neckline seam to allow a minimum of space equal to one half the diameter of your button plus $\frac{1}{4}$ inch? A little more than this amount might be desirable if the button is fairly large and the neckline is to be collarless. The last buttonhole should be placed 3 to 4 inches above the lower edge of a dress or skirt, and 2 to 3 inches above in a jacket. A buttonhole is never made through a hem. For a smooth set in the front bodice, one of the buttonholes should be located approximately in line with the fullest part of the bust, e.

It will be safe to relocate the buttonholes in a vertical direction along the CF or CB line, if necessary; but they should not be shifted off the center line in a horizontal direction. If more or less width is needed in the overlap, find another way to adjust this difference.

SUPPORT FOR BUTTONHOLES   Any type of buttonhole probably will require an underlining or interfacing fabric for stability and strength. Both the fabric, design, and the type of buttonhole will influence the choice of a supporting fabric (considered earlier in Chapter 7). With the proper support, buttonholes often can be made in materials that, otherwise, would be completely unsatisfactory for this type of fastener.

If you are using interfacing that is heavy, stiff, or bulky, make the buttonhole through the fabric and the underlining only, before attaching the interfacing. Cut the openings in the interfacing slightly larger than the buttonhole opening; after placing the interfacing on the garment, pull the buttonholes through the opening. With overcasting stitches, sew the edges of the buttonhole to the interfacing.

A featherweight, pressed-on interfacing can add sufficient stability to prevent raveling. Also, try extra rows of machine stitching—straight or zigzag—on the buttonhole seams, applied before slashing the opening. Slashing from the center to the corner of the buttonhole may increase the durability of these seams.

Fabric Buttonholes

MODIFIED TUCK METHOD

The *modified tuck method* of making buttonholes consists of the following steps:

Plan location and size. The minimum length of buttonhole will equal the diameter plus the thickness of the button. An extra allowance may be desirable if the fabric has a nap or the button is unusual in shape. Try a sample slash in the fabric to determine the correct length. Plan buttonholes far enough back from the edge so that the edge of the button will lie at least $\frac{1}{4}$ inch back of the garment

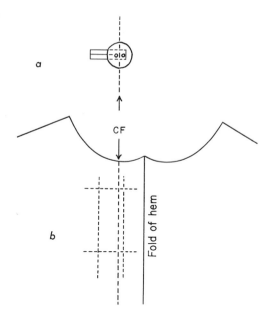

Figure 24-10. Preparation for fabric buttonholes.

edge; generally, buttons are placed on the CF or CB line. Buttonholes would usually be on the right front or back overlap of the garment, belt, or cuff. Plan the spaces to make the design interesting and balanced and to insure a sufficient number to keep the garment closed (determined at preliminary fitting). An odd number of buttons is considered more attractive, as a rule, than an even number.

Mark location and size. An interfacing used on the wrong side of the garment serves as a reinforcement for buttonholes (p. 330). Determine the location of the ends of the buttonhole. A study of Fig. 24-10, *a*, will show that stitches attaching the button will be made on each side of the CF. In order that the CF line of the right half of the garment will coincide with the CF line of the left half, the end of the buttonhole nearest the opening of the garment should extend across the CF a distance equal to one half the length of the space between the holes of the button. Although many patterns show this end of the buttonhole to be located ⅛ inch over the CF, this amount will be modified by the button selected. Make two rows of bastings parallel to the CF as far apart as the determined ends of the buttonhole. Make *crosswise bastings ¼ inch above* the desired center of the buttonholes, extending ½ inch beyond the vertical bastings that mark the ends, *b*. Be sure that all bastings are on grainlines of the fabric.

Prepare the piping *strip* for buttonholes: Cut the strip on the lengthwise grain of fabric, making it 2½ inches in width. (For stripes, plaids, or coarse, loosely woven fabrics, it is better to cut the strip on the bias.) For each buttonhole, allow the length of the buttonhole plus 1 inch for seam allowances (½ inch at each end). For example, if the buttonhole is to be 1¼ inches long, the length needed for each will be 2¼ inches. Multiply this by the total number of buttonholes to be made, as 2¼″ × 3 = 6¾″.

Cut a 2½-inch-wide strip of lined notebook paper with ¼-inch spaces (Fig. 24-11, *a*). Place the strip of paper on the strip of fabric, matching the edges of paper and fabric. For each buttonhole, baste-stitch on two centrally located lines of the paper ½ inch apart. Tear off the paper.

Fold the strip, right side out, on one of the baste-stitched lines and stitch a tuck ⅛ inch from the fold, *b*.

Fold on the other baste-stitched line and stitch another tuck ⅛ inch from the folded edge, being careful to keep the cut edge of the first tuck free, *c*; result will be two ⅛-inch tucks ¼ inch apart. Cut them into sections for buttonholes so that each section is as long as the buttonhole is to be made, plus one inch.

Place the tucked strip, loose edges upward, so that the edge of the tuck will lie along the marked location line of the buttonhole, on the right side of the garment, *d*. Stitch the marked length of the buttonhole on the original tuck stitching, leaving threads dangling. At the machine, bend forward, so that the eye is directly above the needle as you lower it on the basting line marking the end of buttonhole. Check the other end as carefully. Short stitches will insure greater accuracy in ending at the exact point desired.

Bring the cut edges of the tucked strip together, with the strip lying flat, and repeat stitching on the other tuck between the size markings, *e*.

When all buttonholes have been stitched, turn to the wrong side, where you can easily see, on the interfacing, whether all stitched lines end as they should. Rip a stitch if necessary (with a pin). Tie square knots at the ends of all lines. Leave the thread ends ¼-inch long.

If you want a corded lip, draw soft yarn through each tuck with a bodkin or tapestry needle, *f*.

Next, fold loose edges of the buttonhole strip away from the center and cut completely through the strip (but not on the garment side), *g*.

On the wrong side of the garment, cut between parallel lines of stitching to within ¼ inch from each end through the interfacing and fabric, *h*. Clip diagonally to the end of each of the stitched lines to leave a triangle of not less than ¼ inch.

Pull the tuck strips through the opening to the wrong side of the garment, *i*. Adjust the ends of the strips to square the corners. (Overhand lips or piping strips loosely together if necessary, or pin with lips just touching.)

Holding the garment away, stitch over the triangle and strip at the end of the buttonhole, stitching as close as possible to the base of the triangle. Two or three lines of stitching across the triangle to catch the base, middle, and point, will give a very durable, flat finish. Repeat at the other end, *i*. Trim all seams around the buttonhole to ¼ inch, *j*. Press lightly.

For finishing the buttonhole through a hem or facing that rests against the back side of the buttonhole, slash through the hem or facing and hand hem into position, according to either plan *k* or *l* as shown. Plan *k* is satisfactory if the wrong side of the buttonhole does not show when the garment is worn. Construction is simpler, and the buttonhole is likely to be more durable, as it has fewer weak corners.

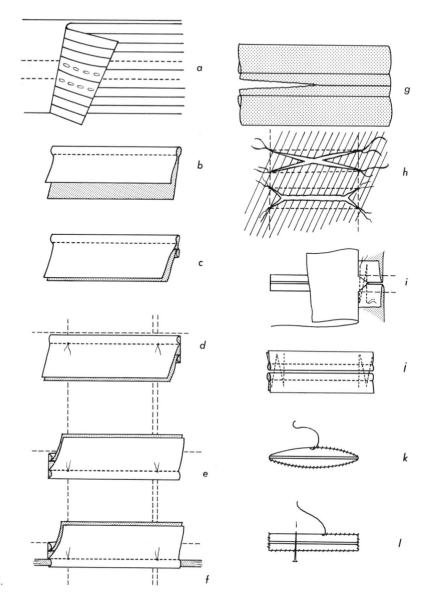

Figure 24-11. Modified tuck method.

BASTED TUCK METHOD

This method differs from the modified tuck method in the manner in which the lips of the buttonhole are formed (Fig. 24-12). In this case, the patch, or strip, for the buttonhole is placed flat into position on the right side of the fabric. Then, on graph paper placed in the identical position on the wrong side, lines stitched directly on the paper provide the accurate measurements needed and, at the same time, stitch the fabric that forms the lips.

437

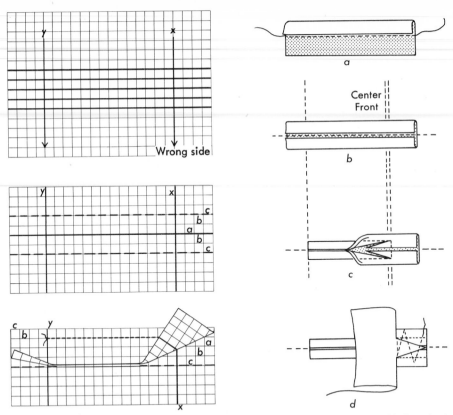

Figure 24-12. Basted tuck method. **Figure 24-13.** One-piece folded method.

STEPS IN THE BASTED TUCK METHOD

1. Follow directions on p. 434, for locating, marking, and cutting the buttonhole patches.
2. For a ⅛-inch lip, select graph paper with eight squares to the inch. Cut the required number of pieces of paper. (Lines could be drawn directly on the interfacing, but using the paper saves time.)
3. On each piece of paper draw the lines x and y, to locate ends of buttonhole. (To speed this process, after the lines are located on the first one, stack the papers and perforate the remainder all at once with a tracing wheel—no carbon needed.)
4. Locate line *a* on the paper; it will be the slash line. Marking these lines is unnecessary if you have them identified in your mind.
5. Pin and/or baste the fabric (bias requires less handling to line up grainlines) on the right side and the graph paper on the wrong side.
6. Baste-stitch on the two *c* lines, the full length of the lines.
7. Examine the right side, to be sure the lines are parallel. Then, use an iron to press the edges of the patch toward the center, creating the two lips. (Test the need for a press cloth. Do not overpress.)
8. Adjust lip carefully, turn to wrong side and stitch on line *b* (with regular-length stitch, or slightly shorter one) starting exactly on line x or y and

ending on the other; stitch just a bit closer to *a* than *c*. Lift the fabric edge back out of the way and repeat the stitching on the other line *b*.

9. Remove the basting threads on lines *c*, and tie the thread ends at *x* and *y*. (At this stage, draw a cord or soft yarn through the lips with a tapestry needle, in case you want the corded lip.)

10. On the right side, cut through the center of the patch *only*. From the wrong side cut through all thicknesses, with slashes to the four knots at the corners. Remove the paper.

11. Pull the strip to the wrong side and stitch the lips across the triangles at the ends.

In heavy fabrics, where slightly more width is needed in the lips, select graph paper in the proportion needed.

ONE-PIECE FOLDED METHOD[1]

This method requires only one fabric strip for each buttonhole (Fig. 24-13).

1. Cut a strip of fabric 1 to $1\frac{1}{8}$ inches wide and 1 inch longer than the button-hole.

2. Mark the center line the length of the strip.

3. With wrong sides together, bring the two edges to the center marking and press lightly, *a*.

4. With the cut edges up, baste the center of the strip on the line that marks the position of the buttonhole. The ends of the strip will extend $\frac{1}{2}$ inch past the marked end of the buttonhole, *b*.

5. Stitch with small stitches, $\frac{1}{8}$ inch from the center, starting at the middle of one side and going completely around, stitching the ends in line with the ends marked on the fabric. Turn square corners, count the stitches across the ends and overlap the beginning stitches.

6. Slash through the center and to the corners. Pull strip to inside and press, *c*.

7. Sew the triangles to the buttonhole strips at the ends, *d*.

Worked Buttonholes

Good-looking standard buttonholes, hand-worked, have the following charac-teristics:

1. Stitches worked through two or more thicknesses.
2. Edges of lips parallel, not wavy.
3. Both edges caught—no fraying.
4. Stitches the width of thread apart.
5. Stitches even in depth, not over $\frac{1}{16}$ inch.
6. Edge purled by buttonhole stitch, not looped by blanket stitch.

[1]*The Vogue Sewing Book*, ed. by Patricia Perry (New York: Vogue Patterns, 1970), p. 293.

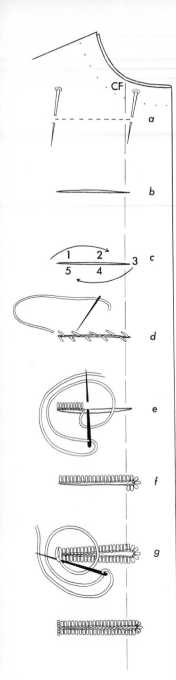

7. A fan at the lapel end or where button rests near fold or overlap—where strain will be.

8. A bar narrow and tight to finish end opposite the end where button rests.

Check for equal spacing. Mark with pins or basting (Fig. 24-14, *a*).

Cut from pin to pin with tiny, sharp-pointed scissors or buttonhole scissors, *b*. Or begin at the center and cut to each end of the buttonhole. If fabric is thick or ravels badly, stitch two parallel rows of machine stitching or machine-buttonholing, and slit between them with a razor, or reinforce between thicknesses of the garment with fine interfacing before cutting. Cut one at a time.

Decide where to begin and end. The strain comes near the outer edge. Hence, work begins at the end farthest from the lapel edge of garment. Work from right to left. The raw edges are up while working the stitch. Hence, you must turn the work upside down to start on the upper edge of slit (at point 1 in *c*; note *e*).

If the material ravels badly, the edges of slit may be *overcast* with the same thread as buttonhole stitch, *d*. Overcasting keeps the two layers from slipping. Begin at the inside or bar end, proceed right to left making small overcastings later to be concealed with the buttonhole stitch. Three or four on each side and none at ends will be enough. Do not use a knot.

Work the buttonhole stitch (not blanket stitch) from right to left, *e*. Insert your needle at right angles to the edge of the slit (Fig. 24-15, *a*). In this position, pick up the two threads at the eye of the needle and bring them around toward you and under the point of the needle from right to left. Pull the needle through and away from you to make a knot or *purl* on the raw edge. Regularity in your tension as you pull up the thread is what makes the buttonhole look even. (Later, gain speed in a simple motion by taking the stitch inside a loop you have thrown, as illustrated.) Try heavy-duty thread except on dainty garments.

When you reach the end, *f*, radiate the stitches so that they match the others in depth and spacing. This makes the *fan,* which reinforces the end of the slit against which the button pulls. Five to seven stitches are needed to make a durable, well-spaced fan. Turn and work the lower edge of the slit.

When the back end is reached, make the *bar.* Place two or three straight stitches across the end directly over the first stitch made and the last, *g*. Cover with five buttonhole stitches, catching *under* the three bar threads for all except the center stitch of the group of five (in which you catch the fabric). Make all these

Figure 24-14. Worked buttonholes.

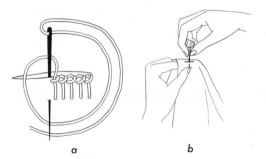

a   *b*   **Figure 24-15.** Buttonhole stitch.

440

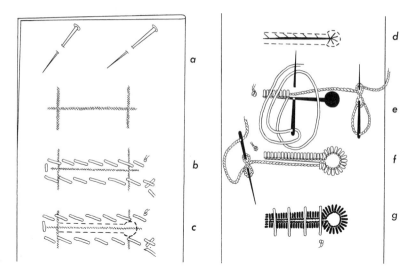

Figure 24-16. Tailor's buttonhole.

stitches close and firm. In a vertical buttonhole make a bar at both ends. Bring thread to the wrong side and fasten it. Large buttonholes need to have lips overcast together and pressed.

COMMON FAULTS If your buttonhole has none of these defects, it is super-excellent! By comparing your work with the standards and by practice, you can overcome these faults:

1. Stitches too deep—too heavy-looking.
2. Stitches too close together.
3. Stitches too shallow—edges ravel out.
4. Stitches too far apart.
5. Purl not produced on edge because a blanket stitch was used instead of a buttonhole stitch.
6. Bar at wrong end.
7. Fan at both ends.
8. Edges wavy.
9. Stitches unevenly spaced.
10. Not enough stitches in the fan.
11. Bar too large or loose.
12. Worked on unsuitable fabric, on one layer of fabric, or with wrong thread.

Tailor's Buttonholes

Tailor's buttonholes are made on the same general plan as worked buttonholes (Fig. 24-14), with added details that make them more durable and attractive. They are usually made through two layers of fabric with an interfacing between them. The interfacing should be firm but pliable. Follow these steps (Fig. 24-16):

441

Mark the location, preferably with a thin chalk line, *a*. Use diagonal basting through the three layers around each marking to prevent slipping during work, *b*. Machine stitch $\frac{1}{16}$-inch from the marked line along each side, *c*. Begin and finish at the inside end, but form a $\frac{3}{16}$- to-$\frac{1}{4}$-inch circle at the outside end. Have the center of this circle exactly on the CF line. Thread the ends into a sewing needle and fasten them with a few back stitches on the wrong side. Clip off closely. Stitch all buttonholes at the same time.

Cut only one buttonhole at a time. Insert one point of fine, sharp scissors in the center of the circle and, with one motion only, cut through all layers exactly midway between the two rows of stitching. To form the eyelet, snip several times around the circle, *d*. Push a stiletto through the circle to form the eyelet. Trim away any excess ravelings. A tailor's buttonhole cutter has a razor-like cutting blade and a punch combined to work at the same time. It is adjustable, and its use insures uniform buttonholes. Press it lightly to make a good outline of the eyelet to follow in stitching.

Overcast the trimmed edges with very fine thread and a needle, stitching almost to the machine stitching, but not over it. Hot beeswax rubbed over the slit keeps the material together and prevents raveling.

Strand or pad the edge of the slit. Use heavy but soft linen or cotton thread, such as no. 10 perle. Use a knot (later to be cut off). Begin $\frac{1}{4}$-inch back of slit; bring your needle out close to the upper side of the slit at the inside end, *e*. Carry the strand to the eyelet and wrap it around the needle to keep it taut. When the upper half of the buttonhole is completed, remove the needle and bring this stranding thread along the lower half. After the buttonhole is complete, insert the needle of the stranding thread exactly at the end of the buttonhole and bring it to the wrong side. Clip off stranded thread and also the knot used at the beginning.

Work the buttonhole, *f*. Use regular silk buttonhole twist (preferably rubbed lightly with beeswax and pressed with a warm iron). Turn the work upside down so that you first can work the upper half of the slit. Use a regular buttonhole stitch (Fig. 24-15). When the eyelet is reached, release the stranding thread and hold it around the circle as you radiate the buttonhole stitches over the strand. Pulling on the strand at this time may aid in keeping the circle a little more uniform. Now turn your work so the lower edge of the slit is toward you; buttonhole stitch over it (over the taut strand). Bring the stranding thread through to the wrong side as explained previously.

Finish the buttonhole with a bar tack, *g*. Turn the work so that the back end is next to you. Take two or three bar stitches across the end with the buttonhole twist exactly in the first and last stitches. Cover these with tiny overhand, button-hole, or blanket stitches. Fasten with two or three over-and-over stitches on the wrong side.

Baste the slit together with diagonal basting. Press well from the wrong side with a damp cloth. While still damp, push a stiletto several times up and down in the eyelet to give it a good shape. Leave these bastings in the buttonhole until the garment is completed. The eyelet provides plenty of room for a large durable shank on the button.

MACHINE BUTTONHOLES

If machine buttonholes are to be used, reinforcing material is usually essential. This was considered, no doubt, in selecting interfacing for your fabric and design.

Specific directions for making these buttonholes are not included here, as this information will be available in the instruction book for your brand and model of machine.

Pockets and Belts

Pockets, in addition to being useful, may add to the decorative design. This emphasizes the importance of the attention given to their size, shape, location, and precise tailoring. Because they attract the eye, they are not to be placed on the bust or hipline, unless one wishes to accent these areas. Knowing how to make the various styles of pockets with ease and accuracy will suggest to a skilled technician many clever and interesting variations—often the only original detail of a good dress.

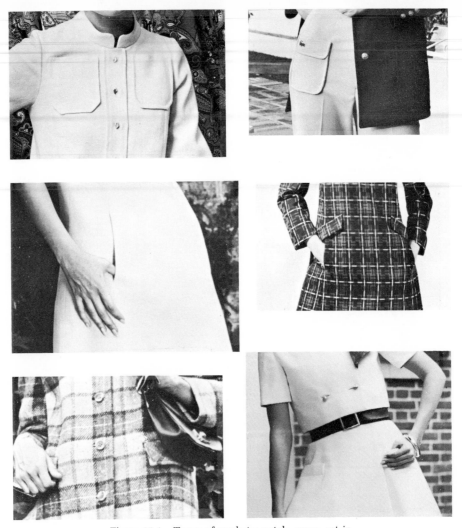

Figure 25-1. Types of pockets: patch, seam, set-in.

Types of Pockets

Pockets may be classified into three types (Fig. 25-1).

1. Patch pocket.
2. Seam pocket.
3. Set-in pocket.

A *patch pocket* consists of a separate piece of fabric attached to the garment. Usually, it is self-fabric, but it might be another material, possibly in a contrasting color.

The *seam pocket,* placed in an opening in the side or front seam, is well hidden and inconspicuous. It is easy to make, as the pocket is constructed along with the seam. This type of pocket in pants, especially in the more tailored designs, is somewhat more complicated to construct.

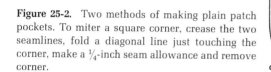

Figure 25-2. Two methods of making plain patch pockets. To miter a square corner, crease the two seamlines, fold a diagonal line just touching the corner, make a $\frac{1}{4}$-inch seam allowance and remove corner.

The *set-in pocket* is based on the principle of design used in a fabric buttonhole—a slash is made into the garment. A variety of designs and techniques are employed to finish the slash and provide an inner pocket.

PATCH POCKETS

Standards to expect in a well-tailored patch pocket are the following:

1. Corners are reinforced.
2. Top hem or facing is in proportion to the shape and size of finished pocket.
3. The pocket is flat and smooth with $\frac{1}{4}$-inch enclosed seams. (Exception: pouch pocket.)
4. It is cut on grain and placed with regard to the grain of the garment.
5. Stitching is perfectly even—and is suitable for the fabric.

HEMMED PATCH POCKET   One method is to staystitch around any curved seams, turn back, and pin or baste. Then hem the top down, being careful that it does not extend beyond the sides of the pocket (Fig. 25-2, *a*).

A second method is to first hem the top, and then crease on the seamline all around, *b*. "Lock" the seams where they cross the hem by clipping the wrong side of the hem only, just above and parallel to the stitching, for about one inch. Then invert both raw edges of the ends into the inside of the hem.

Lower square corners are *mitered*, by first creasing across the corner before creasing adjacent seams. Clip off the corner.

FACED OR LINED PATCH POCKET   Staystitch interfacing to the wrong side of the pocket. Trim interfacing seams. Fold and pin the seamline of the material over to the wrong side of the interfacing. Miter, slash, or notch corners and curves as needed. Baste $\frac{1}{8}$ inch back from the foldline. Press.

Cut the lining about $\frac{1}{8}$ inch smaller than the pocket on all sides, matching the grain. Pin in position. Turn under raw edges so the fold of the lining is kept slightly back from the fold of the pocket. Pin and hem the lining by hand neatly to the pocket. Press. Apply it to the garment in a decorative yet durable style of stitching.

LINED POCKET WITH A HEM   Stitch the right side of the lining to the right side of the lower edge of the pocket hem in a $\frac{1}{4}$-inch plain seam. Press the seam down toward the lining (Fig. 25-3, *a*).

Turn the hem and lining to the right side of the pocket and stitch a plain seam across the ends of the pocket hem the depth of the hem, *b*. Press seams open.

Turn right side out, and baste along the seamline around the edge of the pocket. Trim enclosed seams to the width of the welt. Remove wedges on convex curves and cut across corners. Press lightly without disturbing the shape or grain, *c*.

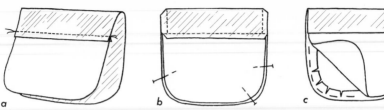

Figure 25-3. Lined or faced patch pocket with a hem.

Fit the lining to the pocket by turning a slightly deeper seam in the lining than on the pocket and slip-stitch it to position, *c*. Press it again.

Stitch to the garment.

The usual width of an enclosed seam is ¼ inch. If, however, for decorative purposes you plan to stitch ½ inch back from the edge of the pocket, leave the enclosed seam just under ½ inch wide. This will make a padded line next to the stitching and make it stand out more effectively to match the welt seams. In this case it might be better to make the lining of self-fabric.

Trim off the seam allowance to leave just ¼ inch for the enclosed seam. Keep stitches short and ⅛ inch from the edge in basting curves (Fig. 25-2, *a*). Finger-crease straight lines but do not baste them. Miter outside corners, clip inside corners and curves, and remove wedges from outside or convex curves (Fig. 21-6). (To be sure that duplicate pockets are identical, try pressing the edges over a thin cardboard pattern of the finished pocket shape before basting.)

Pin the pocket in place and stitch evenly to preserve the designed shape. Reinforce by retracing or by a decorative second row of stitching at least the depth of the hem (Fig. 25-4).

ATTACHING A POCKET BY HAND

Whether a pocket is finished with topstitching or without visible stitching, it can be attached with hand stitches. It is often simpler to do precision stitching on the pocket before it is attached, especially if the fabric is rather bulky.

STEPS IN ATTACHING A POCKET BY HAND

1. Finish the pocket with lining or self-lining.
2. Pin and baste it into place.
3. Use method *a*, *b*, or *c* for attaching a pocket.
   a. Working on the *right side* slightly under the pocket's edge, slip-stitch the pocket to the garment with strong thread. Keep the stitches short and add extras near the upper edges for greater durability (Fig. 25-4).
   b. From the *wrong side*, backstitch with short stitches through garment and pocket, keeping the stitches back from the edge far enough to make them invisible.
   c. Attach the pocket with the prickstitch. (See p. 430.)

SEAM POCKETS

Standards for seam pockets.

1. The seamline is smooth and unbroken at the pocket opening.
2. The inner pocket is flat and smooth.

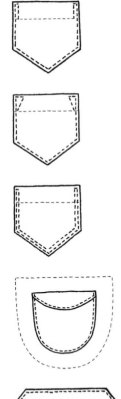

Figure 25-4. Methods of stitching and reinforcing.

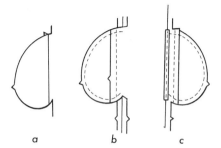

Figure 25-5. Seam pocket in a dress.   *a*   *b*   *c*

POCKET IN A SIDE-FRONT SEAM

A wider seam allowance is an advantage at the pocket opening, in order to move the seam back from the edge where it will not show on the right side (Fig. 25-5, *a*). Self-fabric can be used in medium- or lightweight fabrics; an underlining or lining fabric is desirable where less bulk is preferred.

STEPS IN CONSTRUCTION

1. Seam the pocket sections to the garment.
2. Press seams open to flatten and then press toward the pocket.
3. Baste garment sections together, including pocket openings.
4. Baste pocket edges together.
5. Stitch the entire seam, going around the pocket edges.
6. Clip one side of lengthwise seam at upper and lower ends of pocket in order that it can be pressed open above and below the pocket, *b. Note:* If seam is to be topstitched, the lines along the opening must be stitched before the pocket is closed.
7. If pocket is not sufficiently reinforced (with underlining), woven seam tape can be hand-hemmed across the opening, *c.*

TAILORED POCKET IN A SEAM

Cut a side pocket to be concealed in a seam as illustrated (Fig. 25-6). Provide facings of garment material about two inches wide (if the pocket is not made of self-material). Apply the facing as a lapped seam, leaving raw edges at the top and side that fit the garment seam.

Fold the pocket lengthwise and seam the lower part up as far as the facings, *b.* Retrace or tie the ends securely.

Pin or baste each side of the pocket opening to the opening left in the side seam of the garment, *c.* Stitch from the top to meet the seam of the garment and retrace ends.

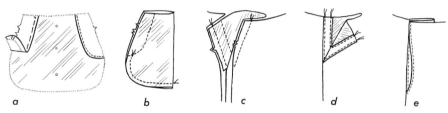

  a   *b*   *c*   *d*   *e*

Figure 25-6. Faced pocket in a seam for pants or skirt.

Press both the pocket and seam toward the front, *d.* Understitch on the overlap and, if desired, on the underlap. Tie the thread ends securely on the wrong side. Pin or baste the top edges of the pocket in position to the waistline of the garment, *e.*

SET-IN POCKETS
Standards for set-in pockets.

1. Flat, not bulky; seams are well-pressed; excessive fabric has been trimmed away to leave $\frac{1}{4}$-inch enclosed seams.
2. Corners are neatly made and square.
3. Lips are even in width.
4. Facings on welts are hidden along the edges.
5. Stitching is durable; seams at ends of pocket are securely anchored.

Set-in pockets are constructed in a manner similar to that used for fabric buttonholes.

ONE-STRIP POCKET
Cut a pocket strip 1 to $1\frac{1}{2}$ inches wider than the opening and about 10 inches long (twice the depth of pocket plus seams and lips).

Make a crosswise crease $1\frac{1}{2}$ inches from top. Place the crease on the marked line for opening of pocket. Pin in place (Fig. 25-7, *a*).

Stitch parallel to the crease to make a rectangle $\frac{3}{8}$ inch wide—$\frac{3}{16}$ inch on each side of the crease. Turn square corners. Count the stitches across the ends to make them equal.

Slash through both thicknesses on the line of marking to within $\frac{3}{8}$ inch of each end. Clip diagonally to, but not through, the corners.

Turn the strip through this opening and press it back flat as a facing on the wrong side, *b.* Then press the piping along the sides toward the slit, but not the seams or the triangles.

Fold the strip so that it forms a piping, or lip, on each side of the opening. Keep the seam pressed back out of opening and lips. Edges should meet in exact center so that the lips are the same width. Baste at the base of each lip but not over the triangle. Use diagonal basting to baste folded edges together along the center of the pocket, *c.*

Turn to the back and adjust the inverted box pleat at each end and tack by hand or stitch to the base of the triangle underneath. Press.

On the wrong side, machine-stitch the lower lip to the seamline of the lower edge of the original rectangle, *c.* This will keep the lip from slipping out of place in use.

Now fold the lower edge of the long pocket strip up so that its raw edge coincides with the raw edge of the top of the strip just above the upper lip, *d.* Shape it in a curve if desired.

Pin, and stitch a seam to hold this strip up, thus forming the inside of the pocket, *e.* The stitching should not go through to the right side of the garment anywhere. A plain seam is made in such a way that it catches the turned-up strip fast to the seamline of the upper lip, continues on down the side exactly on the stitching at the base of the triangle (which has the inverted pleat tacked to it), through both layers of pocket, up on the other side, and is retraced or tied where it meets the beginning stitch.

Press, trim, and overcast or pink. Leave diagonal basting in place until the garment is finished, *f*. The ends are sometimes finished with arrowheads (Fig. 27-13).

Refer to Figure 24-11. Note that at the completion of a regular fabric buttonhole, *f*, a strip can be attached to the seams of the two lips in order to make a pocket.

Welt Pocket

A simplified welt pocket is made like a piped pocket, except that you develop the lower lip into one wide band instead of having two narrow lips (Fig. 25-8).

Cut a pocket strip about 4-by-10 inches. Crease it crosswise in the center and place this crease on the marking for the pocket, right side to right side. Pin and baste in place, *a*.

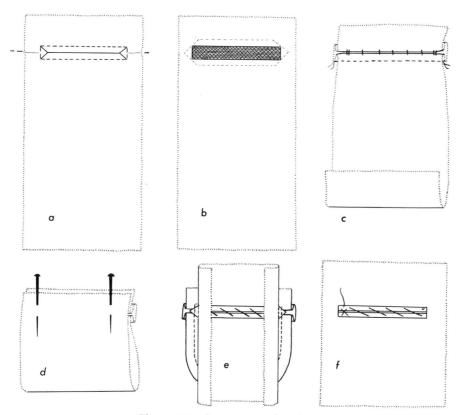

Figure 25-7. One-strip piped pocket.

Stitch a rectangle parallel to and ¼ inch from the marking. Count stitches across ends to make them equal. Turn square corners. Begin on a long side and end by retracing. Slash through both thicknesses on the line of marking to within ¼ inch of end. Clip diagonally to each corner, *b*, but not through stitching.

Turn the strip through this opening and press it flat on the wrong side as for a facing, *c*. Then press the upper seam, strip down, and pin up out of the way. Press the lower piping up, but not the lower seam or the triangles.

Use the lower end of the strip to form a piping or *welt* the width of the stitched rectangle. Keep the seam turned down out of this welt. Baste along the base of the welt. Use diagonal basting to hold the upper fold of the welt to the upper edge of the pocket opening, *d* and *e*. Press neatly.

On the wrong side, stitch welt to seam along the lower edge of the rectangle only, *f*.

Pull the top of the strip down flat onto the lower end of the strip, thus forming the back of the pocket. Shape the two ends of the pocket strip in a curve, *g*. Stitch the two strips together in a plain seam, catching the ends of the welt to the triangle at each end.

Tie thread ends or retrace and finish seam, *h*.

STAND POCKET

A regulation stand pocket is made by preparing the welt or "stand" separately. It may be stitched and turned (Fig. 25-9, *a*) or first interfaced. Cut two pocket pieces one inch wider than finished stand, and as deep as desired—the underpiece ⅜ inch deeper than the upper pieces.

Baste the stand face down where planned (better reinforced there). Place the shorter (upper) piece over stand and stitch ¼-inch seam. Fasten ends exactly, on stand. Place the longer (under) piece above with raw edges matching stand; stitch to match other ¼-inch seam, *b*.

Slash through garment only (as in piped buttonhole, tuck method) leaving ⅜-inch triangles at ends, *c*. Slip pocket pieces through to wrong side. Pull the stand upright, overcast into position, and press. On wrong side, stitch pocket sections together in a seam catching base of triangle but not the stand; use catch stitches to tack stand upright, but invisibly, *d*.

This method applies to slanting shapes as well.

Separate Belts

Even though you have followed a pattern carefully, ravel edges to see that the belt is cut exactly on the straight of the fabric. If a fabric buttonhole is to be used, make it before closing the belt.

SOFT BELT

For a *nonstiff belt,* fold the fabric lengthwise, wrong side out, and stitch on the seamline. Close both ends, leaving two inches unstitched at a desirable location, or leave one end open. Trim the seam to ¼ inch, cut off corners, and press it open along the edge of the ironing board or over a sharpened dowel stick.

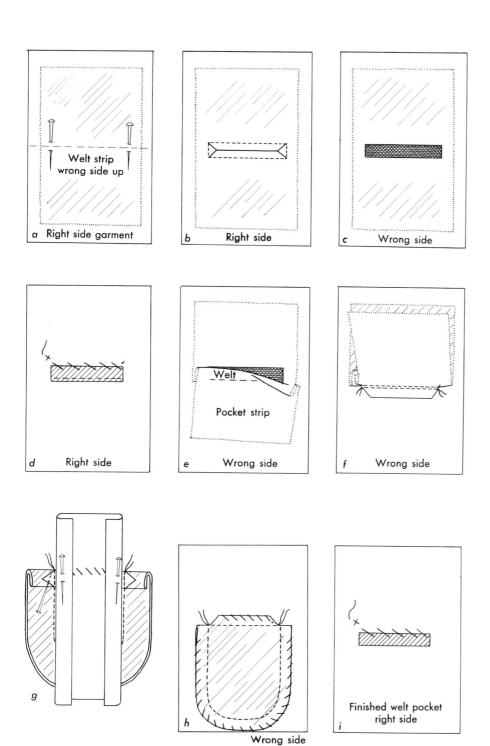

Figure 25-8. Simplified welt pocket.

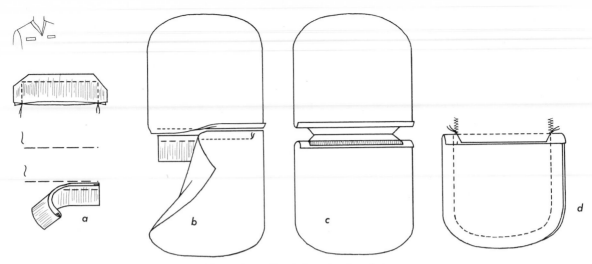

Figure 25-9. Regulation stand pocket.

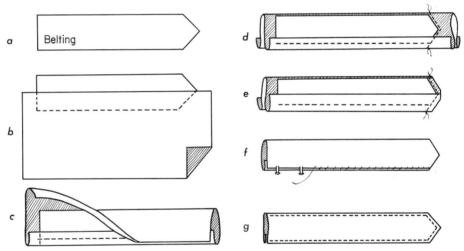

Figure 25-10. Fabric belt with stiff interfacing.

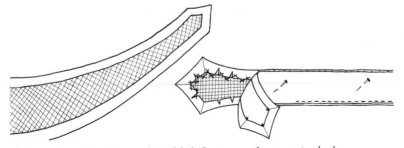

Figure 25-11. Interfacing a shaped belt for a smoother, smarter look.

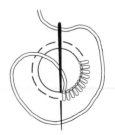

Figure 25-12. Worked eyelet for tongue of belt buckle.

454

Use the end of the dowel to turn the belt right side out. Work the *enclosed seam* out just off the edge so it will not show on the outside of the belt; baste or press it to establish a straight, flat edge. Close opening by hand. Topstitch or quilt if preferred. Attach the buckle.

STIFF BELT

A *stiffened belt* may be made in several ways:

1. Use grosgrain ribbon or belting as a foundation. Turn under the raw edges of a fabric strip until they meet in the center, and stitch them to the ribbon. The ribbon may or may not show at edge, but your work must be even.
2. Use commercial belting or cut your own the desired length and shape from heavy interfacing material. If the garment is to be washed, be sure to select interfacing that will not shrink. Read the label! Shape one end of the belting (Fig. 25-10, *a*).

    Cut the fabric three times the width of the belt plus a ½-inch seam allowance, the length of the belting plus two inches, *b*. Place the wrong side of one edge of the belt fabric along the center of the wrong side of the belting. Baste stitch midway between the center and edge of the belt, *c*.

    Fold the fabric around the belting and crease the other edge of the belt, *c*. Finger-crease the edge near the point. Reverse the fold, *d*, and stitch on fabric around the point of the belting, very close to, but not catching, the belting in the line of stitching, *d*. Trim the seam to ⅛ inch, snip off corners, and turn the belt. Turn the raw edge under and pin slightly back of the edge of the belt, pinning through the fabric but not into the belting, *f*. Stitch on the right side, beginning at the unfinished end and stitching around the point back to the open end, *g*. If machine stitching is not desired, hand-hem along the back edge of the belt, *f*. Use metal or thread-worked eyelets.

    Cover your own buckle from kits available; have them made commercially; or find a distinctive ready-made buckle.

CONTOUR BELT

Choose appropriate interfacing for the outer belt of *shaped belts* that cannot be folded and turned (Fig. 25-11). Cut the interfacing the exact shape of the finished belt. Pin it on the wrong side of the outer belt. Turn the seams of the belt over the edge of the interfacing. Fold corners as a miter, slash on curves, and catch-stitch the raw edge to the interfacing. Press. Turn in the edges of the underbelt or lining, pin, and baste so that it is about ¹⁄₁₆ inch smaller than the outer belt. Pin it to the belt arched in position to be worn. Slip-stitch or hand-hem along the edges, or topstitch if desired.

EYELETS

For *worked eyelets*, locate the position with pins (Fig. 25-12). Outline a circle of the size desired with tiny running stitches. Punch a hole through the circle with a stiletto or an orange stick. Buttonhole or overhand over the edge with stitches close together.

Hems

Standards for a Professional-Looking Skirt Hem

1. A well-made skirt hem is a uniform distance from the floor all around.
2. It is uniform in width throughout.
3. It is well-proportioned as to width and heavy enough to hang well.
4. It is suited to present styles.
5. It is inconspicuous—either hemmed by hand or blind stitched on a machine. If topstitched for a tailored effect, machine hemming is standard throughout and corresponds to other stitching on the garment.
6. Hand stitches are about $\frac{1}{2}$ inch apart—uniformly spaced; loose, not drawn.
7. It is flat and smooth.
8. It is free from the appearance of oversewing or overpressing.

9. Any excess fullness in circular hems is controlled by easing and shrinking.
10. The entering seamlines are pressed open in bulky hems, and clipped at the back edges of pleats.
11. There are no pleats in the tape. It must not be tighter than the garment on which it rests.

Skirt Hems

To Establish a Hemline

At the second fitting of a dress, after approving the waistline and placket, you can save time by marking the hemline of the skirt (and of short sleeves) at this point. This plan is safe if your skirt is relatively straight, is made of firm fabric, and has been hanging for some time to allow stretching or sagging of bias or circular parts.

Examine the construction lines that enter the hemline. On sagging skirts you will sometimes find seams that draw. The weight of the skirt has stretched the fabric so that the fabric yarns are longer than the stitching thread. Stretch the seam somewhat to break threads and release the puckering. Restitch.

Pin the placket or opening in place and put on the belt. The lengthwise seams have been finished and pressed. Be sure to wear the type of shoes and undergarments you will wear with it and assume your best posture throughout the process. The person being fitted should be standing on a table or other platform, so that the fitter has her eye level with the hemline and so that she can do the moving rather than the one being fitted. The fitter stands back frequently to view her line of pins and check wherever the line seems uneven.

During the first fitting, a hem pinned up temporarily should have helped you decide on a preferred distance from the floor. Consider the fashionable length for this type of garment and adapt it to your own proportions, shape of legs, and weight and fullness of the skirt. The hemline in firm fabrics may need no marking if the garment has been correctly fitted.

Measure from the floor with a yardstick or hem marker (Fig. 26-1, *a*). Do not turn up the hem, but place a line of pins or chalk on one thickness of fabric, parallel with the floor, at the exact line desired for the finished length. Hem markers, which either form a chalk line or hold the skirt while a pin is inserted in a slot to make two stitches, are effective for measuring. The pins can be four or five inches apart on a fairly straight skirt, but they should be closer on a more circular skirt. Extra pins will be needed under folds and pleats and at openings.

To Check Skirt Length

Remove the garment and examine the marked line to see if the curve is gradual (Fig. 26-1, *b*). Generally, the right half should not vary greatly from the left half. Correct slight irregularities by replacing pins, *b*.

A short cut consists of marking with four pins only: the CF, CB, and side seams; on the table match pattern pieces to these pins to establish a new gradual curve—removing sag and the like.

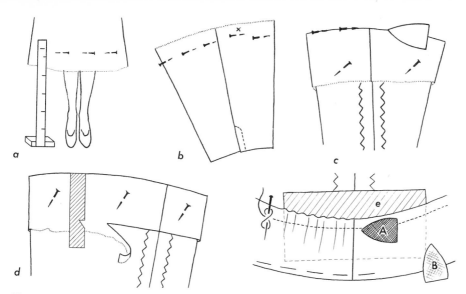

Figure 26-1. Steps in preparing hem for finish. *a*, Mark length; *b*, on table, correct line; *c*, fold, pin upper edge, remove pins from marked line and press lightly (might baste difficult fabrics); *d*, trim to desired, even width; *e*, control ease at upper edge.

Turn to the wrong side (with the bulk toward you) and fold the hem back (toward you) along the line of pins, *c*. Keep the fold in place by other pins, matching seams, pleat creases, and CF and CB grainlines. Pin or baste about ⅛ inch from the fold through two thicknesses, on difficult fabrics or circular skirts. Or you may prefer to place the pins about halfway between the fold and the upper edge of the hem, *d*. This plan permits you to crease the fold lightly (after removing the marking pins on the fold) and leaves the upper edge free for trimming after you have approved the hemline. It is obvious that you will not want a crease if there is any question that it might need changing.

Stop! Have the third or final fitting. Check for becomingness as well as evenness of length.

To Prepare for Hemming

After approving the hemline at the third fitting, press the fold. Be sure that all the pins along this fold are removed to avoid imprints. A gathering thread (hand or machine) helps to control extreme fullness but is usually unnecessary. If pleats persist, press in several small ones rather than a few wide ones, but it is more satisfactory to reduce the hem width in circular skirts. Use paper, as in *e*.

Place the skirt on a table, wrong side up, and use a gauge to mark and cut a hem of the desired width in an even curve, *d*.

The narrowest point of the hem determines its maximum width, but if there is plenty of hem allowance, adjust the width in a straight skirt to suit your taste or the fashion; in curved hemlines adjust the width to the degree of curvature. In general, make hems in full, sheer straight-cut skirts (chiffon or organdy) 7 to 12 inches wide; in short-skirt styles about 2½ inches; and in very full, long evening dresses, especially if circular, ⅛ inch.

Hem Finishes

There are a number of finishes for dress and skirt hems. The hem edge can be taped; clean-finished, zigzagged; overedged; staystitched $\frac{1}{4}$ inch from the edge—pinked or left raw; or unstitched—pinked or left raw. Your choice of finish will depend on your fabric, function of the garment, cut of the skirt, and care required.

The *tape finish* is chosen when material ravels and where clean-finishing would be too bulky. Stretch lace is used for a more decorative finish.

Clean-finishing is reserved for lightweight fabrics. Omit the machine stitching if it makes an imprint or shows through on a sheer or semisheer. It is valuable on fabrics that do not finger-crease readily.

On knitted fabrics, a *zigzagged finish* may be chosen to allow for flexibility and to prevent rolling. However, a finish on knits is optional.

Staystitching, or ease-stitching where fullness is present, is not objectionable on a firm, nonraveling fabric such as wool flannel or laminated jersey. A durable-press cotton might be ease-stitched and left raw, or overedged.

A *plain edge, turned under*, is best on very sheer fabrics, such as organza or chiffon. It may be used on average-weight materials easily finger-creased where a softer finish is desired.

To Dispose of Fullness

If there is very little fullness, and if the fabric is soft or lightweight, ease in the fullness as you pin, baste, or stitch, and depend on pressing to dispose of it (Fig. 26-2, *a*). If a tape finish is used, the fullness can be eased on to the tape as it is pinned to the raw edge of the hem. Be sure the tape is not tighter than the skirt on which it rests. After stitching, more fullness can be removed by shrinking. Stretch-bias tape is a good short cut—when relaxed it absorbs the ease in the hem.

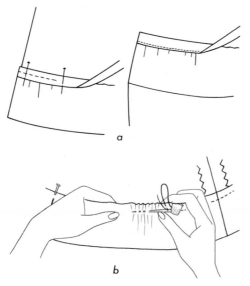

a

b

Figure 26-2. Decide on ways for disposing of fullness and method of treating raw edge. *a*, Easing garment to tape; *b*, use an ease line, if very full.

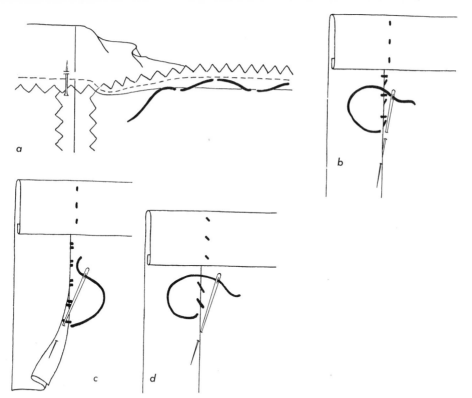

Figure 26-3. Standard hemming stitches: *a*, running hemming; *b*, vertical hemming; *c*, slip hemming; *d*, slant hemming.

Where the material is full, ease-stitch—by hand or machine—$\frac{1}{4}$ inch from the raw edge and draw it up to fit the skirt (Fig. 26-2, *b*). Ease must be shrunk out before the edge finish is applied.

Hand-Hemming Stitches

All hemming stitches are more professional if not too close together and if loose and done with a fine needle. You will be surprised to see how much better your work appears when the needle used is not coarser than No. 9. Hand hemming should be invisible. In underlined garments, stitches are made only into the underlining fabric.

To hold the hem in place, we ordinarily use running hemming, vertical hemming, slip hemming, slant hemming, or catch stitching. *Although hand stitches are loose, they must be fastened securely at the ends.*

Where durability is a factor, make hand stitches close together. Where appearance is important, durability is sacrificed, as on a skirt hem.

Running hemming is plain basting between the hem edge and the garment. With the garment wrong side out, roll it back about $\frac{1}{8}$ to $\frac{1}{4}$ inch from the raw edge of the hem. A taped hem will appear less conspicuous if the stitches are under the raw edge of the fabric under the seam tape rather than in the tape. Run the needle along to take tiny stitches first in the garment and then in the hem about $\frac{1}{2}$ inch apart (Fig. 26-3, *a*).

Vertical hemming, b, sometimes called straight hemming, looks better on the grain of cloth and shows less float on the wrong side than does slant hemming, *d.* It is used on better dresses, flat textures, ties, ruffle edges, and luncheon linens, which need to be as inconspicuous on the wrong as on the right side. After fastening the thread in the hem proper, take a tiny stitch in the one layer of the garment close to the fold of the hem and parallel with the hem. The needle does not slant but is pointed straight along the hem. Proceed at once to insert the needle forward in the hem and pull the needle and thread out. Take the next stitch in the single thickness of the garment right beside where the last stitch came out of the hem; then slip the needle forward as before—slightly under the fold. The floats are partially concealed under the fold. Where using this stitch on the wrong side of bands or bindings, catch the needle in the machine stitching or close to it on the seam, permitting the needle to stay between layers of cloth. This results in a firmly stitched, inconspicuous line.

Slipstitch resembles vertical hemming on the right side in that the stitches parallel the hem, but the floats are completely concealed inside the fold of the hem, *c.* After fastening the thread in the fold, take a tiny stitch in the single thickness of the garment parallel to the hem right beside the point where the thread emerged from the fold. Pull the needle and thread through. In a second motion insert the needle back in the fold of the hem at a point directly opposite the point of the ending of the tiny stitch. Slip the needle along in the fold and pull it out. (It is difficult to slip the needle through the fold if the clean-finish is too close to the edge.) Then make the tiny stitch right beside it. Repeat. After some practice you will be able to make the tiny (right side) stitch and the floating stitch ahead in one operation. Avoid having floats exposed; the floats are visible only as little cross links and not as long slanting floats because they are in the fold. In skirt hems the floats are at least $\frac{1}{2}$ inch long; in overdraperies, they are about 1 inch long; in the back of an upholstered chair $\frac{1}{8}$ inch; in joining seams in millinery or making a blind closing in a belt ending, about $\frac{1}{8}$ inch long. They do not give a firm, straight line on the wrong side as does vertical or slant hemming, but the right-side appearance is identical with that of the vertical hemming stitch.

Slant hemming (Fig. 26-3, *d*) may be used on plain hems and to fasten down bands, bindings, collars, and cuffs where the stitches will be concealed or can be caught in a previous line of machine stitching. However, it is less attractive than vertical hemming for these uses. It is fairly conspicuous (except as noted) and can be used on skirt hems only if the fabric is of very rough texture or has a printed design. After fastening the first stitch in the hem proper, take a tiny slanting stitch in the single thickness of the garment close to the hem edge. Before pulling the needle out, push it on to pick up the edge of the fold—keep the needle slanting toward your left shoulder. Repeat. Make the stitches about $\frac{1}{8}$ inch apart. Stitches may be $\frac{1}{2}$ to $\frac{3}{4}$ inch apart on wide dress hems.

Note that in slant hemming you progress and then stitch, whereas in vertical hemming you stitch and then progress. This is the only difference in the technique of making, but the slant hemming stitches, on both right and wrong sides, are much more conspicuous and are more likely to be pulled in wear.

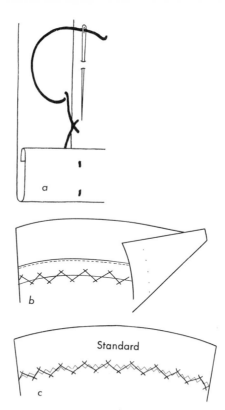

Figure 26-4. *a*, Herringbone or catch stitch; *b*, used on taped hem; *c*, covering a raw edge.

The *herringbone stitch*, or *catch stitch*, is worked left to right. It consists of a series of back stitches along two imaginary parallel lines (Fig. 26-4, *a*). Fasten your thread on hem tape, then take a tiny stitch ½ to ¾ inch to the right, not on the tape but close to it in the single thickness of the garment. This stitch is parallel to the tape, so the needle is parallel to the tape also. Pull out the needle and thread, then take another back stitch on the tape about ¾ inch farther along and about ¼ inch back from the edge. This stitch should catch the tape but not go through to catch the outside layer of the garment, *b*. Continue the stitching, first on the garment, then on the tape. Throw or hold the thread to one side to avoid making a lock stitch. Pick up just a few threads of the cloth and do not draw the thread tight. Practice keeping the stitches uniform in length and spacing. Many dressmakers object to its use over tape, as the crossing adds weight; they reserve it for use over raw edges, *c*. Because of the long floats it is more likely to be pulled in wear. It may leave more of an imprint in pressing.

PLEATS AND REVERSED SEAMS IN HEMS   Clip the seam at the back of a pleat where it enters the hem, to make it lie flat and permit the pleat to set correctly (Fig. 26-5, *a*). Press this seam open through the hem and trim it to ¼ inch, as in *b*, to remove bulk. A line of stitching along the underfold of the pleat holds it in position.

Where a hem is turned to the right side, *b*, the seam must be reversed (see also p. 374).

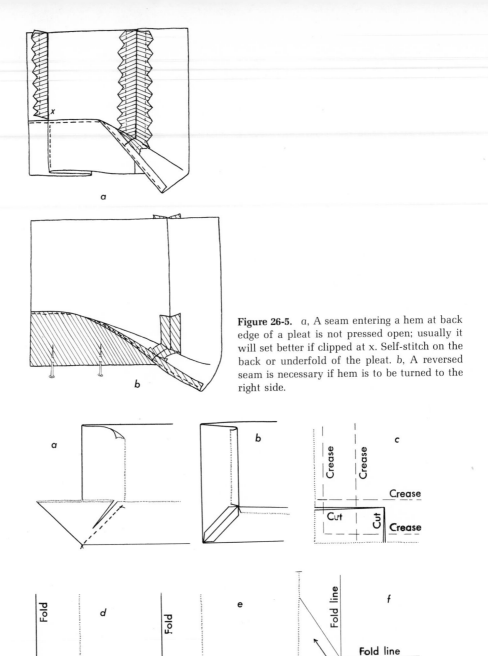

Figure 26-5. *a*, A seam entering a hem at back edge of a pleat is not pressed open; usually it will set better if clipped at x. Self-stitch on the back or underfold of the pleat. *b*, A reversed seam is necessary if hem is to be turned to the right side.

Figure 26-6. *a* and *b*, Mitering a corner in a hem. Fold and cut a mitered square corner. *c*, Squared corner prepared by cutting away a rectangle. *d*. Steps in cutting mitered corner with adjoining hems of unequal width.

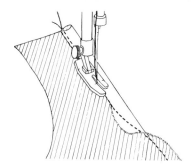

Figure 26-7. To turn and stitch a narrow hem is a simpler process when the edge is first staystitched ¼ inch from the edge. Trim to ⅛ inch if desired to remove bulk, as the stitching keeps the edge under control.

MITERING A HEMMED CORNER   Steps for folding and cutting a mitered square corner, with hems even in width and hems uneven in width, are shown in Figure 26-6.

BLIND-STITCHED HEMS BY MACHINE
Blind stitching produces a durable hem finish that is almost invisible. It is best suited to straight or slightly curved hems. This stitch can be used with a variety of edge finishes—taped, bound, clean-finished, or unfinished.

NARROW-STITCHED HEM
For ease in turning and stitching a hem along off-grain edges, there is an advantage in first staystitching ¼ inch from the edge (Fig. 26-7).

INTERFACED HEM
See p. 477.

UNDERLINED GARMENT
Hemming an underlined garment may involve the same decisions and processes as hemming other garments, except that one has the advantage of hemming invisibly, through underlining only (Fig. 26-8).

Figure 26-8. In an underlined garment, the hem is attached only to the underlining fabric and the seams that are crossed.

Finishing and Couture Touches

Well-chosen, neat finishes, even though they are invisible on the right side of a garment, add greatly to its appearance and to your satisfaction in wearing it.

Finishing Details

BUTTONS

To locate positions for buttons, arrange overlap on underlap, centers (CF or CB) matched. Insert a pin at the end of the buttonhole nearest the closing to mark underlap (Fig. 27-1).

467

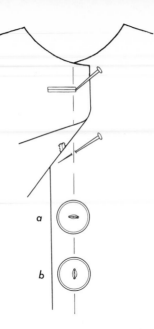

Figure 27-1. Marking location for buttons: *a*, correct direction of stitch for horizontal buttonhole; *b*, incorrect for horizontal buttonhole, but correct for vertical buttonhole.

Using a double thread, begin on the right side with a small knot under the button. Bring the needle up through the button so that the stitches will be parallel with the slit of the buttonhole, in a vertical direction for vertical buttonholes and in a horizontal position for horizontal buttonholes. Keep a pin across the top of the button and take stitches over it as you stab the layers of the underlap (Fig. 27-2, *a*). Remove the pin and bring the needle up between the button and fabric, close to the center. Form a stem or shank by winding the thread closely around the stitches, *b*. Bring the needle to the wrong side and fasten the thread securely.

The pin prevents sewing the button too close to the garment, which puts a strain on the button and pulls the buttonholes too closely, giving a puckered effect to the overlap. The thicker the buttonhole, the longer the shank should be. On coats, a match or nail used in place of the pin will make a longer shank. If plastic shanks are preferred, they are available in a variety of sizes, to lift the button the proper distance above the fabric.

The button will not be very secure if sewn through but one thickness of material. A small piece of the fabric or a tape may be held underneath to reinforce the garment if it is not interfaced. On some coats a small button is caught on the wrong side with the same stitches that hold the large button on the outside, thus forming a brace to keep the stitches from pulling out the fabric.

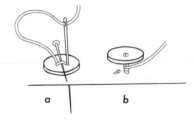

Figure 27-2. Make a shank in sewing on a button, or use a button neck.

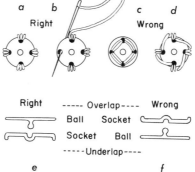

Figure 27-3. Sewing on snaps: *a*, correct finish, over the edge; *b*, correct method of carrying needle *under* the snap from hole to hole; *c*, incorrect—thread carried on top will prevent tight closing; *d*, poor. The thin, ball part preferably belongs on the overlap, the thicker socket part on underlap, *e*. Wrong location, *f*. Why? Which plan gives a smoother overlap, placing the flat, ball part or the irregular socket part against the overlap?

An automatic machine set with a lowered feed-dog and zigzag disc sews buttons on very well, even with a thread shank.

The shank is usually omitted when buttons are put on as decoration not intended to be functional. Buttons with metal shanks are sewed on firmly with plain over-and-over stitches. Secure the thread on the wrong side without making a stem. They also can be inserted through eyelets and fastened on the wrong side with tiny safety pins or clips. Special safety pins are available for pinning buttons with shanks on garments needing frequent laundering.

Snaps

Snaps are placed near enough to the edge to hold the overlap in position, and sufficiently close together to prevent gapping. Stitches that fasten snaps to the underlap should stab through to the wrong side if durability is desired. Usually there is an interfacing or an enclosed seam to support the stitches in the overlap, so they will not show on the right side.

Place the ball part (with the thinner base) on the wrong side of the overlap, usually about ⅛ inch back from the edge. The thinner base does not distort the smooth surface of the overlap. After the snap is sewed to the overlap, chalk the ball to imprint the position on the underlap for the correct location of the thicker (socket) part of the snap.

Sew over the edge of each hole in the snap (Fig. 27-3, *a*). Carry the thread from one hole to the next by passing the needle under the snap for a neater appearance, *b*. Either buttonhole or overhanding stitches are satisfactory, considering durability, but the former give a neater appearance and provide a flat, firm finish.

The small extended snap is a suitable fastener at the neckline of a zipper placket (Fig. 27-4). If there is a possibility of its showing, it might be covered with matching fabric. (See p. 471.)

Figure 27-4. Extended snap.

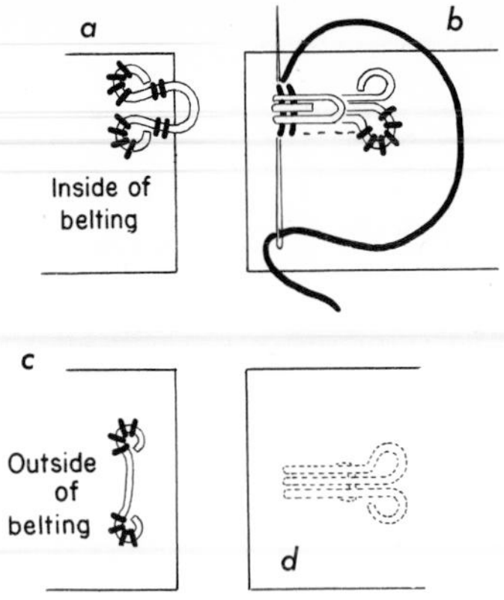

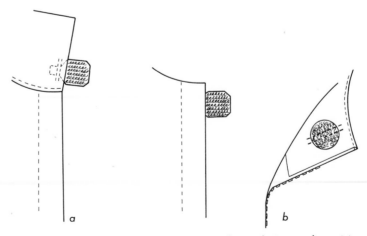

Figure 27-5. *a* and *b,* Hooks and eyes are placed on inside of skirt belting so that ends exactly meet. If round eye is used, *a,* it must extend as far as the bill of hook, *b,* is back from other end. Be sure to tack end of bill as well as neck of eye. *c,* Flat eye belongs on *outside* of underlap far enough back to be concealed by overlap. *d,* Hook is then set on underside of overlap far enough back for desired overlap.

HOOK AND EYE

To attach hooks and eyes, use the round eye where the edges are just to meet, as on inside linings, inside belts of skirts, or coat edges. Use the straight eye where edges are to overlap.

If the round eye is used, sew it on first; it must extend beyond the edge of the underlap about $\frac{1}{16}$ inch, so that the edges of the garment just meet. Test it before sewing. It is placed on the wrong or underside of the underlap (Fig. 27-5, *a*).

If the straight eye is used, sew the hook on first; place the hook $\frac{1}{16}$ to $\frac{1}{8}$ inch back from the edge on the wrong side of the overlap, *d.* Place the straight eye on the upper side of the underlap, *c,* and far enough back from the edge to hold the hook. (Place the overlap on the underlap and mark the point with a pin.) Place the eye so the hook will pull with the curve, not against it.

To sew on the hook, hold it down firmly under the left hand and sew around one ring, then slip the needle under the hook out to the point slightly beyond the end of the bill or loop of the hook, *b.* Take several stitches there across and under the loop of the hook to hold the end firmly; then return to the other ring and sew it down firmly. Fasten off at one side with a few tiny back or knot stitches. The

Figure 27-6. Velcro tab—press sections together to fasten; peel apart to unfasten.

round eye also needs tacking to keep it from flopping back in use, *a*. Of course, stitches must not show through on the right side of the garment, but on the underlap one may stab all the way through the layers.

Instead of using two or three regular hooks and eyes on a skirt or pants band, you may prefer to use one larger one specially designed for this purpose. Attach it according to directions on the package.

VELCRO FASTENERS

Nylon and polyester fibers constructed into grip-type fasteners function efficiently for a variety of uses, including dresses, blouses, jackets, and waistbands. They consist of two parts, one covered with small loops and the other with hooks. When pressed together, a firm grip occurs. To be unfastened, they are easily peeled apart. A synthetic heat setting should be used for ironing or pressing them.

The techniques for attaching a Velcro tab at the neckline end of a placket follow (Fig. 27-6):

1. Press the loop half to the facing, ¼ inch from the edges of the fabric, *b*. (Adhesive backing holds it in place for stitching.)
2. Hand stitch it in place or open the facing out and machine stitch it back and forth across the section.
3. Slip the stem of the hook section between the facing and the garment in line with the loop section, *with the hooks facing away from the body*. Hand or machine stitch across the stem, as for the loop section, *a*.
4. Hand-hem ends of neck facing to zipper tape.

Couture Touches

Extra couture touches, well chosen to enhance your garment and emphasize its beauty, individuality, and quality, can multiply your enjoyment and pride in your creation.

PICKSTITCH

This hand stitch, used as a decorative finish, appears the same as prickstitch. Dots of thread lie on the surface of the fabric, with the stitches caught through only one thickness. Otherwise, it is made in the same manner as prickstitch.

SADDLESTITCH This stitch, usually applied to a finished garment, can be very decorative. It consists of running stitches, about ¼ inch long, evenly spaced, and made of embroidery floss, yarn, or buttonhole twist.

COVERED SNAP

Cover both sections of the snap with an underlining or lining fabric that is not heavy. Cut two circles of the fabric twice the diameter of the snap. Sew a hand-gathering thread around the edge of the circles and place a section of the snap face down, centered on each (Fig. 27-7, *a*). Work the ball of the snap through the fabric, gather the thread, and sew it securely with overhand stitches, *b*.

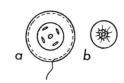

Figure 27-7. Covered snap.

COVERED HOOK AND EYE

Use a double strand of matching thread and cover the hook and eye completely with blanket stitches, working from right to left (Fig. 27-8). Large fasteners may be covered with buttonhole twist.

Figure 27-8. Hooks and eyes may be covered with thread for a couture touch.

WEIGHTS

Weights are sometimes necessary to give the desired effects at certain points in a design, as in holding the folds at a cowl neckline or a hemline in position.

Select a circular flat weight in your fabric shop and enclose it in a small, square bag, made similar to a pillow case. Stitch a seam around the bag—making it barely large enough to slip the weight into—turn right side out, slip the weight in and hand-sew it across the opening. Tack it to the garment or attach it with a French tack (Fig. 27-9).

Metal chains may be used in the hems of tailored coats and suits. The chain is tacked to the fabric.

TACKS

Bar tacks are used to finish and reinforce the ending of a placket; on a weak corner caused by slashing the seam, as in a V-neck or at end of a placket; in place of buttonholes for small buttons; or in place of the more bulky eye in a hook-and-eye set. To make a tack or loop, take several stitches about $3/16$ inch long across the place desired, then make overhand, buttonhole, or blanket stitches over them until covered; fasten off firmly, neatly, and invisibly (Fig. 27-10, a). These buttonhole stitches should be around the threads and not caught in the fabric, exactly like the bar at the end of a buttonhole.

Swing tacks or French tacks, d, are made in the same way as bar tacks but longer. They are used to tack a lining hem to a coat hem in three or four places or to tack a belt to a dress in order to avoid visible keepers or a tight, oversewed effect.

Crocheted tacks or *loops, e,* are often used in place of the buttonhole tacks. Use a double thread in a sewing needle. Fasten the tack securely and invisibly on an inside seam with several over-and-over stitches. Bring through to the outside and make one stitch to produce a loop. With your fingers reach through the loop and draw out the thread to make a second loop. Draw it up snugly and reach through the second to make the third, and so on until the chain is long enough.

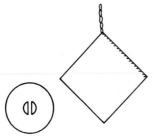

Figure 27-9. Weight encased in fabric.

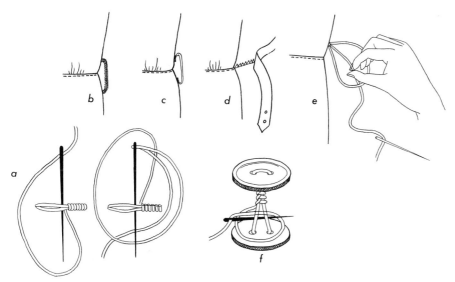

Figure 27-10. *a*, Making a bar tack; *b*, tack used as a belt carrier; *c*, fabric carrier; *d*, swing or French tack; *e*, crocheted chain carrier; *f*, tack used to join buttons.

At the end, pull the thread and needle entirely through the last loop to fasten it. Stick the needle through to the inside of the dress again and fasten the thread securely to the seam so it is invisible from the right side. You may prefer a crochet hook instead of your fingers to crochet the chain.

BELT CARRIERS   *Belt carriers* or keepers may be made with fabric, French tacks, or crocheted tacks. Adjust them to fit the belt in width.

LINGERIE STRAPS OR TACKS   In shoulder seams of dresses, better dressmakers provide tapes or French tacks with snaps at the end to hold *lingerie straps* (Fig. 27-11). A tape or tack about $1\frac{1}{2}$ inches long is fastened to the shoulder seam or shoulder pad near the armhole and to the ball part of a snap fastener near the neck. The socket part of the snap is sewed to the shoulder seam. The best location is determined by fitting.

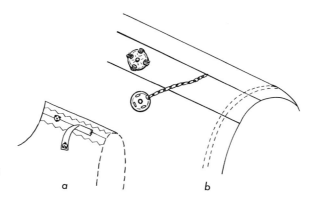

Figure 27-11. *a*, Tape lingerie strap; *b*, crocheted chain.

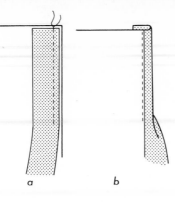

a   *b*

Figure 27-12. Hong Kong finish, suitable for seam, facing, or hem edges.

HONG KONG FINISH

This finish gives the appearance of bound edges; the process involves the steps in applying a binding, down to the last one where the raw edge of the strip is not turned inside the binding.

One-inch bias strips cut from underlining or lining fabric, which is lightweight and flexible, or double-fold bias tape may be used (Fig. 27-12). Place the bias strip on the seam allowance and stitch ¼ inch from the edges, *a*. Turn the bias over the seam and stitch very close to where the strip was joined to it, *b*.

LACE

A more decorative finish for hem and facing edges is the use of lace, in preference to seam binding. Flexible lace can be shaped to fit curved lines; select stretch lace for extreme curves and stretchy fabrics.

ARROWHEADS

An arrowhead is used to finish the ends of pockets, pleats, or darts. Mark all the triangles with tiny bastings before beginning the first one. Bring the needle out at the lower left corner. Take a tiny stitch across the top point and then a stitch across the base of the triangle. Work down from the top and in from the bottom until the triangle is closed (Fig. 27-13).

COVERED CORDS

Covered cords (Fig. 27-14) may be used to decorate the edges of hems, waistlines, necklines, wristlines. They may be used as piping in seams, in braiding, and

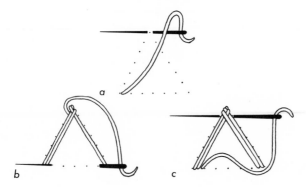

a

b   *c*

Figure 27-13. Arrowhead.

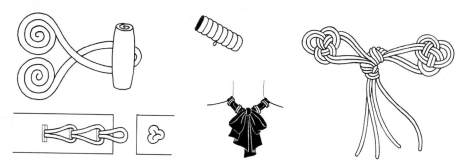

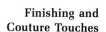

Figure 27-14. Covered cords.

in loosely twisted sets of two or more. They may be tacked in close lines to some foundation material or to the garment. Long cord ends may be drawn through slits in seams or buttonholes. They may be wound around and around to form buttons, balls, or buckles. Free ends may look more finished by the addition of beads, buttons, tassels, or knots. Clever closings may be made by twisting and tying the cords in various styles of frogs and knots. Experiment with any common string or cord until you develop a design you like.

FABRIC LOOPS

Cable cord covered with fabric has endless possibilities for finishing and decorating a garment. The diameter of the cord varies with the type of garment and fashion. It makes loops, piping, knots, buttons, fringes, and frogs.

To cover the cord for *loop fasteners*, cut true-bias strips wide enough to go around the cord plus two seam allowances (Fig. 27-15). Seams should be on the warp, flatly pressed together in the direction of the cord's pull, and trimmed to ⅛ inch in width. Stretch the bias well, then fold *right sides together* over the cord. Pin or baste only if necessary. Have a cord twice as long as the cloth. Begin by tacking the folded-in end of the bias strip to the middle of the cord, *a*. With a cording foot, stitch fairly close to the cord, but leave enough room for the seam to be turned. Have the beginning and ending of the tube wider than the rest of it for ease in turning. Stretch the bias as you stitch to insure having the machine

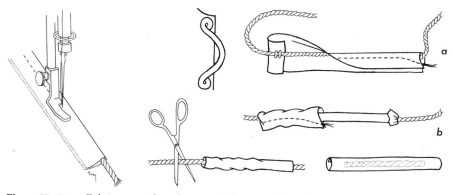

Figure 27-15. *a*, Fabric-covered cord prepared for covered cord; *b*, turned for loops and ties. For piping have piecing seams (on warp of bias strip) on the inside and fabric right side out as you stitch, *a*; leave some space for a second line of stitching when applying to a welt seam.

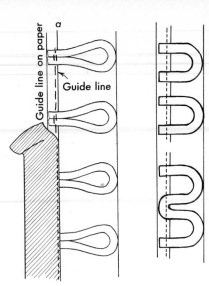

Figure 27-16. Fabric loops for buttonholes. Baste first to paper to insure even sizes and spaces.

stitch elastic. Trim off the seam. Turn the tube right side out by drawing the cord so that the bias turns right side out onto the uncovered half of the cord, *b*. Estimate the width of the strip, closeness of stitching, and amount of trimming by trying out a sample first.

When cord loops are to be used as a series in place of buttonholes, cut them all the same length, which is determined by testing them over a button and allowing for seams. The loops may be closed, as in Figure 27-16, or shortened with the ends spread apart. Attach the loops first to a piece of thin tape. If only two or three loops are to be used, they may be tacked directly to the garment just back of the seam line.

To be more accurate for a series of loops, draw three parallel lines on a piece of paper and baste the loops in place (Fig. 27-16). Tape may be placed over the ends and caught as the machine stitches along line *a*. Tear the paper away and baste the row of loops in position on the garment with line *a* on the seamline of the garment and with the raw edges of the loops following the raw edge of the garment. Cover with a facing and stitch on the seamline. Press very lightly to avoid making an impression of the inside ends of these loops on the outside of the garment. The loops may be used without the cord to keep them softer. The seam of the tube should be kept on the inside curve of the loops and the folded edge on the outside.

Purchase good ready-made frogs, loops, or other novelty closures for an extra, professional-looking touch if you are lacking in time and precision.

THE BRAIDED BELT

Use four to eight strands of covered cord or yarn. About ten feet of each strand will be needed to finish a six-ply belt one yard in length. Tie the several lengths together in a knot or to a belt buckle. Fasten to a nail, peg, or clamp to permit you to use both hands and maintain an even tension while braiding (Fig. 27-17). To begin with six strands, cut three twice the desired length and fold each one in two to form a loop over the nail or peg, *b*. Then start weaving.

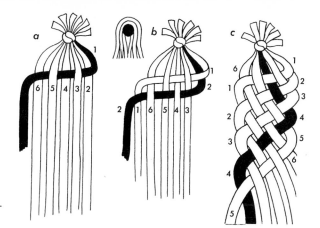
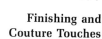

Fig. 27-17. Braiding a belt—weaving on the diagonal.

Braiding is simply plain weaving over and under, then under and over. Keep your work rather tight, straight, and free of tangles. To begin, take the last strand at the right, 1, and pass it over strand 2, under strand 3, over 4, under 5, and over 6, and end the strand at the left. Pull strand 1 down in line parallel with 6.

Then pick up strand 2, *c,* farthest on the right, and weave it over and under all the strands, including the strand, 1, you just placed at the left of strand 6. End by pulling strand 2 down in parallel line at the left of the former strand 1. Now pick up strand 3 and continue.

Finish the ends with a tassel, bead, or knot.

TASSELS AND FRINGES

Covered cords and yarns of varying thicknesses can be made into tassels and fringes. Many ready-made types are now on the market; they are also easy for you to make.[1] They relieve the monotony of uninteresting fabrics or styles, and lengthen skirts, jackets, and sleeves.

THE CHINESE KNOT

Weave a cord in the steps shown (Fig. 27-18). Tighten into any desired shape. If a tight knot is formed, it makes an individual and useful button; sew the cut ends as a shank underneath. Endless variations are obtained by continuing to follow the first weaving as a pattern—twice around for a double knot, *a,* or three times for a triple knot. Certain loops pulled out loosely produce interesting flat frogs, *b* and *c.* Chinese knot used as a button, *d.*

INTERFACED OR PADDED HEM

For a soft, padded appearance in a hem, an interfacing may be all that is needed. A more pronounced effect is achieved by adding a one-inch strip of cotton flannel, lamb's wool, or soft cable cord in the fold (Fig. 27-19, *a*).

The interfacing—cut on the bias—can be applied to the garment by hand, as in *a,* or stitched partly by machine, *b.*

[1]Mary Thomas, *Embroidery Book* (London: Hodder & Stoughton, 1960), pp. 50, 53.

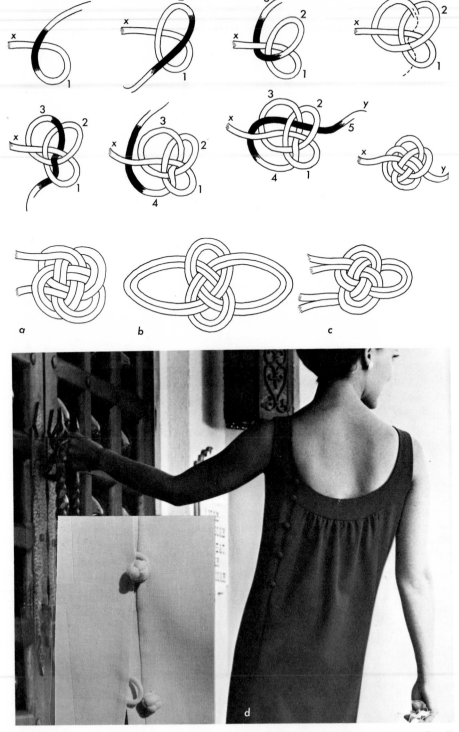

Figure 27-18. Weaving a Chinese knot: *a*, repeat weaving; draw up tightly and conceal ends for a button; *b* and *c*, loops adjusted for frogs; *d*, loop and Chinese knot used as fastener.

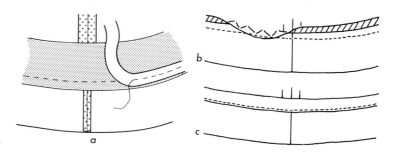

Figure 27-19. Interfaced and padded hems.

For the method shown in *a*, the interfacing is cut the width of the hem. Place its lower edge about ½ inch below the foldline, and shape it to follow the curve of the hem. Use the running-hemming stitch to fasten it along the fold of the hem and along the upper edge of the bias strip. The herringbone stitch may be used at the upper edge if desired, although this stitch is less flexible. Without an underlining, use of the running-hemming stitch might result in a less conspicuous line, especially in lighter-weight or smoother-textured fabric. Lightly baste the padding to the interfacing along the fold of the hem; fold the hem into position and finish the upper edge as desired.

For a softer effect, the bias strip may be cut from two to six inches in width and lamb's wool enclosed in the strip. It is manipulated in the same way as any corded welt, piping, or binding.

For the interfaced hem shown in *b*, cut the interfacing ¼ inch wider than the hem. Turn the hem into its finished position; slip the interfacing between the hem and the garment, with its lower edge at the foldline and its upper edge projecting ¼ inch above the edge of the hem. Pin the two edges together, shape, and machine-stitch ¼ inch below the edge of the fashion fabric, stitching only through these two thicknesses. Attach hem to garment with running-hemming stitches. If garment is unlined, trim away ⅛ inch from the edge of the interfacing (leaving ⅛ inch to cushion the edge of the fashion fabric) and cover the edge with lace or seam binding, *c*.

Narrow Hems

Rolled hems are used on fine linen handkerchiefs, lingerie materials, edges of frills, and baby clothes (Fig. 27-20, *a*). Roll the freshly cut raw edge toward you between the left thumb and forefinger. Aim to enclose about ⅛ inch into a $\frac{1}{16}$-inch roll. Work from right to left and roll only one or two inches at a time. Use over-handing stitches about $\frac{3}{16}$ inch apart by slipping the needle under the roll and slanting it out at the top of the roll, which is the outer edge of the hem. Be careful across seams. Materials that fray easily or are very soft are improved by first staystitching ⅛ inch from the edge; better still, stitch ¼ inch from edge and trim to ⅛ inch to give a crisp, unraveled edge.

A lace edging may be held on the right side and caught in the overhanding stitch as you roll, *b*.

The *shell-edged hem, c,* is a decorative scalloped effect used on thin fabrics. Baste in a narrow hem about ¼ to ⅜ inch wide. Work from right to left with the wrong side toward you. Fasten the thread at the edge of the hem as usual, then take two or three overhand stitches over or around the hem. Draw up each stitch tightly to crush the outer edge down to make a scallop. Slide the needle in the

479

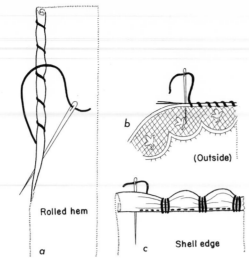

Rolled hem

a

b

(Outside)

c

Shell edge

Figure 27-20. Dainty hem finishes: *a*, rolled hem; *b*, lace overhanded to rolled hem; *c* shell edge created by overhand stitch.

fold of the hem forward $\frac{1}{4}$ to $\frac{3}{8}$ inch, then repeat the overhand stitches. If the scallops are $\frac{1}{2}$ inch apart, you might need to use tiny running stitches in between to hold the hem down.

LINING

A lining, cut and marked in the same manner as the garment, is constructed separately, but should be altered and constructed along with the garment.

TO LINE A SKIRT (FIG. 27-21)

1. Finish and press all darts and lengthwise seams in both outer fabric and lining.
2. Place wrong sides of the two garments' fronts together and pin along the center front lines.
3. Pin side seam allowances of lining to the seam allowances of garment and

a

b

Figure 27-21. *a*, Skirt lining hand-hemmed to zipper tape; *b*, skirt and lining hemmed separately.

hand baste together with loose basting stitches, beginning a few inches above the hem and finishing at the waistline.

4. Turn the lining right side out over the skirt and pin and/or baste the skirt and lining together at the waistline.
5. Turn lining edges under along the placket and hand-hem to zipper tape.
6. Attach band and hem skirt, and lining separately, *b*.
7. Hem the lining, to hang about 1 inch shorter than the garment.

TO LINE A DRESS   The general technique for lining a dress is the same as for lining a skirt: (1) make the two garments separately, (2) baste seam allowances together loosely, turn under, pin in position, and (3) hand-hem edges of the lining to the zipper tape; turn under edges of lining and pin in position to cover such raw edges in the garment as neck or armhole facing edges; and hand hem lining to garment. The armhole seams of the lining and garment may be basted together as with the other seams, or the sleeve may be left unattached to the garment and hand hemmed around the armhole, with the sleeve edge turned under and covering the other raw edges.

The lower edges of a skirt or dress are allowed to hang free at the hem lines, but in a lined jacket or sleeve, the lining may be turned under and hand-hemmed to the hem of jacket or sleeve. In this situation, a slight overhang of lining length is needed to prevent tightness and drawing (Fig. 27-22).

Figure 27-22. Interfaced hem covered with lining. Edge of lining held flat by vertical-hemming stitches. Note extra length in lining; this overhanging fold prevents tightness and drawing in the lining.

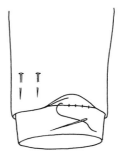

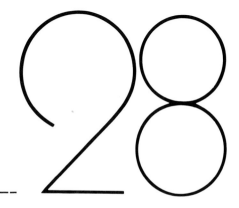

Decoration in Dress

Travel and our interest in countries of all continents have developed a trend toward handwork, both dainty and bold. There is a renewed interest in the wealth of ideas in museums and libraries (Fig. 28-1). Using good patterns, skillful fitting, and good tailoring are of first consideration, but decoration challenges attention and relieves the plainness of simply cut garments.

Contemporary Revival of Stitchery

In earlier centuries, needlepoint was a lady's art. Worked in a beautiful handcrafted frame, it was both a forerunner and an adaptation of handwoven

483

tapestries. Contemporary French and American artists draw and paint designs on paper, called *cartoons,* from which tapestry weavers select the colors for their weaving. Lurçat, foremost of modern tapestry designers, uses few colors, not over twenty or thirty—forty at the most—and often as few as nine, for his palette (of wools). Designs are not pictorial but flat and stylized. They may be abstract or representative forms, carefully distinguished from "easel-painted" pictures. Few people have access to a loom, although handweaving in America is making great strides as an art form as well as a hobby. Tapestry was essentially a wall covering (Fig. 2-1). Today, wall hangings are developed either by tapestry weaving or by stitchery. Their textures may be needed to relieve the coldness of walls or the monotony of many easel pictures.

Modern stitchery does away with the fine, intricate handwork of past years. Various textures and colors of yarns, appropriate materials, and free forms or imaginative shapes are desired. Directions or patterns for such designs in pattern books are difficult to find, so the best thing to do is to learn a few basic stitches, decide on the fabric suitable for your project (skirt, sweater, handbag, overblouse, diaper shirt, upholstery, or wall hanging), and then find a design in harmony with these limitations that is free or original in concept. Adapt it to the space you have.

Not everyone wants to be original, and many will not try; for them the best plan is to be critical in selections of ready-made designs. Gradually such a person may adapt these ideas. Selection of one's own colors is a step in that direction. Most women today, more daring in dress or in home decoration, might well use better taste in choosing stitchery projects than they do. The poor quality of handwork on a modern dress is just plain dowdy. Many imported so-called "hand-made" blouses are in this category.

A bit of handwork to pick up at the TV hour, or when callers drop in, or when one is quite alone, will take the place of "worry" beads and release many modern tensions.

STRUCTURAL AND APPLIED DECORATION

It is important to recognize the fact that there are two kinds of decoration—structural and applied. Good *structural* design in a dress refers to its shape: the silhouette is graceful, well proportioned, and in harmony with its use and the shape of the body; the parts (yokes, pleats, insets, collar, belt, pockets) are cut by lines into pleasing *shapes* related to each other as well as to the whole garment. It should be simple, beautiful, and functional. Crooked stitching and puckered lines illustrate poor structural design. Luxurious material needs little or no applied decoration.

These Are the Goldstein Standards for Good Decorative Design

1. It is used in moderation.
2. It is placed at structural points and strengthens the shape of the part. It seems "to grow out of the structure."

Figure 28-1. (facing page) Regional costumes from other countries are worn now only for festivals. However, the aprons, laced bodices, embroidery, and so on, contribute to our heritage of dress and inspire contemporary designers.

Polish

Czech

Swiss

Italian

Greek

Lebanese

3. It has enough background space to give the effect of simplicity and dignity to the design.
4. Decorative patterns cover the surface quietly.
5. The decoration is suitable for the material and the service it must give.
6. The artist's idea (a flower or other motif) is fitted to the shape of the object, its function, and the limitations of the material and tools to be used. Thus, stylized or conventionalized design is preferred to a naturalistic design.

A good decorative design must be more than "pretty," "sweet," or "cute"; it must have character. Decoration on cloth should give a sense of flatness rather than padded-up roundness or perspective—that is, naturalism. Good decoration obeys basic art principles. "Trimming," an outmoded expression, so often cheapens the effect and adds to the basic cost; it should not be used to cover careless workmanship. The *shift* mode resulted in rather plain garments; if a print is not used, a touch of decoration to accent the face or give weight to a hem might seem desirable.

Applied decoration may consist of self-materials, as well as contrasting textures and colors, worked up ingeniously and applied with restraint. In this classification would come braiding, puffing, appliqué, lace, embroidery, sequins, buttons, and bows. Any good decoration should make the garment distinctive—beautify and enhance it—never destroy one's sense of orderliness, refinement, or harmony. Simple details—bows, bindings and folds—may give a finished look.

Because decoration is intended to enrich a garment, it should be of as good or better quality than the fabric in the garment. Too-heavy decoration on lightweight material will look cheap or pull the garment out of line. The decoration should be able to withstand the cleaning and wear that the dress will undergo. Buttons, belts, and other closures should be practical and usable (functional), not just sewed on.

An overuse of any form of decoration generally results in garments of poor taste, whereas restraint in decoration characterizes garments of good taste. Of course, there is danger in being too timid, leaving an effect of plainness or lack of interest and character. The design may appear weak or out of scale.

A small bit of well-executed decoration is better than a lavish use of ordinary work or commonplace design. It is important to select a type of decoration within one's capabilities and resources of time or money (Fig. 28-2).

It is better to plan the decoration while planning the design of the dress, but this first plan should be of a general type; leave details to be worked out later. For example, if you plan a self-scalloped edge around the collar, do not draw the scallops on your pattern until your blouse is fitted, the neckline and shoulder seam corrected, and the collar tried on and altered for roll, width, and shape becoming to you.

APPLICATION OF ART PRINCIPLES TO DECORATION

1. Decoration should emphasize a good line in the garment. Borders along edges of collars, pockets, garment slits, and yokes are used in this way.

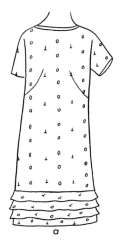

Figure 28-2. Self-material is often more refined and effective than ready-made trimmings. In *a,* bias folds cut of strips about 3 inches wide, folded and applied in groups, add a soft semiruffled, textured effect. They fit curves where tucks would not and strengthen a basic structural line. In *b,* simple basic stitches add the simplicity of childhood. For an adult's garment in denim, use large stitches with crewel or tapestry wool or coarse cotton.

2. In planning two areas of decoration, make one dominant and one subordinate. Plan the dominant area first; for example, do not make a border around the sleeves or cuffs the same width as one around the collar. The dominant area calls attention to that part of the body. Decoration near the face is usually preferable to one near the hands or the abdomen. On the other hand, a tiny waist might be emphasized. Decoration may be located to draw attention away from an undesirable feature.

3. Shapes of decorative motifs should be adjusted to harmonize with the area they occupy. A curved design looks better fitted in the corner of a round collar or round yoke than would a diamond or square. Avoid cater-cornered designs, because they are not in harmony with the structural shape.

4. The decoration should harmonize with the design in the fabric. Patterned materials are pleasing with solid fabric for decoration, or self-material such as folds, tucks, and loops. Stripes and plaids demand straight-line or bias treatments such as bands and corners. Consider the harmony of both color and texture.

5. Good proportions should be observed throughout. Avoid obvious divisions and equal spaces such as halves or thirds; work for subtle, well-balanced, and interesting space arrangements.

6. Conventionalized designs are more satisfactory than naturalistic ones, because the latter usually lack harmony of shape and are frequently childish, too elementary, or unorganized in arrangement.

7. Stripes arranged in new ways illustrate the idea of structural decoration.

8. Self-fabric decorative details usually look less homemade than hand embroidery. The average American girl has not perfected this skill.

Embroidery

Embroidery is but one of many good methods of applying decoration. Because it is fascinating work, danger lies in its overuse. Good work is often slow work; some girls hurry and spoil the results. Simple stitches that are effective and not too time-consuming are recommended. The satin stitch used on dainty French handmades is not advisable. It is hard on the eyes, requires much practice to be good, and is seldom effective on dresses.

Hand embroidery can look professional and beautiful if exceptionally well done and of good design in itself. Long floats, straggly stitches, too much surface decoration, or raised work will appear "stuck on"—not a unified, inherent, or *structural* part of the article. Rows of stitching, quilting, and cross-stitching seem to merge with the weave of the fabric. The stitches themselves should follow the feeling of the shape of the design and the grain, as a rule, and be short enough and of thread fine enough that they appear to be a part of the cloth itself when completed. Threads like No. 10 perle cotton are good on average cotton materials. Experiment in using six-strand embroidery cotton. Rayon embroidery thread is usually too shiny, coarse, and wiry. Crewel and tapestry wools are used for crewel embroidery, needlepoint, decorating sweaters, dresses, and curtains.

Select a method of transferring the design so as not to soil the fabric. A light mark or yellow tracing paper is acceptable. Never use regular carbon paper. A few pins often are the only guides needed.

Avoid beginning or ending the work in a corner; it should receive careful planning for balance in design. Do not begin with a knot, but use two or three back stitches or running stitches inconspicuously concealed in the hem on the wrong side or under the proposed line of embroidery. End in the same manner on the wrong side. When you run out of thread, fasten—loosely but well—on the wrong side, both the old and the new thread, and bring the needle out on the right side exactly where the old thread would have come out.

Basic Embroidery Stitches

BACK STITCH

Plan your work from right to left. Bring the thread through $\frac{1}{16}$ inch ahead of the beginning of the line. Insert the needle $\frac{1}{16}$ inch back and bring it out $\frac{1}{16}$ inch ahead (Fig. 28-3, *a*). Short stitches resemble machine stitching. Keep stitches uniform in size and fairly firm. *Hand picking* is a *half* back stitch (a variation of back stitching) used in place of topstitching on lapels, collars, pockets, and *plackets, b.* It is produced by using fine thread and one tiny back stitch at a time, with the needle sliding underneath from one stitch to the next about $\frac{1}{4}$ inch or two spaces apart. (*Saddle-* or *tailor-stitching* is nothing but running or basting stitches, too often far from professional-looking because of irregularity or oversized stitches.) We use the back or half-back stitches to tack down another thread (and call it *couching*) and to attach beads and sequins.

OUTLINE STITCH

Fasten the thread underneath on the line so as to work from left to right. Bring the thread out at a space ahead of the end of the line (Fig. 28-3, *d*). Take a back stitch as short as possible, $\frac{1}{16}$ to $\frac{1}{8}$ inch long. Hold the thread below the line with your left thumb. Take the next stitch farther along so that the point of the needle

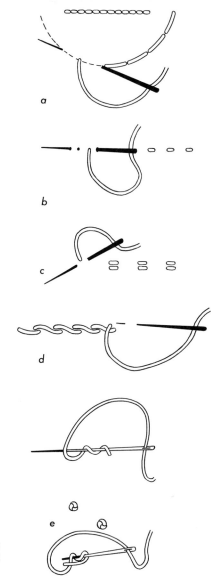

Figure 28-3. Basic stitches (from top down): back, halfback or prickstitch, seed, outline, and French knot.

comes out where the previous stitch ended. When well done, the outline stitch resembles a twisted cord or rope. It is a back stitch worked backward.

In working around curves, throw the thread above the line for an outward (convex) curve and below the line for an inward (concave) curve. At points or corners, take an extra stitch over the edge of the stitch to keep it from slipping back from the corner.

SEED STITCH

The seed stitch is used to fill in solid areas or backgrounds and to tack down narrow hems from the right side in a decorative manner. It consists of a *pair* of tiny *back* stitches side by side spaced $\frac{1}{4}$ to $\frac{3}{8}$ inch apart (Fig. 28-3, c).

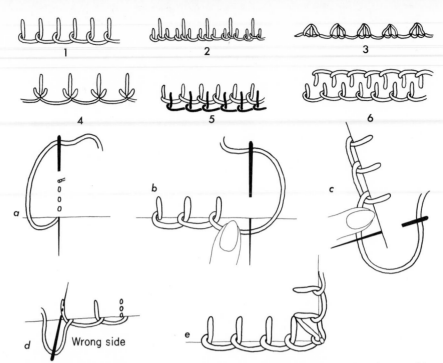

Figure 28-4. Blanket stitch: *a–c*, steps in making; *d*, finishing off on underside; *e*, tacking the corner. Design variations, 1–6.

FRENCH KNOT

With the thread pulled through to the right side (Fig. 28-3, *e*), wind thread two or three times around the needle near the point. Hold it firmly and insert the needle as close as possible back of where it came out. Hold it under finger and thumb while pulling the thread to the wrong side.

BLANKET STITCH

Work with the edge to be finished next to you—the bulk is thrown back in a horizontal position. Work from left to right.

Fasten the thread by inserting the needle underneath ¼ inch back from the edge and making two or three running stitches out to the edge, ending with a back stitch there (Fig. 28-4, *a*).

Hold the thread under your left thumb. Insert the needle directly back of the first stitch on the top side. Bring the needle out at the edge. Draw the needle through the loop, thereby placing this first stitch over the running or fastening stitches. Repeat, inserting the needle always the same distance, ⅛ or ¼ inch to the right of the last stitch made, *b*.

For speed, after you have a good start, turn the bulk of the material to the right and hold your work vertically across the left index finger, *c*. Thus the needle will go in horizontally or slightly slanting.

To fasten the thread, turn the material to the wrong side and weave a few stitches back into the material directly under the last stitch, ending with a back

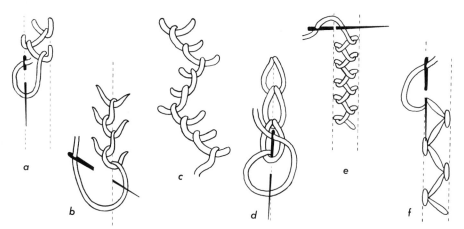

Figure 28-5. Looped stitches: *a*, briar; *b*, feather; *c*, triple feather; *d*, chain; *e*, cretan; *f*, chevron.

stitch, *d*. To begin a new thread, weave in the same place and bring the needle out on the right, inside the last loop made at the very edge.

Before reaching the corner, plan to secure balance in the spacing, *e*. The stitch on the corner needs an extra back stitch to anchor it at the very corner.

BRIAR STITCH

The briar stitch follows double imaginary lines about $\frac{1}{4}$ inch apart. It is a variation of the blanket stitch placed alternately on the line at the right and then on the line at the left. Take stitches about $\frac{1}{8}$ inch deep with the needle pointing straight toward you. The beginning of each stitch should be on the same level as the ending of the last stitch (Fig. 28-5, *a*).

FEATHER STITCH

The feather stitch is made like the briar stitch, but the stitches slant toward a center (imaginary or traced) line (Fig. 28-5, *b*). Bring the thread out on the line. Hold it down under the needle from left to right as you insert the needle to make a slanting stitch from right to left. Then hold the thread down from right to left as you make a slanting stitch from left to right, and so on.

A triple feather stitch consists of three slanting stitches to the left, then three to the right, *c*. Keep stitches short and evenly spaced.

CHAIN STITCH

The chain stitch (Fig. 28-5, *d*) is worked down toward you. Each loop or link of the chain is closed at the tip and comes out through the loop of the previous stitch. Bring the thread out at the top of the line. Hold it under your thumb a little to the left of the line. Put the needle back in the same hole and bring it out $\frac{1}{8}$ inch below, on the line, so that the needle passes over the thread held down. Draw the thread up to form a loop but not too tight. Continue to the end. Make one short stitch over the last loop to hold it in place. Fasten it inconspicuously on the wrong side.

The chain stitch is the basic stitch of crewel embroidery—fine wool thread on linen.

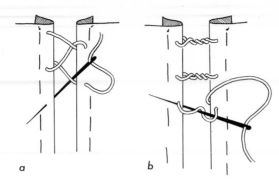

a   b

Figure 28-6. Fagoting: a, plain; b, bar.

CRETAN STITCH

This stitch (Fig. 28-5, e) is a variation of the feather stitch—flattened out—or of fagoting (Fig. 28-6, a).

CHEVRON STITCH

The chevron stitch (Fig. 28-5, f) is similar to the catch stitch or herringbone stitch (Fig. 26-4).

Fagoting

PLAIN FAGOTING

Fold the material back, not on the seamline but ⅛ inch farther into the garment. The fold may be a hem or may be left raw. Draw on a piece of paper two lines exactly ¼ inch apart. For straight seams, draw these lines with a ruler. For seams such as a yoke line, follow the shape of the pattern.

Pin and baste the edges of the folds on these lines. Fasten the thread inconspicuously on the wrong side. Bring your needle from under the fold up to the right side (Fig. 28-6, a). Slant back to the other side, always putting the needle under the last stitch taken. Stitches are not opposite each other but always a step ahead.

Slightly dampen the fabric to *press before removing paper*. In this way the work does not slip.

BAR FAGOTING

Prepare and finish your work as for plain fagoting. Fasten the thread in the left fold (Fig. 28-6, b). Take a stitch over the right fold directly opposite. Twist the needle two or three times around this horizontal stitch and bring it out on the left fold and draw it up to make the twisted bar. Reinsert the needle in the same point, slip the needle along the fold, and bring it out ³⁄₁₆ inch ahead for next stitch.

Hemstitching

Threads are removed from the cloth to leave a space about ⅛ inch wide. Locate the place for drawing threads by first folding in the hem, if there is to be one, or placing the dress pattern on the fabric to locate the lines desired. Do not draw threads across the hem at the corners, but leave enough of the cut threads to catch in the hem to prevent raveling. After threads are pulled, baste in the hem close to the first pulled thread. As in any hemming, hold the bulk of the cloth toward you and the hem up in your hand (Fig. 14-4). Work on the wrong side and from right to left. Fasten the thread with a back stitch on a fold of the hem. After the first stitch, hold the hem across the left forefinger (Fig. 28-7).

Point the needle toward you and slanting to the left shoulder. Take up a cluster of three or four threads. Draw the needle and thread out without catching any loop or knot. Throw the thread back out of your way. Place the needle back of the same cluster of threads, this time inserting it into the fabric ahead and into the fold of the hem in a regular hemming stitch. Pull the stitch up slightly taut. Repeat.

PUNTO QUADRO

Punto Quadro, or Italian hemstitching (Fig. 28-8), is based on two rows of pulled threads of four each with a space of four between. For clusters, pull four, skip four, pull eight, skip four, pull four. Generally, leave a ½-inch space for the hem, if any. (Slant or vertical hemming is done after the hemstitching.) Use a blunt tapestry needle.

1. On the right side of the material, work toward the left, hem uppermost. Fasten on the underside and bring the thread down to the lower (second) space by taking up four threads; pull needle out.
2. Make a back stitch over the same four, but bring the needle out diagonally above.
3. Complete the second back stitch by inserting the needle four threads to the right; carry the needle under the same four and out.

This completes one unit; come down (on top) to the lower space and start over. Thus the unit forms a modified square (only slant stitches are on the wrong side).

4. For clusters, first complete the row above, then make a complete unit (two back stitches) directly below the first unit in the top row.
5. Take the lower back stitch of the second unit, then bring the needle out diagonally above, ready for the upper back stitch. Insert the needle to catch

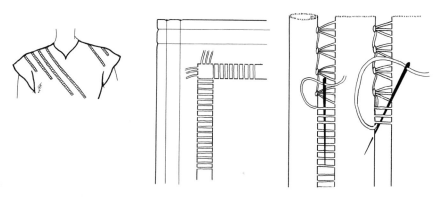

Figure 28-7. Hand hemstitching.

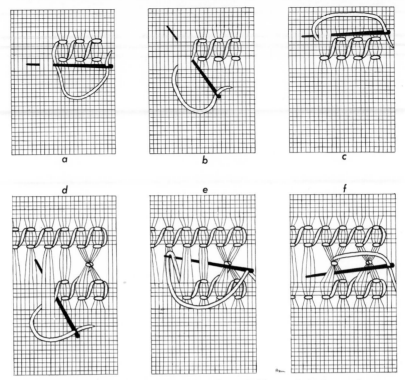

Figure 28-8. Punto quadro—Italian hemstitching and cluster work.

up cluster units 1 and 2; throw the thread around the needle point as for a knot or buttonhole stitch. Pull the needle up away from you to tighten the knot in the center of the cluster.

6. Complete by bringing the needle under the second unit of the cluster, out and down, ready to start over. Note that the back stitch at the top of the lower second unit in the cluster is missing; it has been used for the knot—to take an extra stitch makes work too heavy.

Cross Stitching

Cross stitches are plain stitches worked diagonally in an imaginary square. Checked gingham or a canvas forms a perfect background. The kind of canvas to buy is Penelope. It is basted to the fabric with grains matching. After the work is completed, the canvas is raveled out. Stamping patterns usually have squares or crosses that are too large. Use a crewel embroidery needle.

Work from left to right, one stitch at a time, poking the needle straight down, then straight up in the proper place. On long rows, make the first line of crosses all the way across the design (Fig. 28-9). Then complete all the crosses. On irregular designs, complete one cross at a time.

Bring your needle out at the lower left of the square, down in the upper right, then up at the lower left of a second square (to the right). This point is directly below the last complete slant. On the wrong side, all the stitches will be vertical.

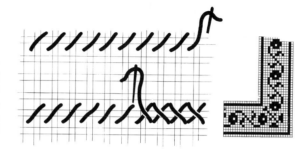

Figure 28-9. Cross-stitch designs are copied by counting squares, as crosses are made over two threads of canvas, later to be raveled away. Checks on gingham make good guides.

Needlepoint

Needlepoint is a variation of the cross stitch; just the first slanting stitch is used. It is worked to cover a permanent canvas solidly, using a wool thread. Tapestry wool, tapestry canvas, and a tapestry needle are used, but the work is called needlepoint. (Real tapestry is a *handwoven* product produced on a loom.) Because the work is relatively heavy, needlepoint is a favorite for upholstery, rugs, and wall hangings. It is also used extensively for bags, pockets, belts, and scuffs. It is a good TV pastime, a conversation piece, and an absorbing hobby for many persons, at a variety of age levels.

There are several ways of proceeding. Although making the stitch shown in the top row of Figure 28-9 has been a popular method for amateurs, it has been found to be too lightweight. Most workers now use the *continental stitch* (Fig. 28-10). Make one slanting stitch on top but bring the needle forward underneath two squares, back one; forward underneath two squares, back one, and so on. The extra backing makes a firmer, smoother product. Backgrounds are best filled in on the diagonal, down as in c and up as in d. The wrong side is thick and appears like basketweave.

Copy your design from cross-section paper by counting squares as you work. Beginners sometimes are content to fill in a background on a commercial piece with the design all worked in. This is not creative work. The designs are seldom stylized. So look elsewhere, then develop your own designs on cross-section paper, ten per inch to match the canvas (Fig. 28-11).

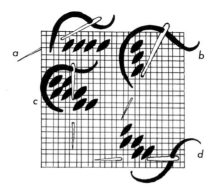

Figure 28-10. Needlepoint. Stitch is half of a cross on permanent canvas. Continental stitch is carried two squares on back.

Figure 28-11. Practice on a piece large enough to make into something useful. Here many kinds of stitches, threads, and colors were tried to be completed later—even the 2-by-4 pincushion.

Smocking

Smocking is done on rows of dots about ¼ inch apart and directly under each other. You may draw these in with a pencil; use a dotted material such as lawn, percale, or Swiss; use the squares of gingham; or use a stamping pattern. Follow the directions that come with the pattern.

Honeycomb smocking is most effective worked up in several groups of two rows each. Simple color combinations are best, such as navy or red on white, red on black, brown on green, and brown on peach. Use No. 10 perle cotton or three or four strands of six-strand embroidery cotton.

Smocking is worked from left to right (Fig. 28-12). Note that after each stitch the thread is pulled at right angles to the work to create little pleats in the fabric. Pull the thread *up* when you have made the horizontal stitch on the *upper* line and pull it *down* when on the *bottom* row (steps 3 and 5).

1. Bring the needle out on dot 1 of the top row.
2. Throw the thread above the needle and take a stitch (⅛ inch long) to the right of the second dot, bringing the point of the needle out on the dot.
3. With the thread still above the needle, pick up the third dot (the second one on row 2—dot 1 in row 2 is never caught). Pull the thread down firmly through dots 1, 2, and 3.
4. With the thread *below* the needle, pick up dot 4 (the third on row 2).
5. Hold the loop thus formed under your left thumb while you pick up dot 5. Then pull the thread *up* firmly through dots 4 and 5.

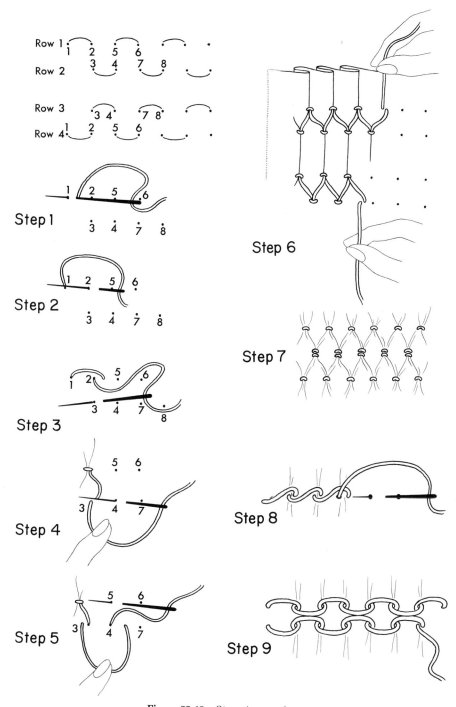

Figure 28-12. Steps in smocking.

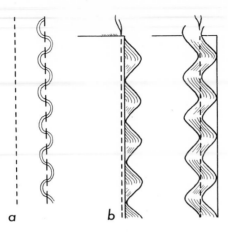

Figure 28-13. Wave stitch and rickrack.

6. Repeat. Holding the thread *above* the needle, pick up dot 6. With the thread still above, pick up dot 7 in the row below and pull *down* to form the next pleat. Dots 5 and 6 are repeats of 1 and 2.

Pull each time with the same amount of tension.

Continue on across rows 1 and 2. The stitches go diagonally from row 1 to row 2, forming neat little pleats. Straighten them by creasing with your fingers when you reach the end of the two rows. When completed correctly, note that a pair of slanting stitches emerges from under the short horizontal stitch that tacks two dots together to make the pleat.

Rows 3 and 4 should be about $\frac{1}{2}$ inch below rows 1 and 2. Note that the first dot picked up is on row 4 directly under dot 1 in row 1 (dot 1 in rows 2 and 3 is omitted). Dots 1 and 2 in row 4 are bound together, then dots 3 and 4 in row 3 above. In this way the pleats are continuous with the ones formed by rows 1 and 2.

Stitches may be carried diagonally underneath instead of on top (step 7). The *outline stitch* may be used along a line of dots (step 8). Pick up one dot at a time working from left to right. Throw the thread above the needle before taking each stitch. Make every stitch the same size and pulled up the same amount. The *cable stitch* is worked like the outline stitch (step 9) except that alternate stitches are held below and above the needle. The second row is worked close to the first, with the thread below the needle opposite the stitch made first with the thread above the needle. *Mock smocking* consists of lines of decorative stitches, such as chain, catch, and feather stitching, made on top of a line of gathers.

Machine Decoration

TAILOR'S STITCH

Fill the bobbin with embroidery thread such as No. 10 perle cotton. Do not thread the bobbin thread through the tension notches of the bobbin case. Thread the machine with ordinary thread that matches the material. Adjust to 8 to 10 stitches per inch. Stitch with the wrong side of the garment up. It is most effective with several parallel rows. Use the presser foot or quilter to keep the lines true.

WAVE STITCH

Set the machine at 8 to 10 stitches per inch. Stitch on the line of the design (Fig. 28-13, *a*). Run a heavy embroidery thread in and out under the machine stitches. Unless it is done neatly and uniformly, this stitch tends to look unprofessional.

Although simple stitching, this will not lack fashion value if a little creativity is used. Choice of thread, color, spacing and careful work can add an attractive touch to a blouse, pocket, a child's dress, as well as household articles.

Edgings

RICKRACK

This is most easily laundered if it is inserted under the edge of pleats or lapped seams. It may be inserted as a piping between two seams, as around the edge of a belt or collar; this method seldom produces regular spacing. An easy method is to baste the rickrack on the right side of the collar so the points just meet the raw edge. Stitch (or zigzag) along the center or at the base of the scallops. Turn over to the wrong side (Fig. 28-13, *b*). If the raw edge shows, trim it back. Press the braid back and stitch a neat distance from the edge of the garment right side up to catch the rickrack and the raw edge underneath.

PIPING

A *piping* is a bias fold (generally a contrasting color) that emphasizes some design line. It may be inserted in a seam or be used as an edge finish. For a *seamline,* after folding the bias strip (without pressing), baste so it will extend away from the finished seam stitching about ⅛ inch. Attach adjoining section as in a regular seam. With first-basted side up, pin (or baste if necessary), and then stitch deeper than previous stitching. Obviously, the original basting line is a guide and should have been quite accurate.

For an *edge finish* the piped seam is easily finished with a facing or lining after first attaching the piped fold.

A welt piping or *welt roll* is the cord shown in Figure 27-15, *a*. Some designers have made them extra large, using bias lamb's wool for a filler instead of heavy welt cord. Keep it soft and not overstuffed. This roll adds softness, yet balance or weight, to shorter skirts and defines necklines. One repeat at the armhole or neckline is effective, but at both places it would be tiresome, overdone, or heavy looking.

Be meticulous or your work will be unprofessional looking and disappointing; in execution apply principles relating to concave and convex curves as well as to corners. But even beginners can do a creditable job if challenged and determined to meet the challenge.

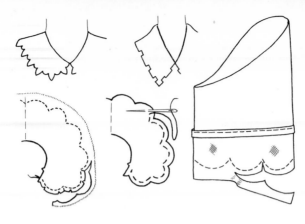

Figure 28-14. Stitch scallops or points before cutting shapes.

SCALLOPS

Scallops form rhythmical edgings popular on garments of simple construction. Do not cut the scallops out before stitching. On the wrong side of the facing, draw the shape of the scallops back $\frac{1}{4}$ inch from the edge. Baste the layers together (Fig. 28-14), and stitch on the scalloped line. Remove bastings and press flat. Then trim to leave a $\frac{1}{8}$- to $\frac{3}{16}$-inch seam allowance with a slash up in the points. Turn and work the seam out to the very edge, pin or baste, and press lightly.

POINTS

Crisp organdy or taffeta points may be used to edge collars, necklines, and seams. For uniformity, begin by cutting the fabric on the grain into $1\frac{1}{4}$-inch strips. Cut across the strips to make perfect squares (Fig. 28-15, a). Fold each square diagonally twice. On the seam to be decorated, raw edges matching, overlap the points so that when stitched the folds meet. Note that one edge is a single fold and one a double fold. Turn all the single folds in the same direction. The edge of the garment is usually faced.

LOOPS

Cut the fabric into lengthwise strips about $1\frac{1}{4}$ inches wide. Fold lengthwise and stitch a $\frac{1}{4}$-inch seam (Fig. 28-15, b). Turn and press with the seam along the edge. Cut in pieces exactly the same length. Fold end to end. Also see Figure 27-16.

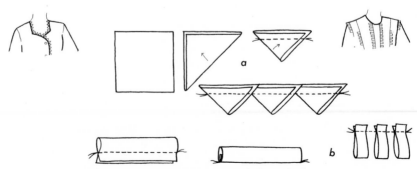

Figure 28-15. a, Pointed edging; b, looped edging.

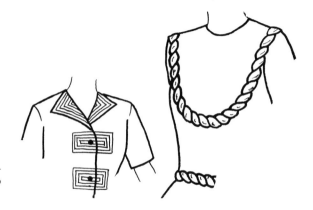

Figure 28-16. Machine stitching is the basis of this *trapunto* quilting.

Quilting

Flat fabrics are given a textured look, weight, and warmth by quilting. The fabric is usually quilted before cutting the pattern because the quilting takes up a little in both width and length.

Place a thin sheet of cotton wadding between the fabric and cheesecloth lining. Baste the three layers so they cannot slip or pucker while stitching. On the wrong side, draw diamonds, checks, or stripes. Serpentine, rope, or ocean-wave designs are more rhythmical but difficult. You may begin with one pencil line as a guide and use the presser foot or quilter attachment for stitching the other rows parallel, or you may cut a cardboard pattern and use it as a guide to draw the repeats.

Stitch with the wrong side up and with the lower tension slightly loose to give a puffy appearance on the right side. Stitch parallel rows in the same direction to prevent puckering. Avoid too-short stitches; they pucker and look homemade. Heavy thread on the bobbin with long stitches makes the design show up better. Do not press!

TRAPUNTO

Trapunto, or Italian quilting (Fig. 28-16), has some areas of the design padded so they will stand out in relief. Find a design with a continuous pair of lines or one with not too many breaks in the line of sewing. Baste firm cheesecloth on the wrong side. Place the design on cheesecloth or paper. Baste around the design to keep the layers smooth. Stitch from the center out—carefully, to avoid blisters. Tie all threads securely on the wrong side.

Thread a blunt needle with heavy wool yarn. Work from the wrong side and pull the yarn through between the lines of stitching to fill in the design. Do not use knots; do not pull the yarn tight. Bring the yarn out at sharp curves or corners. Do not fasten off, but leave short ends of yarn. Cut a slit in the lining to insert extra yarn or lamb's wool where the spaces are wide or where the design needs to be thicker. Avoid pressing after padding.

Appliqué

Contrasting material is applied like a patch in a flat, decorative manner. An easy method consists of basting in the proper position a piece of the decorative

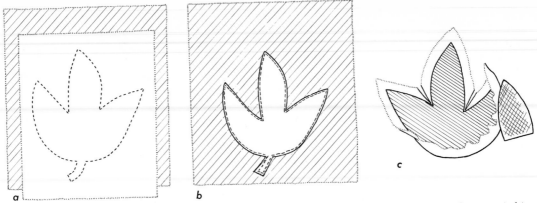

Figure 28-17. Appliqué by machine: *a*, stitch to outline design; *b*, cut away close to stitching and cover raw edge with fine stitches; or *c*, shape over thin cardboard and trim to narrow hem: hem by hand or use Point Turc.

material right side up on the outside of the garment, matching grains. On the wrong side, trace the design. Or you may pin a paper pattern on the right side (Fig. 28-17, *a*). Baste through the three layers rather close to the design lines. Machine-stitch on the design line with short stitches, then tear the paper away. Tie the thread ends. Steam press it.

On the right side, use fine embroidery scissors to trim close to the stitching, *b*, leaving a raw edge, which is often covered with chain stitches. Of course, this decoration cannot be washed vigorously. Use crêpe, linen, or organdy, which will not ravel; try velvet on crêpe and taffeta, leather on tweed.

Scrolls and other simple but graceful shapes are hemmed down by hand. They are used both on wash garments and tailored suits. A professional method, *c*, consists of cutting the design first in thin cardboard, then cutting the fabric with a ¼-inch seam allowance all around. Use the side of the iron to press the edge of the fabric smoothly over the cardboard. Clip corners where needed. Remove

Figure 28-18. *a*, Heavy knit wool skirt and shirt with suede trim; *b*, detail of suede appliqué and skirt border; *c*, appliqué combined with embroidery across the pocket of a long skirt. (Courtesy of Janet Heineman, *a* and *b*.)

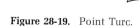

Figure 28-19. Point Turc.

the cardboard and pin appliqué in place. Hem the edges with short vertical-hemming stitches. This method is used on patchwork (not pieced) quilts. *Intarsia* is work inlaid or set under.

Holes have been punched around the circle of suede (Fig. 28-18, *b*) to accommodate the overhand stitches.

Point Turc

Point Turc is a sort of punch stitch resembling fine hemstitching. No threads are drawn, hence it can be worked on any grain. It is used around the edge of fine linen motifs appliquéd on organdy; the edge of the motif is basted under about $\frac{1}{16}$ to $\frac{1}{8}$ inch (Fig. 28-19).

With a fine thread and a coarse needle, hold the single layer away from you with the folded part toward you; work from right to left, *a*. Take a $\frac{1}{16}$-inch back stitch close to the fold on the single layer, then a hemming stitch, starting over the back stitch and bringing the needle out on the fold, *b*. These two back stitches, one on the other, complete one unit. Repeat. Draw back stitches tight; place the needle in the same holes to emphasize them, *c*.

REFERENCES

BEITLER, ETHEL JANE. *Create with Yarn.* Scranton, Pa. International Textbook Company, 1964.

COX, DORIS, AND BARBARA WARREN WEISMANN. *Creative Hands.* New York: John Wiley & Sons, 1945.

DAVIS, MILDRED J. *The Art of Crewel Embroidery.* New York: Crown Publishers, Inc., 1962.

DE DILLMONT, THERESE. *Encyclopedia of Needlework.* Mullhouse, France: D. M. C. Library, n.d.

GOLDSTEIN, HARRIET AND VETTA. *Art in Everyday Life.* New York: Macmillan Publishing Co., Inc., 1954.

HOGARTH, MARY. *Modern Embroidery.* New York: Studio Publications, 1941.

NICHOLSON, JOAN. *Creative Embroidery.* New York: Sterling Publishing Co., 1966.

THOMAS, MARY. *Dictionary of Embroidery Stitches.* New York: John Wiley & Sons, 1961.

WILSON, ERICA. *Crewel Embroidery.* New York: Charles Scribner's Sons, 1962.

Index